William Arthur Cornaby

A String of Chinese Peach-Stones

William Arthur Cornaby

A String of Chinese Peach-Stones

ISBN/EAN: 9783743351004

Manufactured in Europe, USA, Canada, Australia, Japa

Cover: Foto ©ninafisch / pixelio.de

Manufactured and distributed by brebook publishing software (www.brebook.com)

William Arthur Cornaby

A String of Chinese Peach-Stones

A String of Chinese Peach-Stones

By W. Arthur Cornaby

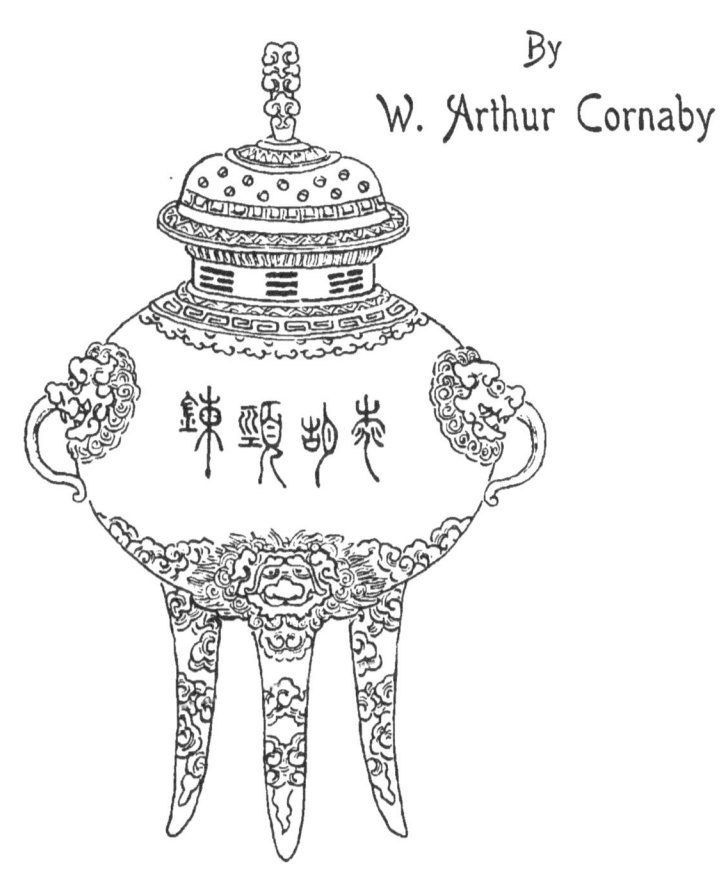

London
CHARLES H. KELLY
2, CASTLE ST., CITY RD.; AND 66, PATERNOSTER ROW, E.C.
1895

TO THE

REVEREND DAVID HILL

THIS RESULT OF THE GATHERED UP FRAGMENTS

OF NINE YEARS

IS DEDICATED WITH HEARTIEST AFFECTION.

Contents.

CHAP.		PAGE
I.	A Village District in Light and Shade	1
II.	Rural Scenes and Sounds	20
III.	The Mandarin in Embryo	47
IV.	Red Letter Days	75
V.	Compensations	94
VI.	Records of an Ancient City	112
VII.	Can any Pathos come out of China?	135
VIII.	An Historical Romance	153
IX.	Problems Domestic and National	187
X.	Gods Many and Lords Many	209
XI.	A Taiping Camp	234
XII.	The Longhaired have come	258
XIII.	Suffering by Deputy	273
XIV.	An Old, Old Story in a New Edition,	290
XV.	Imperial Pop-guns	306
XVI.	The Mart of Central China	322
XVII.	Four Miles of Flame	347
XVIII.	Imperialists to the Front	356

CHAP.		PAGE
XIX.	ART AND ARTISTS	372
XX.	HOW TO BECOME A DEMIGOD	386
XXI.	CHANGING SCENES	404
XXII.	FATHER AND DAUGHTER	421
XXIII.	RESURRECTION	442
XXIV.	FOR BETTER, FOR WORSE	457

Note on the Illustrations.

THE seals on the back of the cover contain the Chinese name, etc., of the author, and the brazier on the title-page has inscribed upon it the title of the book in Chinese.

The illustrations are, many of them (reduced) facsimiles of Chinese pictures of various penmanship, while the bulk are composed on the style of the best drawings in one or other of the two native (photo-lithographed) illustrated papers of Shanghai, to whose artists (unknown) the writer must here express his indebtedness.

Thanks are also due to Dr. Fryer of the Kiang-nan Arsenal, Shanghai, for his kind loan of the one surviving impression from a block (since stolen), engraved with the portrait of Cheng Kwoh-fan.

At the other end of the scale, thanks have already been rendered to a vendor of watermelon slices in Hankow streets, who was generous enough to give to a passing foreigner a character-formed picture of an ox, whose doleful proportions he was studying. Such little incidents are as cheering as willow trees in the somewhat dreary expanse, as it seems, of many parts of China.

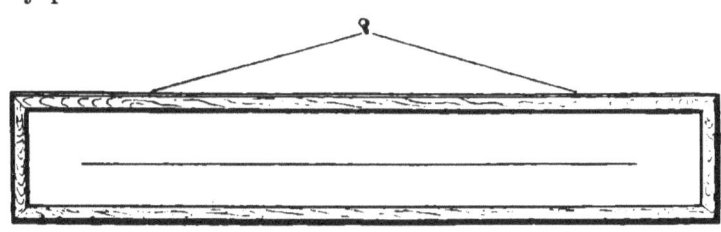

VIEW OF THE PLAIN NORTH OF HANKOW.

Introduction.

RESPECTED READER,—May I be allowed to dispense with conventionalities, take a seat by your side, and have a chat with you about the book you hold in your hand?

The title? It may be taken to indicate that you are in possession of a collection of desiccated tales, legends, and the like, picked up here and there along the highways and byways of China. Or if you should be charitable enough to regard the body of the book as a story in itself, the title will still apply; for a string of peach-stone charms, literal enough to hang upon a study wall, does certainly figure in these pages.

In that narrative, my object has not been to attempt anything like a novel, but by means of a series of character sketches, in which the details are drawn from the life, to picture the normal village life of Central China, to describe some leading incidents in the earlier Taiping Rebellion, and to indicate how Chinese character may be modified under the changes which come, and must come, even in "the changeless East."

To many, China is merely an old curiosity shop, to others a land of easily-scared soldiers or of anti-foreign mobs. The present need is for information. A symmetrical work of art would hardly meet this need, and at the expense of what may be called literary fluency, the author has endeavoured to give as much reliable information as may be crammed into four hundred and eighty pages.

Since returning from China, it has been my privilege to visit many an English home, tell many a Chinese tale, and answer questions by the hour, until the hands of the clock have united in upward suggestions for all early risers. A direct or indirect answer to most of these questions may be found somewhere or other between the covers of this volume.

The book, indeed, is the result of many a fireside chat out yonder—with the fire eliminated; for at the outset of my residence in the middle of the Middle Kingdom, I gained a Chinese friend of my own age, a young man of more than ordinary intelligence and communicativeness—a walking encyclopædia of anecdote, who had been schoolboy, "houseboy," colporteur's assistant, a partner in a little firm, pottery painter, and opium smoker. A serious illness having destroyed the opium craving, he came to live under my roof, accompanying me in my journeyings, and our companionship (yes, we plied our chopsticks together for a long time) only ceased when I buried him,—and buried a bit of my heart with him.

It was his custom to tell me a Chinese tale every night, and my custom to jot down all he told me. With such an introduction, it became easy, after due study, to read various Chinese tale-books as an after-work recreation, and to continue my researches into the comparative folk-lore of the district in which my lot was cast.

In this region of folk-lore, unexpected correspondences were found between Far East and West, sufficient as it seems to reverse the once prevalent notion that China is emphatically a realm of Topsyturvydom. In order to bring out these correspondences, a rather formidable array of footnotes has been necessary, readable it is hoped and interesting to the more studious reader, but capable of being passed over by the juveniles who are hereby introduced to a few typical Chinamen at home.

China was once regarded as such an out-of-the-way place that Walpole has a story of the Duchess of Kingston, who, on being told that the end of the world was close at hand, declared that she would start for China without delay. In which outlandish region certain of her countrymen have been in close touch with the natives for years, feeling as much at home among them for days together as though it were their own land.

It used to be a truism that the study of the written hieroglyphs was "the passage of the wilderness of the Chinese language to reach the desert of Chinese literature." That there is much desert, and few willow trees in some parts, no one will deny. But there are many spots where the varied foliage of the hill-slopes lends a grateful colour to the dull brown villages, and even the willow tree affords a touch of nature to the grey and white mazes of a city of slums. Nor are pavilions and pagodas to be despised—they are bricks and tiles in blossom.

Being interested therein, the writer seeks to interest others—a sentence which will recall to any Chinese student who may honour the "younger brother" with its perusal, a quotation from the desert-like books of orthodoxy, specimens of whose classical sand will be offered for inspection, Professor Legge having been guide. For semi-classical references, W. F. Mayer's *Chinese Students' Manual* and J. H. S. Lockhart's *Chinese Quotations* have been consulted. My indebtedness to other scholars is noted in the right place.

The connecting thread of narrative on which the varied tales are strung has to do with the years 1849 to 1867. It involves the Taiping Rebellion which affected Central

China in the years 1850 to 1860, after which it continued to be an Eastern China fact until it was finally put down by General Gordon and his "ever-victorious army," for an admirable account of whose achievements, the reader is referred to the large volume of A. E. Hake, *Events in the Taiping Rebellion.*

The leader of the Rebellion, being early possessed of Christian books, commenced his career as an exponent of their contents, but more especially of certain dream revelations of which he professed to be the recipient. Like Mohammed, he was a man with a mission, but before long the man himself predominated. The Scriptures, however, were actually read, and Christian doxologies were sung in the Taiping camps of Central China nearly ten years before any European Christians came to reside there. Once masters of a given locality, the Taipings were undoubtedly popular in Central China. The movement rapidly degenerated in various ways, but not before it had given a deathblow to idolatry as a religion—nowadays it is little more than a "luck-pigeon." By breaking up many of the old isolations and monopolies of the land, it has also done more than perhaps any other modern event towards the opening up of China.

Apart from historical and legendary characters, the reader will have to be troubled with the following Chinese names:—

Nieh (Shü-k'ing), a village schoolmaster;
Lieu (Fuh-t'ang), a tea-shop proprietor;
(Lieu) Fah, his son;
Li (Sung-seu), a farmer;
(Li) Seng-teh, his son;
Li, the Crouching Tiger, a Taiping captain;
Yang, the Golden Ox, an Imperialist commander;
Tai, a young pottery painter;
Chü, the future brother-in-law of Nieh;

INTRODUCTION. xv

besides those of some ladies related to some of the above, and those of a few lesser personages.

For further light upon the Chinese character and more readable literature, such delightful books as *Chinese Characteristics*, by Rev. A. Smith; *Gems of Chinese Literature*, by H. A. Giles; and *A Collection of Chinese Proverbs*, by Rev. W. Scarborough, are to be highly recommended.

W. A. C.

A String of Chinese Peach-Stones.

Chapter I.

A Village District in Light and Shade.

ITS WHEREABOUTS — FISH — FOWL — DIETARY — FOOD FOR THOUGHT—AUTUMN SORROWS AND THEIR ONLY REMEDY.

> " Rain torrents have ceased, flood waters subside;
> Clouds chased to the westward, behind the hills hide;
> The lake one wide mirror, all heaven shining there,
> The trees autumn tinted, autumnal the air.
> The fishermen's boats like wild geese return,
> And oh, with the wild fowl for cloudland I yearn!
> The wavelets beyond, where are hills higher still,
> By storm billows circled, each wave crest a hill.
> But look, here are yellow flowers laughing with glee,
> Like thousands of wine cups proffered to me;
> The wine is as golden, as fragrant, I ween,
> As ever of yore in yon ruin was seen."

WITH some such words as these, a visitor to the Hill of the Nine Recluses recorded his impressions of the scenery therefrom, some two hundred years ago, little thinking that from over the "storm billows" could come by and by an "ocean man," to stand on the spot where he stood; still less that he would offer his Western readers some sort of a translation of the officially preserved poem he there indited.

As yet, the hill in question has hardly had more than one foreign visitor, if the priest-monk on the hill-top is to be believed; but that countryside well repays a visit. It is an almost lovely neighbourhood; the lake waters ever blue, the banks ever fertile; the towering hill peaks, the highest in the Hanyang county, shutting in the scene from the sounds and distractions of the outer world.

That world, however, is not far distant. An hour by boat and another by land brings the traveller to the kiln-dotted town of Ki-ma-kow (so called because some grandee in ancient times *tied* his *horse* to a tree on the bank of the Han by the *mouth* of a creek, since silted up). From hence come the grey tiles and the brown pots and pans of the neighbourhood. Ten miles to the north, on the banks of the same winding Han, is the mart of Tsaitien (vegetable enclosure), and twenty miles to the east is the hub of the Chinese universe: Hanyang (virility of the Han), with its literary pretensions, the densely populated mart of Hankow (Han mouth), opposite which two important places, on the eastern bank of the mile-wide Yangtse (popularly explained as son of ocean), is the spacious city of Wuchang (military effulgence), the capital of Central China, where reigns the Viceroy in a state befitting his powers of almost absolute monarchy over the fifty millions of Hupeh and Hunan (northern and southern lake district).

The neighbourhood of the Hill of the Nine Recluses is in more than physical configuration a world in itself, a world which supplies nearly all the wants of its denizens. We who are accustomed to sit down before tables spread with various products from every continent, can hardly realise how independent of the outer universe are many country districts in China. The necessities which have to be imported can be counted on the fingers of one hand. Given a bowl of salt, a packet of tea, an iron pot, an earthen pan or two, and whole country districts can afford to be well-nigh hermetically sealed, self-contained and self-supporting. When the farmer does go to town, it is to sell rather than to buy. But he

A VILLAGE DISTRICT IN LIGHT AND SHADE.

seldom goes. He is essentially a stay-at-home, where home means such fields and lakes as these. As a fact the produce of the land in this region is bought by traders, whose large boats ply on the lakes for this purpose.

The waters are stocked with a variety of fish, most of them familiar to the English angler, such as the bream, pike, roach, tench, barbel, gudgeon, dace, and carp, the latter being *known*, by those who have watched the process, to change into a dragon! Among the

Fresh-Water Fish.

fish, which it is presumed must be peculiar to China, is the oft-quoted "time-knowing fish," which, if only possessed of a loud voice, might throw many a night watchman out of employment. It leaps out of the water once for the first watch, twice for the second, and so on till the fifth watch sees the stars pale before the rising sun. The idiotic tom-toming of the old Charleys, some of which make night hideous with their cry of "Sleep carefully!—Burglars about!" might make the most sober-minded fish leap in wonder. But this explanation is untenable, for there are no such nocturnal distractions around the country lakes where such fish abound. All fish, however, are not voiceless. There is the "baby-fish," which cries like an infant when caught; at least so the "compleat anglers" of China affirm, which affirmation is supported by the proverb, "Those who are near the water know the disposition of fishes."

Leaving such wonders to the Chinese piscatologist, we

note that several varieties of eel are to be caught here, together with speckled water snakes, also that there are shoals of fresh-water shrimps in the stiller reaches of the hill stream, and that now and then a cockle or mussel shell is found to have been washed up on to the shores of the lake. These have probably been swept inland in high flood-time from the Han, on the banks of some of whose tributary streams such shells abound. The mussel is mentioned in what is perhaps the earliest specimen of a complete fable on record in Chinese literature. "A mussel was sunning itself by the river bank, when a bittern came by and pecked at it. The mussel closed its shell and nipped the bird's beak. Hereupon the bittern said, 'If you don't let me go to-day, if you don't let me go to-morrow, there will be a dead mussel.' The shell-fish answered, 'If I don't come out to-day, if I don't come out to-morrow, there will surely be a dead bittern.' Just then a fisherman came by and seized the pair of them." The moral of which word to the wise will be sufficiently obvious to the youngest reader.

Fable of the Bittern and the Mussel.

Fishing by means of cormorants is one of the "hundred methods," and is largely practised on these lakes. These birds fish best when hungry, and deliver up what they have caught without extorting commission, owing to the fact that a ring is fixed round their neck, which makes swallowing a task too arduous to be attempted. The feeding of these ungainly birds would afford more amusement to English

youngsters than any sight in the Zoo at three o'clock. The
fisherman puts the end of his bamboo rod
into the water among the crowd of expectant
birds, whose united cry sounds like the distant yelping
of dogs, takes the ring off the neck of the first cormorant,
which, having perched upon the rod, is lifted into the boat,
and holds the bird aloft by the neck in mid-air. He then
introduces a small fish between its beak, then another, and
another. Should its swallowing powers be of too tardy a
nature for his patience, he rams the fish down the bird's
throat with his thumb. He may have lost count of the fish
thus administered, in which case he bases his calculations
upon the plumpness of the bird's "bread basket." This
having distended sufficiently, he refastens the ring, and
throwing his black feathered assistant into the water, takes
up number two, then three and four, until the long-necked
multitude is reduced to a state of after-dinner contentment.

Cormorant Feeding.

Water-fowl abound in the form of wild duck, and wild
geese are frequently seen, as the poem at the head of the
chapter indicates.

The favourite bird with the poetasters (though not such
a universal subject for art as in Japan) is the crane. It
ranks next to the phœnix in Chinese legends.
Its plumage is usually white, but there are
yellow cranes, as the historical Yellow Crane Tower of
Wuchang bears witness; also blue and black cranes, as
Chinese literature attests. The crane, together with the pine
(and the tortoise), is the emblem of longevity. The black
variety, after six hundred years, drinks but eats not.

The Crane.

With such traditions it is not to be wondered that cranes
are prized by the wealthy as fit adornments for their
rock-scattered gardens, harmonising with the weirdly twisted
fragments of antiquity as naturally as the peacock (also
known in China)[1] with the terraces of an old English mansion.

[1] In the Middle Ages cranes used to be at least as numerous in England as peacocks. Among the miscellaneous entries in the books of the Goldsmiths' Company (1480), we find that foreigners were not only subject to restrictions n practising the art, but the foreigner vanquished in a trade exhibit had to pay to the winner a crane, with the appurtenances, in a dinner to be made at the trade hall to the wardens and others.—*Christopher Barker.*

A certain prince of the seventh century B.C. (Yi Kung of the State of Wei) carried his fondness for cranes to the point of folly. The people were uncared for, while the royal park became an aviary for his pet birds, upon the choicest of which he conferred patents of nobility. When he rode forth, one of these favourites must accompany him in a special chariot.

By and by the northern barbarians invaded his frontiers. He must arouse, and assemble an army; but the militia would not enrol themselves. Upon a number of the fugitives being captured by his guards, they exclaimed, "You have wherewith to defend the country: why do you want us?" "What mean you?" "The cranes." "Of what use are they to defend the country?" "Why then nourish the useless, and neglect the populace?" The battle was "lost by a crane."

The Immortals, however, who have no kingdom to lose, seem to cherish the crane lovingly. They are wont to use it as their courser through the cerulean, gliding along through upper air with a speed and gracefulness which would quite obliterate Shakespeare's Ariel "on the bat's back."[1]

The emblem of vigilance among the Greeks and Romans, the crane is credited in the Far East with wondrous sagacity. A tyrant of the seventh century A.D., having determined to add birds' feathers to the costume of his guards, a crane from her nest on a high tree, seeing the fowlers beneath, and fearing for her brood if she were pierced with an arrow, tore out her own feathers and threw them down to satisfy the hunters.

Sportsmen from the treaty ports go out shooting in the season, to return with heightened spirits and robuster health, and with a burden more or less heavy, of pheasants, partridges, snipe, blackcock, and the like, all of which are known to the Nine Recluses region.

Birds in General.

High above the little village is heard

"The wheeling kite's wild solitary cry,"

which changes to "a cackle like that of a hen" when any stray chickens newly hatched are in sight. The falcon, perched upon a jutting rock, presents the picture of dignity, maintained in spite of the noisy impudence of chattering magpies which fly around, daring it with mischievous beak-snappings to prove its prowess.

The blue jay is very common. It is often taken in hand by the fortune-tellers of the town, and made to pick out the particular roll of dirty red paper which contains the precise destiny of the client.

Rooks and crows are numerous, a large white-necked variety among them. A smaller bird is the *pako*, so called from the sound of its cry. It looks quite black when at rest, but displays white patches when the wings are opened. It is a merry bird, and so tame as to make friends with the

[1] The bat, however, being blessed with a name of the same sound as the word for happiness, is a favourite emblem of good luck.

heavy, lumbering water-oxen, or even with their juvenile riders. White gulls are sometimes seen; seagulls they seem to be. Perhaps they have followed the junks up the broad Yangtse. The wagtail haunts the shallower shores of the lake. On the overhanging branches is seen the gorgeous kingfisher, for the colour of whose back the Chinese have a special character. The golden oriole is not unknown. Perhaps it has suggested the term *golden crow* (or *bird*, for the characters are very similar), which is applied to the sun.

When the dawn breaks to hush the hootings of the ill-omened owl, the lark, unconscious of its heathen birthplace, trills its morning psalm, which in the early months of the year is answered by a sound of a "delightful visitant," whose cry is reduplicated into *cu-cuckoo*. Soon after it has begun to add its note to the many joys of the spring-tide, come the swallows from the south (from the Kwangtung province, it is said), whose cry is "understanded of the common people" of Foochow! The cooing of the wood-pigeon is heard above the twitterings of the ubiquitous sparrow, while song-birds of varied note and with only Chinese names, round off the list. One of these is called "Cut the corn, weed the fields," from

the resemblance of its cry to the Chinese sounds for these operations.

But we have wandered as far as the swallows fly. The text was the necessities of life, or, at anyrate, the utilities thereof. The world on wings counts little to the farmer. The dictum of Victor Hugo's good bishop, that "the beautiful is as useful as the useful, perhaps more so," finds no parallel here, except for perhaps the merry Chinese youngsters, who may even do a little amateur birdnesting. Cormorants, ducks, geese, and

A VILLAGE DISTRICT IN LIGHT AND SHADE. 9

poultry—this is the extent of the utilitarian countryman's ornithology.

His domestic birds supply him with daily eggs, to be beaten up into a salted custard, or pickled in various ways. A succeeding race of foreigner-instructed children will have to teach their grandmothers to suck eggs, for the achievement is unknown as yet. The birds may be killed and eaten with "meat" (that is pork) on state occasions. The "yellow oxen" and water buffalos which plough the fields are not eaten unless they die naturally. The benevolent

argue thus: "Here is your most faithful servant, who has toiled hard for many a long year; is it not opposed to all principles of righteous retribution to kill and eat him in his old age?" as in the doleful ditty reproduced above.

The Buddhist priest-monk of the hill-top temple, indeed, exhorts the country folk never to destroy life. How do you know, he argues, that yon fat pig is not your great-grandfather come back to earth in that disguise? At an execution at Hanyang, a man once cursed the executioner, saying, "In a future life you will be turned into a pig, and I will eat you." A cooked executioner might be tolerated by an appetite whetted with revenge. But one's great-grandfather! Think of it, gentle

The Rationale of Vegetarianism.

readers, who do not worship your distant progenitors as the Chinese do. Boiled grandfather! Oh the cannibalism! So, many are vegetarians on principle, accumulating stores of merit which shall appear on the credit side of their account by and by, when they kneel before the judgment-seat of the King of Hades. (That king is a deified Chinaman, and belongs to Taoism, but the popular theology is a composite photograph of beings Chinese and Hindoo.) And the King of Hades, it is hoped, will find that their abstinence in this one particular has just overbalanced their demerit in many others. He will say: "Punish not this man; he has abstained from boiling and eating his great-grandfather."

But even these vegetarians have a variety of foodstuffs to add to their rice.

From the lake shores upwards are numerous fields in terraces, divided by many curved paths to baffle demons, who *Three Crops a Year.* can only go in a straight line. Pestilence and famine having been averted by this much-approved method, the fields yield the laborious farmer three crops a year; and that from year to year, for there is no ground lying fallow where there are hands to work in the genial sunshine, and ordure to enrich the soil This latter is supplemented by water-weed from the lake, and the ash of corn and rice husks (which ash is also used for making potash lye for washing, but can rarely be spared for that purpose).

First comes the wheat or barley, some of which will fill the flour-bin and the primitive baker's oven, to be eaten between the two chief meals, in the form of rather gritty cakes, reminiscent of the threshing-floor, with a husk now and then as a reminder that the shovel-winnowing process has been deemed sufficient. But fully half is made to ferment, and distilled into native spirit.

The corn having been cut, the fields are flooded from a pond at the top of the terrace-like series, and plots of sunlit emerald deepen in tint until the rice ears have well formed; then, having yellowed into ripeness, the cut grain is beaten out with flails as the corn had been. Then it is hulled in a stone mortar by means of a huge stone-headed hammer, worked by the foot.

A VILLAGE DISTRICT IN LIGHT AND SHADE. 11

After this, if another crop of rice (of smaller grain than the former) is not wanted, the fields are clothed once more, it may be with sesame, the seeds of which yield oil for cooking and lighting, or perhaps with beans to supply the needed nitrogenous elements in the form of bean curd (the poorer country folk, however, may not be able to afford this; they eat boiled bran instead); or it may be with plantations of white or buff-coloured cotton; or perhaps with indigo to dye the former when it shall have been put through the rustic cotton-gin, spun on the goodwife's wheel, and woven on a simple loom into material for garments.

Land which is too high and dry for all this is covered with the sweet potato plant, or with the yam (called "mountain medicine"), or various kinds of melons. Near the water's edge, in fields ever flooded, grows the taro, the graceful contour of whose leaf, however, is eclipsed by the lotus, which demands more than a passing note.

The broad leaves at first float upon the waters when they appear in the third month, then with many a graceful scollop **The Chinese** are lifted up into a vision of possibilities in **Lotus.** tender green; then fully opened, sway gently at the bidding of every breeze, or offer a green jade goblet for the rain pearls, cherishing and rocking the treasure lovingly, until it is found to be only water, too heavy a load to be borne, and so poured out into the lake; then more pearl-catchings and more water-pourings till the clouds break. Anon in the sixth month, in poetry "the lotus month," the buds burst forth into an inflorate emblem of a realm of serenest calm and ethereally fragrant beatitude, which the Buddhist dreamers of old time—when men had not lost the art of dreaming, but had lost the ideal hopes which to us are no dream—interpreted into Nirvana. The poetic elements of theoretical Buddhism have been evolved out of lotus petals.

But in these unpoetic days the aesthetic sense has well-nigh died out in Chinese country places. The priest-monk in the accompanying picture is not Chinese at all, but Japanese. The characteristic admiration of flowers among these "Eastern oceaners" exists but as a well-nigh forgotten tradition among the populace of the Flowery Land. The very last man "within the four seas" to be seen sitting in rapt contemplation of the lotus flower, is the illiterate mendicant who acts as temple-keeper. The wealthy may plant their rock-ornamented grottos with various flowers and flowering shrubs, may peer at times into their miniature lotus tank, or watch the growth of the flower in an earthen pan, calling their literary friends to "taste the flowers," as the phrase goes, perhaps pouring their wine through the hollow stalks of the lotus flower; then, with such wine before them, they may engage in rhythmical puzzles redolent more of wine fumes than of lotus fragrance; but as the proverb has it, life is now a mere matter of "fuel, rice, oil, salt, soy, pickles, and tea."

As a fact, the only poetical saying on the lotus which is at all current is to the effect that, "The lotus may be severed, but the silk is not broken," which is doubtless inexplicable to the Western reader until it is explained that there is no reference here to the lotus flower[1] at all, but only to the excavated tubers, and these after boiling for food. In biting such lumps, the fibrovascular tissue is uncoiled, and stretches from the piece held between the teeth to that held between the chopsticks. To the lotus

---

[1] The lotus flower appears in one or two Chinese sayings, but it is hardly idealised in any of them.

A VILLAGE DISTRICT IN LIGHT AND SHADE.

cater [1] is thus suggested the silken cords of affection between two far-severed friends. Thus we see that poetry lies dormant in the black mud of the lotus pond for three of the seasons, emerging therefrom in the winter to hide in the kitchen, but pays a flying visit to the dinner-table occasionally.

Enough has been said to show that the Nine Sages Region is a little world to itself. Were it actually isolated by an impregnable wall, it would stand a thousand years' siege. It is self-contained, and somewhat self-opinionated. It professes to have a complete knowledge of the facts concerning itself. The Athenian dictum, "Know thyself," it has kept from its youth up. The rest is dreamland. Everybody knows everything about everybody within the charmed circle. Those who are said to earn a dishonest livelihood in the towns by means of an iron abacus, on which they can reckon up all the earthly belongings of the house at whose door they use their magical instrument to meditate burglary in person, or perhaps by means of a monkey trained for that purpose, bring not their iron abacus here. The exact state of a man's belongings is known. There are no burglars, for they would be caught at early dawn. *(The Iron Abacus.)*

In the times with which we have to do—the historic present of the '40's—they have just heard of the existence of foreigners, though ancient traditions affirmed their presence in various parts of the outer dreamland. A

---

[1] Homer seems to use the word "lotos" in a double sense. The term seems now to denote a water plant, now a tree. This double use of the word is not unknown in China, for besides the much-quoted water lotus of Buddhism, there is a tree mallow (*hibiscus mutabilis*), which in poetry is sometimes called the lotus tree. It, however, has no

". . . enchanted stem,
Laden with flowers and fruit,"

such as that concerning which Tennyson (in elucidation of Homer's *Island of the Lotophagi*) sings. No part of the tree mallow is used for food, and the insipid tubers and seeds of the lotus proper have no toxic properties. This water plant, or one similar, Homer seems to have in mind, in the lines—

"The flakes continuous fall,
. . . .
And lotus-cover'd meads are buried deep,
And man's productive labours of the field."
Iliad, xii. 306-9 (Lord Derby's Trans.).

14   A STRING OF CHINESE PEACH-STONES.

Perforated Chest Kingdom. would-be oracle of the tea-shop, who boasts that he once travelled a thousand *li* (a *li* is a third of a mile) in the train of a mandarin, "a distant relative of his," claims the respect due to a man of such world-wide explorations. He affirms that foreigners have holes in their chests, which render the use of the sedan chair unnecessary; the wealthier of them being

transported from place to place by means of a bamboo passed through the said hole.

But a rival of his, a fisherman, who once went down the Han to Hanyang, though not doubting the fact of such a kingdom, denies both the originality of the information and the universality of the phenomenon. The village teacher's grandfather once showed him an ancient book, *The Hill and Sea Classic*,[1] wherein that and also many other kingdoms are

---

[1] *The Hill and Sea Classic* is almost the oldest geographical treatise extant in the Far East. Its compiler lived, it is supposed, somewhere in the dynasty which saw the Scripture Proverbs written and collected in Old Judæa. Like Solomon himself, the Chinese scholar "spake of beasts, and of fowl, and of creeping things, and of fishes," but his marvellous collection points to an early "community of goods," for the birds, beasts, and fishes have, doubtless from

described, such as the women kingdom,[1] the dog-head kingdom, and others. He himself can state with confidence that the river Han flows into the Yangtse, the Yangtse into the Southern Sea, the Southern Sea into the Northern Ocean, which feeds the source of the Heavenly River (the milky way), which feeds the source of the Yellow River, and so on. In proof whereof he appeals to the very authoritative tea-shop keeper, who "often" goes to Hanyang, and has therefore seen the Han flowing into the Yangtse over and over again. As to the Heavenly River, the schoolmaster's grandfather related to him, also from an old book, the story of the "Cowboy and the Spinning Maiden," who love, but are doomed to live apart on opposite banks of the river, until, on the seventh of the seventh month, the magpies collect and form a bridge, over which the youth may safely travel to meet his lady love.[2] "This must be so," he would add whenever he asserted his dignity by repeating

The Water-ways of the Universe.

The Legend of the Heavenly River.

the best motives, exchanged arms, legs, wings, and fins. Our schoolboy friends would describe them as "decidedly mixed up." The book in question is responsible for much modern pride of knowledge in matters ancient, and of much assurance in fables modern.

[1] Could this be a reference to the Amazons? The commentary on the "Never-dying people" passage contains what seems to be an Eden tradition. "On a certain hill grows the tree of deathlessness, those who eat thereof live on, and the red fountain, those who drink of which never grow old."

[2] Persia (according to Torpelius) has a somewhat different legend, which

the tale, "for it is in an old book, a very old book, which contains a poem thereon by an Emperor" (535-552)—in fact that heaven and earth are wider than the "frog-in-the-well"[1] mind of the tea-shop oracle imagined.

On this expressive metaphor, it may be remarked that there is no such thing as complete isolation in the universe.

Frog in the Well. The Chinese well contains some drops, highly impregnated indeed with earthly salts, but which have fallen upon a wide area. The atmosphere in the well, moreover, though stagnant, is subject to the law of the diffusion of gases, which sure but tardy process even the croaking of the frog serves to hasten.

Our little worlds with their little systems are bounded by nearer or farther horizons, at best contracted. Our own horizon is happily broader than that of the Chinese countryman; our universe is watered by purely celestial drops. Heavenly visitants, neither cowboys nor spinning maidens, but which we so often materialise into earthly forms, or forget altogether, do guide us in our dreams unless we have materialised their spiritual realms and turned our highest formulas from paths into well-wall barriers.

The world of the Chinaman is so contracted that he is forced to dream; so monotonous that he is forced to dream somewhat wildly. But some of the farmers' dreams are ugly, realistic nightmares. In the ninth or tenth month the

Tax Extortions at the root of Chinese Exclusiveness. dreaded time of tax extortion comes round, when the rapacity of the rulers is supplemented by the grasping efforts of their underlings. That the Chinese are voluntarily exclusive need excite no wonder. The lake is made up of "little drops of water"; its banks of "little grains of sand." The little

represents the milky way as a bridge constructed in a thousand years by far separated lovers. The completion of this bridge is thus described :—
"Fear seized the Cherubim; to God they spake,
 'See what amongst Thy works, Almighty, these can make!'
God smiled, and smiling lit the spheres with joy—
 'What in my world love builds,' He said, "shall I, shall Love
    itself destroy?'"—(Trans. by E. Keary).

[1] A semi-classical expression of similar import is, "The animalcules in a jar, how can they have wide experience?"

A VILLAGE DISTRICT IN LIGHT AND SHADE. 17

country districts know the outer world chiefly in connection with such extortion, and the aggregate of such country districts, which form the basis of the Empire, naturally look upon outsiders as harmful intruders. The feeling has grown with the centuries. The *yamun* runners of the present dynasty, moreover, are in the end representatives of powers not Chinese; and to these go a large proportion of the crops, not easily spared, especially in years of flood or drought.

As to these extortions, a modern instance may suffice. A certain man sold a little plot of land not twenty feet square. The land-tax on this was two tael cents, one-fiftieth of an ounce of silver, thirty copper cash, or one penny. The new owner, not being asked for the money, did not pay it until four or five years had gone by, when a representative of the powers that be came round with the tax papers, whereon the sum was marked in plain figures, but demanding a hundred and fifty cash for each one,—five hundred per cent. Woe be to the widow and orphan who do not volunteer to pay at the right time! The phrase, "a heathen and *a publican*," needs no commentary for Chinese readers.

With regard to the tax on crops, the old law quoted by Mencius (B.C. 372–289) decrees that every field shall be divided by means of imaginary lines like those of the Chinese character for well (井) into nine parts. The produce of one of the nine divisions is to be regarded as the property of the Emperor. But the Emperor's representatives must live. The mandarin, though always from another part (to prevent collusion with his relatives), is not so much of a foreigner as to be transported from place to place by means of one piecee bamboo passed through a hole in the chest. He must have his gorgeous chair with its four or more bearers, his red umbrellas of state, the bearers thereof, and his inevitable retinue of grown-up ragamuffins, hardly one of them paid by him. These too must live, partly upon hush-money from their bosom friends the burglars and blacklegs; principally upon their extortions in the autumn tax collecting.

If anyone would interview a mandarin of any rank he must "pay Mr. Li and fee Mr. Wang," until, in the case of a

Viceroy, a sum not less, often much more, than ten ounces of silver has been paid before his card can be presented. Should an audience be granted, the minimum ten must be multiplied by a minimum ten before the "great man" will move a little finger to help him. The motto of the justice-seeker is in full accord with an aphorism of our old poet Herrick—

> "Fight thou with shafts of silver and o'ercome
> When no force else can gain the masterdom."

But perhaps his adversary's quiver is fuller than his. What then? Let the Chinese themselves answer.

The case is set forth in an oft-quoted, almost hackneyed tale. A wronged man sought justice of a certain magistrate, and in course of his appeal happened to recollect that he had a hundred taels (ounces of silver) on his person. The magistrate assured him that he would see that he had the "right." Exit justice-seeker; enter his opponent with two hundred taels. On the morrow the verdict was given against the former applicant, who naturally expostulated. Quoth the justice of the peace, "You have a certain amount of right on your side; but he has double as much, so I decide for him."

The Price of Justice.

The old version of a Chinese proverb declares that, "Riches are as dung and filth, righteousness is worth thousands of gold"; the practical application of which is, that a man has often to treat his riches as so much muck, and perhaps spend his thousands—thousands of cash at the very least—to buy the otherwise unobtainable righteousness and justice. The market price is decidedly high.

But then the mandarin to whom he appeals is an underling of the next higher mandarin. He has not only to live,— and his orthodox stipend may not be more than ten taels per month, the wages of a good servant in Shanghai,—but he has to contribute towards the expenses of his superiors. So that the Chinese science of officialdom has come to be expressed in the formula, "Big fish eat little fish, little fish eat shrimps, shrimps eat mud."[1]

[1] Compare Sibbes (b. 1577). "As they say great fishes grow big by devour-

Where one's adversaries are in official employ, the case is hard indeed. Summoning the police would be a hopeless procedure in the East. So from time immemorial they have gone their own sweet way. Yamun underlings are ignorant and unlearned men. They do not know character. The simple "oughts and crosses" diagram is too complicated for their caligraphic abilities. Sometimes a figure formed of two strokes is therefore substituted, sometimes just one straight line is deemed sufficient, and the representatives of the law seize half the results of a year's hard toil.

In the Jewish mind publicans were classed as lower than heathens. In the Chinese mind they are earthly types of the fiercest kind of demons. The tormentors of the Chinese purgatories are represented, many of them, as dressed in the garb of yamun underlings.

Is there no remedy? Not far from the Nine Recluses Hill lives, in these more contented times, a man who had gained a military button, the equivalent of that worn by the literary "B.A." He once tried to resist the extortioners. The only result was the loss of his degree, with all its privileges, and lifelong disgrace into the bargain. That "law-defying" man could hardly get a case put through the law courts, however clear his "right" might be, or however much money he used. He is a marked man.

"Is there no remedy?" whispered the country folk fifty years ago. And through the years the whisper rose to an audible cry, and the cry to a wide resounding roar. And the answer came back in one big ugly word, blood-written, the word Rebellion.

Early in the '50's the Taiping Rebellion had spread from the south upwards, attracting under its banner many of those who had whole generations of wrong to avenge, and with ever-swelling ranks threatened to invest the greater part of Hupeh, if not the Empire itself.

ing many little ones, as a dragon comes to be great by devouring many little serpents, so many grow great by the ruin of others" (vol. i. p. 347).

Chapter JJ.

Rural Scenes and Sounds.

A NATION OF VILLAGERS—INVISIBLE ONLOOKERS—VEGETABLE
AND OTHER LIFE—CHILDISH SPORTS AND STUDIES—AIDS
TO VISION.

> "Declining daybeams light each rustic home,
> Along the lanes the flocks returning come,
> The aged men their herdsmen sons await,
> And, staff-supported, stand beside the gate;
> The wildfowl fly o'er fields of ripening corn,
> The silkworms sleep 'mid mulberry boughs half shorn;
> With shouldered hoe the farmers homeward stride,
> To spend, in social chat, the eventide."
> — Wang Wei (699-759).[1]

Before dealing with the excitements of the Taiping Rebellion, it may be worth our while to "seek retirement" among the "mild scenes"—mild at times to insipidity—of a quiet village district.

Chinese exclusiveness, as we have seen, is to be accounted

[1] A celebrated poet-artist of the Tang dynasty. It was said of him, as in modern times of D. G. Rosetti, "His poems are pictures, and his pictures poems." The above lines are translated very literally. In five and six the reader will note the Chinese antithetical method—wild wings in motion, homely worms curled in rest; also of harvest fulness and sparcity of leaf. The poet adds two other lines, which may be more freely rendered thus:—

> "'Mid such mild scenes I seek retirement sweet,
> From misruled courts, where crowd the idly great."

The accompanying illustration is a composite from ten pictures, chiefly those of the imperial artists of Kang Shi (r. 1662-1723), but in the foreground is a tree ascribed by tradition to the brush-pen of the above eighth century poet-artist himself.

RURAL SCENES AND SOUNDS. 21

for by our regarding the great Empire as an aggregate of little country districts. And perhaps most Chinese characteristics are best explained by referring them to the life of the village. These little communities are larger families, sometimes of but one surname, with the head of the clan as the parent of the whole, or, if several surnames are represented, some man of light and leading is looked up to instead.

The little divisions, answering to our "hundreds," are a still larger family, with a small mandarin as parent. And so on, until each province—a very big village district—has a Viceroy for parent. At the triennial examinations in such large cities as Wuchang, the graduates who seek for the next higher degree come, many of them, in boats, which all display little red flags bearing the inscription, " In respectful accordance with the Decree. Village Examination." This depreciative epithet is partly explainable from the fact that at such times the provincial capital is brought into regimen with the imperial palace,

A Big Village.

whose glories cause the lesser lights to fade away (an excellent illustration of Christian humility), but also from the point of view we are studying.

The Emperor is but a bigger mandarin; the mandarin, as we have seen, is regarded as the patriarch of a larger or smaller village community. The Emperor is called the parent of the people. The government of China is eminently patriarchal.

The monopolising of the worship of the Ruler on High may be traced to the days (described in some passages in the Books of Genesis and Job) when the father of the family was also its priest. Anon the patriarchal priest became the king-priest (as Melchisedec). *Melek* is perhaps related to the old root, *malel*, "to speak." As a fact, the early kings, as the patriarchs before them, voiced the wants of the family to God, and God's decrees to the family. In China their relation to God seems to have been regarded as bound up with such recognition of their people's wants. "Before the sovereigns of Yin [B.C. 1766–1154]. lost the hearts of the people," says Confucius, "they could appear before God." In later days the Chinese sovereigns have proudly arrogated to themselves the sole right to appear before a Great Unknown, who through the ages has been volatilised into a mere phrase. From such exclusiveness, and from such volatilisation of the divine essence, the Hebrews were spared, at first through the medium of a lawgiver, then a representative priesthood, until the Supreme drew near, and the "priesthood" widened in anticipation of the climax where all are found to be king-priests in a heavenly family.

The Imperial Prerogative of Worship.

Another link which binds the ancient Chinese to patriarchal times is found in some of the characters still in use. They were originally a pastoral people. Righteousness is represented by a character made up of *sheep* and *my*; the shepherd who recognised the distinction of *meum* and *tuum* was the righteous man. From their later agricultural tendencies we should have expected the sign for *field* and *my*. Admirable is represented by a combination of the signs for *sheep* and *large*.

The Chinese at first a Pastoral People.

RURAL SCENES AND SOUNDS. 23

An ancient name for governors of provinces was *pastors*, which term Mencius applies to rulers generally.

The fact that the Chinese originally came from the West is more than suggested in like manner. Chinese characters are classed under 214 headings, according to the ruling "radical." The only one of the four quarters which is used as a "radical" is the West. It is always used in a good sense, and seems to express some of the feelings of the emigrant looking back with affection to the old country. *West* and *woman* form the character for desirable, important, or want. *West* and to *return* give the idea of unstable. *West* and *mouth* mean a happy smile. This traditional affection for the West may have smoothed the path of the Buddhist missionaries, who came in the year A.D. 67. The history of Chinese Buddhism might have been a blank if Buddha had been born in Japan.

<small>They immigrated from the West.</small>

Having settled down in the north-east, and spreading therefrom to occupy what is now known as China,[1] pastoral characteristics became exchanged for agricultural, in which the heads of the clans seem to have led the way. Twice a year the Son of Heaven handles the plough, as do the mandarins at "the reception of spring," the latter being supposed to wear straw sandals during the ceremony.

<small>Development of Agriculture.</small>

After a while, the early settlers divided themselves into four classes: Scholars, Agriculturists, Artificers, and (travelling) Traders. In this classification the recognition of the village as the unit of which the Empire is the multiple is evident. It is the order of importance to villagers. The solitary scholar claims their highest respect; the bulk of the villagers are agriculturists, whose supply of their own necessities is supplemented by the artisan and the travelling pedlar.

<small>The Four Classes of the populace referable to the Village.</small>

The Sacred Edict of the Emperor Yung Cheng (R. 1723–1736) is written from the same standpoint. Its sixteen injunctions, texts for sixteen imperially classical style expansions, and stilted colloquial sermonettes, deal largely with village life.

[1] The name being derived from the Tsin kingdom, which was nearest to the West (Hebrew, Sinim). Compare the term "Palestine" derived from Philistia.

Individual loyalty and national prosperity are to be fulfilled by the renovation of village life, and the recognition of such relations and duties as are found in such family-like communities. The Empire, then, is a big village; the village family an empire in miniature.

The miniature empire which we have chosen for the subject of our contemplation, like the great Empire itself, can boast of a northern great wall (of hills) and an isolating sea (of lakes). Its capital is undoubtedly the hamlet called the Yang Family Pavilion. Whether it be true, as is fondly imagined, that a remote ancestor of these Yangs held office, we need not decide. With fifteen or twenty houses, mostly built of burnt brick and surrounded by a wall of the same material, who would be cynical enough to dispute the name? In China the music of politeness is all written in the key of seven sharps, with a double sharp here and there. The musician "goes up one" with every note. The hamlet is therefore a pavilion.

The foreigner's contemplation of normal village life, however, is attended with difficulties which may be set forth by reference to a familiar story of Hume the historian. "I have never seen a cheerful Christian," he grumbled one day. "How should you?" was the rejoinder; "the sight of you would be enough to make any Christian melancholy." Many a *Crythrawl Sassenach* (or "devil of a Saxon") complains that he has never seen a normal Chinaman at home. His approach is greeted by cries of *Fan Kwei* in the south, and *Yang Kwei tsz* in the mandarin-speaking districts; and he may have to abandon his original intention, and ponder over the fact that in Chinese, and in another still older language (as Welshmen affirm), he is described as being a native of a somewhat unearthly realm, the singularity of which coincidence he would commend to the philologists. Can they not construct a theory thereon?

<small>The Foreigner's Difficulties.</small>

The foreigner, having had a lesson on the points of contact between ancient languages, has to be content therewith, and must defer his contemplation of quiet village life a decade or so.

A way out of the difficulty of seeing the villagers minus the disturbing effect of the foreigner's presence, was once proposed by a friendly native. It may be given in the spirit in which it was received. According to the country folk, many a district is blessedly haunted by a certain personage, for whose delectation they are wont to set aside a little bowl of rice now and then. They strive to avoid hurting his feelings by cautioning their children against tying empty egg-shells on the ends of a stick when playing at water coolies, seeing which, the dwarf— for he is a very tiny little fellow—might think they were stealing his buckets. Grandfather Three, as he is called, is invisible. The discovery of his existence happened on this wise. An ox-boy was once hitting his beast with a switch. As he did so, he saw a tiny hat fall to the ground, and a dwarf run away for fear of receiving a second blow. He picked up the hat, put it on, and went home. "Rice is ready!" cried his mother, as she saw the ox come back, but where was her lad? "Here!" he shouted. "Where?" "Standing in the doorway," was the reply, which, being accompanied by a removal of the magic head-gear, made the lad apparent to her ocular demonstration. He seems to have returned the hat.

The Solution thereof being an Invisible Hat.

"Goddess of Mercy"

Now, if the foreigner could but meet this dwarf, and knock off his hat with his stick, he could go anywhere unmolested, unseen but seeing. Availing ourselves of some such method, we put our heads together, and proceed in peace. One other qualification is needed besides the invisible hat, however. It is an appreciative heart, such as the favourite deity, *Kwan Yin*, is credited with possessing. *Kwan Yin* means "sound contemplator," a god in the north, and a goddess in China and Japan, who "looks down and listens to the sounds of earth and the voices of men." Unseen as this fabled onlooker, we must have a little of his or her kindliness; without that we shall see very little to interest us.

<small>And a Heart like that of Kwan Yin.</small>

As English men and women, we note that where in our own land there is found a solitary farmhouse, the more rapidly bearing soil of mid-China (more highly seasoned than ours, and with a tropical sun overhead for half the year) supports one or two little communities.

Most of the denizens of the "Pavilion" before us are of the surname Yang, but one or two other surnames are represented. The hamlet is built on a slope; the hill begins from the hinder wall. In front are the threshing-floors of rolled and dried mud, which are fringed with trees of varied leaf, the majority being buckthorn (*Zizyphus jujuba*), the fruit of which, though resembling when ripe the taste of a half-ripe acorn with the least suspicion of sugar added, is sometimes preserved in honey, and rendered pleasant to the palate of the most fastidious. Here and there are graceful pomegranate bush trees. Their bright scarlet flowers are almost dazzling to the eye, as they catch the sun amidst the rich green leaves of the slender twig branches. Each branch tip displayed a beautiful gradation of tints, from russet to red, when the new leaf buds appeared. A grove of pomegranate trees would appear autumn-tinted in the later spring. For genuine autumn tints, China is largely dependent upon the planes and maples, several of which are to be recognised here. The characteristic aster-like touches seen on some Chinese drawings are derived from the sturdy "medlar trees," known to South Sea colonists as the pibo or bewa (*Eriobotrya japonica*), which grow to a large size in Japan. The pine adds dignity to the verdant village fringe. It is much revered, much painted, and its evergreen virtues often sung by Chinese poets. Its "sworn friend" is the bamboo, over a clump of which it spreads one of its longer

<small>Trees.</small>

branches by way of ægis. The inevitable willow thrives near the long irregular pond, which occupies an important place at the head of the forty or more terraced fields which stretch away down to the shores of the lake.

As with the common herbage of the region, so with the microscopical riches of the lake shores, very little unknown in England is to be found. The microscopist is somewhat disappointed, but the familiar wild flowers help one to feel at home here. A dwarf lilac is characteristic of the district. It is scentless, as are all the violets we may find in spring. Wild pinks, also scentless, abound here and there. Pale-purple daisies enliven many a hollow. Buttercups brighten the never emerald grass. Many familiar butterflies flit around, the common sulphur butterfly being most frequent. But splendid black and yellow, or black and purple varieties, large and swallow-tailed, tell us we are not in the homeland. The warmer nights are

<small>The Herb-age.</small>

<small>Butterflies and Moths.</small>

made melancholy from the suicide of many a moth in the flame of the rush pith wick'd saucer-lamps. A paraffin oil lamp will slay its thousands of smaller moths each summer evening. It is hard to write then. Public opinion is aroused by one's literary efforts, and critics, only too friendly, swarm around. Among the unbidden, but in this case not unwelcome guests, are the pure white silkworm moths in the autumn. If butterflies are the fairies of the insect world, surely these are the angels. But the entomology of China would need a volume to do it justice. A larger volume of imprecations might be compiled from numberless authorities upon the subject of mosquitos, with a tale once told at the tea-shop on the Main "Road," a hundred yards from the "Pavilion," to enliven its dreary, woe-filled pages. "The country mosquitos once invited their cousins of the town to a banquet. Plenty of human flesh

<small>Mosquitos.</small>

was provided, but it was thick-skinned and tough. Town manners, however, made it necessary to return the invitation. On their way back the town-bred connoisseurs of flesh consulted as to what was to be done. Mosquito-nets were on the increase, and country cousins are so voracious. There would be no food left for the hosts. 'Take them to the temples,' suggested the wisest of them. The suggestion was received with buzzing acclamation. The guests came, and had to try the points of their knives and lancets upon gilded and painted stucco. They declared, however, with all politeness, that they had enjoyed the repast, but inwardly resolved never to invite or accept such invitations again."

The story, though related in English more elegant than the original, could be proved by internal evidence to be thoroughly Chinese. A foreigner would have modified it to say, that in the spirit-filled idols the mosquitos recognised their relatives grown large. Had Milton visited China in the summer, he would surely have described the demon council as contracted to the size of mosquitos, not bees.

"They anon,
With hundreds and with thousands, trooping came,"

would then have served for the motto of the massive volume. But to our rustic contemplations.

The "sounds of earth"—chirpings, tickings, whirrings, and buzzings being eliminated—are chiefly harmonious. There is an occasional dispute at the tea-shop,—wine is sold there,—and occasional squabbles among the women in the hamlet itself, not unconnected with the unregenerate nature of a neighbouring youngster, pig, chicken, or dog.[1] And amid the prevailing monotony such little excitements are regarded by the Chinese country folk as almost welcome diversions. In every town light, however, there are sure to be a couple of peacemakers. Without these, a fight would be as unorthodox as a duel without seconds. Peace with excitement is a country ideal, but genuine happy

The Monotony of Life.

[1] "Our domestic dogs are descended from wolves and jackals" (Darwin's *Descent of Man*, sec. 130), with which part of the evolution theory every resident in China fully agrees.

excitement is rare. Minor squabbles must supply the place.

The "voices of men" here remind one of Leigh Hunt's definition of bagpipe music, "a tune tied to a post." Here there are two posts, crops and cash. The women add one or two more. With them it is clothes, marriage, babies, crops, and cash.

Babies are a perpetual break in the monotony of life. They refuse to be tied to any post, actual or metaphorical. They do their utmost to raise life above the dead level. Their cries belong to a universal language, the one music common to all the nations of the earth. Has music been developed up from their cries? Ancient music seems to have been minor and plaintive.

Babies.

Such cries may indeed have had their part in the formation of the Chinese language. An Englishman once amused a little crowd in a village tea-shop by remarking that the baby was crying in English. But on carefully noting the sounds uttered by his own babies, he seems to have discovered that it was rather they who cried or chuckled in Chinese. It is a curious fact, that Chinese characters could be found for most infantile sounds. Most "mandarin Chinese" sounds (in Central Hupeh there are only about three hundred) are at one time or another uttered by infants, it is presumed, the wide world over. "Foreign children" born in China show a tendency to pick up Chinese far more readily, under evenly-balanced conditions, than the more complex sounds of their parents. The bearing of all this must be left to the philologist. But the fact is hereby recorded that *we all begin life by talking Chinese.*

The Place of Infant Cries in Philology.

If the Goddess of Mercy be a philologist as well as a linguist, such facts may assist her in her contemplation of the growing, prattling treasures of Chinese villages. But such contemplation, if indefinitely prolonged, would need all the patience and superhuman motherliness with which she is said to be endowed. The Chinese father, and, perhaps, at times, the patient Chinese mother, sees not so much the infant, as the future boy, or just " half a girl."[1]

[1] This is a genuine Chinese book phrase, and gives us the converse of the

The "Pavilion" is unusually gay at the Chinese New Year. Red paper mottoes, antithetical and learned,—for there is scholarship represented here,—adorn some of the doorposts. On New Year's morning everybody goes out and fires as many crackers as he can well afford,—a necessary precaution against evil, and an indispensable accompaniment of worship then. Mere child's play it all seems to us. And if the gods and goddesses existed, it would seem such to the kindest of them. But after the mutual congratulations of the early daylight, some of the more favoured children get a handful of loose crackers given them. Without dealing with higher mathematics, we may safely set down the equation—Chinese child + handful of crackers = intense delight. Nay, it is almost deification. The lad in question becomes a juvenile god of war. Who can withstand him? But several are armed in the same way. And the deification goes to the lad whose crackers last the longest. On this particular day the victor in the mimic battles is a certain Li Seng-teh (*Li* is the Smith surname of China; *Seng-teh* is "victorious virtue.") But no. Here comes the bully Lieu Fah (*Lieu* is a surname as common as Li; *Fah* means to display), who displays certain characteristics which make him the bugbear of the neighbourhood. His father is the tea-shop keeper and cracker-vendor. He thus boasts an easy supremacy, as far as force is concerned. But he does not count. No amount of crackers would deify him. He does not play fair. The threshing-floor is half cleared till he sulks away.

The Children at their Sports.

Meanwhile Seng-teh has gone up to the village school teacher, who is standing at the gate; and, being an intelligent little lad, asks a question, which may be quoted: "Why is it, sir, that the character for cracker is the same as that for whip?" "Because," replies the teacher, with a brightened face full of hope for the boy's future, "in ancient times, before crackers were known, bamboo

The Philosophy of the Cracker.

plural of majesty which is so frequent in Hebrew, concerning which it has been well said that it multiplies the conception not externally, but internally. In Chinese, by the way, *two* stands for a few, while *three*, the extent of the infantile powers of counting, stands for many.

whip-like rods were used instead. These being dried, were lit at the end, and brandished about. As each knot was reached, the bamboo 'whip' gave a loud pop."

"And this frightened away the evil?"[1] Seng-teh is a well-instructed youth, and so does not utter the word demon on New Year's morn. The mention of evil spirits is supposed to bring them.[2] They come when they hear their names called.

Some well-instructed youngsters, however, on New Year's day come up to mother and father, saying, "I must not say demon to-day, must I?" "Hush!" "Yes, I know; nor death, nor coffin, nor lion, or tiger, or elephant, or snake." Until the bewildered parent sticks up in his house a slip of red paper, which says, "Children's words do not count," or over his front door the words, "Heaven, Earth, Yin, Yang [Male and Female principles]; all things without danger from unlucky words." But well nigh trembles at the sound of any unlucky word nevertheless. For the Chinese flower of happiness is so delicate, that "one rough blast" in the form of an unlucky phrase may cause it forthwith to droop and die.

But the school teacher's reply has not yet been given. "No," he says; "hardly that, for, as the *Household Treasury* says [a work of twenty odd volumes, full of concentrated essence of goody-goodiness], 'these sounds agitate the Yang principle [the productive principle] and dispense that of the Yin [which is merely absorptive], and so ensure good luck.'"

With the "crossing of the year" begins the lantern **Feast of Lanterns.** making for the festival of the fifteenth.[3] In the villages near the towns and cities, that evening is marked by processions carrying illuminated dragon

---

[1] There is a legend to the effect that there was once a demon a little more than a foot in height, who lived among the Western hills, and that all persons who saw him became ill. A certain man of the Sung dynasty fired at him with crackers, and put him to flight; hence the origin of cracker-firing in modern times.—*Lockhart*. The teacher's explanation, however, goes back before the days of crackers, and is probably the earlier one.

[2] The Chinese proverb answering to ours, however, is "Talk of Tsao-Tsao, and he is sure to come." Which striking figure of the third century A.D. we shall meet by and by (pp. 117-120).

[3] This festival is said to date back to the second century B.C., originating in the worship of a certain spirit by the Military Emperor of the Han dynasty.

32   A STRING OF CHINESE PEACH-STONES.

lamps, long enough to require perhaps ten or more men to manipulate them so as to imitate the writhings of that monster by a dexterous rotary motion given to the rods which bear the lanterns. The children in such parts are the happy possessors of lamps in the form of fishes (which represent the carp, of dragon - turning propensities), the rabbit (which represents the moon), and other equally significant shapes.

There are no dragon-lamp processions here. The children's lanterns are all home-made. Clumsy and indefinite they are, but still possessing the undoubted charm of being made "all by myself." The mimic processions of juveniles armed with such lanterns, as

RURAL SCENES AND SOUNDS. 33

their cracker-firing at the New Year, are idolatrous, if you like; as idolatrous as our own fifth of November squibs and bonfires are anti-papist.

Soon after the New Year, the kite-flying season begins. Kites being more packable and portable than the bulky lanterns, are supplied by Lien of the tea-shop, from Tsaitien. But in this part, with due apologies to early writers, it is the youngsters who fly the kites, and the elders (if they are not too dignified) who look on. There are, however, traditions in vogue at the present day, that in Hankow kite-flying was quite an art before the Rebellion. Enormous centipede kites (the centipede is the rival of the dragon, creeping in at its ears and eating its brains out), fabulously large birds, butterflies and dragon flies used to engage the attention of the wealthier youths, who may have been fathers. Messages are sent up the line; and see, Seng-teh has attached a lighted lantern to the string, —a new and very erratic star in the evening gloom.

Kites.

A more earthly excitement is derived from whipping tops, which appear at intervals all the year round. They are just like those of our own land. These afford a mild recreation for the little girls too, almost the only one, besides playing at ball (made of cotton thread), which they possess. We may defer our further consideration of the year's sports to notice the pretty dress of these mild spectators, who are as interested in the rougher games as the fair ladies of old were in the tournaments of chivalry.

Whipping Tops.

The Little Girls.

On New Year's day they appear with faces somewhat ghastly by reason of the application of flour in place of finer face powder. They have also red patches on their cheeks, suggestive of exceedingly hectic flushes, and their lips are wonderfully scarlet. Each face is adorned with a coronet of satin or cloth, with large "gems" or gilded miniatures of the eight Immortals of Taoism thereon. But notice that from the coronet depends a black silk fringe reaching almost to the neck over each ear. These surely are most interesting survivals of early classical days. Compare them with the

Their Head-gear, a Survival of Trojan Times.

3

golden headband and fringe brought by Dr. Schliemann from Hissarlik, and described by Homer in the scene where Andromache bewails her lost Hector. He tells us that her head-dress was fourfold, two of the parts being of textile fabric. The remaining two alone have survived; to wit, a gold frontlet, and a fringe of golden pendants [1] dropping over the brow, and then at greater length down the side face. The sight of these at the South Kensington Museum suggested the lines—

> "Gauds that once glittered, spite their present rust,
> In the ears of maidens fair as could be seen,
> Sprightly-voiced maidens of soul-gladdening mien." [2]

Similar fringes, but of silk, are to be found in China, that wonderful museum of antiquities, and comely too are some of the bright little faces that peer forth from such a classical adornment. Poets have belauded the famous beauties of China, but have forgotten these. Let us greet them at least with the poetry of chivalrous emotions. Life will be a very battle around them. But some of them will be as brave, if as sad, as Andromache.

As the weather grows warmer, hats and coronets are laid aside, and boys and girls grow slender. The difference between the broad-as-long style and the later slenderness, is, however, a matter of clothes. Long before midsummer the boys follow the example of their fathers, and when the sun comes out retain but one lower garment. The little girls look sweeter in summer; their garments are clean with frequent washing. Their younger brothers gain in comfort, if not in elegance. Like the newly-transformed Tom in Kingsley's *Water Babies*, "they feel how comfortable it is to have nothing on but

Summer Attenuations.

---

[1] In Judæa, these seem to have become in after centuries the ten pieces of silver worn on the brow, one of which was lost in the parable, Luke xv. 8-10. The number ten, rather than seven, would seem to argue an early origin of the custom. The Egyptian perfect number (hence ten plagues, seven in the Revelation) seems to have predominated in the popular phraseology for about three or four hundred years, then to have taken a secondary place, to be finally ousted by the distinctively Jewish seven.

[2] J. W. Hales.

RURAL SCENES AND SOUNDS. 35

themselves." But how they avoid sunstroke, with their clean-shaven pates, is an inexplicable mystery.

With the fifth month come the double horse-power castinet cicadas. These have been dormant until now, but may be seen emerging from the ground as ugly "bugs" (see American dictionaries), which make for the nearest tree, split the middle seam of their coat at the back, and walk out. They may be seen doing all this, but now they claim a hearing as well. The maiden speech is duly hesitating. The sound of its voice seems at first to frighten the beastie itself. But with growing confidence comes growing fluency. Only the voice is a rattling apparatus.

Summer Recreations.
With Cicadas.

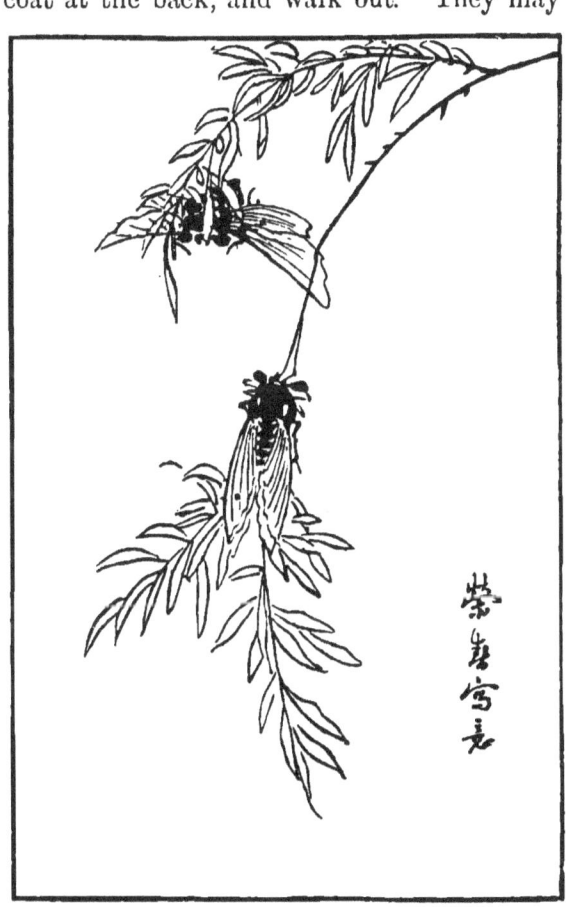

Here again we are back in classical times. A Greek poet,[1] noticing the fact that only the male insects are noisy, vented his spleen on the fair sex in the couplet—

"Happy the cicadas' lives,
Since they all have voiceless wives."

Like many of the Greeks of old, the Chinese youngster

[1] The Rhodian Xenarchus.

catches the cicada, and delights in its song. But it is only charitable to the Greek nation to assume that the *tettix* of the Greeks must have had a quite different voice, more soft surely, and melodious. This, however, makes the author of the above couplet the most uncharitable of men.

But the cicadas are far outrivalled, as far as recreative pleasure is concerned, by the fighting crickets. Their duels are of little harm to the vanquished, and of wondrous interest to the seconds. An elaborate little treatise is published, giving the habitat and characteristics of the best fighters, with equally explicit hints as to the nurture of their bodies and the development of their martial spirit. But such volumes are unneeded here. The lads have their own theories. Fighting crickets, and centipedes also, they affirm to have been produced from feathers buried in the earth. A good cricket is often found to be guarded by two centipedes, they say. But one lad declares that the very best fighters have a bodyguard of snakes. He found two snakes the year before, and went looking for the champion cricket. His *à priori* argument did not have a very palpable conclusion. He did not find the cricket, but (he says) the two snakes found him, and fastened on his hand. He shook them off, and ran.

Fighting Crickets.

In this village the youngsters do not gamble. They have no cash to gamble with. Victory means a name for the owner of the cricket, rather than gain. The former is the higher of the two supreme ideals of China. Such fame may be appreciated by the British schoolboy who is himself the champion fighter of the school. Here there are few such fights, and no hitting out from the shoulder. All fighting is done by deputy, the deputy being a cricket. Fighting crickets, moreover, are quoted by grown-up scholars as being typical of the human race. A man who is defeated in any undertaking or discussion (and Chinese undertakings always involve lengthy and sonorous discussions) is described as "a defeated cricket, which gives up its mouth."

All feathers are not destined to be buried to bring forth centipedes or crickets, however (most are used for the enriching of the soil), some are rescued to be tied into a bit of rag stretched round a cash to form a shuttlecock. This is kicked about with many a nimble contortion. Some can kick the shuttlecock a hundred times without letting it fall, and have great fame in consequence.

Shuttlecocks.

Stilt-walking enlivens many an evening. The spills afford much amusement to even the women, while the winning of a race at breakneck speed brings deserved renown.

Stilts.

The very little folk occupy the time that can be spared from mud-pies by the recital of noisy nursery rhymes, mostly full of puns, and so not easily translatable. In earlier days Seng-teh's mud-pies were voted most artistic, and he still occupies an evening now and then in moulding yellow clay into elaborate but fragile vases. Will he become a kiln-owner at the great pot-and-pan centre so many miles away? His fond parents almost shudder at the thought. He is an only son, and the kilns are so far off, quite out of the world indeed.

Nursery Rhymes.

And Mud-pies.

Meanwhile he must do his best at study. He seems to have powers beyond his years. And so he is found at the village school soon after daylight, with the ten or more other scholars who can be spared at times from ox-tending. His tasks, however, are sooner learned than theirs, and his spare time is devoted to artistic, if impossible, designs for an ideal series of birds, beasts, and fishes.

The Village School.

The first book to be devoured for future rumination in more advanced years is the *Three Character Classic,* the author of which is said to have gained the idea for this universally admired text-book from a girl's primer written by his mother, a highly-educated

The Curriculum thereof.

lady, some of whose literary productions are still extant. The work begins—

"Men at first,
Disposition radically good."[1]

The first honoured name it mentions, perhaps out of respect to the author's own mother, is that of the mother of Mencius, who, with careful regard for her son's morals, "selected a place of residence," and when her son would not study, cut the web in the loom to show her grief.

Inducements to study and to virtue generally are given in varied language, and supported by numerous ancient examples; but before the galaxy of great scholars appears, such things pass before the view as the decimal numbers, the powers of the universe, universal obligations, the seasons, the elements, the virtues, grain, domestic animals, emotions, musical instruments, kindred, the classics, philosophical authors and commentators, emperors and dynasties down to the Sung (960–1280, during which the author lived); then by a later hand the stream of history is descended, the rapids at the fall of the Mings' are shot, and the "Great Pure" waters reached. Then the original author resumes with his stories of precocious infants, indefatigable scholars,[2] and a grand old man of antiquity, who at eighty-two was

"In the great court
The foremost scholar,"

and statesman. But watch-dogs and morning chanticleers, silkworms and bees, add their quota to the peroration in favour of the glorifying of ancestors and the attainment of learning's priceless treasure.

Another spelling-book is the Hundred Surname list, with its equivalents of Smith, Brown, Jones, Robinson. Another is the Thousand Character Classic, the origin of which is thus accounted for: The "Military Emperor" (B. 502–550)

[1] Compare and contrast the old-fashioned "New England Primer" for children, which begins—

"In Adames fall
We sinned all."

[2] One of these reminds us of Foote's recluse, "Reading his breviary by the light of a glowworm."

ordered his son to write a number of characters after the style of a certain Wang, a noted caligraphist of earlier days. A thousand of the best of these were selected and shown to the Emperor, who called one of his statesmen named Chow, and said, "You are a man of ability. Arrange these for me." Chow did so in a single night, and offered the result for imperial inspection. The effort had turned his hair quite white. He received a liberal recompense. The wonderful jumble[1] certainly suggests midnight oil and whitening locks, if nothing else.

The Hundred Surnames and the Thousand Character Classic.

Then come the Confucian Analects, The Great Learning, The (Golden) Mean, and Mencius, which complete the "Four Books." For more advanced scholars the Book of Odes, one of "the Five Classics," is added; also the Three Hundred Tang dynasty poems (an attempted rendering of one of which appears at the head of the present chapter). These works are not devoid of interest to the intelligent scholar, but are a mere jumble of inexplicable characters to the schoolboy. As in old Judæa, the Chinese juveniles begin right away at their sacred writings, the explanation of which is deferred. Here, however, it is never the "sincere milk of the Word"; rather a ponderous cheese, too heavy for the youngsters to carry away with them, too hard to bite at, and somewhat indigestible if bitten.

The Classics proper.

Not at all understandable by Schoolboys.

A vital necessity for the Chinese pedagogue's work is "one piecee bamboo." It affords frequent incentives to diligence. It is by no means reserved for mere naughtiness. Nay, should it lie idle for any length of time, it administers heart-stinging chastisement upon the teacher himself, for engraven on its hollow side are the words—

Forcible Aids.

"To instruct without severity
Shows the laziness of the teacher."[2]

---

[1] Its chief modern use is to number the balls of imported opium, after the manner of the alphabetical numbering of the sheets of our red postage stamps.

[2] "Correction in itself is not cruel ; children, being not reasonable, can only be governed by fear. To impress this fear is therefore one of the first duties of those who have the care of children. . . . It is the duty of a schoolmaster." So Dr. Johnson, *Boswell's Life*, 1827, p. 195.

Thus we see that in some cases the old descriptions of China as topsy-turveydom have more or less justification in fact. Our early instructors assured us that the rod hurt the hand which wielded it. In China the rod hurts the heart of him who handles it not.

Two of the "Pavilion" scholars, however, are remarkably free from aches and pains ferrulean. Li Seng-teh seldom needs it, while Lieu Fah has been sent to school on the express condition that the preceptor shall not punish him.

The man who made this most un-Chinese stipulation—doubly un-Chinese from the fact that the bully-dunce of the school is big-boned and anything but delicate—is possessed of a face which does not impress us favourably at first sight. It is always well to make a note of your first impressions of a Chinaman. In many cases they will change on what seems to be closer acquaintance, but which is often a growing prejudice to his advantage or otherwise, nurtured on the one hand by some occult art of suspicion disarming, or, on the other, by equally occult influences from the man's rivals. The full analysis and tabulation of first impressions might save much after regret. But such an analysis, even were one possessed of the requisite "reagents," is not always feasible. In medical phraseology, it is diagnosis through a curtain if your Chinaman meets you full face. The full face is often a habitually-worn mask in this part of the world. Side face is better; the mask does not reach quite so far. It is also a fact that the mask drops considerably during moments of slumber. Caught thus unawares, the task of character-reading is not so intricate. If only phrenology were an exact science, the Chinaman's semi-baldness might reveal much more than half his scalp skin. Head charts, however, being, as the learned affirm, as reliable as Chinese maps of the universe, that method must be eliminated. Chinamen not always being sleeping beauties when our princely forms first approach them, we must do our little best with first impressions. By the neglect of such precautions, even Chinamen themselves may go wrong. The frequenters of the tea-shop have really forgotten what their

The Reading of Character.

first impressions of Lieu were. They have themselves constructed for him an almost magic mask of nobleness. The school teacher, still young, has never forgotten his early impressions of the man. He was a little boy when he first caught sight of that palimpsest countenance. Children's first impressions are not to be despised. No English child seems to take to a Chinese mandarin, for instance. And before the juvenile, now schoolmaster, appeared on the scene, Lieu Fuh-tang (Hall of Happiness) was practically a high mandarin here.

In his case, whatever our age, we find ourselves in sympathy with the little lad aforesaid. When we do catch the full face, the mask is so obvious as to suggest something which needs a great deal of hiding. His smile is more repulsive than his scowl. The head is habitually bowed, so that we hardly see anything lower than the conspicuous eyebrows. But were we to doff our invisible hats and turn to him our side face, we should feel that something from under those dark eyebrows was scanning us. The evil eye (not quoted in these parts) would be a fitting name for that something.

But see, the villagers come in. Something within them bows low indeed. And something within the man claims and proudly accepts the homage. Are they bewitched? Possibly subjected to demi-semi-hypnotism.

What is the sudden excitement about? Enter a crowd of small boys gasping out "Spectacle-seller." Yes, the black goggle seller, seller of real goggles, supposed to be real pebble, has come on his quarterly round. Notice him as he enters. Something within him nods, but bows not. The " I know you, old fellow " is almost audible. Then slipping out of the shoulder-strap which has borne his little cabinet, he puts the box of tricks on the rickety table, worn to corrugation point, sits down upon a bench equally rickety and yet more corrugated, and sips the proffered decoction which (on the seven sharps scale) we may call tea. Fah has strayed in from the school, and begins to elbow the young cowherds aside in order to inspect the contents of the several drawers of the cabinet. A forcible exclamation escapes the

Spectacles.

pedlar's lips, but he checks himself with another look at Lieu when he sees who the youth is.

The neighbourhood is now fairly aroused. The schoolmaster has saved his dignity by permitting the remaining scholars to stop fidgeting and run to see. The force of parental example certainly urges in the direction of the tea-shop; the women have left their spinning-wheels and washing-tubs, and the farmers their farming. The shop is crowded out. Cabinet, table, and all are brought outside under the thatched awning in front. And no wonder. Here are goggles black and goggles grey, goggles of clear "stone" and clouded, goggle frames without glasses, glasses without goggle frames, tweezers, files, hammers, scissors, a bow drill with bits of steel wire to replenish it, whole coils of brass wire to be chopped up for rivets, and quite a museum of spectacle cases,—cheap lacquer, and those of better quality with floral and poetical adornments,—cases for "folders" of carved peachwood, and full-sized cases of shark skin. The latter material, in response to numerous inquiries, is declared to be the hide of a foreigner; but the more knowing twinkle their appreciation of the "big word." They know the skin to have belonged to a foreign beastie.

In their minds, however, the polished case of "sand skin" (shark skin being the sandpaper of the town joiner) and the man who would part with it, if paid his price, seem connected in uncanniness. They have both come from far beyond the horizon. They both belong to the farther bounds of *terra incognita*.

There must be something in it apart from *à priori* considerations, for once or twice there pass between the sand- skin man and the tea-shop functionary words which the crowd cannot catch. The sounds seem Chinese, but Chinese is, after all, a language of phrases. The secret of the matter is this, the two friends are conversing with the aid of a system of occult phraseology.[1]

_{Occult Phraseology.}

---

[1] The occult phraseology of China would require a small volume to itself. A couple of men will sit down in a crowded tea-shop in town and carry on a conversation, the gist of which may be quite unknown to the man opposite; the nouns and verbs being foreignised by previous agreement. There is a

At last a sharp ear is quite sure of one of the phrases. It sounds like "eyebrow beast," which may be another name for shark, but the third sound may be "number." That is it, "eyebrow number." He sees at a glance that he is right. Little is gained, however, for when that particular number is to be mentioned again, there are other available words less obvious, which are as familiar to the hopeful pair as they are unguessable by the uninitiated.

But something within us bows low before the august presence of the reader. We hasten to explain that the Chinese figure for 8 consists of two strokes of an angle corresponding to that of a coolie hat, or, say, a cottage roof. Our momentary occultness having been pardoned, we are, however, landed in a field of controversy by the phrase in question.

Are not the Chinese a race of folks with little buttonhole slits inclined obliquely downward towards the nose? Would it not be rank heresy to dispute it? It is so by their own showing. What can be more reliable than Chinese and Japanese portraits of themselves (*and portraits of mountains standing upon their peaks*)? The fact is, that tipping up the outer ends of the eyebrows, as of overturning mountains, is a method of idealisation. Overhanging rocks do exist; and in Central China, about once a month, may be seen in the crowded cities a pair of eyebrows which point slightly upwards outwardly. But the architecture of the face of the earth, as of that portion of the Chinese face under criticism, is generally otherwise,—that is, in Central China.

<small>Chinese Eyes.</small>

But we cling, at anyrate, to the buttonhole slits. Does not Moore sing of

"Persia's eyes of full and fawn-like ray,
And the half-shut glances of Kathay"?

---

common basis for most of this cypher talk. It is in use among fortune-tellers, often for the deception of country folk. With them a father is "heaven-elder"; mother, "earth-elder"; elder brother, "bow up"; younger, "bow down"; eyes are "shiners"; ears, "fair-winders"; a foot, "kicking horn." Numbers may be disguised in many ways. One method is to fix upon ten characters which shall serve the purpose according to their projecting strokes. Thus 卄, already given, is 8.

Yes, and Addison promised in No. 583 of the *Spectator* to give in his next paper a history which he had "found among the accounts of China, and which may be looked on as an antediluvian novel." And Goldsmith wrote a surprising amount of information about Chinese customs in his *Citizen of the World*, and Lamb a luscious history of roast pig, and someone in the East wrote about Chinese princes and princesses, cities and citizens, in *Arabian Nights*; and quite a host of "old masters" decorated what were once standard books on China, with elaborations in woodcut and steel plate, wherein coolies are crowned with incipient pagodas, and high mandarins luxuriate in their drawing-rooms, forgetting to put down their ginghams, or shall we say to remove their oilskin sou'-westers? *i.e.* to take off from their own classical pericrania their water-carrier's bad-weather rain hats! All of which afford delicious diversions to the resident in China, and confirm his Chinese friends who are favoured with a peep, in their idea that *foreign* countries are indeed the haunt of marvellous beings.

Don't, pray don't tell them they were meant for China! They will open their eyes too widely, unless for untold generations their family has been afflicted with ophthalmia sufficient to "half-shut" the most "full and fawn-like eyes" that Persia possesses.

It is a thankless task, however, to attack the "old masters" and the classical dreamers. Suffice it to say that many a Chinaman whose years have long since left behind a "cycle of Cathay" (who is far more than *sixty*) possesses as wide-open binoculars as most men of Europe after their "fifty years" are passed.

From the relative shape of the eye, we may change the subject to that of relative powers of vision. And here many a European knows to his cost that while the Chinaman has seen him through and through, he has but seen the outer surface of the Chinaman's mask. Foreigners, you know, as Mohammedans in China (whose intelligence has been quickened by journeys to Mecca), are credited with the power of seeing into the earth. It is the treasures thus discovered that make them rich. But few, alas! spite of all maxims, can see into a Chinaman.

And with regard to even the surface of the earth, are we not half blind? Let us launch out into the lake, and make a sketch, taking a photograph of the Hill of the Nine Recluses, to make sure. Alas! even our cyclopic, demon-eyed, special landscape lens is a delusion and a snare. Compare what it has recorded with the very vigorous old Chinese woodcut below. Its result is entirely innocent of pagoda; the

photograph but contains one hill-top temple and none beneath. These perchance have disappeared during the many years (no one knows how many) since the officially appointed artist drew his design. But the everlasting hills themselves, how flat and meaningless in the photograph! Here they are jaunty, heaven-aspiring peaks. The nine recluses of old must have been, as they are reported to have been, acquainted with secrets of nature not yet unfolded to ordinary mortals, still less to foreigners, or they would never have managed to balance themselves year after year upon the apex of each rocky pinnacle. The fact that they discovered the much quoted "immortality pill" seems also to be established, for how could they come down to market? These rocky perches, moreover, as everyone will admit, were specially adapted for their ascending to the skies when their initiation was complete.

We cynics of the school of Diogenes who have never seen a "true man"—for such is the Taoist phrase we have translated "recluse"— can hardly understand how such a drawing as the one before us came to adorn the pages of an official topography. Yet are we from the West, that region whose iridescent poetry is seen in mirage at sunset by Chinamen who know nothing of the mirage of our science books, but see the gates of the West wide opened to display the glories of a paradise lost, to be regained one day for them who confide in the "man of the West country"; such hopes being attested by bannerets carried aloft in funeral processions, inscribed in varied phraseology, "Westward Ho!"

But the artist whose inner eye saw the nine lovely maidens—for report says they were such—perched upon nine pinnacles, might surely be excused if he depicted those peaks as emulating one another in vigorous attempts to follow them to the regions of higher empyrean. Which attempts, to our purblind eyes, they seem long since to have abandoned in despair.

Oh for a pair of Chinese spectacles! Metaphorical spectacles! Dream spectacles! No dollars will buy them. We can but purchase a pair of black goggles, such as Chinese elders affect.

The school teacher, though not an elder, must perforce possess such a pair, which, like an academical gown, may be worn on state occasions, and give weight to *ex cathedra* utterances. For he has come to occupy the onerous post of referee to the community. Moreover, the resplendent doctrines of the sages necessitate dark glasses. They are too dazzling for the ordinary eye. But the school teacher's history, his claims for veneration, and how he came little by little to oust him of the tea-shop, must be relegated to another chapter.

Chapter III.

The Mandarin in Embryo.

PROBLEMS LITERARY AND PHILOSOPHICAL—AN EXILE AT HOME
—SYMPATHETIC TREES AND FARMERS.

> "Nine mouths are found in me,
> The 'Hundred Surnames' see;
> Give him who guesses the answer complete
> A bottle of wine and a catty of meat."
> —*A Chinese Riddle.*

THE answer not being very obvious to the Chinese, it is hardly to be expected that the Westerner, whose education (in the contents of the book in question) has been so sadly neglected, will have any chance of success, and its accompanying feast. Happily, as fat Chinese pork and, especially, Chinese gin afford little attraction to us, we may be content to give it up. The answer to the obscure conundrum, however, gives us the surname of the school teacher, as will be presently explained.

Every Chinese character takes us back to the blue distances where all seems heavenly, and where fancy, aided *The Origin* by tradition-telescopes, sees a wondrous sage *of Chinese* some forty-six centuries away, "laying bare the *Characters.* permutations of nature, and devising a system of written records." Having succeeded so far as to oust the earlier system of knotted cords, "heaven caused showers of grain to descend from on high; the disembodied spirits wept in the darkness; and the dragons withdrew themselves from

48 A STRING OF CHINESE PEACH-STONES.

human gaze." The demigod Ts'ang Hieh[1] it was who thus caused some very signal "permutations of nature." His portrait is given herewith. The four eyes are probably meant to indicate his extraordinary power of insight.

Once Rounded Characters now Angular.

The earliest specimens of Chinese caligraphy which have come down to us are evidently the descendants

of signs (yet more) pictorial. The earliest characters for

[1] An interesting theory of Professor Terrien de Lacouperie (*Babylonian and Oriental Record*, May 1888) makes this Ts'ang Hieh to be none other than the celebrated Chaldean king Dungi, known for his numerous inscriptions. He says that an examination of many early Chinese characters shows that they are derived in a cursive or rounded form from the later cuneiform characters. The date he fixes for this is B.C. 2500.

THE MANDARIN IN EMBRYO.

"ear" and "mouth," given in the illustration, will more than suggest this. In earliest days, folks drew a picture of an ear and of a mouth, and in those two cases the pictures remain to this day, squared, however, instead of rounded. This angularity arose from the fact that "books" in old time were bamboo slips, on which it was far easier to engrave in straightened lines than in curves.

The sign for the surname of the teacher is formed of that for ear thrice repeated; and as the angular form of the character for ear contains three openings or mouths, some witty scholar unknown made bold to concoct and propound the above riddle.

The sound of this character could not be guessed by any Chinaman who saw it for the first time. The elements of Chinese characters seem to combine chemically, and afford an excellent illustration for a lecture to Chinese students upon that science. The (central) Chinese sound for ear is *erh*, that for the three-eared character is *nieh*, which is very close, considering. The meaning (now forgotten in the surname) seems to have been a sound which needed a triple ear to hear it, *i.e.* a whisper.

The Sound of each Character a Riddle.

The teacher's surname is therefore Nieh, and his other name (one cannot say the "Christian name" of a "heathen Chinee") is Shu-k'ing, which means "Book Noble," or more elegantly, Prince of Literature.

Nieh Shu-k'ing was not born here. One early morn, a venerable man, evidently of good family, appeared at the teashop, his only attendant being a little boy, his grandson. In process of time (Li Seng-teh's grandfather having put him up for a while) he bought a house in the village, which had been long empty, because of the ghost or ghosts known to haunt it at nights.

Nieh senior, however, nothing daunted, watched there one night, bade the ghosts begone, and they forthwith departed from the popular imagination, to leave in their room a great name for the demon-vanquisher. The exorcist then bought a plot of land, planted it with mulberry slips, and the vegetables of the season, and cast in his lot among the country folk.

Who he was, and what he had been, could only be guessed. Even Lieu could not read his past. "A wronged man, who will be righted some day," was his own scanty explanation. Every time the keeper of the tea-shop and general store went to Hanyang, the old man commissioned him to procure copies of the *Peking Gazette* (the oldest newspaper, or rather court circular, in the world), which he could get through some "friends" at the Hanyang *Yamun*, and also a few books, chiefly of high literary style, for which, having brought a heavy bundle of silver with him, he was able to pay Lieu's price. When he died, he left his grandson, of seventeen years, a well-selected library, and knowledge enough of classical intricacies to make the volumes intelligible to him. This grandson had thus become the literary genius of the place, and the days of mourning for his father being ended, had opened a school in the village.

The Scholar's Position in Country Districts. In order to understand the position of a scholar in Chinese country districts, we must first consider the fact that one of the prominent characteristics of China is respect for precedent. "First on the field" means undoubted superiority. Precedent is a national deity.

Filial piety is largely buttressed by the fact that parents existed before their children. They are one generation nearer to the ideal, but incalculably distant, days of old. They are, moreover, links in the chain of ancestry which binds their offspring to the days of the half-deified emperors, whose beams of grace glorified the golden ages of antiquity.

From these premisses, illustrated as they have been by expression in terms derived from family life, further conclusions may be drawn concerning the relative positions of the tea-shop Lieu and the literary Nieh. Lieu came into his business some years before Nieh was thought of. He was first on the field by some years; he had a few years of actual precedent. Therefore by most of the tea-shop frequenters he was worshipped as the living abode of the deity Precedent.

Added to such principles there was his personality. He

was fairly on in years, years of varied experience which seemed universal to his rustic worshippers, the sincerity of whose worship was by no means disannulled by the fact that he was very sparing in his communications. Perpetual mystery as of a half-veiled idol; the reverse of cheapness in his oracular responses,—these made him a demigod indeed. He was a link to the outer world of utter mystery, and could, if he would, discourse in short tantalising sentences on everything ancient and modern.

Nieh, on the other hand, was an actual link to the ideal past. Lieu's antique fables paled before his exact "text-behind-every-syllable" communications. Lieu had therefore to entrench himself in more recent events, which none could disprove. The unobtrusive Nieh could justly claim to be the authority on things ancient.

"But for such as he," argued the villagers unconsciously, "how should we know anything definite concerning the early ideal times?" In some respects even parents compare unfavourably with the *literati*, for the average parent is but a dumb survival of the good old days; whereas the village teacher (and mandarins are but glorified *literati*, instructing and admonishing larger villages) represents the ideal times themselves.

The ideal emperors died long ago; the deity they worshipped was (to them) a mere memory of a luminous cloud appearing in the early dawn of the world's day. Here is a man, however, who "knows all about" the ancient emperors, together with all that is known of the deity they sought to propitiate (somewhat needlessly, it is thought by Confucians nowadays); a man who can quote their very words, ideal in meaning, ideal in style, and written in ideally perfect, ancient, and inexplicable characters. He is clothed in the mantle of the sacred sages, so sacred as to possess never-to-be-written names.[1] He is a living stream which has flowed unpolluted

---

[1] This form of respect, familiar to us in connection with the early substitution of other vowel points for those properly belonging to the Divine name we pronounce Jehovah, and the continued substitution of Adonai for those altered sounds by the more devout Hebrews, is applied in China to the personal name of Confucius (first altered in writing, and commonly avoided altogether by a

from a sacred fountain, whose every drop is liquid gold. "Yellow gold has its price, books are priceless," as one proverb has it, but another declares that, "Each character is worth thousands of gold." With regard to the man who imparts this priceless enrichment, another proverb reads: "One day a teacher, your father for a lifetime." Fellow-scholars, by reason of their relation to the teacher, become elder and younger brothers.

A link between the present and the past, the teacher is also a link between the populace and the Son of Heaven. He gives to those who can hold it, the pound which has the potentialities not only of five or ten pounds, but five or ten cities. Learning opens a dazzling vista of official emolument, at the end of which sits the demigod on the Dragon throne. The schoolmaster is thus a sage by survival—an imperial statesman in prospect. The honours due to him are partly parental and well-nigh imperial.

Realising all of which, can we wonder that in isolated country districts so many of the *literati* are proud despots, whose bamboo rod of correction for youngsters is sometimes dropped for an iron rod of something like terrorism when anyone crosses their path? This is especially so when they have taken their degree. Their position, in the event of any law cases, would then correspond in many respects to that of Roman citizens in our own classical times. *Romanus sum* becomes to the country folk almost *Consul Romanus*, the phrase which haunted De Quincey in some of his opium dreams. It happens that in China the word for learning and that for poison are of identical sound. Hence there is a saying, "Don't offend him; there is an air of learning [poison] about his house." Instead of the "frog in the well," they are thus the upas tree in the hollow. China would be a different land if all those country scholars whose learning has curdled into "pride, vainglory, hypocrisy, envy, hatred, malice," were kept in check. The subject, indeed, occupied the attention of

word like So-and-So), and to those of the emperors of the reigning dynasty. The term Kwang Shü of the present emperor is but a kind of signboard appellation. His personal name is learnt by scholars only, that they may avoid the use of that pair of characters, to use which would be a grave misdemeanour.

the imperially appointed expositor of the Sacred Edict. He has no words too scathing for these "bare stick"[1] B.A.'s.

From such an abuse of learning Nieh Shu-ki'ng is happily free. He can read the Sacred Edict through without wincing. He has not taken his degree, however, nor even attempted to take it. He does not wish to explore the outer world as yet. And his not wishing means not daring. Blameless as he is, according to ordinary standards, he dare not fill up the required schedule with the names of his progenitors. The reason thereof is only known to himself.

A place among the competitors in the imperial examinations is denied to men who live by immorality or robbery, to chair-bearers, to barbers, to professional minstrels and others, and to their descendants for three generations. But surely he does not come under any of these headings. Yet he has a secret which, for the life of him, he must keep to himself. It has been well said that he who would effectually keep a secret, must hide the fact that he has a secret to keep. And this has hardly been done, at least from Lieu of the tea-shop.

The near presence of that objectionable man, who, among other characteristics, has that of being extremely hospitable to those rascals the tax collectors when they come, is on this score, as on others, an exceedingly uncomfortable, but, perhaps, salutary check. It prevents the "rod of pride" from either blossoming or budding.[2] Any move towards self-assertion has been checkmated, and life has long been with Nieh a very game of chess, in which every move has had to be most cautiously made. There are heavy stakes at issue in this life game, and he cannot afford to lose.

He knows that Lieu looks upon him as an interloper of "shady" origin. He also feels that Lieu has for him a craven kind of respect. Lieu seems to have his own secrets, but his dislike is no secret. It is partly fed by the necessity for such respect. Of the two, hatred is the predominant characteristic. What but dislike could have caused Lieu to make the un-Chinese stipulation that his son was not to be punished? The

---

[1] The force of the expression comes out in contrast to the Chinese for "B.A.," literally *budding*, or, perhaps, fertile, *talent*.
[2] Ezek. vii. 10.

great hulking youth is not delicate, and his father is in the habit of administering many a fisticuff, accompanied by much unclean abuse. Lieu evidently imagines that with such a pupil the schoolmaster's powers of self-restraint will be more than tested. Nieh rightly guesses that any slip in that direction will be followed by a declaration of war. And he cannot afford that. Fewer polite phrases are current in the country than in the town. There is less of that bribery of flattery, which is so effectual in winning the day against the other's accusing thoughts. But still the art of keeping another in something like good humour has to be studied. Every civility toward such a man involves a certain loss of self-respect, but is also a cause for self-gratulation. Nieh has been uniformly, if coldly, polite to the man he dreads and despises.

He has also kept strictly to the letter of the agreement, and really has more command over the lazy lad in school hours than many a Chinese pedagogue, stick and all, possesses over his pet blockhead. How it has come about puzzles the other lads. Outside the school walls a bully, Fah is but a dunce within them. Yet "I'll tell your father" never supplied the place of the rod. And no other scholar's person[1] has been made to serve as substitute for the rod's due "falling place." The latter would hardly have renovated the lad, and it would have been sure to have given rise to enmity among the families concerned. Such family feuds, often starting after pre-existing soreness from very slight causes, are most undesirable things in villages, as they are most difficult to allay. They mean civil war in its worst forms, and the calling out of all the militia of the parties concerned, the diversion of all the energies from their proper spheres of exercise, and the concentration of effort toward the hurt of the hated adversary. Everyone has to take sides, and there is general alienation. Victory has no

---

[1] Young emperors, like our early princes with their "whipping boys," are punished by proxy. A few years ago there was a tale going the round of the graduates assembled for examination at Wuchang, to the effect that young Kwang Shü had escaped into the streets disguised to see a bit of life. He was mobbed, the offenders were punished, and a certain statesman's son was banished by way of punishment due to him.

attendant laurels. Defeat means revengeful plottings. A feud of a generation back has isolated the "Pavilion" from the large village of Soho (across a few miles of land and lake), which would otherwise figure in our narrative.

Unlike the English schoolmaster, the Chinese teacher has jurisdiction over his scholars out of school hours, and many a blow in school is administered in connection with offences committed outside. It was this which made Nieh's palm to itch so frequently, and the rod's silent message to become at times a very peal of thunder in his ears. When school was over, Lieu Fah defied him.

The next biggest boy and second dunce in the school is a lad who wears the garb of a Taoist priest, his early death having been predicted by the village doctor and general prognosticator. Such a dress, however, would deceive the gods into the idea that the lad was dedicated unto them, and thus render him invulnerable. The case of another village lad having been deemed more desperate still, he was apprenticed to the Buddhist priest-monk on the hill. By an act of pre-arranged disobedience, he will one day be turned out of the temple when the crisis shall have passed. But of him at present we have nothing further to relate.

One morning, however, the "Taoist" lad had had a deserved beating before the school had been dismissed for morning meal. The scholars having dispersed, the teacher went into the rustic kitchen, placed in the stove some bundles of dried grass and a few split branches of the smaller pines from the hillside, then, with black flint, steel, and paper spill, lit the fire and cooked his breakfast. There are neither clocks, watches, nor sundials in the country (in later days all of these, however, have been imported), and so the breakfast hour is a variable quantity with the scholars, whose fathers may be away in the fields. In place of gong, various shouts are heard when the meal is ready. These shouts do not synchronise. So the literary Nieh, having had his breakfast earlier than the generality, was in the habit of repairing to his mulberry plot, the ground of which was a well-tended and productive vegetable garden. The school fees were by no means a fortune, and he had need of this very important means of supplementing his slender income. The garden was enclosed by a wall of rough stone, over which Mother Nature's decorative fingers had woven many a verdant web, and over which he himself trained his annual pumpkins.

His occupation this morning was chiefly weeding. He had cleared the ground up to the low wall, the other side of which was one of the main thoroughfares—a path actually two feet wide (country roads being so narrow, it might be resented as an act of something like "Cockney" impertinence if cities had wide streets). It happened then that the teacher was squatting down on his heels very near to, but completely hidden from, any but full-grown passengers who might pass along the narrow but important highway, when he heard voices, and familiar ones, and his own name mentioned by them. He did not stoop down lower still, for he was no eavesdropper, nor did he rise, but went on with his weeding. The voices were those of the "Taoist" and Fah. As they drew nearer, the latter said, "He never hits me, the —— [a reflection, as all Chinese bad language is, on the parentage of the man in question]; he daren't. He has no ancestral tablet, and the 'old head' [instead of the usual "my venerable father"] says he is ashamed of his ancestors. And no wonder. The old runaway, I have heard, brought a heap of silver. The 'old head' knows,"— but they were gone.

Nieh had received a bite as from the most venomous reptile known in China. Where ancestry is everything, where the antecedents of a man occupy a place only to be compared with the thought of eternal destiny in the West a century or two back, it would not have been possible to have chosen a more refined form of mental torture than that under which Nieh writhed. He was excommunicated, and by such a pope; the message of excommunication being bruited abroad by such a mean ——. Poor Nieh! no vile word passed his lips, but sometimes it was suggested to his heart. "You complain when you are angry; I curse," once said a foul-mouthed coolie to his Western master. Yes, the language of complaint in China is derived from a dictionary of unclean slang. Nieh's complaining was extreme, and his memory recalled the strongest phrase in that unprinted dictionary.

For a while he seemed stunned, then rose, looking old and livid, and walked away from the village along a narrow hill path. He stamped the ground, and moved his arms convulsively. He walked on mechanically until the village was out of sight by reason of a bend in the hill-path, when he met Seng-teh's father, his one real friend, coming home to his breakfast. "Still early," said Li, with a bow and a smile. But no answer from Nieh. "Are you poorly?" he asked, alarmed at the strange look in the teacher's face. This seemed to remove the rocky seal from an overcharged subterranean spring. With a sudden jerk the young man raised his trembling hands to heaven, and cried, "High heaven! High heaven! bear witness and avenge! High heaven! High heaven! right a wronged man! All-seeing heaven, right me! vindicate me! Reward virtue! Punish vice!"[1] Then he burst into a flood of tears, and the impassioned appeal was changed to a dreary wail. He would not be comforted, nor could he explain himself. "Fah," at length he stammered out; "unspeakable insult;" then he started to run, and Li had to put forth all his strength to restrain him. "Let me go! let me go! I'll thrash the slanderer to death, and his father too. No ancestors? High heaven! High

---

[1] The reader may note that the sentences quoted approach the point of rhythm. This is frequently the case among the Chinese, especially Chinese women, when they are announcing their woes to the universe [the Eastern equivalent, as Rev. A. Smith says, of writing a letter to the *Times*]. "When a man warms and becomes aglow with emotion, not only is there a certain run in his sentences, but also a certain flow in his speech" (J. H. Morgan on the *Welsh Hwyl*). "Various intermediate forms between speech and song may be heard in the ordinary speech of certain races [presumably in their excited moments], notably in Italians, Welshmen, and others. The Puritans, as is well known, uttered their formal and affected diction in a peculiar nasal tone; and the term 'cant,' though properly belonging to their singing, came to be applied to the sentiments expressed by it. Many of the ancient orators . . . would seem to have sung their speeches, the style of declamation being termed *cantus obscurior*" (Sir Morrel Mackenzie). We may apply this to the case of the Hebrew prophets. The Chinese (Preface to the *Ancient Book of Odes*) find in it the origin of poetry. "Poetry is the product of earnest thought. Thought [cherished] in the mind becomes earnest; exhibited in words, it becomes poetry. . . . When sighs and exclamations are insufficient for the feelings, recourse is had to . . . song. When song . . . is insufficient for them, the hands begin to move, and the feet to dance."

heaven! Hear it. Avenge!—avenge!" Overpowered by Li, he sank down on the grass, and moaned afresh. "It is only one man," Li urged, "and we all know him." "No; he has told everybody, and everybody worships him as a god: I will go, and you shall not stop me!" "Lieu has gone to Hanyang early this morning," urged Li. "I will follow him to the Yamun, and appeal. No, I cannot. I am wronged, I am wronged, and heaven has no recompense." "Do not say no recompense, the day has not come," broke in Li, quoting a frequent saying; then, pleadingly, "Nieh Shen-seng." The words, and especially the sound of his name, with the term of respect after it, seemed to act with magical effect. He was himself again. "I have lost face with you," he said. "A myriad times No, Nieh Shen-seng! And I guarantee you will be righted soon!" exclaimed Li with fervour. Thus soothed, Nieh washed his eyes in the hillside brook, and went back to school with no outward signs of any inward struggle. Chinese masks are almost more unbuyable than Chinese "spectacles."

After a while we see him sitting at his table amid the shoutings of the scholars over their tasks, now and then striking the table with a block of wood, not for silence, but that any scholar who has ceased to shout may resume such vocal exercise. One merit of the Chinese system may be seen in the fact that a youngster cannot be shouting, say, the four Chinese surnames, Field, Black, White, Bell, and at the same time be whispering something else. Then the use of the voice does undoubtedly assist the memory, on the same principle as that which is at present operating on the mind of the teacher. The placidity of his countenance, though artificial and the result of long training, backed, perhaps, by force of heredity, suggests placidity to his mind. Fah has no idea that he has been overheard, and when his turn comes to show his ignorance of the appointed task by "backing the book" (that he shall not see it), and stammering out more Chinese "hums and haws" than sounds of character, the teacher is unusually gentle in his tones of censure. Pride sits on the safety-valve. Pride whispers, "You are a superior man to control yourself thus." And something, which is not altogether pride, repeats a task for the teacher to learn: "It is not that there is no retribution; the day has not come."

One true statement made this morning was that Nieh had no ancestral tablet.[1] There were few in the village. Li pur-

ANCESTRAL TABLET.

chased one on the death of his father. Nieh "ought to have one" if Li had. But instead he keeps his grandfather's tomb

[1] Chinese ancestral worship so far resembles that of ancient Greece and Rome in theory, that some words applied to the latter may serve to describe that of the Far East. "The supreme object of veneration in the home is the progenitor, who is supposed to protect and preserve the life which has sprung from him [in China, however, the various offerings of cash paper, etc., are supposed to be of actual value to the now needy ancestors]. None but direct descendants can claim a share in the sacrifices. 'The dead who left no son receives no offerings,' says Lucian. The woman only takes part in the domestic worship through the man . . ." (Pressence). Images of ancestors are seldom used, but in the *Twenty-Four Examples of Filial Piety* there is a story of a filial son, in the Han dynasty, who was early bereaved, and who therefore

in specially good repair. Behind his "mantelpiece" (no fireplace underneath), with its looking-glass of uncertain surface, a couple of painted glass candleboxes, a three-legged brazier for incense in the centre, and a large cheap vase at the right hand, is a large red scroll, on which is written, "The Philosopher Chü's 'Household Maxims.'" On either side of this are too narrow scrolls, whereon are the words—

"A heart of diamond (fanned by) zephyrs from the crocus;
Righteousness for a friend, virtue for an instructor."

Which words in the original exactly match each other, a noun for a noun, a particle for a particle. There is also a contrast in the tones of the characters (somewhat suggestive of Western counterpoint), which makes such parallel antithetical sentences the essence of Chinese poetry.

From the large central scroll we may quote the words, "Do not covet the riches of unrighteousness; do not drink wine beyond measure. Let economy characterise all the affairs of the household. . . . Let those who have give to those who have not. . . . Let the instruction of youth be in accord with rules of right. When you have done a kindness, do not think about it; when you have received a kindness, do not forget it. . . . In your intercourse with the world, let your words be few; in a multitude of words there are sure to be errors."

The whole list might be quoted, but these maxims will suffice to show that the great commentator of the Classics (1130–1200, whose house still stands in a lovely spot not far from Kiukiang) has some claim to our respect.

School over, Nieh went by invitation to dine with his friend Li, for that worthy rightly divined that he was in need of mental ventilation. After all, the teacher lived a very pent-up life. His chief friends were the authors of his books.

---

made wooden images of his parents for his own consolation. His wife, however, pricked these images with an iron skewer, whereupon blood trickled forth. The filial son discovered the crime, and divorced his wife.

There is also a curious custom in which one of the juvenile sons of the family is dressed up in the ancestral robes, and receives the worship of which they are the real objects.

He held nightly converse with departed sages, philosophers, and other old-time authors.

Li, whose "other name" was Sung-seu (*Li* means plum, also baggage; *Sung-seu* is pine-like longevity), met him with the exclamation, "The pine load I brought home this morning" (Nieh winced inwardly, for Li was somewhat " honest," which in Chinese often means "too simply true") "was unusually dry." "It is all right," thought Nieh. "Dry weather. And as I was cutting it I noticed that fine old pine up the hill. 'Eh, my old namesake,' said I, 'you look wondrously well. I hope I am as well when I am as old.' Not bad, was it?" and Li laughed his demure guest into a manifest smile. "I'd like to meet the spirit of that pine. I'd bow to him, and call him 'old namesake' too." This sublime utterance, and the one little cup of warm wine together, for the two met under his epiglottis, nearly choked him. "I suppose it has a spirit?" he added inquiringly, when he had subsided sufficiently to wipe his eyes with a very dirty bit of rag inserted in his left sleeve preparatory to the feast, if not in anticipation of the catastrophe. "What do your books say, Shen-seng?"[1]

"You remind me," began the teacher, "of an old hermit on a certain hill, who, on being asked who was his best friend, used to point to an old pine hard by, and say, 'That faithful old man.'" "But *I* do not say the old pine was my best friend. He is here," interrupted Li, laughing in wonder at his wit.

The Pine-tree in Folklore.

"*I* can point to Pinelike Longevity, and say, 'There is my best friend, and the son of my venerable grandfather's best friend too.'" This was irresistible. It brought down the house, or rather caused Li's arm to gyrate so as to bring down his chopsticks. His son picked them up, uttering the words "*Kwai loh,*" a frequent pun meaning nimble (lads) fallen, or *sprightly joy.* The aptness of the remark called forth the proud father's approbation in the form of, "He has a good

---

[1] The corresponding English word Scholar is also used as a term of address in the *Compleat Angler.* Literally translated, the word is Signior (or elder). But without going away from our own English phraseology of to-day, Sir is from Senior (Lat.) through the French.

teacher," which Nieh acknowledged by asking Seng-teh the composition of the character for pine. "Wood and duke," he replied readily, which his father (who could not read) saw at once from the look on the teacher's face to be right. "And so, according to an old book upon trees, it is the duke of the forest. Now the sign for wood consists of a cross and two strokes, as though it were the number eighteen. It is not that number. It was originally a picture of a tree, but it looks like eighteen now; and so another writer has described the sound of a high wind blowing through the old pine branches as that of eighteen dukes leading their retainers on to victory."

"Good; very good. It will stand a high wind too."

"Well, the old book says that a famous hermit was once deep in his meditations, when he saw a form standing before him, who introduced himself as the spirit of the hills, and said he had come for instruction in doctrine. Having received it, he asked what recompense he could give. The hermit answered, 'The hill where I generally meditate has no pines; could you move these thither for me?' 'Your humble servant,' replied the spirit; 'never fear.' And he bowed exit. That night there was a great thunderstorm, and the morning saw all the pines transplanted around the dwelling of the hermit."

"Hai Ya! He must have been a scholar. Be diligent at your books, Seng-teh."

"As to the pine spirit, on a certain hill a countryman met a traveller dressed in strange clothing, leading a white dog. On asking where he lived, the traveller replied by pointing to a neighbouring hill. The countryman followed him as far as an old pine tree, where both man and dog disappeared. The traveller was the spirit of the pine, and the dog was that of the fungus[1] around its root!"

---

[1] This fungus (the *pachyma cocos*) is used as a medicine. The Chinese say it is the sap of the tree converted into that form after a thousand years, and that after the second thousand years it will have turned to amber (Williams' *Dictionary*). The attractive powers of rubbed amber do not seem to be quoted as evidence of the indwelling spirit, but were probably thought to be such in old time.

"Hai Yeh! I saw the dog this morning, unless it was the watch-dog of the temple. And it barked at me! I didn't see the spirit, but only met the priest's apprentice soon after. He was cutting wood too!"

Nieh was not quite so credulous as his friend; but to avoid being asked for his opinion as to the present visibility of pine spirits and the identity of white dogs, related how that when the "Military Emperor" of the Liang dynasty,— in whose reign the Thousand Character Classic came to be,— who was a very pious ruler, went to worship on the hills, he used to weep profusely at his own unworthiness, at which the pines "changed colour," a phrase which Nieh explained might be taken literally or otherwise, but either way was a sign of emotion. Such sympathy of trees with good rulers he further illustrated by the story of the cypress[1] in the front of the temple of Confucius, at his birthplace in Shantung. It is said to have been planted by his own hand. Its high trunk puts forth no fresh branches until moved to do so by the advent of a good sovereign. The beginning of the present dynasty and the birth of the Emperor Yung Cheng — he of Sacred Edict fame — were marked by this wonder.

The Cypress.

"Confucius was exceedingly 'spirit-moving,'" said Li, somewhat missing the exact point of the argument, and using a term which illustrates the wide difference between the common phraseology of China and that of Christian lands. Spiritual influence is not so often quoted here. Man is the palpable fact of the universe—spirits are less obvious, some very shadowy indeed, but are open to influence from either strikingly good or bad men.

But Nieh had a story of a cypress made famous by a magpie, which bird had actually "moved" the Supreme. The "Military Emperor" of the Han dynasty (R. 140–86 B.C.),

---

[1] With some of the above legends, compare that of Cyparissus, son of Telephus, beloved by Apollo, or else Silvanus (who is represented as carrying the trunk of a cypress). One or other of these deities—for the story is variously told—once killed by accident a hind belonging to the youth, who died of grief, and was metamorphosed into a cypress (Smith's *Classical Dict.*, pp. 201 and 707). Compare also the legends concerning Dryades, Hamadryades, and Melides.

whose long reign, like that of the Liang dynasty emperor aforesaid, gave rise to many an anecdote, was one day—a showery day—having a feast with some of his courtiers, when his favourite associate and adviser, Tung Fang-so,[1] a

gifted scholar and man of genius, who is now ranked as one of the Immortals, appeared under the dripping eaves, holding a weapon in his hand. On the Emperor asking the reason of his appearance, Tung Fang-so smiled, and said he had been sent for by the Supreme, who told him there was a magpie on a withered cypress behind the palace cackling vigorously toward the East. "So I was commanded to go and find out the reason of the noise it was making." "And how should you know?" asked the Emperor, who had risen from the now finished feast. "Oh, I know a thing or two about the affairs of men," he replied, with a laugh. "I saw the wind was in the East, so, by reason of the bird's long tail, it must perforce turn its head that way. Moreover the branch was slippery with the rain,

---

[1] On one occasion when the Emperor intended to present his courtiers with some sacrificial meat, Tung Fang-so, being the only one present, did not wait till the others arrived, but cut off a piece of the meat and departed. On being ordered to apologise, he replied, "How impolite not to wait for the imperial bidding to receive the gift which had been made! How bold of me to draw my sword and cut the meat! How generous of me not to cut too much! How kind of me to take it home as a present for my little lady!" The Emperor laughed at the apology, and gave him another present of meat and wine for his wife.

for which two reasons the magpie began to cackle. What a joke!"

"Then if birds' cries are heard," exclaimed Li, for once logical, "the cries of men are too, and Heaven will right the wronged."

"I look upon the story," said Nieh, "as a gentle reproof administered to the Emperor, the argument being that if Heaven cared for birds, he ought to do something besides sit at idle feasts; he ought to hear the cry of his people."

This strange dream parallel between the above story and certain words concerning the cry of birds, young ravens and others, with which we are happily familiar, will not be lost upon the reader, who will see, moreover, that the superstitious may at times catch glimpses of high truths which the more coldly critical put from them in their times of need.

"Are there any stories about the maple?" asked Li, who had accepted the scholar's explanation, and felt a little abashed at his presumption; "the leaves are beginning to redden."

"Not much that is at all interesting. A term for the Imperial Palace is Maple Rooms; because in the Han dynasty maple trees were planted in the imperial courtyard. My old book says: 'There is an old maple tree in the south called the maple demon, its trunk being somewhat like a man's body. It has also been called the prayer-answering maple. In other parts, the maple is found to make prayer-answering idols.' Another passage says: 'The maple spirit is that invoked by the Nine Recluses [which may mean some nine recluses of another part], and the tree is very precious in consequence.'"

The Maple.

"There is one law for all under heaven," said Li, feeling he had a firm footing when held up by quotation crutches. "Anything about the willow?" he asked, pointing to one outside the door.

"Yes," said Nieh. "A scholar, who was afterwards famous, was walking under an old willow tree, when he heard sounds as of a harpsichord. On asking who the minstrel was, a voice replied, 'I am the spirit of the willow'; and the spirit sprinkled the garments of the

The Willow.

5

inquirer with willow sap, saying, 'You will, without fail, gain the highest degree of the Empire. But you must come afterwards and make me offerings of date-cake.' The scholar promised he would, and sure enough got the foretold degree."

"You must take your degree, Nieh Shen-seng," was the practical application.

To avoid discussion, Nieh continued by relating the story of a certain young scholar, in whose house was a picture of a very lovely maiden. "The scholar's eyes used to wander up from his orthodox task to the picture; he spent many a moment trying to discover what was the secret of its wondrous fascination. The lines were well drawn, and the colour well applied, but there was something—Eh! the eyes blinked! No, he was dreaming. He rose and gazed once more. There it was again! 'Speak!' he cried, 'if you can.' The picture smiled. In process of time the lips moved as if to speak. 'Little sister,' he said, 'you love me'; excuse the folly [this by Nieh to his audience, which now numbered three, Mrs. Li having been attracted at the sound of a word or two in this promising legend]. The picture reddened, and said, 'I do.' 'How can I possess you?' [was the somewhat natural question]. 'I am the spirit of the willow tree yonder. Get me suitable garments, and I will enter them.' 'And will you be my wife?' 'Yes, after proper betrothal and the marriage ceremony.' These, with the compliance of his mother, being fulfilled, they were married" (and lived as happily afterwards, we hope, as Pygmalion and his vivified statue).

Li looked out of the door, half-expecting to see the willow trunk open and disclose a similar maiden. But he said solemnly and decisively, "Nieh Shen-seng, you must get married."

Nieh's face became suddenly gloomy. He was still a young man, and had not brought his mask with him to Li's house. The privilege of being himself was so rare, that he clung to the few opportunities he had. He would have to assume such a mask perpetually by and by. He had already accepted other limitations of his position; one of which was the unspoken command, "Thou shalt not take thee a wife, neither shalt thou have sons and daughters in this place." He was undoubtedly the superior of these country folk, yet not so free to act as they. The words Fah had blurted out (except the last insinuation of unjust gain), had some basis of fact behind them, sufficient, he had persuaded himself, to tie his hands. Lieu the elder had some theory as to his origin, and perhaps spite enough to get that theory accepted at the *yamun*, with whose underlings he was a sworn brother. He might even then be perfecting his schemes for his extinction. A man who is "in" with the *yamun* blacklegs is to be dreaded. He had money too. He undoubtedly had; more than his country business would bring in. This would pave his way, unless, indeed, his own secrets were such that he dare not "lift his head" in the *yamun*. Nieh was involved in the misfortunes of his grandfather; he was in the eye of the law a criminal, whose punishment, at the least, disgrace, might be much more if that eye were but anointed with silver eye-salve. Till he was "righted," he had no chance of taking his degree, and he would not undertake fresh relations which might, with a man as Lieu for an informer, involve others in something more than ignominy, and, apart from *yamun* proceedings, Lieu might at any time use his influence to close the school, and thus cut off his chief means of livelihood.

"'No household,'" urged Li, supported on quotation crutches, "'is complete without three sounds: the sound of study, the sound of children crying, and the sound of spinning.'"

"My household," replied Nieh, with a forced smile, "has the first. And when my scholars are lazy, it has the second."

"Not wrong!" exclaimed Li with a loud laugh; "your doctrine is deep, inexplicably deep. But how about the third?"

"I have no fair maiden picture," said the other, "but I have my 'central hall scroll,' and I will hold its doctrines instead."

"'Righteousness for a friend, virtue for an instructor'; but still, you might have a woman for a wife. The daughter of that humble relative of mine on the other side of the lake, for instance. She knows 'the coolie pole character' [—, the numeral one] when she sees it. She is of good disposition, and has 'teeny weeny' feet compared with those of ordinary country girls. 'Not to deceive you,' I am told her feet were specially bound with you in prospect, if I may say it without offence. But you are a 'superior man,' and 'the tree mallow weds the camellia,' not the 'dog flower' [the wild rose]."

"Don't! don't!" cried Nieh in pain; "wait till Lieu comes back from Hanyang."

"With the *Imperial Almanac* to fix a lucky day," said Li, laughing at the audacity of his wit.

"No, not that," half moaned the school teacher; "I want to do a little reading. I have been poor company."

"Don't hurry away," responded Li, using the customary phrase in real earnest.

Besides the *Peking Gazette*, Lieu, as will be gathered from this conversation, used to bring back the *Imperial Almanac* towards the end of the year. This has the fortunate days for marriages, burials, and the like marked thereon, and also the unlucky ones, the importance of which would have been very real to our grandfathers. The choice of an unlucky day might be as disastrous (mark the word) as setting sail from port on a Friday! In China, however, it is the emperors, rather than the stars, which "ban the days."[1] The anniversary of the death of any emperor of the present dynasty is a day so unlucky, so filled with possibilities of calamity, that, as the Almanac maintains, it is positively unlawful " to have stage plays or weddings, to pay or receive calls, to buy official buttons, to start on a journey, to remove one's bed from one room to another, to cut out clothes, to resume studies in a school, to call the doctor if you are ill, to call the barber [however much your pate may itch], to remove goods and chattels, to open a new shop, to have a bath, to strike a bargain, to rent a house or repair it, to cut wood from the

---

[1] Compare Job ii. 8 : " Let those that ban the days, ban it."

" Not from the stars do I my judgment pluck ;
And yet methinks I have astronomy ;
. . . to tell of good, or evil luck."
SHAKESPEARE, *Sonnet XIV.*

THE MANDARIN IN EMBRYO. 69

hills, to level the ground, to grind corn, to brush the underside of the tiles, or to shoot birds or beasts."

These regulations, Nieh Shen-seng, Almanac in hand, did his best to enforce, with complete success as regards at least one item. The villagers were loyal enough to abstain from cleansing their persons on that *one* day.[1] But with such

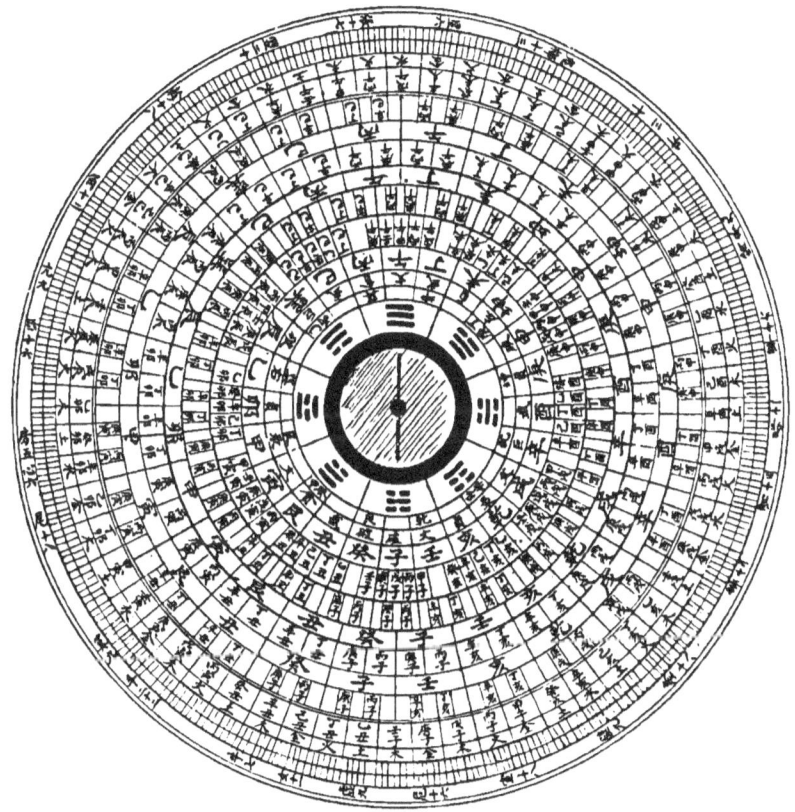

"FUNG SHUI" DIAL.

multifarious restrictions, it can hardly be wondered that the Chinese salute for the Emperor is practically the same as the Babylonian, "O king, live for ever!"[2]

[1] In the Ta'ng dynasty the ministers received their pay every ten days. This pay was called "washing money," the ministers being supposed to wash every ten days. The terms upper, middle, and lower "wash" are still used for the three divisions of a month.

[2] It is literally "a myriad years." The Military Emperor of the Han dynasty ascended a certain hill, when his attendants heard the cry (from out of the heavens) thrice repeated, "A myriad years."

Possessed of this Almanac, moreover, the teacher was able to foretell eclipses,[1] so that the villagers might be prepared with their gongs and cymbals, and the priest-monk with his big drum and bigger bell, to frighten the heavenly dog into disgorging his tender morsel of sun or moon as the case might be. Such a duty, is it necessary to remark, is incumbent on all patriotic souls?

This Almanac, moreover, gave the true interpretation of dreams. A man dreamt that he saw his front door open. This, according to Imperial exegesis, meant that great happiness was in store for him. A woman dreamt that she saw her door shut. This was a sure portent of calamity. The next time her baby fell ill, she would see a fulfilment of such prophecy, and perhaps procure a charm, an old coin, or perhaps, if means allowed, a circlet of silver wire for his neck.

The teacher, having this Almanac, had ousted the fortune-telling doctor from his occupation in the matter of dreams, but the "doctor" held his own in the matter of *fung shui*, having a special geomantic dial, with a compass in the middle, with a few hundred characters around it, which he could not read, but in which the priest-monk on the hill-top was giving him instruction as far as his abilities went, what time he visited the temple while out on a medico-botanical ramble among the hills. Thus provided, he could look wise, and talk ambiguously about sites for graves, and possible house building. He was chiefly in request at a distance; all travelling expenses paid, besides the professional fee.

The present temple-keeper was a youngish man, who had appeared one day duly branded on the head, and with shoes worn with long travel. He had been accepted as helper by the old priest, who was getting feeble, and needed someone to fetch water for him, if not to cut wood. He found his helper very ignorant of Buddhism, but as he knew half the characters in the mass books, and could learn those on the slips chosen by lot according to the number of the bamboo tally picked out of a jar for suppliants, he would do. When the old priest died, the young man, having cremated him, and

---
[1] The Emperors, from the time of Kang Shi (b. 1662–1723), having enlisted the services of the Roman Catholic astronomers.

buried him in a jar with all due ceremony, was voted his successor *nem. con.* He thus represented the Church, as Nieh Shen-seng the State.

The days dragged on, and at length Lien Fuh-tang returned with a barrow load. Nieh Shen-seng's packet was delivered to him for a consideration, and having gone round to Li's house, he prepared to devour the contents. The Almanac had come. Li wanted to begin with that. But Nieh, with visible trepidation, began to turn over the pages of the *Gazette*. Folks in England can hardly conceive the excitement which may attend the delivery of a mail to one of their countrymen away in a Chinese village. It is exhilaration almost to the point of pain. The hands of the strong well-nigh tremble if bad news is anticipated. With the arrival of the mail everything receives a new centre of gravity. Monotonous peace is exchanged for a declaration of war, in which the combatants are conflicting emotions. Which will win?

"Ah! which?" asked Nieh, until he was tired of asking such a question concerning such forlorn-hope expeditions. With quickened breath, he turned over the leaves of the oldest newspaper in the world. At last he fairly broke down, tears blotted out the page, and Li had to support him to a chair. "Bring some tea," he cried to Mrs. Li, "and put some salt and ginger in it. And warm a little wine too." Then to his friend, "What has happened?" "It is all over!" he gasped. "What is over?" "I am righted." "I said so! I said so! Ancestors' protection! Heaven's recompense! Stand up, that I may bow my congratulations." Nieh rose, and his good friend bowed again and again, with "respectful congratulations" each time. To which Nieh bowed his acknowledgments. Then, with a voice tremulous with emotion, he read—

"The Governor-General of Hupeh and Hunan reports that the present magistrate of Fancheng has captured a criminal, who, on being examined, confesses that from motives of spite he stole the seal of a former magistrate there, named Nieh, which is now forwarded to the capital. Memorialist has made diligent inquiries, and has received many testimonies as to the probity and benevolence of the said Nieh, and pleads that the deceased mandarin's family, if any members yet live, may be pardoned. Rescript. Sanctioned."

At which stage, Lieu Fah was seen to be looking through a crack in the closed door. "You young ——, you spy, you may go home and say that the great official Nieh is righted now." But Fah needed no hurrying. Li's words were loud enough for him to hear nevertheless.

"This refers to my venerable grandfather," began the schoolmaster, having pulled his impulsive friend back by the sleeve. "My venerable father and mother ["venerable" is always prefixed by dutiful sons to the words] died when I was young, died of smallpox, and I was brought up in my grandfather's *yamun*, which was soon changed to that of Fancheng. He was an upright man, 'only taking a cup of water from the place,' as the saying is. So he was not wealthy, but was benevolent as far as his means allowed. One day the occupants of his jail, with one exception, were found to be ill. They were all retainers of a certain wealthy man of the city who had died, it was thought from poison, and from whose house some chests of silver and clothes were missing. The illness of the prisoners was traced to the fact that the oldest of them had on his person a little of a suspicious yellow-white powder, which was found to be a deadly poison when administered to a dog. He had half-poisoned them with arsenic, and had vainly attempted to do the same to the prison-keeper, so as to make good his escape. The rest recovered. The old villain, my grandfather beheaded. Hardly had he done this, when the chest containing his seal was missing. One of his confidential servants had decamped with the son of the decapitated man. Without saying what was lost, my grandfather sent his runners in all directions to capture the thieves. The case was desperate, for, as you know, the loss of the imperially-bestowed seal[1] is a capital crime and involves the family."

---

[1] The moulds of all the official seals are kept at Peking. A lost seal can thus be renewed and reissued by the Emperor, but any rascal possessing the lost seal can of course work great damage. It is like possessing the orthodox signature to any number of blank cheques. If the seal becomes worn, it can be sent to Peking with a corner filed off to make it unusable. On every occasion of a mandarin's leaving his *yamun* to go out anywhere, the seal is supposed to be entrusted to his wife. On each resumption of office, the seal is worshipped as coming from the Emperor's sacred person.

THE MANDARIN IN EMBRYO.

"Hai Yeh!' was Li's comment. "But he wasn't killed, was he?"

"No trace could be found of the robbers. And in a few days an important deed had to be signed. The truth must leak out then. An under-mandarin from another part, an old friend of my grandfather, was passing through the city, and being unwell, stayed a day or two.

"One moonlight night, my grandfather, having seen his guest to rest, for this Wen had a son about my age, called in a trustworthy old servant, and got into his visitor's chair, getting the old man to call the bearers, quietly so as not to awake 'the mandarin Nieh,' and to order them to start down the river at once, under the pretence that Wen's mother had just died, and he must be off immediately and attend to the customary ceremonies which filial piety requires."

"Good plan! Good plan! And then?"

"The bearers seeing my grandfather's servant, and thinking they had the mandarin Wen to carry, went straight for the boat. The city gate was not yet shut.[1] The boatmen were deceived too, and the faithful servant came on board on the pretence that he had been engaged by Wen as his personal attendant. The supposed Wen kept himself closely confined to his room, and I with him 'nursing.' The only other person admitted was the old man."

"Heaven-granted wisdom!"

"The flight would not be known till the morning, so we had some hours' start. The current was swift, and the rowers worked with a will, being promised extra wine money."

"Ancestors' protection!"

"They were anxious hours, but the boat folks suspected nothing; and, after rowing by relays day and night, we reached at length a point just below Tsaitien. Here the boat was stopped at a village on the north bank, where the grappling irons were thrown on shore, and a general feed, with plenty of wine, given to all on board. The faithful old man had hardly slept at all, and was wearied out.

"When all was quiet but for their snores,—and they

[1] The gates of such cities as Wuchang close at sunset, but in smaller cities they are left open till nearly midnight.

snored like thunder,—my grandfather and I crept on shore. He was in plain clothes, but had his official robes in a bundle. Another bundle—a heavy one—contained silver. I had a lighter one too. We went down the river bank some way, when my grandfather undid his bundle of clothes, and hung his robe on a tree stump, half in the water, letting his hat drift down.

"Some distance farther, we found a boat. We got in, and he rowed across; then letting it float down, he and I went inland up the river, and arrived here at daybreak. He changed his name (not the surname), and also gave me the name of Shu-ki'ng. And now"—

"Nieh Shu-ki'ng, Nieh Shen-seng, Nieh the official, respectful congratulations," interrupted Li with a deep bow. "Now you will get married, and take your degree, and 'ascend to the highest grade.'"

"Yes, to the former," replied the teacher. "As to the latter, I await Heaven's decree."

Chapter IV.

RED LETTER DAYS.

THE NEW GIRL—FAT PORK—ACADEMICAL HONOURS.

"A day of triple joy: A son born in the morning; an ingot of silver kicked up outside; arrival of a messenger with the news of a brother's success in the examinations."—*A Chinese Saying.*

WITHOUT binding ourselves to the inevitable fulfilment of a prophecy quoted by our friend Li in the above terms, in which the school teacher was both the man and his brother rolled into one, it behoves us to relate that, one day in the early spring of 1849, there was considerable excitement around the Yang Family Pavilion. Little processions of country folk were wending their way from the neighbouring hamlets, to join the groups which formed picturesque patches against the "village" walls. Other little processions were already wending their way, somewhat Blondin fashion, along the narrow and irregular field paths which led to the shores of the lake. School was disbanded for the day, and the scholars added their quota to the strings of youngsters running along, tumbling at times along the little ditches beside fields of incipient wheat and barley. It was a national holiday.

A sound as of a musket was heard in the distance; whereupon all eyes were directed, and not a few lips pouted, towards the lake. Pouting is the coolie's only available method of pointing when both his hands are occupied with his load. But no one is a coolie, or even a farmer, to-day. All are gentlemen—and ladies, fine birds with fine feathers. Respectability reigns smilingly everywhere in such a garb that had a tax-collector turned up to-day he would have certain qualms of what stands him in stead of conscience that he had extorted so little.

On the lake are the usual fishing-boats, but there in the distance is a speck. It moves. It is red. It emits a little puff of white smoke. Listen, there is the corresponding bang at pianissimo. The speck becomes a boat, the boat is full of living forms—and that bit of sun-reflecting red. It shoots a flash of light across the waters; it is partly of glass. The craft which does duty for the dragon boat, on the festival of the fifth day of the fifth moon,[1] has been brought into

requisition, and now, as then, is being propelled by a numerous crew, armed with short-handled, shovel-like paddles. It is broad enough for two paddlers to sit side by side, with a clarionet player, a gong and cymbal beater, and others in the centre before and behind that wonderful red object, never to be too much quoted.

The rowers keep excellent time, impelled thereto by the clang, clang of gong and cymbal. Thus stimulated, they are doing their best to drown the musical cadences of the clarionets, yes, and the flutes too—we had forgotten these.

---

[1] This festival commemorates the death of a worthy but maligned statesman of about 314 B.C., whose appeals being disregarded, clasped a stone to his bosom and plunged into a certain river. Attempts were made to recover the body, but in vain. The modern dragon boats are a survival of these.

But every now and then feeling their rustic ditty to be too "slow," too refined an expression of their jubilance, they break out into a loud neighing sound, decidedly heathenish to Western ears. Dragon boat excitements "pale their ineffectual fires" before the exhilaration of to-day, for is there not in that very boat a brand-new bridal chair, wherein is imprisoned a real live "new girl"?

A detachment had gone in the early morning to the "Tung Family Lip," which pouts considerably lakewards, some five or six miles away. Having landed at a spot where (six cash) ferryboats start to carry travellers across a mile and a half of water towards Soho of lawsuit fame, they made their way to a somewhat isolated cottage, picturesque and picturesquely situated hard by a large pond. The door was found to be barred, as if in defence—as effectually as little Jack Horner's Christmas pie may be supposed to have been crusted over, and with a like sequel.

This barring of the door seems to be the other half of the tally corresponding to our custom of throwing the shoe. Put the two together, and we have a survival of the good old times, when brides were procured by

"The good old rule, the simple plan,
 That he should take who has the chance,
 And he should keep who can."

No stealing has been done in this case, however; the door is unbarred—unlocked we ought to say by two thousand keys (circular, with a square hole in the middle—good large Imperial cash). The elder Chü is happy indeed to have his daughter disposed of to one whom he already considers a mandarin-elect, perchance a prime minister. She herself weeps a bit as she says farewell to her parents, whom custom requires to stay and bemoan her fate, if they can. Her brother, a host in himself, packs her resplendent form into the chair, which we can only idealise by calling "Coach and four," and they are off.

Nay, the cry now is, "Coming! Coming!" A cry which grows every moment; a theme with variations of explosive hand-claps, of soprano melodies from the little girls and their mothers; of shouts which are not reducible to musical nomenclature from the boys, of falsetto peals from the youths, and baritone exclamations from their elders.

Excitement is, as we may imagine, a Chinese ideal. Just as with the ever-present indigo-dyed garments, and the green and brown landscape, they love bright red, so with their life of monotony, they revel in noisy excitement. Owing, it is thought, to a peculiar construction of the bovine eye, oxen are disagreeably excited by red contrasts, and two thousand years B.C., we are told, black was the lucky colour; but we of China are neither bulls of Bashan nor colour-blind ancients. Red tints, metaphorical and literal, are the order of our festal days. The bride's chair is red, as we have surely done our best to persuade the reader. It is hung with red lanterns. The teacher's house glows in the morning sunlight, a veritable ruby. Red is the prevailing colour of the holiday costumes, which flash out from the green and brown everywhere.

"It is better than a play," cries young Li, of the artistic soul, who had seen a few "ox plays," as they are called, from the fact that the histrionic representation upon open-air stagings of the deeds of demigods is calculated to draw down their protection upon beasts brown or water loving, for which protection from murrain a sum of three hundred cash is subscribed as a capitation tax upon every "brown ox," and six hundred upon each (stronger) water buffalo.

Better than a play? Who would doubt it? When nearing the shore, crackers, interspersed with squibs, are fired off in volleys. It is a Liliputian battle, a battle against evil influences, with Gulliver assisting. Another method of demon-scaring is embodied in a round red victory trophy, in the centre of which is a "brass mirror," the one Chinese survival of the days when all mirrors were metallic. The ugly sprite catching a glimpse of his face therein must flee aghast at the sight. He is thus assailed through both ear and eye. He had better flee, or it will be bad for him.

The boat rasps against the pebbly shore, and the lantern-hung chair, with its emblematic decorations in tinsel and red panels, among which is sure to be the celestial unicorn, ridden by a Chinese cherub, indicative of an honourable perpetuation of the family on the male side, and other designs too recondite to be explained here—the whole contraption is taken up tenderly and lifted on shore, to remain on the grass a moment until the procession has duly formed.

First comes the huge red trophy, then two large red lanterns with golden characters of "double joy" thereon, then two

"torches of display," then a couple of flutes, then the gong, then a couple of clarionets, then a double pair of cymbals, then the coach and four. A whole string of Lieu's best crackers is fired as the gorgeous pageant starts; to get a full view of which, certain youngsters make a box seat of a tree, impressing their plastic minds with materials for a future and amateur encore.

The hills resound with such manifold exultation, that the

solitary priest-monk must surely rue the day when he took his vows of celibacy.

The particular chair of the day, we repeat, is a brand-new one, an importation; an investment also, for a marriage chair may be more profitable than an ox or two. Apart from chair hire, everyone expects double wages in connection with marriages, the building of kitchen stoves (the residence of the action-recording kitchen god), and funerals. Hai Ya! an unlucky word, has slipped out. We can only atone for it by contributing our quota of red to the fortunes of the day. If we had been Chinese, no amount of blushing, however, would suffice.

We scorn to be coupled with Lieu of the evil eye. "If it blows hard, she will not prove a good wife; if it rains, she will not live long," was the proverb he quoted but yesterday. We would rather have our portion with the sunshine and zephyrs. Lieu's sour looks have been robbed of some of their acidity to-day by the fact that he is general purveyor by appointment. Classing him as the inevitable exception which proves (tests) the rule, we may say that everyone is in an ideal temper on this day of ideal weather, the marriage day of the ideal village teacher. And spite of customs differing from our own, let us rejoice with them that do rejoice. Perhaps before many years have passed—but no, not a whisper of a gloomy foreboding to-day.

The bridal chair again. Was ever such a wonder seen in the whole mundane universe? Woe be to the man who drops a shadow of a hint that more gorgeous ones exist. No such comparisons could be made. Rather do they deal with the old faded red (shall we say Pompeian red?) relic which has done duty for a bridal chair on many previous occasions. Everyone shouts his admiration, and (another inevitable phenomenon in China) everyone asks how much it cost, and how much its hire *per diem* will come to. Several guesses are made, but the guessers are extinguished with two words (不 只), which, with the tones of the speaker, have to be spun out in English to the length of, "You ignoramus, you wild man of the woods, you untaught barbarian, you 'potato,' to give such an inadequate estimate! It is far more than that!" But here is Chü, the owner thereof, who can perhaps settle the matter. A rush is made; he is surrounded and cross-examined.

"Hai Ya!" is the general interjection; "so much as that! And the cost *per diem*?" "She is my sister," is the reply; whereat Miss Chü's brother is voted an incarnate deity of generosity by all except Lieu. He tells his son (who, by the way, has of set purpose neglected anything like a wedding garment) that Chü is a "potato" of the first quality.

After a slow and stately progress, the triumphal procession arrives at the gate of the village, where the new chair is found to be too wide for the side-posts. Nothing daunted, the bearers unhook the lanterns, dismantle it of its gorgeous panels, and bring to light a plain red chair, which forms the basis of such decoration. With a loud exhortation to the youngsters to avoid touching the panels,—in which are some untranslatable reflections upon their ancestry, which expressions do not seem to count as unlucky words,—the chair-bearers proceed to the teacher's domicile.

The bridegroom has not yet emerged. A Chinese bridegroom is often a pitiable object, a necessary parenthesis. He hides away before and after the ceremony, taking no part in the wedding-feast. In Western language, he eats his dinner on the stairs. But here it is a national event, and the hero of the day, who is soon to be doubly so, is not allowed to be as retiring as he would like. He must submit to the unavertable.

The chair enters, and the door of the dark prison is unlocked, to disclose a gaily-dressed figure, whose face is hidden under a red cloth, each corner of which is weighted by five large cash.[1]

Every neck is bent round for the first look, for everyone wants to be first in the mental arithmetic handicap as to cost of garments, and adjudication of the important question as to whether the robes and crown are the bride's own or only hired. The latter will open up a wide field for speculation as to whether her brother lent them as well as the chair, and if so, how much he has lost through his already known

[1] Five visits of the unicorn aforesaid.

munificence. Before these matters have been at all settled, the chair is taken out of the door, and the "new girl," supported by Mrs. Li and an old crony, is led to the red kneeling-mat, where, sure enough, stands Nieh Shen-seng in a long plum-black satin robe and dress hat. His scholars are wonder-struck at the sight. He looks a mandarin, every inch of him.

But hush! Both are kneeling, and bow low to their

ancestors. There is a tablet now, blotting out some of the maxims on the scroll, hiding up a bit of the red, but supposed to represent those who, being dead, more than exemplify the highest virtue of the classics and classical commentators, and, from their seats of heavenly influence, shower down ruby-red felicity. In ancient days the patriarchal priests represented their families to the Supreme. In later years the ancestors have become more than mediators. The human "angel" is worshipped, the fact of his being but a servant overlooked; for who could be a servant to an abstraction, a messenger sent on his errands by a mere phrase? Nieh would call to mind his grandfather. Perhaps he looked beyond, perhaps not. But it may be pleaded that he went to the full extent of his known privilege.

The bride, whose small feet have been lavishly admired, is again supported by the two women, and led to the chamber prepared for her, where the bridegroom lifts the cloth and catches a hasty glimpse (his first) of the features of his bride. His usually pale face seems to reflect the prevailing red. Two cups of wine are then taken, the wine mingled and given to the pair. This done, the bridegroom retires with the shamefaced look of one who has lost his dignity. The crowd elbows its way in, to pass noisy comments; and when the outer room is clear enough, the tables are brought in, and preparations for the feast are evident.

The kitchen has been made for the occasion. It consists of two mud-brick stoves built outside the house in the open air. Here the smoke from the dwarf pine branches will not irritate so many eyes. But many are they who endeavour to prove the invulnerable nature of their binoculars by crowding round. The feast will not be covered by the gigantic sum of ten thousand cash (£2 in our money, as cash then was), and part of the interest is due to the fact that all except the trifles for dessert (which precedes the feast proper) are in this case presents. These trifles consist of bits of sugar-cane, orange quarters, pea nuts, "water chestnuts," melon seeds, pickled eggs, sweets, honey "dates," and candied pork—literal sweet meat. For the feast itself Li Sung-seu has given half a pig, another a peck or so of rice, others ducks, chickens, fish, eggs, and vegetables. Be it known that there are neither birds' nests, puppy or kitten chops provided, and few indeed of such things as we were perhaps taught to consider indispensable on such occasions. Glutinous birds' nests are rarities, for which rare prices are charged. Dogs are not common items of diet in these parts, still less are cats. The town beggars may eat them when reduced to extremity. It is said, however, that in some parts of Hunan a feast is not complete without dog's flesh. In some parts of Hupeh dog hams properly cured are to be purchased. In Mencius, too, dog's flesh is mentioned among the five kinds of meat. But in this case the dogs have their place under the table. There is a feast going on "below stairs."

Though these feasts are glorified dinners, part of the glorification being in the form of viands dyed red, certain things in the ordinary dietary of the various classes ought not to be found on the tables. These are mutton, small fish, beancurd, beans, cabbage, and turnips. Most of these are regarded as too common to be glorified.

But what have the guests been doing all this while? They have been struggling for places. Not by any means for the chief seats, but for the lowest. There is much clutching of sleeves, pushing, and dragging. Which is top and which bottom is a subject that would require a chart of the room; the direction of the grain of the central pieces of wood in the "eight immortals" tables being indicated. Such things belong to the region of higher mathematics, which require a specific education.

The places having been fixed, with many protestations of "Familiars need not stand on ceremony," the heated wine is poured out from a pewter vessel into tiny cups holding less than a fluid ounce. Each drinks to the other, and with his own chopsticks helps the friend he wishes to honour to the trifles before him. These are placed in his china spoon or dropped into his little saucer of soy. Nieh has been forced not only to appear, but to take a chief seat. This is unusual, but he is an unusual man, as his new "brother" Li assures everyone.

The guests look bland if ever they did, and blandness seems to merge into supreme felicity as the feast progresses. Not many cups of wine are taken, and it is incorrect to drink when once the rice (a mere addendum in a feast) arrives, with the climatic bowl of fat pork. In a Chinese feast, then, Western customs are reversed,—last is first; but a Hebrew ideal is retained. It is eminently a feast of fat things.

Everyone in the village, to the babies, has some part in this marriage feast. It is perfectly correct to take some goodies home to the children, and the quantity provided is more than the comparatively few invited guests can get through. Although the viands are mostly presents, the donors have their share. Is it cruel to suggest that this helped to make some of them so generous? An elderly man of more recent days, a graduate, was once asked what would be an appropriate present for a certain couple about to be married. "Oh, pork, of course," he replied, with scholarly accents; "then the bridegroom will invite us to have some."

The conversation at one of the tables has been marked with unusual brilliancy. The bride's brother is, as we have said, a host in himself. When at Han-yang,—at Hanyang, mind, for he had been to town himself to negotiate for the chair,—he heard of a couple of brides who got mixed. Two chairs started from different houses, one poor and the other wealthy; but these chairs were so much alike, that when the two sets of bearers came out of a wine shop, whither they went to refresh themselves, they took the wrong one. And the folks were really married thus, and could not be unspliced again, though the case was *sub judice* when he left, being referred to the "parent of the people" in the very city he had visited, and near the shop from whence that identical chair came. Lieu of the tea-shop was at the other table among his special admirers, and having heard the story, said that was nothing. He had a tale about nothing less than pork. All ears were bent, for the other "eight immortals" were decidedly noisy though by no means inebriated, and Lieu's utterances were generally exceedingly laconic criticisms. It has been said that the world is composed of two sets of folks, one of which sets about and does something, the other consisting of those who ask, "Why was it not done the other way?" Lieu belonged to the latter. Also to the class of those who give very little to their worshippers, but manage to get a great deal out of them. But here, warmed up on this festal occasion, he was going to tell a tale. He still paused, for the others were laughing at something fresh. "Pork, you said." "Yes, pork," chimed in several. But those of the other table

Mixed-up Brides.

Legend of a Pork-eater.

would never hear him, and he would defer the story. "I am accustomed to be listened to," he said imperiously. "We are all listening," was the reply, and indeed they were in a state of painful suspense, their chopsticks laid down, with actual pork—and the fattest of pork too—before them undevoured. But the story came at last. "There was once a mandarin at Hanyang who was in the habit of eating three catties [four pounds] of pork every day."

"Three catties, did you say? *Three* catties? Hai Ya!"

"Ah!" sighed another, adding solemnly, "Three catties a day!"

"I said three catties, and you might have heard it if that man Chü was not making such a row. And one of his underlings said he was a happy man to be able to eat so much, and to have so much to eat."

"Ha! ha! ha!" roared the seven listeners, who thought that the story (a long one for Lieu) was over. "Good! good! They can't come up to that! Ha! ha! ha!"

Lieu, however, looked round with inexpressible scorn at his flatterers; and, taking up his sticks, helped himself to a luscious morsel, saying, "I have not finished yet!"

"Nor have we," and they attacked the pork.

"The tale, you stupids, not the pork."

"Yes, the tale! Ha! ha! ha! They don't come up to "—

"But his fellow said," resumed Lieu, "'Yes, to have the pork; but three catties is nothing.'"

"That's true. Nothing at all!"

"Of course not," said another, shaking his head.

"'Three catties is nothing,' I repeat," continued the narrator; "'I could eat as much if I had it.'"

"So you could. So you could," several exclaimed in unison.

"No, not I myself. I am speaking of the *yamun* runner," said Lieu in a not very amiable tone.

"Not himself, you hear, but the *yamun* runner. That's true."

"Which *yamun* runner?" asked the densest of the lot.

"The fat man Wang, I guess, he used to "—

This was too much for Lieu. He refused to proceed. But that night, after due solicitation, he condescended to finish the narrative in his own house, which, being told without note or comment, though not delivered thus, was to the effect that the mandarin, overhearing the boast, demanded that the speaker should prove his words by eating the three catties in his presence daily for a whole year. If he utterly failed he was to have a hundred blows. For the first month the man succeeded, but afterwards had to come down to two and a half, and eventually to one and a half catties. He was beaten correspondingly. Soon he could take very little, and the full hundred blows were inflicted daily. This was as expensive as painful, for he had to fee his lictors " to the tune of " (a Chinese expression) two hundred cash a day to " lay it on lightly."

It is an established fact that cross fertilisation results in sterilisation, and Lieu had conferred a distinct boon by the importation of such a prolific topic of conversation as his tale about pork proved to be.

Not long after his marriage, Nieh Shen-seng's scholars had another and a longer holiday. He had gone off to Hanyang to try for his degree. What sort of a parting he had from his wife, we can only guess. There was mutual suitability, but as yet an utter absence of anything like sentiment. A refreshing amount of this glows in many a poem in the classical Book of Odes, however; though not in the commentaries thereon. The supremest efforts of the fossilised paraphrasts are directed towards its extirpation. And the Chinese scholar, like the later Hebrew searcher of Scripture, presumes not to receive his morsel except from the hands of a commentator.

Yet perhaps there may be something to be said in favour of the Chinese custom for the Chinese in matters matrimonial, especially if the alternative be such as is expressed by Goldsmith's *Lien Chi Altangi*, who swears by the head of Confucius (!), but seems to have some faculties of observation concerning Eighteenth-Century England. He says: "Many of the English marry in order to have one happy month in their lives; they seem incapable of looking beyond that period; they unite in hopes of finding rapture, and, disappointed in that, disdain ever to accept of happiness."

In China, where so many young couples have no previous personal knowledge of one another, and where there are such sayings as " Ten matchmakers, nine liars!" there may be a gradual approach in process of time towards the honeymoon state. And in some cases there undoubtedly is.[1]

The parting in this instance, as far as the outward world saw, was marked with calm decorum. There was no " Write soon, dearest," and the like. There are no letters in China. They are all epistles. If a wife gets a note written to her husband, it probably begins with " Princely husband [or hero], beneath whose lightning throne," etc. etc. And the epistle never falls below the level of the introduction. Our word "dear" means also "beloved"; the Chinese equivalent means also " honourable."

And as there is little sentiment, so there is no humour in a Chinese epistle. It would be as incongruous as a joke sculptured on a recent tombstone; and is not modern Chinese literature but an inscription on the tombstone of the dead and dust-turned past? What that past was like, however, in affection and human nature generally, we may perhaps guess from a glimpse or two by and by. The ancients were not all born grave and stolid sages, whatever the stilted scholarship of present-day China may pretend.

There are three examinations before our friend. The first is that in which the county mandarin is examiner. Should

Taking a Degree.

he not be a scholar, or have only a bought degree, his secretary does the greater part of the text-choosing and paper-scanning. The examination work consists of two essays on some classical passage, and one poem (of twelve lines, with five characters in each). About a fortnight after the county examination, the candidate,

---

[1] " We have been married for eight years," said a young Chinaman once, "and I think we know a little of your Western affection. My wife always cries when I go away on a journey"; and the speaker had only of late come under Western influence. His wife, moreover, as far as features went, was not exactly the kind of woman with whom a youth might fall in love at first sight. Her age suggested that one of the "nine liars" had had the task of matchmaking. And, further, she had but one very sickly child.

RED LETTER DAYS.

bearing his previous essays with him, has to write two essays and a poem, with the prefectural mandarin as his examiner. A prefecture contains from, say, seven to ten counties. Hanyang happens to be both a prefectural and a county capital, so the two examinations take place within the same city walls.

The prefectural examination over, the candidate, bringing with him the result, has to pass a like examination at the bidding of an examiner sent down from the capital by the Emperor. This examination is held in the same enclosure as the previous one.

The difficulty of attaining the degree of "budding talent," which we call the Chinese B.A., consists not only in the fact that the required standard of excellence is a high one (and however good the essay, the slightest fault in the writing of any one character is fatal), but also from the very limited number of degrees which the examiner is authorised to confer. The number of candidates usually present at the Hanyang examinations is about 1500; the number of degrees conferred is 32.

Moreover, it is a curious fact, explain it how you will, that though the examiner is not supposed to know whose paper he is examining, a considerable percentage of those who gain the coveted degree are the sons of wealthy families. Is it that literary genius and wealth are usually associated? The Chinese have a different explanation, as will be seen by the following, which was told by a "B.A." of some note:—

<small>Side Passages thereto.</small> "A certain scholar had known a certain Imperial examiner in past years. He tried to intercept him on his way to Hanyang, but failed [the possibility of his succeeding opens a wide field of thought]. So the examiner arrived, and became an imprisoned guest in a certain guild in Hankow, till the examination day should arrive. The scholar sent the messenger with a note, which was handed to the examiner in the presence of several witnesses. He glanced through it, stamped his foot in righteous indignation, had the messenger called in and a hundred blows administered. 'Now go back and tell your master to "take and put a heaven-directed conscience [*lit.*

virtuous heart] in the middle [of his body,[1] where that of the upright is supposed to be, thus answering to the position of China in the universe!]"'

"The messenger returned sore and angry. 'Well, what did he say to you?' 'He gave me a hundred blows.' 'Nothing more?' 'Surely that was enough.' 'But did he say nothing?' 'Say? Why he told me to tell you to take and put a heaven-directed conscience in the middle!"'

"At this, the scholar's face brightened. He put a 'heaven-directed conscience' in the middle of his essay. His essay was thus recognised by his friend, and he received his degree."

The narrator of this not improbable tale holds the position of surety to the new candidates. The first work of a candidate is to get such a surety, who will introduce him to the examiner, and be answerable for his good conduct. The post of surety is not always a sinecure. Students the world over, added to their characteristic studiousness, often manifest a considerable capacity for rowdyism. And the examination month or so is an anxious time for the mandarins. It takes little provocation to make the young gentlemen, strong by reason of union, very determined law-breakers. In some cases they tear down the tablets whereon the names of previously accepted candidates are inscribed. They may even deface the entrance gates of the temple of the sages. One year the county examiner of Hanyang, on entering his *yamun*, saw two students gambling at the very doors. Gambling is illegal,[2] though everyone (mandarins sometimes included) is addicted thereto. In a fit of anger, and probably the throes of dyspepsia, the mandarin ordered the young men to be seized and put into jail. Some bystanders informed the thousand odd students, who met and consulted, then went

Sureties against Rowdyism.

---

[1] Compare Eccles. x. 2: "A wise man's heart is at his right hand; but a fool's heart at his left." See also Trapp (1656) on John vi. 43: "You carry your galls in your ears as some creatures are said to do, hence you are so embittered."

[2] Except in the first few days of the New Year, during which certain laws are suspended. On the first three days of the year no customs dues are ever exacted, so many a boat starts at such a time; and as to gambling, it is as indispensable a part of the Chinese New Year as our pudding is of Christmas.

en masse to the *yamun*, broke open the prison, and carried off their two friends in triumph. In China—

"Stone walls do not a prison make,
 Nor iron bars a cage."

They are both made of wood. The keeper drew his sword and

managed to make a gash in the calf of one of the rioters, the wealthiest of them. Whereupon the candidates refused to a man to sit for the examination. This would have resulted in the deposition of the mandarin from his post of ruler over a million or two of folks, had he not bowed his abject apologies and restored peace.

It may be remarked here that whereas our own Government may be typified by the dolomite-built Houses of Parliament, with Westminster Abbey in the background, that of China resembles a flagstaff held in position by the aid of many a cord pulling in opposite directions. From the top of the flagstaff floats the dragon flag, and behind it stands an ancestral temple.

But to return to our narrative. Nieh Shu-ki‘ng having readily obtained a surety, to whom he could now fully introduce himself, filled up the required form with the names of his father, grandfather, and great-grandfather, the presence or absence of moustache or beard on his face, and other items connected with his identity; and, after other formalities, went, with a considerable amount of trepidation, to take his place in the examination enclosure.

The day of the third examination, he was entering the gates, when he saw the Imperial examiner walking along with that gentle swaying motion so frequently assumed by the *literati*. Two students were standing near, and were heard to remark, "You need not 'swell about' in that fashion; you are no bigger than the rest of us." But the examiner, who must have heard the impudent remark, had sufficient command of his feelings not to take any notice. Perhaps he dare not. His virtue was necessitated by circumstances.

The final examination over, a certain candidate was asked for by the Imperial examiner, who evidently thought him a man of no ordinary ability. With upturned thumb rotating, —the acted superlative of China,—the examiner told the flattered young man that he had written a splendid essay, characterised by "flowers and fire" and suchlike. The young scholar bowed his acknowledgments, and proceeded to depart, but in the outer courtyard his good fortune made him leap for joy. The doors being open to the farther recesses of the building, the examiner saw the performance, and called him back, exclaiming, "Aha! I perceive you are too light-headed for the onerous duties of magistracy. I cannot give you a degree." Nor did he.

That young man's surname was not Nieh, but his removal procured for our friend the first place on the list.

Chapter V.

COMPENSATIONS.

LAWS OF THE REALM AND OF THE UNIVERSE—FOXES AND VIXENS—THE CUP THAT CHEERS.

"Sweet musk imparts its fragrance to a paper in which it is wrapped; and a mud turtle communicates its stench to the willow-twig run through its body."—*Chinese Proverb.*

It would be difficult to find a land on the face of the wide earth where public spirit is at such a low ebb as in China. It is the balance of contending interests which keeps the Empire from falling. But the ropes which thus pull at the flagstaff are composed of twisted twine. In plainer language, it would be difficult to find a land where the principle of solidarity in families and village communities is more fully exemplified.

The loss of a mandarin's seal involves the whole family, at the least, in extreme disgrace. Some great crimes, such as high treason, may involve the "nine degrees of kindred," —from great-great-grandfather to great-great-grandson. Other offences may involve a whole village, and the office of the mandarin, "parent of the people," in whose district that village is situated.

While Nieh Shen-seng (he has surely earned the appellation now) was taking his degree, a tragedy was being enacted close by one of the low rounded hills within sight of Hanyang battlements. A wild youth named Sen Yuen-pao (ingot of silver), while away on a boat journey, heard that his father's younger brother had sold a house to which he professed to have a part claim. He came home in a rage, demanding his share of the money. His uncle was out, and so he wreaked his vengeance on his younger brother. His mother, interposing to save the youth, was also killed. The Chinese law is, as in old Judæa, "Whosoever curseth father or mother, let him die the death." Knowing such a penalty to be inevitable, it is said (printed in some rhyming song books issued at the time) that he went to the hillside and lit some cash paper in a circle around him, as he knew that no one else would provide means for the repose of his soul. He was caught there; and as he had committed most of the sins possible to a young man, with a climax of matricide, the spoilt child would have been the cause of the degradation of the Hanyang mandarin if something desperate in the way of lynch law were not done. So the country folk, themselves endangered by the crime, wrapped the offender up in cotton-wool saturated with oil, and, on a spot which may still be pointed out, " burnt him with fire." Thus was justice appeased, and the matter hushed up.

Nieh Shen-seng proceeded homewards with an exhilaration that not even such a tragedy could dispel; and somehow, in the dense population of China, a single death even from burning hardly affects the hearer of the news as it would in the West. His feet were already upon the first flight of the Imperial throne steps, and the existence of such criminals but sobered the graduate to a due contemplation of his possible position as future mandarin.

His path for several miles lay in the midst of numberless grave mounds, and at times that path lay over a coffin-lid. The "mandarin road" from Hanyang westwards has several coffin-lid bridges. Coffin-lid-snatching would seem to be a somewhat frequent practice. And the coffin-lids being in good condition, suggest comparatively new graves. This might well cause a feeling of revulsion; but here, again, the graves are so numerous, so endless, as it seems to the traveller, from Hanyang westward, that he soon gets atrophied on that score. There is no cemetery feeling; the dust seems to have returned so completely to dust, that the grave-mounds seem to be but mounds. Stones there are, but no epitaphs;

no pathos, no poetry, no hope; and but such remembrance of the dust-turned bones as near relatives feel it their duty to pay at the festival which resembles in name and time that of our old-time Eostre, but differs (as far as the worshippers of the dead are concerned) from that of the Christian Easter.

Nieh Shen-seng chose to return by road that he might visit one grave, however, which is to be found at the foot of the Horse Saddle Hill, as will be related before many pages have been turned over. Instead of resurrection, many of the departed are honoured with demi-deification; and instead of everlasting life, some few are rewarded with posthumous "immortality."

The grave of one who has dignified the county in the hearts of Chinese, and perhaps a few Western scholars, having been visited, the graduate proceeded on his way with "an unusual share of somethingness in his whole appearance," notwithstanding the fact that he carried his own bundle. He rightly felt that in his high honour the whole neighbourhood of the Nine Recluses was uplifted and glorified. The thought crossed his mind as to whether, had he waited a year or two, he might not have made a better match. But he dismissed such an unworthy suggestion. He was everlastingly indebted to the Li family. And his wife, who would make up in appreciation, almost adoration, what she lacked in position, was lady enough to fill any possible sphere in store for her. Moreover, she was free from many of the disagreeable tempers exhibited by those brought up in luxurious "public residences," otherwise the mansions of the wealthy and scholarly.

The familiar hill came in sight. He was walking along the identical path where he had once met his good friend Li; anon the tree-tops around the village were seen, and his own little vegetable plot appeared. His heart beat wildly as he undid his bundle and extracted therefrom a gilt button, which, if the truth be told, he had felt over and over again through the cloth, as he walked along, to make sure that it was really there. The slanting sunbeams glanced upon it, and Nieh's heart, if not his feet, danced for joy. He was the very man who had come in early days heavily laden with an outward and ponderous burden of silver, and an inner burden of sorrow, heavy indeed for a child to carry. And the young man in whose genial presence he had felt at home, as his grandfather had in the presence of his father, was now his "brother." Simple, he might be, and unpolished, but friends true to the core do not predominate—in China.

"What wind blew you here, Nieh Shen-seng? I was just thinking of you."

"And I of my 'brother'; but look here," and to Li's enchanted gaze was exhibited the golden knob. He did not wait for more. Running down the hill path, he made straight for the tea-shop, and, to the bewilderment of all the villagers assembled there, to say nothing of Lieu himself, jumped on to the counter, seized a bundle of the largest squibs obtainable, some of which had been left over from the marriage, caught up a spill from the hand of a sleepy old fellow with a water-pipe, and rushed out again toward the village; let off one to arouse all the world and his wife; then shouting for gong and cymbals, pointed in wild excitement to the approaching figure of the scholar. The musical instruments seemed hours coming, but they arrived, nevertheless; and amid a veritable cannonade, the loudest gong beats, and the most " cloud-shaking cries " of rapture, the victor was escorted to the threshing-floor, then to his house—nay, his palace. Everyone had reserved their bows till this moment, and now there was universal bobbing. Soon red candles were presented, incense lit, and the gold knob was well-nigh worshipped. And then, and not till then, did the crowd hear that Nieh's name was top of the list. Three bliss-filled folks conversed till a late hour—the other two were Mrs. Nieh and Li. There were indeed four, for Seng-teh was present.

There is, however, another side to everything in China; the flagstaff of "truth" is kept in position by theories the most opposite, and, to our minds, most contradictory. There is first, and chiefly, the cord of Sadducean Confucianism, opposite to which is the rope of ancestral worship, and the cord of Buddhism is kept from overbalancing the pole by that of Taoism. "It is so and so" on the one hand, and "it is quite otherwise" on the other. But note how, because of these very contradictions, the flagstaff stands firm. Really it is very simple, when thus illustrated!

While our friends were chatting,—Nieh Shen-seng with dignity, Mrs. Nieh somewhat sparingly, but with a most eloquent pride-flushed face,—and Li was bringing out all the quotations he had ever heard, and many more, there was a gathering of philosophers in the tea-shop.

Sudden and overwhelming shocks have been known to bring speech to the dumb, and Lieu was positively garrulous. He was unfolding the Chinese theory of fixed proportions of happiness. His harangue may be condensed thus: "It is well known," quoth he, "that in the street 'lantern processions' in honour of various idols, the Imperial tablet is carried in a chair, to prevent any disturbance. In front of it sits a girl to personate the heir-apparent, not a boy, for one hour of such personification would absorb all the happiness of his life.[1] But what concerns us is this, that it is unlucky for a city to bring forth a prime minister or a viceroy, for he absorbs in his person all the happiness of the district. Now, here is a little village, and a young upstart comes in somehow or other, and is a criminal for years—a criminal, I repeat, who ought to have been decapitated; and this criminal goes and gets his degree, —gets top of the list,—and absorbs into his criminal person all the happiness of the village." And if our keenest logicians (having granted the premisses and eliminated the "criminal") could find no possible flaw in the conclusion deduced therefrom, what flaw could be discovered by country farmers and farm labourers in the conclusions of their flawless deity? "Something will happen! Mark my words! Something will surely happen!" he added, subsiding into his ordinary terseness of expression.

Fixed Proportions of Happiness.

"Ay, that is so; something will happen," echoed everybody, and everybody had to have a cup of the hottest and most fiery spirit to cheer them into facing a fact so inevitable

---

[1] Compare Richard Jefferies: "The family of Idens had endured two hundred years of unhappiness and discordance for no original fault of theirs, simply because they had once been fortunate of old time, and therefore they had to work out that hour of sunshine to the utmost depths of shadow" (*Amaryllis*).

and gloomy. And Lieu actually "treated" them! Unprecedented generosity! One cup not being enough, another, and yet another, was warmed and drunk; and in the small hours, just as Li and his son were rising to depart, they heard, and Nieh Shen-seng heard too, voices thick with "wine" exclaiming, as their owners returned, "Something will happen! He said so! Yes, something will happen!" From which Nieh guessed that Lieu had been doing his best to prevent his flagstaff from being pulled over by the big rope of pride.

Meanwhile Nieh determined to keep steadily on his way. He was up early weeding his vegetable plot, for in his absence there had been a prolific growth of couch grass and the like. It had only invested half the plot, however; which fact might puzzle even a B.A.

"How can a 'country potato' explain such a wonder?" exclaimed Li. "But you are surely omniscient now. At any rate, you can get some doctrine out of it."

"Half cleared and half weed-filled, such is the life of men on earth. And—I know, it was you who did that 'good deed.'"

"There is no deceiving you. Truly omniscient!" was the reply.

But some weeds are not so easily uprooted. If maxims and doctrines were as omnipotent as their propagators were supposed to be omniscient, what roots of bitterness would remain? The red scroll in the schoolroom had plainly written thereon: "Do not hurriedly take in every rumour; how do you know it has not sprung from malice? . . . When others are happy and fortunate, do not envy them; when they are in trouble and distress, do not regard it with complacency. . . . Concealed hatred and the secret arrow will end in calamity to one's own family." But the concluding maxims, though partly hidden by the ancestral tablet, were not altogether lost upon Nieh Shen-seng. They were: "Do things at the right time. Obey Heaven. When a man acts thus, he is not far from right."

Nieh Shen-seng kept steadily on his way. That is, as far as his numerous visitors would allow. For was he not now a greater wonder than a "new girl"? For the first three evenings after a marriage, it is an unwritten law in China, much enforced in country districts, that everybody shall crowd in to see the new phenomenon, make as many remarks as they can, be as audacious as they please, and as rough and noisy,—a law which might be rescinded with advantage, and which was somewhat modified in the case of Mrs. Nieh when she was a "new girl." At such time, however, the horizon opens to admit of the advent of a gorgeously dressed visitant, and everybody must use all possible means to satisfy themselves that the visitant is human. Ye brides of far Cathay, some of us foreigners can sympathise with you, dropping down (for have we not come up?) into a noisy, blatant world of critics, whose five senses must have full play. Ye are indeed prisoners,—prisoners, however, who may long in vain for wooden barriers; caged birds who would give anything for solid cage bars.

But a real live "B.A." top of the list! Nieh might be a bit of a wonder, but think of a full-fledged Nieh Shen-seng! A *rara avis* indeed! The horizon, the utmost horizon discernible from the top of the hill, had opened to let a man with a golden knob through. Was that region beyond made of golden knobs? And so, to satisfy ourselves, we must come from all parts, drop into the schoolroom, have a cup of tea and a smoke, and ask for an exact and detailed account of everything in the outer universe. "Is it not pleasant to study with constant application and diligence?" the Confucian *Analects* asks in the opening sentence.[1] "Is it not delightful to have friends [attracted by the fame of your learning, the commentators explain] coming from distant parts?" Yes, but all earthly delights bring satiety in the end, as Nieh Shen-seng found when streams of button-worshippers invested his schoolroom and his school hours day after day.

At last he was compelled to ask them to call in the evening, after school work was over, when he would answer their questions to the best of his ability. And thus began a series of Chinese Nights' Entertainments, at which we may be unseen guests.

[1] An incentive to learning corresponding to the word "Be strong" found in the Hebrew Bible at the end of each of the opening books.

Nieh Shen-seng's cottage not being big enough, these were at first held at Li's home, who, being the largest landowner of these parts, has the biggest house. The guest hall is somewhat like the schoolmaster's, but behind the ancestral tablet there hangs a red scroll, with the character for longevity in gold written a hundred different ways. On the top of this is pasted a slip inscribed : " Heaven, earth, sovereign, parents, teacher," which is often the only adornment of a country " hall," and represents the comprehensive sum of all things adorable. On one side wall are four scrolls in which the four seasons are typified by somewhat crude paintings of the plum blossom, bamboo, Chinese crocus, and chrysanthemum. On the opposite wall are four still cruder specimens of landscape paintings, also representing the four seasons. Upon the crossbeams, from post to post, rest a few boards, which serve as shelves for such things as an extinguisher-like fishing frame, and the two-pronged spear used with it, a bundle or two of hay, a ladder, a jar or two, also a long rotary pump. From these crossbeams depend sundry baskets and sieves, and a dust-covered, cobweb-decorated bunch of gold and silver ingots (of paper), and a sprig of " Christmas tree," for the reason that the name of that tree (*pch tsz*) is identical in sound with that of "a hundred sons." Such bundles are commonly hung up on either side of the shop fronts at New Year's time. This bundle was a wedding present, and survives as do orange blossom decorations of bride-cakes nearer home.

The furniture consists of an "eight immortals" table against the back wall under the " mantelpiece," which, as in Nieh's house, is a rather rough, thick board, supported on two tea-poys ; a couple of chairs each side, with a tea-poy in the middle; and, finally, a short form or two, completing the accommodation for guests. But in this same guest hall is a wheel-barrow, various farming implements, such as a plough stuck up on end, with a harrow behind, various sized bins and sacks, a few roosting chickens, and two or three miry pigs.

The presence of the latter seemed in early Chinese days to constitute home. "Old home" is generally defined as one's country birthplace (where the old folks may yet live, unless they have gone to the "old home" above), but the same tender word used of birthplace, and of heaven itself, consists of the signs for *pig* and *shelter*. A *pig* under a *shelter*, then, is the universally used sign for what to the Chinaman comes nearest to our "home," earthly or heavenly, with suggestions of festal gatherings and fat pork,—the fatter the better in either place.

In this country home we find a company gathered, hungry and expectant; not, however, for fat pork, but for mental food. Eyes beaming with admiration are turned to Nieh Shen-seng, who has been forced to sit in the highest seat of all, that on the left of the table (the right hand to anyone entering the door).

He has to retail the texts for the various essays and poems, describe the examination enclosure, and especially the "heavenly messenger" (heavenly meaning Imperial) who gave him his degree. This personage, as Nieh relates, on coming to an examination centre, first lights three sticks of incense and worships the foxes of the place.

The fox, as the reader will know, is regarded in China and Japan as far more than a mere beastie. It has wondrous powers of transformation. While, according to Buddhism, you can never be quite sure that your pig is not after all your grandfather, or someone else's, according to the popular notions, you cannot tell whether your visitor from a distance, or even the wife of your bosom, is not a transmogrified fox. The fox, or is it the foxen (the old non-technical form of the word vixen)? is specially addicted to taking the form of beautiful women, often to prove a very "vixen" after all. The last monarch of the Yin (or Sha) dynasty (B. 1154–1122 B.C.), who, "having lost the hearts of the people, could not appear before God," had a wife yet more infamous than himself. Jezebel of Scripture and Shakespeare's Lady Macbeth were infirm of purpose compared with her. They were human after all. This woman, however, united to peerless beauty and consummate witchery the most inhuman passion for deeds of cruelty. A noble statesman's heart was cut out to see the

The Fox in Chinese Folklore.

colour thereof; folk's legs were amputated to see what it was that made some endure the cold so well. In short, the Emperor, at her instigation, undertook a series of vivisection experiments, in which the victims operated upon were human beings. This Ta Ki, as her name was, also invented copper

A Vixen

cylinders, round which the victim was secured, fire being applied to make the tube red-hot. All of which is now explained on the theory that as the beautiful and innocent girl was on the way to the capital, a specially malicious old fox killed her, assumed her form, and personated her ever afterwards. Which Nich Shen-seng duly related, adding that if the story be true, that old fox is responsible for some of the finest poems in the *Book of Odes*, which welled forth to express the admiring gratitude of a people rescued from such enormities by the half-deified Literary King and his son the Military Monarch. "But among those old poems," he said, "foxes are only mentioned as 'solitary and suspicious'; their fur, together with lamb's skin, being made into winter robes for the courtiers. One poem speaks of 'fox firs so yellow,' another says, 'Our fox firs are frayed and worn.' The down on the fox's ribs is of peculiar fineness, and would make rich garments. Hence the phrase of modern scholars, 'gathering the fox hair from the ribs [choice literary extracts] to make robes.' There is no trace of demon foxes[1] in the early records.

"The present ideas about foxes seem to be of later growth. But in the oldest dictionary of China, it is stated that the fox is the courser upon which ghostly beings ride [as the Immortals on the back of cranes]. Nowadays they are regarded as mischievous fairies. They can make the seals of higher mandarins disappear. My grandfather, though not a high mandarin, thought this might account for his own seal's disappearance, until he found that two men were missing. So the viceroy, when he comes into office, does his best to propitiate the fairy foxes; and in the north, rich men have a 'fox chamber,' wherein victuals are daily provided.

"The suspicious nature of the fox is proved by its listening to the sound of the ice under its feet when it crosses it."

"But they are artful!" interjected one of the listeners.

"Yes; there is a fable spoken to a king of old time by one of his ministers. 'A she fox was overtaken by a tiger, which was about to devour her. The fox remonstrated with the tiger, and claimed that she possessed a superiority over other animals, all of whom she declared stood in awe of her. In proof of this, she invited the tiger to accompany her, and

---

[1] It is a curious fact that the aspergillum used to sprinkle holy water, and thus to drive away offending demons, in oldtime France, "was occasionally a fox's brush, as is indicated by the modern French name *goupillon*" (*Christian Iconography*, vol. ii. p. 145). Can there have been any trace here of "Satan casting out Satan," of demon-driving homœopathy?

witness her power. The tiger consented, and quietly followed. Every beast fled at their approach, and the tiger dare not attack the fox, not considering that the terror was caused by his own appearance. Thereafter, whenever the fox was seen in public, the other animals suspected that the tiger—with whom she seemed to be on such intimate terms—was at her heels. Hence the saying, "The fox arrogating the tiger's power to terrify."'"[1]

"It is the female foxes that have the greatest power of transformation, I have heard," said Li. "Our Scholar's brother-in-law told me of the case of a countryman who lived near his home. He was very poor, and lived in a mud-brick hut with thatched roof. Having no wife, he was wont to cook one meal a day, and eat the cold leavings in the morning. A fox took pity upon him, and, when he was out, entered the house, changed herself into a woman, cleaned up the place, cooked a meal for him, and then disappeared. This went on for some days, until the farmer determined to watch and find out who his kind and unknown visitor was. So he crouched behind a water jar and waited. Soon he observed a fox entering through a hole in the wall, then turn a somersault, landing on her feet a handsome woman, the fox's skin falling to the ground. The farmer got hold of the skin, and secreted it under the pig trough. When all her good deeds were done, she came and searched, but not finding the skin, had to remain a woman, and become the farmer's wife. In after years he said jokingly to one of his children, 'Your mother is a fox.' The mother asked for his proof of such a statement. He produced the fox skin, when, turning a somersault, his wife entered the skin and ran off, never to return again. Yes, as I said, it is the female fox that has the power of transformation, is it not, Shen-seng?"

But before Shen-seng could reply, another said, "Undoubtedly it is. There was once a tailor living a hundred *li* from,—I forget where,—who had a fairy fox for wife. No one else saw her but himself. But she taught him about all sorts of medicinal herbs, and he was looked upon as a great doctor."

[1] A. H. Smith's *Proverbs and Common Sayings of the Chinese*.

"Well," said Nieh Shen-seng, "the *Book of Odes* does say that the male fox is solitary and suspicious."

"There, I said so!" cried Li triumphantly.

"But the male fox is also credited with transforming powers," added Nieh Shen-seng, "as the following story will show: The scholarly son of a high military official, having himself come into a mandarinship, went one evening to study in a hitherto disused chamber. The door was shut close, but from a crack in the window there entered a thin form, which, having rubbed its body for a while, filled out into a man's shape. The strange visitor advanced with a bow, and described himself as a reynard Immortal who had occupied that room for a hundred years, the former mandarins permitting him to do so. 'But as you have come here, I cannot stand in the way of an Imperial statesman; and so have come to explain that if you must study here, I will give way, if I may be allowed three days' grace. But perhaps you will be compassionate, and have the door closed as before.' The mandarin laughed, saying, 'There are scholars then among the foxes?' 'There are examinations for foxes held every year by the Lady of the Tai San [a hill in West Shantung],' replied the fox, 'where degrees are given to those worthy of them; the rest are regarded as wild foxes, and are not, like the others, allowed to compete for the rank of immortals. If I may exhort you, it seems sad that honourable men do not seek after that state. It is so much harder for us; we have first to learn to change into men's shape, then study their speech; in order to which latter, we have to learn the cries of all the birds within the four seas and nine continents. Altogether it takes us five hundred years, whereas men are spared this first five hundred years' painstaking. Honourable and literary men, moreover, have a further advantage over ordinary mortals of three hundred years, and as a rule can gain the desired rank of immortals in a thousand years.' The mandarin, accepting this explanation, retired from that chamber. In after years he used to tell his son that his only regret was that he had not inquired into the topics set by the Lady of the Tai San."

At this stage tea was handed round, real tea brought by

Nieh Shen-seng from Hanyang, which, when brewed into a pale golden liquid, was the more fragrant and palatable owing to the presence of jasmine flowers which floated on the top.

The conversation therefore turned on the subject of tea. Had the Shen-seng anything to relate as to its origin? someone asked. Nieh Shen-seng, now duly lubricated, began by saying that the "Military Emperor" of the Sui dynasty (R. 589–605) was once afflicted with bad dreams, in which a spirit seemed to move his brain bones about until his head ached frightfully. He met a Buddhist monk, however, who told him that on the mountains grew a certain plant called *c'ha*,[1] which would heal him. The Emperor followed his advice with complete success. From that time the beneficial effects of tea became known the wide Empire over.

<small>Origin of Tea-Drinking.</small>

The village "doctor," who is one of the company, feels that his province has been invaded. He has heard the true and authentic history of the discovery of the tea plant. "There was a man in ancient times, in ancient times," he would beg to repeat, "who was lying down in the forest ' on the occasion of' his dying, ' on the occasion of' his having been bitten by a large centipede. He lay almost helpless, but ' on the occasion of' his seeing a bush near, and being dry in the mouth, began to chew the leaves. ' On the occasion of' his doing so he revived, and [doubtless on all possible occasions] recommended the plant to all his friends. And what was that plant? It was tea. Ancient times! Sick man! Very sick! ' On the occasion of' his chewing! Quite well! Origin of tea-drinking!" And he buried his nose in the inclined cup of medicine, and looked out over the rim to see at a glance that Nieh Shen-seng was *facile princeps* now, and that he had lost rather than gained position by his true and authentic contradiction of what the living encyclopædia said.

---

[1] The earliest authentic advertisement of tea in England reads: "That Excellent and by all Physitians approved *Chinee* Drink, called by the *Chineants Tcha*, by other Nations *Tay alias Tee*, is sold at the *Sultaness Head Cophee-House*, in *Sweetings Rents*, by the Royal Exchange, London" (*Mercurius Politicus*, Sept. 20, 1658).

Need we say that "Mr. Occasion"—for that was his nickname—resolved never to put his nose within Li's portals, still less within his teacups again. Having an important commission early next morning, a long way off, a long way off, he would beg to repeat, he wished to retire early. He had "disturbed the assembly," he had been "poor company" himself, and so on, and so on (as every polite guest confesses to have been). "Don't hurry away," was of course the reply, but no one rose as they said it. So he hurried away the faster.

"There is indeed another account of the origin of tea," said Nieh, "according to the Buddhists. There was a monk named Ta Ma [Darma, the third son of Kasiuwo, an Indian king] who came from the West to China [about 519 A.D.] to 'enlighten the Chinese.' He exposed himself to every possible hardship, being self-denying in the extreme,—but self-denial in the Imperial dictionary is interpreted as the mortification of the 'private,' selfish, disconnected self,[1] on behalf of the 'public spirit,' the related self, which may not involve abstinence from the necessities of life. This monk, however, lived only upon the herbs of the field; and, in order to attain to the highest degree of sanctity, determined to pass his nights as well as days in contemplation of doctrine. After some time spent thus, he became so weary that he fell asleep. This lapse troubled him sorely. He did not consider that his denying the five relations of sovereign and statesman, father and son, elder and younger brother, husband and wife, friend and companion, was at all contrary to doctrine. Though this was the main point in the Memorial of Han Wen Kung [of whom more anon] against Buddhism.

"On awaking the next morning he determined to expiate his vow-breaking sin by cutting off his eyelids! Returning to the place the following day, he was surprised to find that each eyelid had become a shrub,—the plant, indeed, which we now call tea. He took of the leaves and ate them, and found that as he did so his heart was filled with extraordinary exhilaration, and that he had acquired renewed strength for

[1] And therefore is a perfect translation of the words used by our Lord to His disciples.

his contemplations. The event being known, his disciples spread the news far and wide."[1]

The reader is hereby warned that the subject of the "soft, sober, sage, and venerable liquid; . . . smile-smoothing, heart-opening, wink-tippling cordial" (for thus a now forgotten poet-laureate of past days described it) is not yet finished; but while lips are smacking over the wonderful decoction of real tea (with none of your willow-leaf adulterations) we may peep into the minds of the hearers and note how perfectly harmonious these differing accounts seemed. Our flagstaff (as indispensable to us as a banner to a Chinese soldier) is now held in place by two main cords and a bit of hemp twine. It is so and so, it is such and such, it is otherwise, give a nett result of perfect reliability. The audience is therefore sipping down indubitable truths with the tea.

Facts having been established in a most orthodox, threeply manner, we are now prepared for poetic decorations. The Eastern mind scorns the merely matter-of-fact. But Nieh Shen-seng has begun to relate how that " in the days of the first Emperor of the Eastern Ts'in dynasty [317–323] an old woman appeared in the streets with a vessel of fine tea in her hand, the contents of which she sold from morning till evening, for the vessel was inexhaustible. The proceeds of such sales she distributed among beggars and the indigent poor generally. But certain folks seized the old lady with the magic teapot and put her in jail. That night, however, both lady and teapot flew out of the window."

"It was the Goddess of Mercy herself!" exclaimed Mrs. Li.

"It must have been!" said everybody else. After which Li protested that they had no right to cause their honoured Shen-seng to split his throat with talking, but that if he had

---

[1] Tea was known in China as early as the third or fourth century. In the "Three-dynasties epoch" (221–263) a certain official who could not drink as heavily as the rest of the courtiers was allowed to substitute tea for wine. Again, in the Ts'in annals (265–420) it is related that a certain præfect, when visited by a prominent general, placed tea and fruit before him (*Notes and Queries on China and Japan*, 1869, p. 80).

"two words" more on the subject they would all "humbly receive his admonition."

He had just "two words." The first referred to the saying of an old monk, that old and new tea when mixed gave a harmonious but varied taste to the palate. There was a saying about the harpsichord, to the effect that the full resonance of the wood was not evident until after a hundred years. It then gave all the delicate gradations answering to the phenomena of clearness and turbidity, of rain and sunshine, of heat and cold, which principle applied to tea also.

The second word was a comparison between the national beverage and the scholar's ink. "Tea-drinkers like a light-coloured decoction, and dislike a dark-coloured liquid. But it is quite otherwise with ink. Ink loses some of its brilliancy on being left in the slab overnight; tea leaves exposed for a day lose some of their scent. In this they resemble one another. New tea is most esteemed, but the more ancient the ink, the more excellent. In this they contrast. Tea for the mouth, and ink for the eye; but in old time there was a man of note who had a chronic complaint which forbade his drinking tea, yet had it brewed to please the eye. And another man there was, who, though he could not write, was fond of collecting good ink, which he would rub and test by tasting—'a joke indeed for all who hear it,' as my old book says." By way of postscript, Nieh added that a certain man of the Táng dynasty, after drinking seven bowls of tea, experienced a stirring of air under the armpits, and felt like flying to heaven.

It was now time for the company to disperse, and there were general lightings of lanterns, and brotherly offers to guide those home who had none. For in China the phrase "outer darkness" is no mere phrase. The skies were overclouded that night, and there was a danger of falling into cesspools and what not. "Hai Ya!" exclaimed the first man who opened the door; "it is raining, just a fine spray; but it must have begun when the doctor left, and the paths are very slippery, no doubt. No one has nail boots, I guess." On the first rainy day, the clay paths are slimy indeed. On the second, they present a pock-marked appearance by reason of boot nails, with sundry double strokes here and there from the awkward wooden clogs. On the third, boots are abandoned in the country for straw sandals or bare feet. It is sloshy rather than slippery along frequented paths. With numerous remarks on the seasonableness of the rain, and some comparisons between such "sweet rain" and the entertainer of the evening (who had watered the parched soil with heaven-granted wisdom), the company dispersed.

When Nieh Shen-seng reached home, his wife's face seemed instinct with emotion. The character written thereon was a complicated one, and the scholar could not "recognise" it all at once. "Are you poorly?" he asked. He did not say "dear." Chinese married couples are not addicted to many terms of address, still less to that. She did not answer, but looked at him expressively—her look expressive of what? "Are you poorly, 'virtuous wife'?" Yes, he used that term of address, and his tones were those of a husband now. In Chinese especially, the real language is that which lies beyond the mere words, which are often used to hide the heart's real feelings, and at best scarcely ever express them. The language of China is that which is to be read between the (vertical) lines. The wife's face grew red. "Will you not entertain the company here to-morrow night?" From which Nieh gathered that she wanted a little excitement and company; from which we may gather that she felt the penalty exacted from those who marry illustrious men; from which we gather, moreover, O book-blinded student, that thy wife is beginning to love thee.

Chapter VI.

Records of an Ancient City.

CHINESE NIGHTS' ENTERTAINMENTS—WHAT'S IN A NAME?—
A CHINESE NOAH AND DIOGENES—STANDARDS OF VIRTUE
—STUNTED LIMBS AND BUDDING BRANCHES—GEOMANTIC
INFLUENCES—WATERY WASTES AND CLEAR HEAVENS.

" The fist-like rocks rise tier on tier above the river clay,
The many-branching mallow trees their verdant wealth display ;
The herbage on the Parrot Isle by ardent sunrays browned,
But round the ancient hill-top shrine, sand white as snow is found ;
The chain across the river wide is broke by dragon's teeth,
The Han-born clouds in bright array, the city turrets wreathe ;
The fragrant deeds of bygone days the traveller still may learn :
On moss-grown tablet deeply cut, the records old discern."
Selected lines from several local poems.

A FEW evenings have passed, and the rain still continues. It was welcome at first, for the ground was dry indeed. " At first it was a fine, gentle rain, then came in close layers, watering the crops and irrigating the farms, where the wild flowers hang down with a weight of glittering gems; invigorating the soil and fertilising the fields, from whose tender blade points the pearls roll down in wild confusion." A welcome rain indeed, but will it wear out its welcome ?

On wet evenings, the simply-built and simply-furnished houses in Chinese country villages seem very homes, especially when the little rush pith saucer lamp has given place to candles, shining with ruddy light through their flower-painted and poem-decorated glass boxes, making the red scrolls gleam out cheerfully from the dull brown walls. Such light, too, gives a Rembrandt effect to the whole scene. The faces of the genial company shine out in strong contrast from a dull background. The very shadows are picturesque; every corner is full of artistic mystery.

The place of resort is no longer Li's house. Mrs. Nieh's hint has prevailed; and, owing to the rain, no visitors from the other hamlets have arrived; only a select company from the immediate neighbourhood, as appreciative as select. Nieh Shen-seng has been consulting several old books, so as to give an accurate and detailed account of the interesting history and legendary lore which belongs to the city of Hanyang.

The scented tea is poured out; a red, unglazed earthen kettle is heard singing on the hob in the adjoining kitchen. It will be needed to replenish the not inexhaustible teapot. Around the same stove are ten or more home-made cakes slightly salted. These are to be eaten warm, half-way through the evening. With teacups at hand, and more tea in prospect, and the savoury prophecy exhaled from such cakes, there is complete satisfaction among the little company gathered to partake of the intellectual feast. The brightest face is undoubtedly that of Mrs. Nieh. She had a sweet face to begin with, and now it is lit with admiration. The next face to arrest our interest is that of little Seng-teh. He duly worships his " uncle," who is sure to add to his worshipfulness to-night.

" The most ancient reference to Hanyang," begins Nieh Shen-seng, " is found in the History Classic in the *Tribute of Yü,* where it says, ' The Kiang and Han pursue their course seawards as if hastening to [the Imperial] court.' Similar words are found in the *Book of Odes*: ' Lo! this mighty current hastens to its audience with the ocean.' A Ming dynasty scholar says: ' These words bring the mighty streams of the united rivers rushing to the sea before our eyes. I have gazed thereon, and the vast flood dashing onwards brought to my mind the idea of a man hurrying with all his speed on some special mission without a thought of anything else.' So I felt myself, when I stood upon the Tortoise Hill and saw the waters rushing by. It was a noble thought of ancient days to liken them to statesmen summoned to an Imperial audience.

"This Tortoise Hill, with rugged, rocky sides, is about two *li* long. It is very low compared with our grand hill here. Why was it so called, did you ask? Well, I found a tortoise crawling over the top, and suppose its name was given owing to the prevalence of these tortoises around it. How that one got on to the top, I cannot tell. Tortoises love flat land and water. And, owing to this, there is a saying that if the Tortoise Hill is not often flooded at its base the luck of the city will be bad. The farmers of the place have often wanted to raise an embankment around their fields to protect them from the Han in flood time. On such seasons of flood they can only get one crop, or perhaps the second is sown and the young plants all drowned."

<small>Medo-Persian Fung Shui Laws.</small>

"Only one crop!" exclaimed Li. "Flood years must be unlucky for them; but who prevents their protecting their own lands; the mandarins?"

"No," said Nieh, slightly reddening.

"Well, I should make an embankment, I know."

"I am sorry to say they have been made and pulled down. I do not know which to be sorry for. All the noted scholars [1] of the place say the tortoise needs water to dabble in. It was my learned surety who told me. I am not up in *fung shui*, and cannot understand it. For the name Tortoise Hill is of recent origin, and could never be put into a poem. The ancient name is the Great Hill of Division. There is the Small Hill of Division some sixty miles up the Han. Both were named thus in connection with the superhuman labours of the Great Yü. One of the seven temples on the Great Hill of Division is dedicated to Yü. Another has a tablet in connection with a certain prince who reigned in

---

[1] As late as 1891 the graduates of Hanyang filed a protest on the Yamun doors to the effect that the embankments made by the Viceroy would keep the flood waters out (of his new ironworks), and that their sons would be prevented from taking degrees by the dessicated and enraged tortoise. They were only pacified by the assurance that a deep ditch (in reality a drain) would be cut at the foot of the hill and be always kept wet.

Hanyang. His story is long and interesting. I hope to tell it one evening.

"But as to Yü the Great. He is said to have been a descendant of the 'Yellow Emperor' [R. 2697–2597] who reigned a hundred years in the days when men's age was greater than it is now. His mother gave birth to him miraculously, after seeing a falling star and swallowing a divine pearl. When his father had failed to control the waters, the sacred Shwin, afterwards Emperor [R. 2255–2205], nominated him to undertake the work. He began his task [in the year B.C. 2286], and by means of constant assiduity succeeded, during the space of nine years, in bringing the waters under control. So devoted was he to his task that he took heed of neither food nor clothing, and thrice passed the door of his home without stopping to enter, although he heard the wailing of his infant son from within. In the following year he was made a prince, afterwards joint-Regent of the Empire, and eventually was appointed successor by the Emperor Shwin, to the exclusion of his own son. The ancient records speak of three great dykes he raised on the banks of the Han.

The Great Yü.

"On this Great Hill of Division I walked about exploring, and found the rocky depressions called the feeding-troughs of the sage Kwan, the god of war. While looking for them, I noticed some red cracker paper at the mouth of a hole or two. This was evidently a trace of the worship of the fairy foxes at the New Year.

"There is a fine view from the hill-top of the three cities of Hanyang, Hankow, and Wuchang. The latter city looked grand in the sunset. The prominent object at the end of the Serpent Hill is the Yellow Crane Tower, on which the drunken poet, Li Tai-peh, composed some verses [699–762]. A reclining image of this celebrated man may be seen in a temple at the back. Beyond the great city is the Red Hill, so called from the colour of the soil. On its side is a fine pagoda, where, I am told, certain devotees ascend, and either starve to death [1] or throw themselves over.

[1] There is a man known to the writer who ascended the present pagoda with this intention, but was dissuaded therefrom on the second day.

"One of the poets, whose lines are preserved in the official records, speaks of an iron chain across the Yangtse [Kiang]. This was in the Ts'in dynasty [265–420] during a war, and was intended to prevent the enemy's boats passing. It seems to have been thrown across about ninety miles [270 li] below Hanyang, where the rocks are inscribed, 'The iron chain enlocks the Kiang.'

"The *Book of Odes* further speaks of the two rivers in the words—

> 'The breadth of the Han
> Cannot be dived across;
> The length of the Kiang
> Cannot be navigated with a raft.'

"There seems to be a reference here [or *vice versâ*] to another ode—

> 'Where the water was deep,
> I crossed it by a raft or a boat;
> Where it was shallow,
> I dived or swam across it.'

"But the final word is—

> 'Grandly flow the Kiang and Han,
> Regulators of the Southern States.'

"The labours of the Great Yü are age-lasting indeed." On saying which, however, a drop of water fell on to the table—only a drop. "Bother the cats!" said Li, "they are always dislocating the tiles." Such is their nature, certainly, as it is the nature of tiles loosely laid on to be dislocated.

"Bother the rain!" muttered another farmer.

At this stage Mrs. Nieh thought it advisable to replenish the pot and hand round the hot cakes. Thus fortified and cheered, Li could regard the cats with almost complacency. And the rain was forgiven too in the excellent tea it made.

"An early historian, P'an Ku [died A.D. 92]," said Nieh Shen-seng, "states that the Kiang and Han flow through the kingdom of Ch'u [now Hupeh], and that the country abounds in streams, woods, lakes, and hills. The inhabitants eat rice and fish, and gain their living by fishing, hunting on the hills, and cutting wood; they possess but little accumulated wealth, believe in devils and sorcerers, and honour numerous petty deities.[1] Troops were often stationed on the Hanyang Hill, which, from its commanding position, was of great importance, and whatever there existed of trade and population was concentrated in Hanyang.

"To the south of Hanyang is the Parrot Islet, which has an interesting story connected with its name.

"During the epoch known as that of the Three Kingdoms [221–265], Ts'ao Ts'ao, a lawless and prominent character of that period, ordered an erratic philosopher named Ti'ao Hen to come to his court. On his arrival, Ts'ao Ts'ao treated him very shabbily, at which he raised his eyes to heaven, saying, 'Heaven and earth are wide; why then are no men to be found?' Ts'ao replied that he had some teens of warrior chieftains under him, and enumerated several, with commendatory remarks on each one. Ti'ao Hen laughed sneeringly, and said, 'The first may do to condole with folks after a bereavement; the second might manage to guard a grave; the third might answer for a doorkeeper; the fourth, a ballad singer; the fifth, a beater of drums and gongs; the sixth, a cowherd; the seventh is good at litigation; the eighth might carry letters; the ninth, sharpen knives and swords; the tenth can drink wine, lees and all; the eleventh might make a fair bricklayer; the twelfth could stick pigs and kill dogs: the rest are mere clothes frames, rice sacks, wine barrels, and meat bags.'

A Chinese Diogenes.

"'And, pray, what abilities may you have?'

"'There is no knowledge, heavenly or earthly, that I have not mastered; the three religions, and the nine professions, I know thoroughly. I can instruct emperors how to rule like the celebrated monarchs of old time; I can display virtue comparable to that of Confucius and his disciples. But I cannot throw myself away among a set of vulgar fellows.'

"At this, one of the bystanders drew his sword to behead the boaster. But Ts'ao stopped him, saying, 'I am in need of a drummer.'

"Next day Ts'ao prepared a great feast, and as the guests

[1] This is interesting, as neither Buddhism nor the subsequent religion of Tao had at that time been introduced.

118   A STRING OF CHINESE PEACH-STONES.

arrived, ordered the drum to be beaten. The philosopher-drummer appeared dressed in shabby old clothes,[1] and began drumming away in such a style that the guests were struck

"The Parrot Philosopher."

with melancholy. An attendant cried out, 'Why did you come in those rags?' At which the philosopher began to strip!

"'Don't you know the proprieties?' shouted Ts'ao.

[1] A like insult to that of the man without the wedding garment.

"'Yes, I do. To deceive and shamefully treat one's monarch is surely a breach of propriety. But my body, see how clean it is!'

"'Clean? Whose is not?'

"'You cannot distinguish between the worthy and the ignoble—there is dirt in your eye. You have never studied any good books—your mouth is dirty. You will not listen to faithful words—your ears are dirty. You know nothing of matters, ancient or modern—your breast is dirty. You are ever planning usurpation and insurrection—your heart is dirty. And then you make me a drummer.' And he began drumming away more erratically than ever.

"One of the guests, fearing that Ts'ao would kill Ti'ao Hen, began to plead for him.

"Ts'ao replied by saying, 'Look here, I will send you to Kingchow [island of thorn bushes], to get Lieu Piao to submit, thus making an ambassador of you.'

"Ti'ao Hen at first refused to go; but three horses were prepared, and a farewell feast provided. He sat down to table with tears in his eyes, exclaiming, 'I am moving amongst dead men living in the midst of coffins.'

"'If we are dead men,' cried one of Ts'ao's followers, 'you are a headless demon.'[1]

"Not so,' he replied; 'I am a statesman of the Han dynasty. You followers of Ts'ao are without a head.'

"Several swords flashed, but one of the generals said, 'Swords should not be defiled with the blood of rats and sparrows.'[2]

"'If I am a rat, I have the heart of a man. You are a mere nest of hornets.' At which they arose and went off in a rage.

"On arriving at Kingchow, Ti'ao Hen bestowed ironical praises upon Lieu Piao, who, making nothing of him, sent him to Kiangsha [summerlike splendour of the Kiang, *i.e.* the Yangtse], the modern Wuchang. On being asked why he did not stop the old fool's tongue by beheading him, Lieu Piao replied, 'He shamed Ts'ao, who dare not kill him for

[1] The state of ghosts whose bodies have been decapitated.
[2] "Why use an ox knife to kill a fowl?" (*Confucian Analects*).

fear of what folks would say.¹ I was not going to do as *he* wanted me to, and thus earn the name of a slayer of good men. I have sent him off to Kiangsha, to show Ts'ao Ts'ao that I have a bit of *nous*.'

"Arrived at Kiangsha, Ti'ao Hen was banqueted. During the feast he was asked his opinion of Ts'ao's men. He gave characteristic replies. 'Well, and what do you think of me?' his host inquired.

"'Oh, you are like an idol in a temple, who receives many an offering, but does nothing in return.'

"'So you make me out to be a mere dummy of clay and wood!' cried the irate host, unsheathing his sword and hacking away at the neck of the mocker, who continued to curse as long as there was any life in him.

"Lieu Piao, however, hearing thereof, mourned for the old man, and ordered him to be buried on the islet to the south of Hanyang, which, in memory of a petition sent by the philosopher to the weak-minded Emperor, called the Parrot Ode, has been named the Parrot Islet to this day.

"The place where I lodged," continued Nieh Shen-seng, "is called the Lake of the Flayed Child.² It is dry now. But on the shores of the pond that used to be, a woman was once frightening a refractory boy by crying, 'Come, mandarin, come! the boy has struck his mother.' Which cries a passing mandarin heard, and stopped his chair. The mother explained that she was talking in sport.

A Horrible Tale, to be omitted by the gentler reader.

She urged that the child was not old enough to know good and evil.

"'We will see about that,' said the magistrate. 'Bring a bowl of rice and a bowl of muck.' The child chose the former. 'He does know, you see. Flay him.' It was done. The mandarin was fully in accord with the law of China, for whosoever curses father or mother is to die."

---

[1] May it not have been for a similar reason that Domitian refrained from beheading St. John, and banished him instead?

[2] The sounds, however, being almost identical with those of *melon seeds*, those two words, and not *flayed child*, may form the more correct name of the place.

"Cruel!" exclaimed Mrs. Nieh from the depths of her motherly heart.

"Unfilial," observed her law-honouring husband.

"Probably a bad man in a previous state of existence," explained Li.

"In Hanyang, not only is filial piety honoured, but there are many remembrances of virtuous women. I will tell you of one. To

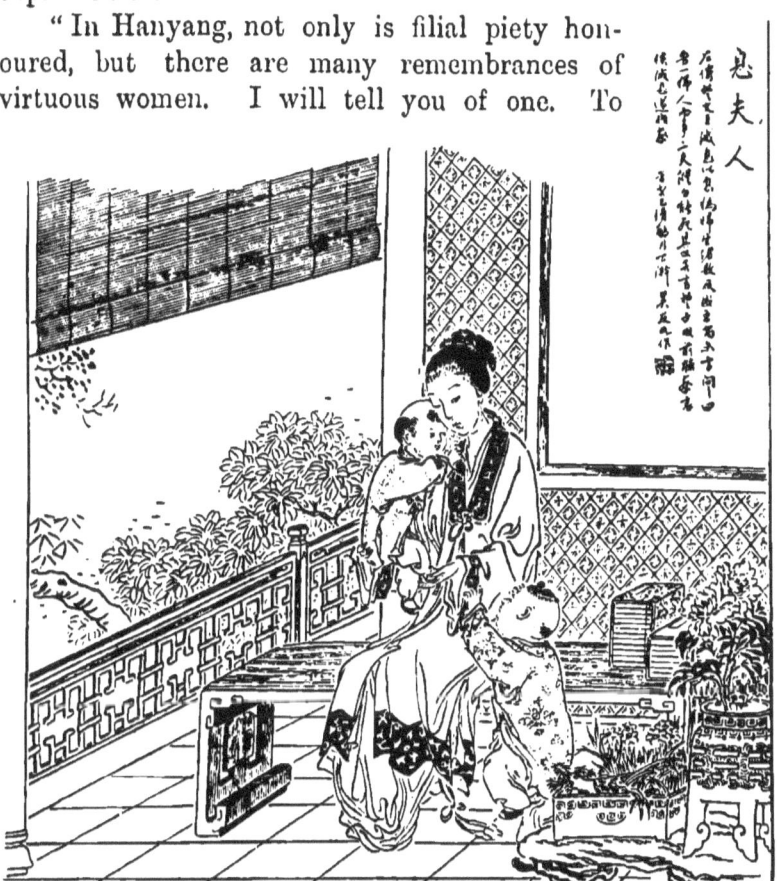

be fair, it must be explained that a different version of the tale exists, but I will relate the one recognised by the Hanyang records.

"In the lawless times of the Chow dynasty, the prince of the State of Ts'ai, who was at enmity with the prince of the small State of Shi [B.C. 682], heard admiring accounts of the unparalleled beauty of the latter's wife, and reported the same to the prince of Ch'u [whose capital was not far from Hanyang]. That

The Silent Woman of Shi.

prince went off at once on a visit to Shi, and was entertained with all due hospitality; which he recompensed by carrying off both husband and wife. The one he made doorkeeper, the other he kept within his palace. She had previously meditated drowning herself in a well, and now she declined to speak for three years. Piqued with her obstinacy, the prince of Ch'u went off to conquer the territory of Shi, but with only partial success.

"While he was away, the faithful wife[1] happening to see her husband from the balcony, broke her long silence by saying to him, 'We can but die once; why then do we consent to prolong this misery and disgrace? Alive we can but live apart, but through death we may at least be united in one grave. Let us die, and thus end our separation.' Saying which she slew herself, and her husband followed her example.

"On his return, the prince was so struck with her fidelity that he restored the State of Shi to its former privileges, buried the lady and her husband in a spot in Hanyang, erecting a temple of some size and splendour to her memory. A modern temple marks the spot to this day. It is called the Temple of the Peach Blossom Woman.

"The peach, you know, besides being credited with magical properties, demon-dispersing and the like, has, from the time of the *Book of Odes*, been an emblem of marriage— later perhaps of marriageableness; while to modern ears the addition of the word *blossom* widens it into a reference to the beauty of ladies, not always without licentious suggestions therein.

"In any case, the name fits her. It fits the tale, which

[1] In this version of an ancient story China joins hands with the classical lands of the West. Panthea, being a captive of Cyrus, had opportunity to desert her husband for the position of queen in the court of that ruler. She refused in touching language. On her release, she persuaded her husband to join the forces of Cyrus, saying as she did so, "Although I care more for you than for my own soul, I certainly would choose to be put under ground with you . . . than to live dishonoured with you in dishonour." Her husband, Abiatus died; and when the corpse was brought home (he probably died in the same way as Uriah the Hittite), she had her maid cover her in the same mantle with her husband. Then she smote herself, put her head upon his breast, and died (Xenophon's *Cyropædia*, vi. chap. iv. Quoted by Rev. J. Cook).

I have not related, which describes her as a wondrous beauty with 'eyes like autumn wavelets, and a complexion like the peach blossom,' a beauty, however, of no great virtue, but the reverse. Or, in its classical sense, it reminds us of the passage in the *Book of Odes*—

> 'Graceful, oh, graceful, you peach tree stands,
> Blooming and bright are its blossoms.
> The maiden comes to her [husband's] abode;
> Well will she order her house and home,'

where the virtues of a prince's well-chosen bride are celebrated.

"That same day, after paying my respects to her memory, I went westward, and came to the West Gate Bridge, where is an indentation in the stone. On the fifteenth day of the eighth moon, the women of Hanyang repair thither, and place their feet in the hollow, to get rid of aches and pains, giving a copper or two to the beggar who stands there with a lantern."

A Cure for Corns.

Mrs. Nieh inwardly wished that the West Gate were nearer, and several looked in the direction where by far the smallest feet in the neighbourhood were to be found.

Those possessed of "nippit foot and clippit foot" gain much admiration in China, though some of them, like a certain young man with brilliant patent leather shoes who shone in society, seem to shine at the wrong end. Not so Mrs. Nieh, however. Her face at the moment shone with veritable peach-blossom hue, and she went into the kitchen— to see if the kettle needed replenishing.

Her husband, proud of her modesty, began to discourse on the origin of bound feet. "Mistress T'ao, a beautiful woman of the Southern T'ang dynasty [which collapsed in A.D. 975], was a most graceful dancer. Her lord the prince ordered an artificer to make a frame of golden lotus lily flowers for her to dance upon. Wishing to please him still further, she caused her very small feet to simulate an unopened lotus bud, which she did with white silk bandages, compressing them until they were only three inches in length. Over these she placed red

Golden Lilies.

124   A STRING OF CHINESE PEACH-STONES.

shoes, and flitted about on the golden lotus flowers, the very beau ideal of gracefulness. She thus set the fashion for small feet.

"By the time of the Sung dynasty [960–1206] foot-binding had become universal. The Manchus, however, allow no small-footed woman to enter the palace precincts. The Emperor Kang Shi, indeed, issued an edict forbidding the practice, but it was never put into effect.[1]

"A little beyond the West Gate Bridge is the execution ground, near to

Golden lotus lilies

Modern mutilations.

which is a little stone erection called 'The Pomegranate

---

[1] The mother of Li Hung-chang, when riding in a chair, is said to show her unbound feet under the chair apron by way of example.

To the present day, small feet are everywhere (except in the capital and in the south) the badge not only of fashion but of respectability.

Flower Pagoda,' the story of which has to do with a virtuous but maligned lady.

"A mandarin's wife of the present dynasty [1818] once prepared a chicken for her invalid mother-in-law, who died soon after. The dutiful daughter was tried and condemned to death as a poisoner. On her way to the execution ground, she passed a pome-

The Lady of the Pomegranate.

granate tree, and plucked a small twig therefrom. This she planted in the crevice of a wall near, and with eyes raised to heaven, cried, 'May the sun bear witness to my innocence. If I am guilty, may this branch soon wither; if I am innocent, it will grow and flourish.'

"Some time after the execution, the sprig was found to be alive and with flower buds thereon. In course of time it became a good-sized tree. The people, taking this to be a proof of her innocence, erected this stone monument to her on the spot where she met her death.

"It has been said that a snake glided down from a beam, tasted the broth, and left poison in the bowl. Or perhaps a little of the comb had got into the broth. We all know that the redness of the crest is due to the poisonous things chickens eat. The poison flies to the comb as wine to the head of man."

<small>Poison Administration.</small>

"Yes, that is it," added Li; "for I remember when I was a child, that a neighbour killed an owl, the flesh of which is very strengthening. But after the feast everyone was seized with dizziness, and the man who had eaten most died,—that is to say, he *almost* died; he died so much, that they bought a coffin from my father, and put him in, but he walked out the next day, and died two years after. The village doctor—not the present one—examined the bird, and found some bones in its gizzard, belonging to a very poisonous kind of snake."

"Grapes are often poisoned from the spittle of lizards," said one of the Yangs; "so they used to say in Soho across the water [a pout of the lips indicating the direction]. And we all know that their tails are very poisonous. They drop off, but will not die till the evening, and of course will kill a man if they are put into his ear. Perhaps a lizard dropped its tail into the lady's ear."

Nieh, however, seemed to cling to his theory of the poison-reddened crest. "The comb of a peacock," he said, "is stated to be a most awful poison. When an official in old time expected sentence of death, he had a thumb-ring made thereof. Being 'permitted to die,' he applied it to his tongue, and thus anticipated the headsman. Now, in the case in point, asafœtida ought to have been tried. It becomes fragrant when in contact with any poison or ill odour."

The next evening was even more black and rainy still; the water dripping from the gutterless eaves had made a wide ditch around the cottage. It served to wash the feet of the audience, and their sandals too. Happily, the floor was of earth. There were no spoiled carpets to distract the good housekeeper. Nor were there any ceilings to get discoloured; tiles easily displaced, are easily put in position. But it was cold for the time of the year, and one or two of the poorer guests, who perhaps came chiefly for the tea and cakes, had already handed in their winter garments to Lieu, who was pawnshop-keeper to the community. The money advanced thereon had been spent in seed,—a frequent state of things among the poorer farmers.

One or two little scholars came shivering in. They might at least have the cheering sight of a couple of candles. The teacher's house was but a schoolroom to them in daylight. At night it was a fairy-lit palace. The instinct of work which the room and the presence of Shen-seng ever called out, and the pressing claims of dire necessity too, urged them to bring little bundles of dried grass under their arms. Taking three of the longest blades, they would twist them into a coarse string by a rotary motion of the palms of the hands. This string would be made into "straw" sandals, at eight cash a pair. They must work thus to redeem their warmer garments.

The subject that night was chiefly the rain and the cold. The farmers only wanted a shower or two; it was coming down in bucketfuls. Nieh could foretell eclipses; had not the *Imperial Almanac* something to say about the weather?

Concerning this, and also the death of his father-in-law, which had just taken place, Nieh's one explanation was Heaven's decree. He was a fatalist, resigned to "an omnipotence either without character, or [which is the same thing] of whose character he was ignorant." "The decree was unanswerable; why trouble to answer it." But one or two who shivered by reason of the present decree would utter a phrase every now and again as though they were firing a minute gun. "Sin's penalty! Sin's penalty!" was their exclamation. Whose sin, they did not specify. It might be their own of course—in a previous state of existence.

All inconvenience and misery is the result of Heaven's decree; and either that decree may be criticised, as in the common phrase, "The way of Heaven [the usual word for weather] is bad," and in actual curses upon the "Heaven way"; or, if we are more submissively inclined, without of course committing ourselves,—that is the present I,—we may exclaim, "Sin's penalty." "Which did sin, this man or his parents?" might be Chinese, but then "there are no faulty parents to be found under heaven," so the orthodox saying goes. They have no faults at anyrate which their offspring dare recognise. If the sin be in the family, it is perhaps the sin of the previous state of existence, the true but not impeccable parent of our present lot. The "sin penalty" being suffered to the full, may redeem us from like trouble in the next state of existence when we shall be born again.[1]

"How cold it is!" exclaimed Mrs. Nieh, as the door was finally closed for the night.

"Yes," replied her husband, "colder than when I filled in the last of my 'nine characters.'"

"Do you mean the 'eight characters' of betrothal?"

"No; have you not heard that on the shortest day of the year scholars take a piece of paper, and write thereon nine characters which read, 'A guest at the front porch; the handmaid brings in the tea'? These characters, are written in outline. They contain eighty-one strokes, one of which is filled in every day. As the eighty-first is completed, the cold weather goes."

The Winter's Requiem.

"I shall get quite learned by and by," laughed the scholar's wife. "And yet I get all this for nothing."

"I suppose you yourself are 'not worth cash!' Confucius said, 'Friendship with the upright; friendship with the sincere—these are advantageous.'"

"I think my husband has omitted a clause," said Mrs. Nieh, reddening, "which is 'friendship with the man of much observation.'"

"Where did you learn that?" asked Nieh in surprised admiration, recalling the remark of Li that Miss Chü knew the coolie pole stroke to mean *one*, when she saw it.

"When they mentioned your name, and before I was

---

[1] The words of Nicodemus (John iii. 4) seem to be best explained as meaning, "Surely you do not advocate the popular notions as to a future bodily state of eligibility for the kingdom of heaven! The orthodox Hebrew can scarcely receive them." As to notions concerning the possibility of a previous life, note John ix. 2, a man sinning so as to be born blind. Concerning a reappearance on the earth, note especially Matt. xiv. 2: "This is John the Baptist; he is risen from the dead," words all the more striking as coming from one who would seem to have been a Sadducee in creed.

'spoken,'"[1] she said, " I did my best to learn the Analects. An old schoolmaster lived in the next village, and he explained a great deal to me."

The scholar's delight was great. His home was getting to be home indeed. It was the picture of snugness, as he looked around; and his wife was fully appreciative, and could actually converse with him on a portion of the classics.

While outside the rain was pouring down in a manner which was well-nigh fierce. And beyond the expanse of nearer blackness were at that moment some Chinese Nights' Entertainments in full swing at the tea-shop.

Tittle-tattle, in China at anyrate, would seem to be quite an ancient, if not quite venerable institution. It may be traced back to the good old classical times of three or four thousand years ago. Did not a poet in the *Book of Odes* sing—

> "They buzz about, the blue flies,
> Lighting on the jujube trees.
> The slanderers' tongues are limitless;
> They throw the realm into confusion"?

Lieu's "Something is beginning to happen. I said so. You don't deceive me," afforded suitable resting-places for the flies, which seem to have been more than mere survivals of the good old times.

The champion buzzer of the evening was the village " doctor " and *fung shui* professor. Having been repulsed so ignominiously when he was doing his best to patronise Li and Co., he has at length found a suitable environment, where he can embody his learning in utterances, not indeed independent of Lieu's, but rather lectures, if not orations, with these for their text.

[1] This expression throws light upon a well-known Scripture passage. By the light of a Chinese lantern, Ps. lxxxvii. 3 reads, "Thou art gloriously betrothed, O city of God." Which makes it a parallel passage to Hosea ii. 19, 20, the Hebrew phrase in the former sentence corresponding to the Chinese colloquialism. Its nearest English equivalent would be *bespoken*. Compare Cant. viii. 8, 1 Sam. xxv. 14. The above interpretation is indeed suggested by Jennings and Lowe, but surely rendered indisputable by the Far Eastern parallel in daily use. The modern Arabic for *betrothed* is also *spoken*.

But in order that we may appreciate the cogency of his remarks, it may be necessary to give some of the acknowledged facts concerning the *fung shui* of the Hanyang county. Among the rounded hills a few miles to the west of the city is one which has a curious lump on its flat top. It is quite natural, and no mere heap of stones, such as is found at the top of Helvellyn—to the ignominy of Skiddaw. It is part of the solid rock which forms the hill. It therefore has a meaning. It resembles an inverted cooking-pan. It *therefore* signifies emptiness of cooking-pans all around. In Hunan, it is said, there is a corresponding hill, but with the cooking-pan upturned. The harvests are always good there. The two form the obverse and the reverse of the stubborn facts behind the exact science of *fung shui*. The Inverted Cooking-pan Hill is the bad spot in the *fung shui* of Hanyang. It was at the foot of this hill, by the way, that the young matricide, "Ingot of Silver," did his deed, and received a fiery recompense, which to some of the Pavilion dwellers might seem to have intensified the untoward influences of the hill of ill-omen. Even Nich himself began to wonder after a while whether a pagoda, a heavenly influence conductor, ought not to have been erected there.

Under ordinary conditions, the Hill of the Nine Recluses seems to be the saving of the county. Beneath its bold configuration it contains the most active "earth-pulse" of the district. In a different way from the scientific conception of matter being ever in a state of molecular vibration, the Chinese think of their hills as alive,[1] and kept in beneficial existence by the throbbing earth-pulse. This throbbing life may be manifest in crops which will support life, or more directly in a life long and happy for those who

---

[1] A notion by no means confined to China. An English farmer, who had made some money and had bought an old country residence, once affirmed that all stones grew, except those killed by the chisel—his marble mantelpiece, for instance. Precious stones seemed to be still more lively, according to old writers. A sixteenth century author calmly tells us that a certain lady had two hereditary diamonds which produced several others, and thus left a posterity. Many Chinese country folk still live in the sixteenth century, some, perhaps, in the sixteenth century B.C.

(Marginal note: Fung Shui of the Hanyang County.)

dwell near, or an alleviation of the lot of those whose bodies are buried within the range of its influence.

Lieu had just been saying that it was not for himself he complained, but for the country district, "for you, my brothers." The first clause had a literal basis; for not being a landowner, he had no taxes to pay, and nowadays his customers were as numerous as the literal blue flies. The second clause marks him out as a public-spirited man.

"The Inverted Cooking-pan Hill, on the occasion of the vile deed done there, on the occasion of the early spring, is far off. It is outside the occasion of our region. And either Nieh, on the occasion of taking his degree, has brought back some of its ill-luck on the occasion of his return, or by concentrating into his person on the occasion of such a degree, and his marriage, which, on the occasion of his father-in-law's death [truly a case of parricide], brought him the prospect of some harvest revenues, unless the rain floods his fields, has robbed us of our rightful happiness, or else on the occasion of such a frightful crime even the Nine Recluses Hill has become revengeful." The speaker will be readily identified as the *fung shui* professor.

As the year advanced, it was still cold instead of tropical. In Hankow, during the "summer" of 1849, fur cloaks were taken out of pawn, and brought home in boats along the Venetian-style streets. Who could wade through twelve feet of water? And such was the registered height in that unprecedented year of flood.[1]

In the country, during the months when one garment usually sufficed, wadded jackets were absolute necessities. Even the mosquitos languished for want of exposed flesh. They resorted, therefore, to Lieu's tea-shop, and held indignation meetings nightly.

Among the human sufferers, many fell poorly, and all the babies born during those dreadful months were lacking in

---

[1] It must be understood that Hankow then stood some feet lower than it does at present. The modern mart is built on the débris of the former houses. In digging foundations for "foreign" houses, the builders have to go down five feet; and in well-sinking, reddened bricks, tiles, and bits of charcoal have been found much deeper.

bone. Bandy-legged, crook-backed toddlers, with white scaly [1] pates, those who survived grew up to be.

At the time of the tax-collector's visit, the waters having subsided, to display a stretch of odorous, poison-breathing mud, the school teacher was "stricken with ague," and his school thinned almost to extinction from the same cause. The "striking" is regarded as the work of demons, unless, indeed, as the form of the expression (being active) leads the Chinese to imagine, the demon is hit by the sufferer, who hopes to recover by making an effort. In either case ague is classed with demon possession. The patient sometimes "makes an effort" by going to see theatricals when they are available. There is some unconscious science here, for pleasant excitement of any sort does often prove efficacious in slight attacks of the complaint. The Chinese explanation is, that in a crowd of playgoers the demons cannot tell Li from Lieu, and so may fix upon the wrong person.

If pleasant excitement be a help, gloomy foreboding is an aggravating influence. Brooding over an addled egg makes it still more addled, until perchance the generated gases, bursting the shell, add their quota to the general contamination.

The tax-collectors certainly afforded material for brooding. They pleaded angrily that, harvest or no harvest, the Emperor wanted his money. The fact being, all the while, that on receiving a memorial from Hupeh, the Emperor Tao Kwang had postponed his requirements in regard to the greater part of the taxes in the flood districts. The memorialist in this case was the noble-mined Tsao, county mandarin of Hanyang, remembered with gratitude by the old folks to this day under the cognomen of "Heavenly Clearness," the epithet which his great generosity and probity won for him; celebrated, moreover, by gorgeous

Tsao the Good (Clear as Heaven).

---

[1] Such white scales, propagated, it is thought, on unhealthy scalps by the barber's razor and comb, are popularly explained as the result of the ancestral tombs being situated in arid places! This *la-li* is perhaps a distant connection of the leprosy of Scripture. It somewhat resembles in appearance the white efflorescence on the walls of some unhealthy houses (Lev. xv. 33-53), which white efflorescence—common enough in 1849—seems to appear under influences which cause malaria. *la-li*, and the like.

processions in the streets of Hankow, until in recent years [1] such rebukeful memories were forbidden by the later mandarins, who felt maligned thereby. He had erected huts upon the Tortoise Hill for the flooded-out refugees, providing means for their maintenance, and eventually for their return home when the waters subsided.

To do this more effectually, he crossed the Yangtse

one day and appealed to the Viceroy for help. That high official—of whom more anon —was known by a nickname answering very closely in meaning and literary grade to the word "Duffer." Interviewing whom, Tsao the Good pleaded the cause of the populace in tones of eloquent sympathy. The reply of the stingy, self-enriching "Duffer" was that he ruled over the land, it is true, but not over the flood waters.

"Great sire," was the reply,—and the suppliant fell on his knees as one of the people might have done,—"the dry land of Hanyang is ruled by 'the younger brother'; must not the waters be also? Must not those who have regularly paid the taxes to the Emperor receive some greater boon than tax postponement in this their time of distress?"

"Yes, if you please to help them, O modern successor of Yü the Great!" was the only help the lordly "Duffer" gave.

[1] This "Tsáo of Heavenly Clearness," afterwards mandarin down East during the Rebellion, was stated by an old man (in 1894) to be still alive, though some years beyond eighty, and to be living in his ancestral home in Shantung.

It was only on the assurance that the Nine Recluses region lay high and dry, that he sent his underlings thither, sent them with strict injunctions that part of the taxes from the happier farmers were to go to enrich the poorer classes. Which facts the underlings studiously forgot, except in whispered communications to "brother Lieu." The flesh-and-blood squeezings they gave to the indigent and poor "runners" (*i.e.* themselves), then returned to report that there was not a cash obtainable, the distress was so great!

Thus defrauded, the small farmers were paupers, with no poorhouse to help them, except the generosity of the larger landowners whose higher fields escaped. The chief of these was our friend Li. He did his little best, chiefly supporting his own household by turning fisherman. Willow leaf decoctions unadulterated served for tea, and willow bark came eventually to be stewed for food in several of the half-dismantled cottages. "Fuel was as cinnamon; food as gems."

"I said so. I said something would happen. Has it not proved true?"

"It has," buzzed the blue flies. "The waters only subsided when the 'parricide' fell ill with ague."

Chapter VII.

CAN ANY PATHOS COME OUT OF CHINA?

"A tale I tell of wondrous sympathy,
For those alone that sympathetic be."

WHILE it was yet (or ought to have been) springtide, Nieh Shen-seng devoted an evening to the ancient story which has made Hanyang famous throughout the eighteen provinces for considerably more than eighteen hundred years. At the foot of the Tortoise Hill, the southern shore of the Moon Lake has for centuries been adorned by a garden, wherein is a "drum tower" and a hall for tea-drinking and poesy. In recent years it has been enlarged by the addition of a handsome "loft," with cloisters built around the stone pattern pathed garden of delights. The gate bears the inscription, "Ancient Harpsichord Pavilion." Thus have sympathetic souls combined their energies to magnify the two names which the people delight to honour. As the story is the most æsthetic of the neutral tint tales of this ancient land, the circle of sympathetic listeners may be (as it deserves to be) indefinitely enlarged.

With the Chinese couplet translated above by way of preface, Nieh proceeded to relate the story of Peh-ya and his sympathetic listener:—

Peh-ya and his Sympathetic Listener.

"In the old days described in the *Spring and Autumn Annals*,[1] when China consisted of a host of rival States hard to amalgamate, there lived a celebrated statesman of the name of Yü Peh-ya. His

[1] Confucius' last literary work, so called because he began it in the spring and finished it in the autumn. It consists of historical jottings of the fifth and

birthplace was the capital of the kingdom of Ch'u, which is now the present Kingchow (the "island of thorn bushes" to which Ts'ao Ts'ao sent his cynical adviser Ti'ao Hen), to the west of the modern Wuchang. But his star of good fortune led him into an official post in the kingdom of Tsin, which occupied what is now the southern half of Shensi, and the north-west of Honan.

"The King of Tsin, wishing to send an embassy of friendly congratulation to the King of Ch'u, Peh-ya sought and obtained the commission. Having reached the capital, he was granted a royal interview, and was entertained in sumptuous style. He naturally wished to visit his ancestral graves, and call upon such of his relatives and friends as the great change-worker Time had spared as yet.

"Public business being ended, he took his leave of his royal host, pleading that he was suffering from ill-health, which would be aggravated by jolting over rough roads; and so provision was made for him to return by water, two boats being fitted up for his accommodation. The fact was, he wished to feast his eyes once more upon the familiar landscapes of ten or twenty years back. All the officials of the capital accompanied [1] him to the river bank, so the parting was even more honourable than the reception had been.

"The wind-filled sails advanced amid the thousand tiers of blue-green wavelets, while beyond the sunlit waters were the distant hills of piled-up turquoise. It was mid-autumn, and Peh-ya enjoyed the varied scenery to the full.

"Passing Hanyang, the boats left the Yangtse; but either the Han had another channel then,[2] or else it was flood time,

---

sixth centuries B.C. Confucius, however, lived some time previous to the days of Peh-ya.

[1] This is a technical term in Chinese, and an exact equivalent to the old-time *convoy*. In *Rutherford's Letters* (No. ccxx.) we read: "It is good that your crosses will but convoy to heaven's gates; in they cannot go." The convoying of guests from the time of Abraham (Gen. xviii. 16) has been an inseparable part of Eastern hospitality. But for "all the officials" to convoy Peh-ya to the bank was a mark of highest respect.

[2] The present channel of the Han, towards its mouth, dates back to the year 1470.

CAN ANY PATHOS COME OUT OF CHINA? 137

for he seems to have entered the chain of lakes which extend from Hanyang to beyond the Hill of the Nine Recluses.

"Peh-ya had not gone many miles before a fierce wind sprang up, and the rain poured in torrents, so that the boats

had to make for the nearest bank, which happened to be not far from the 'Horse Saddle' Hill.

"After sundown the storm abated, and the full-orbed moon shone forth, all the brighter for the rain. Peh-ya being alone, with nothing to occupy his thoughts, ordered his lad to light the incense brazier and bring out his harpsichord. The sweet instrument [which sounds like a piano with both pedals down] being brought, the musician adjusted the strings, and commenced a plaintive strain. Before he had played many notes, however, one of the strings snapped with a loud noise. At this he was very much startled, and told his lad to go outside and inquire what manner of place it was. The head boatman replied that it was a mere uncultivated hill, with no cottages in sight. 'A mere uncultivated hill?' the musician exclaimed. 'Had it been a city or village near which we were stopping, there might have been some scholar or other listening to my instrument, and thus causing the string to break.[1] I have it! There is some villain or other near who owes me a grudge, or a robber bent on stealing the treasure in the boats. If he is not among the trees yonder, he is certainly hiding among the tall reeds.'

"The boatmen went to look, when they heard a voice exclaim, 'The high official need not disturb himself; I do not belong to the robber class. I am a woodcutter caught in the storm, and so took refuge here. Then hearing the classical strains of the harpsichord, I stopped to listen.'

"'A likely tale,' laughed the statesman; 'a hillside woodcutter a musical connoisseur'; and his attendants ordered the intruder off. But he remained expostulating, saying, 'The high official is wrong. Has he not heard that "in a village of ten houses there is sure to be found loyalty and truth?"[2] And where there is a true gentleman, there will be gentlemanly visitors. If you, sir, make out that on a wild hill there are none capable of appreciating music, it may be argued that there will be no guest at the foot of such a hill playing at midnight.'

"Surprised to hear such a clever reply, Peh-ya went to the door, and said, half in sarcasm, 'As the gentleman upon the bank has been listening thus attentively, perhaps he will tell me what sort of a tune I was playing!'

---

[1] It being an idea among the Chinese that the presence of an unauthorised listener will break a harpsichord string. The principle involved will be readily understood, especially by the musical novice. An unsympathetic listener, or a senior perhaps, who is above such elementary attempts, does seem to break some string and spoil the music.

[2] A sentence from the *Book of Odes*.

"'If I had not understood the meaning of the music, is it likely that I should have remained listening? The poem you were expressing in musical notes was that in which Confucius bemoans the early death of his favourite disciple Yen Hwui.[1] The words are these—

> "Alas, Yen Hwui, so soon to die!
> My hair with grief is turned to grey.
> Thy frugal joys, thy humble home,"—

at which point the string snapped. But the fourth line I remember to be—

> "Shall charm the ages yet to come."'

"'You, sir, are no ordinary countryman!' exclaimed Peh-ya. 'The bank is too distant for conversation; will you not come nearer?' So he ordered the boatmen to throw out a plank, and assist the scholar on to the boat.

"The attendants did so, and the young man came on board—a veritable woodcutter, clad in straw cape and rain hat, grasping an iron-shod coolie pole; a hatchet was stuck in his girdle, and he had straw sandals on his feet! What did the underlings know about intelligent conversation? They saw a mere woodcutter. 'Be sure and knock your head on the ground in the presence of the official,' they said. 'And when he speaks to you, be careful how you answer him. He is a high statesman.'

"'Do not insult me,' was the reply. 'Wait till I have adjusted my apparel for the interview.' And he proceeded to divest himself of rain hat, to display a blue cloth wrapped round his head; then his grass cape, to display to view a cotton jacket, bound round with a white girdle, with drawers to match. Not a whit flurried, he placed his rain hat and grass cape, his spiked pole and hatchet, outside the door, took

---

[1] B.C. 514-483. At the age of twenty-nine his hair had grown white, and at thirty-two he died (Mayers). The lines which follow may have some reference to this. Their ambiguity is thus represented—
"Causing men to ponder { [over thy] frosted hair
{ till their hair is frosted."

off his straw sandals, wrung the dirty water from them, put them on afresh, and entered.

"The statesman was sitting upon the divan, amid the brilliant glow of lamps and candles. Seeing whom, the woodcutter just made a deep bow, saying, 'I pay you my respects, Sir.'"

"An official of Peh-ya's standing could hardly be expected to give a common woodcutter a polite reception. But having invited him on board, he could hardly drive him away. He just waved his hand slightly, saying, 'No need for ceremony,' and called the lad to bring a seat. A long bench being brought, the official pouted out, 'Sit down.' The woodcutter, without any phrase of abject appreciation of the honour, took his seat with the utmost composure. At this Peh-ya was rather put out, and neither asked his name nor ordered the usual tea.

"They sat in awkward silence for a long time, till the official, in an irritated tone of voice, exclaimed, 'So you are the listener on the bank?' to which the woodcutter replied with the usual phrase, 'I do not presume!'

"'Well, as you were listening, you doubtless know the origin of the instrument, who invented the harpsichord, and what good there is in playing it?'

"'Receiving your questions with all due deference, I may, however, delay the boat with my tedious replies!' For the boatman had just been to say there was nothing to prevent their starting.

"'I fear you know nothing about it. If you answer rightly, I shall look upon my official post as a thing of no consequence, much less will a little delay matter.'

"'In that case, I may venture to trouble you with my inordinate chatter. The harpsichord was made by Fu Shi [the first of the fabulous Emperors of China, 2852–2737 B.C.]. He saw that the virtue of the five planets[1] was concentrated in the *tung* tree [*Elæococca Sinensis*], and that the phœnix chose it for its resting-place. The phœnix is the king of birds, only eating bamboo sprouts, only drinking spring

---

[1] Named according to the "five elements"; metal star—Venus; wood star—Jupiter; water star—Mercury; fire star—Mars; soil star—Saturn.

water. Fu Shi, therefore, seeing the princely nature of the *tung* tree, gathering into itself as it does the choicest essences of creation, argued that its wood might be expected to emit the choicest music. He therefore ordered a man to cut one down. This particular tree was 33 ft. 3 in. [tenths of a foot] high, according with the number of the thirty-three heavens. He then had its trunk cut into three pieces, corresponding to the three powers of nature,—heaven, earth, man.

"'On sounding the upper block it was found to ring with too high a note, while the lower block emitted too dull a sound. That of the middle block, however, was found to be a happy medium between the two. It was placed in a running stream for seventy-two days, according to the seventy-two periods of the year,—an ancient mode of division, each period being five days; then being dried in the shade, an exceptionally propitious time was chosen, and the Emperor employed a skilful workman to make it into a musical instrument.'"

At this stage Nieh related how that a celebrated politician and man of letters named Ts'ai Yung (133–192), when a refugee in the State of Wu, was one day seated at the fireside when his attention was attracted by the sound emitted by a log of *tung* wood which lay burning there. Believing that its tone gave promise of rare excellence, he converted it into a lute. As the handle of this instrument still retained signs of scorching, it gave rise to the expression, "the scorched tail [lute]."[1]

"In recent poetry," continued Nieh, "this incident is combined with that of Peh-ya. A Hanyang poet sings—

> 'Now would I follow poesy and song,
> Renewed in readiness the silken string,
> My "heart's interpreter" at length has come.
> The "scorched tail" interprets every wish;
> The swiftly-flowing stream is heard once more,
> Swells to the clouds the highest melody;
> As whirlwinds now o'er myriad mountains borne,
> Rises the melody sublime.'

"But to return to the story of the 'heart's interpreter'

[1] Compare "two tails of smoking firebrands," Isa. vii. 4.

referred to. The woodcutter proceeded: 'When completed, the harpsichord was thirty-six inches and a tenth long, according to the three hundred and sixty-one days in a [lunar] year At the broad end it was eight inches across, according to the eight festivals; at the narrow end, four inches across, according to the four seasons. It was two inches thick, according to the masculine and feminine principles of nature. It had a golden youth's head and a gemmous maiden's waist, a back like that of an immortal, a dragon tank, and a phœnix bath [all of which frequent phrases of idealisation seem perfectly natural in the Chinese].[1] It had jade pegs and golden stops, which stops [let into the wood as a guide to the fingering] are thirteen, according to the twelve months of the year, plus the intercalary month.

"'At first the harpsichord had five strings, according to the five elements, their sounds being called respectively Kung, Shang, Kioh, Tsz, and Yu [antediluvian tonic sol-fa!]. In the time of the Emperors Yao and Shuin this five-stringed instrument was used to accompany the populace renovating odes of the day. A thousand years later, the literary monarch being in exile from his State, and lamenting over the death of his son Peh Yih-kao,[2] added another string of pure and pathetic note, since called the literary string. Another son of his [almost a contemporary of King David] having defeated and slain the tyrant, and gained for himself the title of Military Monarch, added a seventh string, which is called after him.

"'The harpsichord has six abhorrences and seven prohibi-

---

[1] In Chinese epistles such expressions abound as "golden face"—your face; "golden peace"—your health; "golden body"—yourself; "pearly opening"—open (this letter) yourself; "gemmous loft"—your shoulder; "gemmous viands"—the eatables provided by you; while "gemmous hall and golden horse" signifies high official rank; and "the pearly words of the golden mouth" means the words of the Emperor. With this latter expression compare the name Chrysostom.

[2] Peh Yih-kao was killed by the tyrant Chow on his playing before the vixen Empress a piece with a reproving strain. His flesh was made into cakes and sent to his father, who thanked the messengers for this token of the Imperial bounty, though he knew well what the present was. Compare the story of Astyges, who invited Harpagus to a dish of meat, telling him afterwards that it was a piece of his son, and asking him how he liked the seasoning. "What pleases your Majesty," replied Harpagus, "must please me."

tions. It abhors intense cold, intense heat, a high wind, a heavy rain, loud thunder, and a heavy fall of snow. It must not be played when wailing sounds are heard, when festive instruments are sounding, when the musician is worried, when his person is not clean, when his clothing is awry, without incense having first been lighted, or in the presence of an unsympathetic listener. Its eight excellences in sound are purity, mystery, obscurity, choiceness, plaintiveness, energy, distance, and resonance. When played by a masterhand in the highest style, the howling tiger will listen, and cease its roar; the screaming monkey will listen, and cease its screeching.'[1]

"Hearing the woodcutter discourse with such fluency and exactness, Peh-ya imagined he must have learned it all by rote, but even then thought him a man not to be despised. Henceforth adopting politer forms of speech, he essayed to test him a little further. 'Confucius was once playing the harpsichord[2] in the house,' he said, 'when Yen Hwui entered. As he listened to its deep and muffled tones, he thought he detected strains of blood-thirstiness, and asked in surprise whether it was so. Confucius answered, "As I was playing, I saw a cat chase a mouse, and smiled at the capture, but fearing it might lose its prey, my blood-thirstiness[!] betrayed itself on the silken strings." 'It was thus that the sacred and sensitive nature of music came to be fully known. Now, suppose I play my instrument with certain thoughts in my mind, can you recognise those thoughts as you listen?'

"Replied the woodcutter: 'In the *Book of Odes* it is written—
"Another's thoughts
I can fathom."

If you, sir, will extemporise a little, I will try and fathom your meaning. Should I guess wrong, pray pardon me.'

---

[1] So much for the solitary Orpheus or Amphion. But a certain Shao Sz (6th century B.C.), a skilled player on the pandean pipes, the *Shao* from which he is named, having married an accomplished lady, instructed her in his favourite art. Their duets "drew phœnixes from the skies," and eventually husband and wife were caught up to heaven, the one by a dragon, the other by a phœnix, for the perpetual delectation of the ideal audience there.

[2] The harpsichord of Confucius is represented on the left, and that of Peh-ya on the right of the illustration on p. 137.

"Peh-ya renewed the broken string and played a while, with mountain scenery in his mind. 'Excellent indeed!' exclaimed the other; 'your far-reaching thoughts were upon the high hills!' At which the musician could hardly believe his ears, and extemporised once more, with the rippling of hillside brooks in his mind. 'Excellent indeed!' cried the woodcutter; 'the flowing brooks are gurgling.'

"With the surprise that such thought-interpretation might well call up, Peh-ya's brusqueness gave place to the geniality of a host, and the woodcutter had to take the place of honour on the left.[1] With fervent apologies, Peh-ya exclaimed, 'Amid the rocks the priceless gem is hidden. And he who judges after the outward appearance and garb cannot fail to slight the most wisely virtuous everywhere.' Then, in the politest terms, he inquired the name of his guest. The reply, given in all due humility, was that his surname was Chung [which we may render as Bushell] Tsz-ki [child of a set time], whereupon Peh-ya introduced himself.

"Tea was brought, then 'wine,'[2] and Peh-ya inquired after Tsz-ki's place of abode.

"'Not far from here,' was the reply. 'I live beside the Horse Saddle Hill, in a hamlet called the Gathering-place of the Virtuous.' 'Truly so called!' exclaimed his host with inclined head. 'And what may your occupation be?'

"'I cut wood for a living.'

"'But how is it that with such abilities you do not seek for a degree, and an honourable official position [*lit.* a name among the bamboo and brocade], instead of hiding your genius among hillside copses and streams, in the company of herdsmen and woodcutters? Why vegetate and wither when you might flourish as a scholar?'

"'Because my parents are both stricken in years, and

---

[1] For the left-hand seat, this much may be said, it leaves the host's right hand free to minister to the wants of his guest. Otherwise the word "left" has little favourable meaning. It often signifies "wide of the mark," as from left-hand clumsiness; applied to a disposition, it means "whimsical" or "faddy," and may be found in the full sense of "sinister."

[2] Probably a feast. Compare Job i. 4, where the words "to feast" and "to drink" are the same. The Scripture word generally translated "feast" is festival, and contains the idea of processions and dances.

CAN ANY PATHOS COME OUT OF CHINA? 145

have no one else to provide for them. Had I the highest possible position offered me, I could not accept it, for they could not do without me for a single day.'

"'Such a true son is hard to find,' exclaimed Peh-ya, whose affection for the young man was deepening. He asked how many 'spring-tides' he had passed? Tsz-ki replied that he had 'emptily passed'[1] twenty-seven years. 'Then I am your senior by some ten odd years'—which was probably a polite understatement of fact. 'And if you will consent to such a relationship, I should like to call you brother, my never-to-be-forgotten thought-interpreter.'

"The meanly-clad young man looked at his friend in silk and fox furs, exclaiming, 'Surely you cannot mean it! You are a noted statesman of an honourable kingdom, and my lot is cast among the rustics. How could I venture to aspire to a friendship so incongruous and unbecoming?'

"To which Peh-ya replied that 'One's acquaintances may fill the earth, but heart-interpreting friends are rare indeed. If I in my various vicissitudes,' he added tenderly, 'may be linked with you in the bonds of sworn brotherhood, it will be an unspeakable enrichment to my whole life.' Then almost pleadingly, 'If you think that I regard such things as riches and poverty as barriers, what manner of man do you take me to be?'

"Incense was added to the brazier, and thus at midnight, in the royally-furnished boat-chamber, the high statesman and the woodcutter went through the eight obeisances[2]

---

[1] Compare a similar polite phrase, Gen. xlvii. 9.
[2] These eight obeisances stand for the eight characters exchanged by the two parties of a betrothal. There are two characters each for the year, month, day, and hour of birth. In the lawless "spring and autumn" days, such yeas on oath crutches often limped to a speedy tumble. But by rights the covenant was as binding as that of marriage. The two above were indeed "weddy'd brethryen." Such a "weddynge" was recognised by old English law (Burrill). An interesting instance of such sworn brotherhood is that which existed between Sir Philip Sydney and his poet friends, Fulk Greville and Edward Dyer. "There is no such touching trinity in all the annals of comradeship," says E. Gosse. "From childhood to the grave of Sydney, where the survivors bore the pall over his body, these three held together without a single flaw, through all the vicissitudes of life" (*Contemporary Review*, Nov. 1886). Perhaps the horizon of the Western world will yet open to admit the names of

which would make them brothers for ever. They were now known to each other by name.

"They changed seats, the elder brother taking the place of honour, and carried on their heart-to-heart conversation until the moon had declined and the stars began to pale. The boatmen having made all preparations for starting [some of them had doubtless been peeping through the window blinds in wonder], Tsz-ki rose to take his leave.

"'My good brother,' said Peh-ya, 'you and I have met too late, and, alas, must part thus early!' At which Tsz-ki could not refrain his tears; and neither of them could bring his mind to the point of separation. 'My feelings are far from spent,' said the elder brother; 'could you not accompany me for some days?'

"'It is not for want of the will that I must decline,' replied the other; 'but how can I leave my aged parents? When the parents are alive, their children should not wander afar.' 'As they are both at home,' Peh-ya responded [with the rest of the quotation from the *Analects* as a basis for his words], 'could you not tell them you would like to go to Tsin to see your brother by and by? Thus, though "wandering afar," you would acquaint them with your whereabouts.'

"'Not to grieve you,' Tsz-ki answered, 'I will not promise, and then break my word. But if I mention it to my parents, they will assuredly object to my going so far.'

"'Let it be as you say, my noble brother. Then I will certainly come again next year and see you.'

"'If you fix a date, I will be here ready to receive you.'

"'Last night was the mid-autumn festival. I shall be looking out for my brother on the fifteenth or sixteenth day of the mid-autumn month next year. I will not break my faith.' 'Then,' said Tsz-ki, 'I will be here on the river bank without fail. It is now daylight, and I must say farewell.'

"'You must really go, my brother?' said Peh-ya, and he ordered the lad to bring two ingots of gold. These he pre-

---

Peh-ya and Tsz-ki. A triple brotherhood between the "god of war" and his two friends, a brotherhood with a military basis, will be instanced later on. Two other instances of Damon and Pythias friendship are noted in Chinese literature.

sented his brother with both hands,[1] saying, 'This little gift will help towards the necessities of your parents. As you are bone of my bone and flesh of my flesh, you will not scorn to receive it.'

"Tsz-ki could not refuse, and took his departure; putting on his rain hat and grass cape, shouldering his spiked pole and sticking his hatchet in his girdle, he was handed along the plank to the shore. The boatmen beat the drums and started. The scenery was grand, but Peh-ya had no heart for it now. All his thoughts were with his heart's interpreter.

"Some days passed thus, when he went ashore, and being recognised as a high official of Tsin, the mandarins of the port provided horses and carriages, accompanying him to the capital.

"Time flies apace! Autumn merged into winter; the spring and summer passed, but not for a single day had Peh-ya ceased to think of his brother. As the autumn was approaching, he petitioned the King of Tsin to allow him to go home a while. It was granted; and the fifteenth of the eighth moon found him once more near the Horse Saddle Hill. The boat was secured by grappling irons and a wooden stake driven into the bank.

"It was a lovely night; the moonbeams came stealing through the blinds. Peh-ya went out and stood on deck. There was hardly a ripple on the waters. The northern constellation was clearly reflected on the glassy surface. Peh-ya opened his heart to the sweet serenity around, and the memories which the spot awakened. 'But my brother promised to be here on the bank waiting for me. There is no trace of him. Can he have broken his word? Nay, it cannot be. There are several boats about, and mine is not the same as I had last year. It was while playing my harpsichord that I discovered him. I will do so again, and he will hear the music and come.'

"So the sweet instrument was brought on deck, and that same brazier emitted clouds of perfume. The musician took

---

[1] A token of highest respect. Compare R. Jefferies: "One fellow happening by chance in the hunting-field to meet the Prince of Wales, took off his hat with *both* hands to express his deep humility" (*Field and Hedgerow*, p. 184).

the harpsichord out of its bag and tuned it, when one of the strings emitted a dirge-like note.

"'How is this?' exclaimed Peh-ya. 'My brother must have some calamity in the house, and so he does not come. He told me both his parents were aged. One or other must be dead. He is a filial son, and has put the first claims first. He would rather break faith with me than neglect his parents, so he has not come. I will go on shore to-morrow and find him.'

"The instrument was brought in again, and he retired for the night. But not a moment's sleep could he get. He longed and looked for the morn. At length the moon declined, and the dawn was about to break over the hills. He arose, washed, and dressed himself, putting on plain garments, and, with the lad bearing his harpsichord and a large quantity of gold, he went ashore. 'If my brother have any mourning in the house,' he said, 'this will cover the ceremonies required of the filial.'

"He walked on until he came to the end of the valley, where he stood still. The road divided to the east and west, and no trace of the hamlet he sought. He sat upon a wayside rock for a while, when an old man with a long, white, silky beard came along, leaning upon his staff. Peh-ya advanced to meet him, and asked which of the two roads led to the desired village.

"'There are two villages of that name, an upper and a lower,' the old man replied; 'which one was it you wished to visit?'

"'My brother is a clear-headed man,' thought Peh-ya; 'why did he speak thus ambiguously? I have it! He did not mean to put me to the trouble of seeking him out.'

"'Your silence, sir, indicates that the person who directed you did not seem to know of the existence of two villages, which are in opposite directions from here. I have lived on the hillside for many a long year, and know everyone here as neighbours or relatives, or else as friends. What is the name of the person you are seeking?'

"'I wish to find out the house of the Chung family.'

"'To seek for whom?'

CAN ANY PATHOS COME OUT OF CHINA? 149

"'To find out Tsz-ki.'

"At this the old man's eyes filled with tears. He sobbed out, 'My own son! Last year at this time, as he was out cutting wood, he met a statesman of Tsin, named Yu Peh-ya, who became attached to him, presenting him with two ingots of gold as he went away. My son bought many books, and studied hard, so as to be worthy of his kindness. Returning with his heavy faggots, he would read on into the night, until he fell ill, and—after—some—months—he—died!'

"With a loud cry, Peh-ya fell down in a swoon. The old man did his best, with the lad's assistance, to restore him; and asked who the traveller was. The lad whispered in his ear, 'The statesman, Yu Peh-ya himself.'

"As consciousness returned, Peh-ya wailed bitterly, 'My brother! my brother! There was I on the boat last night talking of broken promises! Little did I think that you were gone!' He rose and saluted the old man, asking whether his son was already buried or not.

"'It cannot be told in one word,' the old man replied. 'As my son was dying, and we were watching at his bedside, he said, "The bounds of my life have been fixed by Heaven. I cannot fulfil my earthly relations. But I beseech you, bury me by and by on the bank near the place where I met the good statesman, so that I may keep my promise with him."[1] Along the road you came there is a new grave by the wayside. It is my son's. I was just going to visit it.'

"'I will accompany you.'

"They proceeded along the path, the aged father and the elder brother, until they reached the grave, when Peh-ya's sobs broke out afresh. 'My brother,' he cried, 'thou art among the higher intelligences now. I bid thee a long farewell.' Thus he wailed until the country folk assembled. They found out who he was, and crowded to the front to stare at the man in his anguish.

---

[1] On the square church tower of Caistor, Norfolk, there is a mound, the story of which is to the effect that a maiden who had a sailor lover promised to be there watching for his return when the time approached. He never came back. She sickened and died, died on the tower, and was buried there, so as not to break her tryst.

150 A STRING OF CHINESE PEACH-STONES.

"The sweet-toned instrument was taken out of its bag, and with streaming eyes Peh-ya played a dirge. The sightseers, hearing the music by the grave side, went off clapping their hands in merriment.[1] The musician asked the reason, when he was thus bewailing his brother. To which the old man replied that the rustics, not discerning his meaning, took the notes to be festal strains.

"'Can that be so? At least *you* will interpret my heart's meaning?'

[1] Playing to the unsympathetic, "thrumming the harpsichord to a herd of buffalos."

CAN ANY PATHOS COME OUT OF CHINA? 151

"'Alas! I am stupid and dull. I played the harpsichord when I was younger, but now in my old age my five senses are half gone.'

"'I have been extemporising a heart-prompted dirge. I will sing it once for you to hear.'

"With tremulous voice the statesman sang—

'I recall the fond hopes of last year,
When my friend on the bank I met here;
I have come back to seek him again,
I have come back to seek him in vain.
But a heap of cold earth do I find,
And sore is my sorrow-filled mind;
My sore heart is stricken with grief,
My tears are my only relief.
I came here in joy; with what grief do I go!
The banks of the river are clouded with woe.
  Tsz-ki! my lost Tsz-ki!
  True as tried gold were we.
  Beyond the heavenly shore
  Thy voice I hear no more.
I sing thee my last song, my last.
The harpsichord's music is past.'

"Then, taking a small knife from his girdle, he cut the silken strings in twain, and lifting the instrument with both hands, as if in sacrifice, he put forth all his strength, and dashed it to pieces upon the grave.

"The old man wonderingly asked the reason of this.

"'Tsz-ki is gone; to whom should I play now? Springtide friends abound, but to find a heart's interpreter is a difficulty of difficulties.'

"'I am too sad,' Peh-ya continued, 'to accompany you home, but have brought with me some gold, half of which will minister to your present needs, and half will buy a little land around, so that [from the crops thereon] the grave may be ever kept in repair. If you will wait till I return to my adopted country, and ask leave to retire from office, I will come and fetch my venerable father and mother to the old home, there to be cared for until the appointed years of Heaven are fulfilled. I was one with Tsz-ki and he with me. Do not think of me as an outsider;' and he handed the gold to the old man, who received it with tearful gratitude.

"A few moments after, each had gone his several way."

Among Nieh's rustic audience were sympathetic listeners, and more than one sleeve was applied to moist eyes. The narrator himself was not unmoved. He added, with emotion, "I visited the grave to weep there a while."

Subdued to silence, the company dispersed.

"My princely husband," said his wife after a pause, "I am 'but a woman,' yet may I be reckoned as your heart's interpreter? I will sympathise in your wrongs, and share your coming joys."

Chapter VIII.

An Historical Romance.

"When Heaven is about to confer a great office on any man, it first exercises his mind with suffering, and his sinews and bones with toil. It exposes his body to hunger, and subjects him to extreme poverty. It confounds his undertakings. By all these methods it stimulates his mind, hardens his nature, and supplies his incompetencies."—
Mencius.

THE evening following that devoted to Peh-ya and Tsz-ki was enlivened with a story which, if the previous one may be described as a drawing in neutral tint, may be likened to a coloured picture. It is one of the best specimens of such to be found in China. It may not be widely known to Western students, nor even among the Chinese themselves, being found only in cheap, roughly-printed booklets, which may have a somewhat local sale. These booklets, moreover, are unlikely to be reprinted in metal types with other light stories, as their contents do not always fit very closely with the historical records. In taking our place, therefore, among Nieh Shen-seng's audience to listen to the story of Li Tan, *Story of Li Tan.* we must be prepared for fiction rather loosely founded on fact. Li Tan is a true historical character, whose imperial grandsire was illustrious for his patronage of learning and generally noble character. Li Tan lived in the times described in the tale; and if the picture of his adventures be coloured with variegated tints borrowed partly from legend, partly from the imagination of the tale-teller, it may still be of merit as a picture, and certainly of interest to us, as its tints are touches of nature which may help to make the "kinship of all within the four seas,"[1]—a phrase of strictly geographical interpretation, those four seas having widened and deepened into oceans.

There being a historical Li Tan, a word or two may be prefaced as to his antecedents. The second emperor of the Ta'ng dynasty adopted as his designation the term Tái Chung (extreme[ly great] ancestor). As his reign extended from 627 to 650, he was a contemporary of Mahomet, who died in 632. He was a liberal-minded monarch. His name occurs, together with that of his imperial father and son, on that interesting monument, the Nestorian tablet, which is still standing hard by his capital city, the modern provincial capital of Shensi. He was ever on the outlook for literary counsellors and heroic statesmen. "Heroic men have come within my bow-shot," was a characteristic exclamation of his. As a monarch he lived up to the ideal embodied in his words: "I look upon myself in my empire as a father in his family. I love my subjects as my children. An emperor who oppresses the people to enrich himself is like a man who cuts off his own flesh to satisfy the cravings of hunger. These may be satisfied, but in a short time his whole body must perish."

On one occasion he allowed a number of prisoners under sentence of death to return to their homes to celebrate the New Year, on the condition that they should come back at a stated time. They all returned according to their promise, which so pleased the Emperor that he permitted them all to go free.

One day, being out in a pleasure boat with his family, he said, "You see, my children, that the boat is supported by the water, which can at any time overwhelm it when it is roused; consider that the people resemble the water, and the Imperial State the boat." One of these children in after years succeeded him, under the designation Kao Chung (exalted ancestor).

---

[1] A somewhat fascinating, if unprovable, theory might make the Scripture-reading Chinophile identify the "four seas" with the Black, the Caspian, the Mediterranean, and the Persian Gulf; and the enclosed land of "brotherhood" with that in the centre of which, the Middle Realm, rose the Tower of Babel. Otherwise the "four seas" of ancient (or modern) China are hard to identify.

AN HISTORICAL ROMANCE. 155

We may now let the school teacher continue the narrative.

"In the tenth year of Tai Chung's reign his Empress

died. She was a woman of no ordinary talent and virtue. He built her a splendid mausoleum, but the next year consoled himself by collecting beautiful damsels for the imperial seraglio. Among these was a young girl of fifteen, named

Wu Chow [martial radiance]. She was of low parentage, but soon procured great favour for herself, and high official posts for her near relatives, by her exceptional beauty and wit.

"An imperial censor, however, predicted calamity to the realm in connection with her name. A test prophecy on another subject—the highest name on the lists of a forthcoming examination—turning out to be true, the Emperor was alarmed, and sent away Wu Chow into a Buddhist nunnery, where her history is involved in some very serious scandals.

"She did not remain long in seclusion, for Kao Chung, in fulfilment of an early vow he had made her, removed her back to Court. The reason given for the step in the orthodox history books is, that Kao Chung's Empress considered it the only means by which the influence of a certain inmate of the palace could be nullified.

"Her reinstatement at Court, if at first desired by the Empress, brought her much misery. It was like 'cutting out the flesh in one part to mend a sore in another.' Mistress Wu soon began to use every artifice to get the Empress deposed.

"Plots thickened around the phœnix consort of the dragon. Her elder brother, being devoted to Taoism, was in the habit of collecting dew for compounding the elixir of perpetual youth, of writing charms, of bowing towards the northern constellation, where the three august ones of Taoism hold their court [but also a Confucian type of the Imperial Court itself], and of praying to heaven and earth. The latter practices were chiefly supplications that his sister might bear a son, and so be of value in the eyes of her lord.

"Such practices, however, were construed into curses against the Emperor. And to make the guilt of the brother and sister fully manifest, Wu Chow had an image made, with the never-to-be-written personal name, date of birth, etc., of the Emperor inscribed thereon.[1] She then struck five large

---

[1] Compare the *Corp Creadh* of the Highlands of Scotland, and similar practices in many countries. Such an image, but of straw, has been seen by the writer in a little shrine by a small guardhouse, the soldiers of which hoped by such means to punish a thief who had stolen one or two of their garments. His

nails of peach wood into its body. [The character for peach tree dissects into the tree of omen. The dictionary says it is a celestial tree. It also adds that when a statesman died, the Emperor used to pay a visit of condolence, to find a spiritualistic medium brandishing a sword of peach wood to avert further calamity. Magic virtues are attributed to peach tree twigs by ancient writers.] This image she managed to secrete in the apartment of the Empress. Then coming in tears before the Emperor, she besought him to institute a search, as her own life and even his were in danger.

"The image was found, and the sin of the Empress seemed certain. The whole story was reported in the conclave of suddenly summoned ministers. One of them pleaded that there must be some mistake. But the Empress' fair name was gone. To render her disgrace more complete, Wu Chow strangled an infant princess, and accused the Empress of the crime. Upon which Kao Chung imprisoned his brother-in-law, who died soon after; banished his Empress to a secluded part of the palace, and raised Wu Chow to her vacated place.

"On the morning after the celebration of this latter event with a magnificent feast, the deposed Empress, who had heard the sounds of revelry, gave birth to a son, whom she called Li Tan [Li was the imperial surname, Tan signifies dawn].[1]

"On receipt of the news, Wu Chow began to fear for her own position, and secretly summoned the eunuch Teu Hwui to her presence, bidding him go that night to the ex-Empress' apartment and murder both mother and son. Teu Hwui bowed assent and took the proffered reward.

"On his reaching the chamber and explaining his commission, a most pathetic scene ensued. But his heart was loyal; and, far from taking life, he was willing to risk his own by carrying the infant to a place of safety. His plan was to

name being unknown, the words "Heaven-regulated conscience" were written thereon, by which means he might be urged to confession, and thus avert the alternative destruction.

[1] Compare the names Haggai, born on a festival; Shabbethai (Ez. x. 15), born on the Sabbath; Hodesh (1 Chron. viii. 9), born at the new moon; Shaharaim (1 Chron. viii. 8), "double dawn."

flee to the King of Kiangsha, whose capital was the present Wuchang, around which city, moreover, the ancient name still lingers, a large portion of the city being in the Kiangsha county.

"If he were really true, the Empress said, she could die without regret. Being at length assured of his sincerity, she bit her finger till it bled, and wrote a gory letter to the King of Kiangsha, a relative of hers. Then embracing her babe, she sobbed out, 'Alas, my child, that you should be born in such evil days, that you and I should have to part so soon. But the good Teu Hwui will take care of you. Do not cry, will you? And when you are grown up, you will see this blood-written letter, and think of your poor mother, won't you?'

"The infant smiled.

"She gave her child to his deliverer, and as they went, her heart was pierced through as with a sword.[1] Then she and her two faithful maids strangled themselves. Hearing of which, Wu Chow exclaimed that a thorn had been plucked from her eye. But, alas, that Li Tan had escaped!

"Teu Hwui with his precious bundle arrived safely at Kiangsha just as the 'King' was feasting with some friends, one of whom was Ma Chow,[2] of whom we shall hear more by and by. After a secret consultation it was agreed to bring up the infant in the inner apartments of his *yamun*, and to publicly announce that the Kiangsha 'King' had a grandson.

"Years passed, and one evening at the capital city of

---

[1] Cf. Luke ii. 35.

[2] Ma Chow (born 601) was a brave warrior and a fearless censor. He rose from a humble station by force of merit. His noble wife he had raised from the occupation of cake-vendor.

Chang-ngan [perpetual peace], the present Shi-ngan [Western peace], provincial capital of Shensi, the lantern festival of the first month was celebrated with unusual splendour, bringing vast crowds from the neighbouring towns and villages. The streets were crammed with sightseers, and, during the excitement, a young man of high rank named Shieh Kang, who had been drinking heavily, created a great disturbance. The Emperor Kao Chung and his favourites were sitting in a turreted loft enjoying the sights, until one of the princes went down and mixed in the crowd, to be killed by a kick from the wine-maddened man. The Emperor hearing thereof, hurried towards the stairs, and having been drinking freely, missed his footing, fell, and died.

"Shieh Kang escaped in the universal panic by opening up a gory road. But a terrible retribution was meted out by the Empress Wu to the loyal and lordly family of the Shiehs. Three hundred and eighty-odd persons—greybeards grown old in the Imperial warfare and service, women of virtue and beauty, and children too, who had been the hope of that ancient clan—all were beheaded in one day. By such means as these did the merciless woman make good her seat upon the coveted throne, occupied long enough, to her thinking, by the Imperial weakling.

"But before openly assuming the Imperial prerogatives, she first raised a son of hers to the nominal post of emperor. He was a mere puppet in the hands of his mother; and before a month had passed, he contentedly resigned the powers of government to his mother, who relegated him to a state of virtual confinement, assuming the full attributes of supreme power[1] [which she continued to wield for nearly twenty years, putting to death many heads of chief families, and committing, if history be true, many unspeakable crimes].

"Meanwhile, in the seclusion of his 'grandfather's' *yamun* at Kiangsha, Li Tan grew up to boyhood, noble of feature and

---

[1] Requiring also, as any emperor might, an imperial seraglio of rouged and powdered favourites. The countenance of one of these (named Leu-lang) was so beautiful (!) that his flatterers said, "Leu-lang is like the lotus lily." "Nay," said another, "the lotus lily is like Leu-lang." A thousand years' slander on that pure flower, as a modern scholar says.

160   A STRING OF CHINESE PEACH-STONES.

undoubtedly clever. He had been carefully trained in book study, in writing and drawing, in the music of the harpsichord and flute, and could play a game of chess with the 'King' himself. Added to this he was a good archer—though only a mere youth when the news came of the deposition of the puppet Emperor.

"Hearing of this turn of affairs, the friends[1] of Li Tan felt that the time had come for his appearance. His true parentage was accordingly explained to him, and the letter

written with his mother's blood put into his hands. He was at first overwhelmed by the knowledge of his true position, then fell in eagerly with the maturing plans of his faithful adherents, who first called away their relatives from the distant capital, then massed their forces around a city called Yangchow.

[1] One of them was Li King-yeh, at whose suggestion an able scholar, Leu Ping-wang, had written a memorial of accusation, setting forth the crimes of the Empress. Its closing sentence we shall find doing duty for the peroration in a proclamation issued by the Taipings (p. 204). The ability of the memorial called forth the admiration of its object. The Empress sought for the scholar to enlist his services! But he had disappeared, disgusted with the world (into a famous monastery on the western lakes of Hangchow).

"A large army was sent to withstand them, commanded by near relatives of the Empress Wu. The city was taken by stratagem of a very ignoble sort, and two of Li Tan's generals were killed. The young prince only saved himself by solitary flight; disguised as a menial, he made his way to the city of Tungchow [Eastern Islet], where, having no resources, the heir-apparent to the throne of the eighteen provinces became a beggar on the streets, who had to be well content with an old temple as his resting-place at night.

"One day he applied for alms at the shop of a wealthy man named Hu Fah, who, seeing a lad of cinnabar lips, clear features, intelligent eyes, and long-lobed ears, guessed that he was no ordinary beggar, and inquired into his history. He replied that his surname was Ma, and his own name Yin [obscurity], that both his parents were dead, and that, in consequence of disturbances at the capital, he had become a refugee. Hu Fah inquired whether he had any abilities. He replied that his grandfather had caused him to be instructed in music, chess, books, and drawing. Whereat Hu Fah said that he was in need of an account-keeper and serving-man who could dust, sweep, bring in the tea and rice, and make himself generally useful. The youth agreed to do so, and his employer altered his name to one more suggestive of good fortune [to the business], calling him Tsin-shing [approaching prosperity].

"Hu Fah had never been noted for overmuch generosity, but his wife was a stingy shrew. She made things very unpleasant for three days, saying that the young vagabond would eat their rice to their own starvation. The sting of her gentle remonstrances lay in the fact that in the house, living on their rice, were a sister-in-law and a niece of Hu Fah's. Their own daughter had been brought up and educated with the said niece by their scholarly, but lately deceased brother-in-law; but this was forgotten now.

"One day when Tsin-shing (as Li Tan was now called) was clearing away the bowls, the scholar's widow noticed that he was very thinly clad, and, though miserably treated herself, managed to find him an old wadded garment, receiving which with all gratitude, Tsin-shing caught a glimpse of her daughter, which glimpse — aroused his interest. And no wonder, for Fung-kiao [phœnix-like gracefulness] was a maiden of incomparable beauty. To a wise and modest disposition, which revealed itself in her features, may be added the fact that she had attained a high degree of proficiency in study, in music, chess, and drawing. Her abilities in one of these directions was soon to be put to the proof.

"The same evening, her mother suggested that Fung-kiao should play on the harpsichord. The plaintive sounds reached the ears of a 'sympathetic listener,' for Tsin-shing's dormitory was the wood-shed adjoining. He walked quietly forth, made a little hole in the tissue paper window, then standing outside until the pathetic strains overcame him, he gently knocked and entered.

"His presence was greeted with due surprise; but what with his refined looks and his apologetic explanations, Fung-kiao's mother began to feel so much at home with him that she persuaded her daughter to continue her music, while she enlarged upon the causes of its plaintiveness. The widow and fatherless were treated as mere slaves by Hu Fah's wife, who subjected them to daily insults. The story of their woes filled the heart of the young prince with tenderest sympathy, and after he had told his somewhat fictitious history, he responded to the invitation of the ill-treated lady to play a while. After doing so, he retired. There are mingled thoughts, the sum total of which may be more restful than sleep. There is a companionship in adversity which may be more heart-soothing than solitary splendour. And so the prince in the wood-shed found that night.

"The night was not destined to be dreamless as far as the widow was concerned. A demigod in golden armour appeared to her, congratulating the lady and her daughter upon much approaching prosperity, uttering a poetic message for her comfort. After which a ruby sun appeared, and sounds as of thunder shook the place.

"She awoke with a start, and related the dream to her daughter. As also the fact that while the serving-lad was playing the harpsichord so well, she observed that he had upon his hand a birth-mark referred to in the dream poem, a mark corresponding to one upon the hand of her daughter. Anon with early dawn came the nurse [of Hu Fah's own daughter]. She too had a dream, in which a demigod clad in golden armour commanded her to become matchmaker between Tsin-shing and Fung-kiao.

"That evening, after the rest of the family had retired, Tsin-shing came in by appointment, and a comparison of hands ensued, the dreams being related also. Tsin-shing replied with all humility that he was unworthy of having his name coupled with that of Fung-kiao. But that maiden's mother represented to him that the match was all the more desirable, as fulfilling the suggestion of Heaven rather than his own. He was more than delighted, and saluted his prospective mother-in-law with a deep obeisance. He then produced a gem (which his Empress-mother had long ago entrusted to Teu Hwui for him), and gave it, with injunctions of secrecy, as a betrothal token to his own affianced bride, then retired for the night.

"They examined the gem in the lamp-light, and were amazed to see that the device thereon consisted of the five-clawed Imperial dragon; which set them wondering what manner of person the serving-lad could be.

"It must be explained that Hu Fah's own daughter had been recently married to a certain Ma Ti, the conceited son of a military graduate. Also that Fung-kiao had another cousin, the daughter of Hu Fah's deceased sister. This cousin was named Lwan-kiao [the gracefulness of the celestial peacock]. She had a worthy husband, whose name was Ch'eng Tsin.

"The day approached when Ma Ti was to come and bring his bride to see her parents, and partake of a feast which should be provided on that occasion. Previous to the intended visit, Hu Fah's wife told the elder of the two ladies that she and her daughter were to keep close, their garments not being fit to be seen. To their great disappointment, she locked them up in an outhouse, with a limited supply of cold rice to keep them alive, and a rather unlimited supply of hemp twine for them to work up into skeins.

"Lwan-kiao, who had ever been a faithful friend, made inquiries of the nurse, and heard how matters stood, including the dreams and consequent betrothal,—this latter after Lwan-kiao had expressed a devout wish that her cousin might soon find a good husband, who would free her and her mother from such treatment. At the betrothal news Lwan-kiao was delightfully surprised.

"Her husband, Ch'eng Tsin, on seeing the serving-lad, treated him with marked respect. He persisted, in spite of Hu Fah's remonstrances, that the lad was no ordinary youth, but was surely destined for a high position some day. At this, Hu Fah exclaimed that like could only produce like, 'the dragon bears dragons; the phœnix, phœnixes. He is of the lower classes. Can a dog grow a horn upon its head and become a celestial unicorn?'

"Ch'eng Tsin continuing to be respectful to the young man, the guests took Hu Fah's part. The leader in such derision was the objectionable Ma Ti, who was inflated with family pride. Matters came to a crisis at the banquet, from which Ma Ti rose in high dudgeon, and went outside to show his skill in archery, hitting a certain branch of a willow tree at the other end of the garden, as he had promised he could. The guests complimented him on his achievement.

"Tsin-shing, however, emboldened by the geniality of Ch'eng Tsin, asked to be allowed to hit a flying crow in the neck. Hu Fah cursed him with such epithets as 'dog-slave.' But Ch'eng Tsin carried the day. The serving-lad took the bow, waited till the looked-for bird came in sight, and shot. The crow came fluttering down with the arrow through his neck. The guests, with one exception, applauded the deed.

"Ma Ti, choking down his wrath and shame, went off in a rage. When the others had dispersed, Hu Fah, with many a curse, ordered his serving-lad to lie down and be beaten. 'I should like to kill the vagabond myself,' cried Ma Ti's bride, who was remaining with her parents. Thus urged, Hu Fah beat the lad most fiercely, and but for Lwan-kiao's entreaties, the story of Li Tan would have ended here.

"'Now, get up, you son of Cerberus!' shouted Hu Fah; but the prince was so battered about that he could not rise.

So a coolie of the house was told to pick him up and throw him on to his bed in the wood-shed. The orders were obeyed with unnecessary violence."

The feelings of Nieh Shen-seng's audience, finding vent in various ways as the story proceeded, were now expressed in no half-hearted way. It is customary to speak of the stolid nature of the Chinaman, but during the not over-realistic performance of certain historical plays in which the hero or heroine is cruelly treated, tears may be seen to flow from the eyes not only of women or the more sympathetic youths present, but even of case-hardened coolies. Audible groans may be heard in the general hush. The common people of China are anything but incapable of emotion when a pathetic tale is told, as every story-teller and some Christian preachers know. In the present narrative, however, the various interjections, the tears and laughter, must be understood rather than indicated.

"The heir-apparent could hardly move, but his sufferings at the hand of Hu Fah called forth the keenest sympathy of Fung-kiao and her mother. The latter managed to secure a little of the leavings of the feast for him, telling him, what her red eyes had already declared, how great was her grief at his woe, telling him also that her daughter was inconsolable.

"He replied by regretting his forgetfulness of his position in daring to show his skill at archery; and making light of his own aches and pains, tried to comfort her. Nor was she to stay too long for fear their kindness might involve them in fresh insults. Then he poured out his gratitude, and finally sent a message to his betrothed. He was already graduating in the school," added Nieh, "of a certain stern pedagogue, whose lessons are bitterness, but, in their after effects, nobility of character, kindly thought for others, and finally the name and portion of the 'princely man.'

"Next day Lwan-kiao greeted the widow and her daughter with all affection, bidding them to take all possible care of Tsin-shing, and urging them to try and get him away out of such a 'heaven-net earth-gauze'[1] house as soon as

[1] An expressive phrase for a place or circumstances in which one is caught with every move.

possible. At which stage Ma Ti's wife passed close by as she was leaving. She saw them, but she pretended she did not.

"It was a full month before the young prince was able to get about, during which time he had repeated visits from the 'nurse' and his mother-in-law, who sometimes brought Fung-kiao with her.

"Soon after his recovery, five soldiers, who had been going about the streets for some time, were driven by a heavy downpour of rain to take shelter under the eaves of Hu Fah's shop. Standing there, and looking in, they saw—their prince. They were trusty followers of Ma Chow, who had been searching everywhere for Li Tan. The leader of the little band was recognised by the prince, who made signs that each should take no notice of the other. They entered, bought an article or two, then went out again. The serving-lad went out too on some pretence, and having reached a secluded spot, the five soldiers knelt down and did their prince homage, beseeching him with all earnestness to mount one of their horses and fly at once to Ma Chow's camp on a certain hill.

"He replied that he had been in Hu Fah's house for seven months, during which time he had received great kindness from his employer's sister-in-law; that he, moreover, was betrothed to her daughter, and could not leave without bidding them farewell. He asked them, therefore, to come again at night, and wait for him outside the back door. They reluctantly assented to the delay, praying him not to divulge his identity. Having assured them that he would not, he returned to his drudgery.

"'When the golden wheel had dropped behind the hills,' and Hu Fah and his household were asleep, the prince went into the kitchen, and told his friends that an uncle of his had sought him out and sent for him. Fung-kiao's mother heard the news with mingled feelings. Her daughter looked at him with a searching glance, then hung her head and wept.[1]

---

[1] The phrase used by the narrator is covered by Young's line—

". . . liquid pearl runs trickling down her cheek."

China, however, likes not to stop at mere metaphor. In many earlier nations, and especially in China, we find fossilised metaphors accepted as matters of

"The widow asked who this uncle really was. He replied that he could only say that he was a rich man who had just come into office, but that he himself would come or send for them at the earliest opportunity. She exhorted him, now that he had come to great honour, not to forget his poor friends, and take some rich beauty to wife. He responded by an appeal to the all-recording Heaven. The faithful matchmaker reminded him of the mark on his hand. Which called forth the prayer that he might be visited with the heaviest retribution if he forgot his much-loved benefactors.

"The five men were then called in, and the two ladies introduced. When lo, they knelt down before them! Which called forth fresh inquiries from the widow. Li Tan explained that such was the custom of the—camp.

"The prince could not leave without bidding farewell to Ch'eng-Tsin. The bodyguard of five protested that the affairs of the camp were urgent, but seeing that his heart was set upon the visit, went with him. The doors were bolted. But at length Ch'eng Tsin appeared, and let them into his study. Nor was the kind-hearted Lwan-kiao far off. She was listening behind a screen. The prince explained the state of affairs, and implored them to take care of his future wife and her mother. Lwan-kiao could remain in hiding no longer, but advanced to add her own to the already received exhortations to fidelity.

"'The affairs of the camp are urgent,' again protested the leader of the band. That parting over, a longer and more lingering farewell was taken of his yet dearer friends.

"'The affairs of the camp are urgent,' again pleaded the soldier, and soon they were safely outside the city gates, which closed at midnight.

"Meanwhile Ma Chow, in his hill-top camp, was in great distress. A party of seekers had returned after a long absence to say that they could find no trace of the prince. At this the brave old veteran was unable to hold back his

history, and so we have a tale of a mermaid who, on being hospitably entertained by a certain mortal, rewarded him at parting by weeping into a vessel, her tears turning to pearls. Which tale is quoted as the origin of the above phrase.

choking sobs.[1] His brother general exhorted him not to lose heart, or the army could not be kept together. So he endeavoured to maintain a forced cheerfulness, hoping for, yet

dreading, the return of the remaining party still away on search. It was hard work as day after day went by.

"But one day a messenger galloped up to the camp, gasping out, 'The prince is found! The prince is found! He is at the foot of the hill.'

[1] "Talk not of grief till thou hast seen the tears of armed men."
MRS. HEMANS.

"Ma Chow's tears burst forth unrestrained now. As for his army, the men leaped and shouted till the earth shook. Then all doubled down the hill, fell into line, and knelt before their rightful monarch. The customary salute for an emperor is 'Myriad years [may you live]'; that for a prince is 'Thousand years!' And now was the prince saluted with cries of 'Thousand years! Thousand years! Thousand thousand years!' Then came confessions of failure on the one hand, and grateful commendations on the other. After which, with the whole army for bodyguard, the prince was escorted up the hill in triumph. Cattle were slaughtered, and a great feast prepared.

"In a few days consultations were held as to the desirability of taking a city where the prince could live in such style as his position warranted. The choice fell upon Hanyang, as being an important place, with rich revenues, and near Kiangsha. A portion of the army was sent thither, but the ruler of the city, a man of great courage and powers, being persuaded at length of Li Tan's claims and Ma Chow's loyalty, received the commander hospitably, and sent him back with injunctions to bring the prince without delay. The news being carried back, Ma Chow congratulated his imperial *protégé* on such a good omen at the initial stage of his career—a city taken without bloodshed. And with all the glories of a triumphal march, the prince entered the gates, and assumed the rulership of the city [whose ancient walls, with the Tortoise hill behind, are depicted over leaf].

"But the news soon reached the capital, and an army of 100,000 strong was sent to dispossess and capture Li Tan. Previous to the battle, as indeed before all old-time battles, the champions from either side stood forth and stated their cause, then indulged in a wordy battle of boastful recrimination. Two of the boasters, brothers of Empress Wu's commander-in-chief, were killed at the first onset, and the over-confident army repulsed. They were rallying for a second attack, when a despatch arrived to say that trouble had broken out on the frontier from the inroads of the barbarian tribes, and that the troops were to march there at once.

Hanyang had thus a breathing space. Would it last, or would the revenge-fiercened hosts return?

"Meanwhile, how went it with Fung-kiao and her mother? On Tsin-shing's disappearance, they suffered fresh

indignities, being accused of facilitating his flight. Nor had they a scrap of news from him.

"One day, when Hu Fah and his wife were out, they went to the shop-door to try and get a change of thought, when Ma Ti came along and caught sight of them. It was his first sight of Fung-kiao. She retreated in haste, but her mother, proceeding rather slowly, was caught up by the objectionable man, who gave her an ounce of silver to buy a new garment or two. With part of it she procured some refreshments for the donor, as Hu Fah did not come back till evening. Ma Ti greeted him with apparent heartiness, and, in a by-the-way style, informed him that 'the young scoundrel Tsin-shing' had been convicted of robbery with violence, and was awaiting sentence of death in prison.

"Fung-kiao's mother was greatly alarmed. Not so the damsel herself. She was highly indignant at such a lie from 'the evil-faced Ma Ti.' Her mother protested that he was a generous man, and had given her an ounce of silver.

"'Yes, for some evil purpose,' exclaimed the discreet maiden.

"That purpose caused him to ask if he might be allowed to remain and study in Hu Fah's house. His own was so noisy [probably from domestic differences]. Hu Fah was only too glad to regain the good graces of his son-in-law, and, having no scholarship himself, longed that he might add the lustre of a degree to the family. The ladies keeping themselves closely concealed for some days, Ma Ti's next move was to feign illness. His mother accordingly sent him an old crony as nurse. He divulged the cause of his indisposition to her, and a preliminary fee of five ounces of silver made her a very 'sympathetic listener' indeed. She promised to get him Fung-kiao for his [second] wife.

"Worn out by long-continued slavery, Fung-kiao's mother replied to the old dame's overtures with evident reluctance. Her daughter was already engaged, though she did not at all like the recent news. Fung-kiao, however, hearing of the old woman's mission, delivered her soul in somewhat forcible style, bidding the go-between make good her exit, or she would accelerate it with what muscular force she possessed.

"Her overtures having failed, the old woman suggested as a palliative that Ma Ti should secrete himself in the kitchen, where mother and daughter went every evening to wash up. He caught at the suggestion with such avidity that he would 'fain have pushed the sun down the hill.' Evening came at last, and he managed with some difficulty to secrete himself within a large hencoop, 'crawling in sideways like the old tortoise that he was.'[1]

"As the two entered to do their work, Fung-Kiao's sharp eyes caught sight of the enemy in ambush, but she said nothing. Instead, she began busying herself shovelling up the hot ashes under the stove, and threw the contents of dustpan after dustpan upon the hencoop. She then scoured the oily cooking-pan with silk-melon fibre [the Egyptian loofah], and wishing it had been oilier, threw the greasy water over the hencoop also.

"Their other occupations over, they retired. But Hu Fah, who had seen them leave the kitchen, felt sure that he heard strange noises there. 'It must be burglars,' he thought to himself. There was the sound again! 'Burglars!' he cried. 'Burglars!' he roared, until the whole household took up the cry, and came in armed with stout cudgels, coolie poles, door bars, and the like. Fung-kiao's mother snatched up a long-handled grass broom; Mrs. Hu a roll of matting. The burglar was hid in the hencoop; and, strong in numbers, the well-armed force belaboured the flimsy structure with might and main, until the burglar moaned for mercy, then emerged with difficulty, to display the bedraggled person of Hu Fah's son-in-law. All but two laughed in their sleeves. But Hu Fah cried, 'He must be mad! And such a promising student! Such a good man! Alas, he is certainly mad!'

"As Ma Ti was so bad as all this, his wife must be sent for to nurse him. But being now 'a thorn in his eye,' her presence did not minister to his happiness. He behaved all the more strangely when she came, staring wildly at her as though he had never seen her before (and, when her back was turned, glaring at her as though he had both seen and heard her once or twice too often). He was therefore sent home to be nursed by motherly hands, his wife and the old go-between electing to stay behind.

"After a few days, Ma Ti thought fit to recover. His first work was now to secure five men, whom he feed con-

---

[1] Sideways, a term used of a man who is the opposite of straightforward. The tortoise is supposed to walk irregularly, literally and metaphorically.

siderably to scatter evil reports[1] about the city, until a story of Tsin-shing's having killed the keeper of the jail was in everybody's mouth.

"At Fung-kiao's request, the 'nurse' besought Ch'eng Tsin to inquire at all the *yamuns* as to whether there was any truth in the current reports. Of course there was none. It was, however, suggested that she should pay a visit to a famous temple to the goddess of mercy, some distance from the city, to learn his actual fate. Her mother well-nigh persecuted her on the subject, until she agreed to go the very next day.

"Hearing which, the old crony counsellor of Ma Ti went and told him. The news disarmed his pent-up anger. He immediately sent for the two Buddhist nuns who had charge of the temple, and gave them a preliminary sum of a hundred taels. He then arranged to secrete himself in an apartment of the lonely place, and force Fung-kiao into a marriage.

"Mother and daughter went and laid the matter before the idol [that is, as with the more intelligent Chinese, before the supposed deity who visits or permanently inhabits it], then drew a lot, which the nun who was at home said she could not interpret,[2] but the other 'sister' would be back very soon, and she was a wondrous scholar. Fung-kiao, however, having her own interpretation of the very ambiguous message, wanted to return at once, but her mother insisted on her staying. So the two occupied themselves in reading the numerous testimonial tablets which adorned the walls, 'Asking brings certain response,' 'Motherly heart granted a son,' 'Great in efficacy,' and the like being the chief mottoes.

"The other 'sister' came at length, panting as though from a long outing. She apologised profusely; then, without asking any particulars concerning Fung-kiao's betrothed, dis-

---

[1] This is often a very formidable outlet for ill-feeling, as many Westerners know full well. The rumours spread quickly enough along the crowded streets, losing nothing in the process. In recent years such rumour-spreading has in nearly all cases been traced to the *yamun* underlings or policemen.

[2] A very frequent state of things. One priest-monk or one nun in a temple who can read is surely enough! Some cannot even tell the names of any but the one or two chief idols in the place.

played a really wonderful knowledge of his history and his awful but deserved doom. The latter Fung-kiao vigorously disputed, and insisted on going back at once. But, lo and behold, their sedan chairs had disappeared! The temple servant being sent for fresh ones, did not return. It was sundown, and the temple doors were shut by the nuns. Then Ma Ti came forth and showed himself.

"They were in sore straits. But Fung-kiao required him to fulfil three conditions. 'A myriad,' was the reply. The first was that the marriage should be celebrated in due form, with red candles, lamps, and all the customary rites; that she should live apart from her cousin; and that Ma Ti would care for her mother. He gave an eager assent. They then retired into a side chamber to wash, and arrange their garments. The old go-between proffered her assistance, but was indignantly refused. The door having been shut, they gave vent to their feelings in tearful lamentations, and resolved to commit suicide.

"The crows outside were cawing. 'Alas, my betrothed, the crows are happy, and we are moaning here.

"The birds have each a roosting-place,"[1]

but what resting-place is there for us this side the yellow springs?[2] Art thou indeed there, as the depraved nun declared? If so, we join thee.' And they wept on each other's necks, then untied their girdles to strangle themselves —when a 'star of rescue' appeared.

"After displaying more patience than his mother would have thought possible in a lifetime, Ma Ti went to the door and peered through a crack. He could see no one there! He called gently, then loudly, but no response. The doors were then opened by being lifted out of the lower hinge sockets. The room was empty! What could have happened? They seemed to have dissolved into thin air! Perhaps they had ascended the skies!

"The red temple lamps, which were to have shed a ruby light over a marriage ceremony, were now taken down and carried all over the temple, then out into the enclosure.

[1] *Book of Odes.*   [2] A name for Hades.

They searched up and down,—the disappointed man, his five men-servants, the old hag, and the two devotees of the motherly-hearted goddess,—but could find no trace of them. 'But look! There, on the wall, the moss has been crushed a little, and the chamber lattice is open.' With fresh energy, the party went outside the wall, but could not even find a footprint.

"'To think,' growled Ma Ti, 'that such a fine piece of mutton[1] should be lost as it was nearing the mouth.' With not even a scent of 'mutton,' the disappointed villain and his servants slouched home, to find Ma Ti's wife returned, and fully prepared to make a few remarks.

"Where had the ladies gone? It happened that a serving-man of their former household, having gone to the city of Tungchow with a present of grain for them, heard that they had not returned, and learning the bent of Ma Ti's mind, left the present in the house, and hurried off in his little boat, rowing might and main to the bank hard by the temple. Then going on shore, he found the doors closed, but an unusually brilliant light in the main building. Following the wall, he discerned a ray of light from a side lattice, thought he heard sounds of wailing, climbed up a willow tree, called to his late mistress, got her to open the window, pulled them one after the other over the moss-grown wall, took them to his boat, and rowed down with the stream.

"The ladies having a rich relative in Lingchow, the boatman took them thither. It was morning when they arrived. The boatman went ashore, found the mansion where they lived, but the lady of the house, being afraid of lowering the family, would not consent to receive them. While the boatman was delivering his message, a heavy shower began. There was no cover to the boat, and its passengers were soon very wet. Seeing which, an old nun, standing in a temple porch on the river bank, asked them in, and hearing of their recent repulse, told them that the son of the lady who had

---

[1] Mutton is double the price of other meat. "Lamb and liquor," as an old book declares, constituted the farmer's joy. The expressive metaphor above is of course equivalent to "A slip 'twixt cup and lip," which may, for all we know to the contrary, refer to a cup of mutton broth!

treated them so shabbily,—a young man of virtuous and generous disposition,—had passed by that way, and would probably return by the same road shortly. Meanwhile they must dry their outer garments, and partake of some frugal refreshments.

"Before long, Wen-teh [literary virtue], the young man referred to, being caught in the rain, came in. He was much grieved at his mother's conduct, went home and expostulated with her. She excused herself by saying she was afraid her son would not like such folks to come into the house. This being the only alleged reason, he soon disposed of her scruples, and entreated her to send a couple of chairs and two changes of garments to the temple. When the guests arrived, she received them with many apologies, and the recital of their misfortunes moved her to tears. But here matters were destined to be complicated by the fact that Wen-teh, from his first sight of Fung-kiao, longed much for her.

"Meanwhile a second army sent against Hanyang had been guilty of such enormities on the way thither, that the citizens of the cities which lay between the capital and Li Tan's district had fled into the country. One of these cities was Tungchow. Its houses and shops were bolted and barred, and the streets emptied, for fear of their own army!

"Wen-teh's longing having reached the point of supplication, Fung-kiao's mother thought it a stroke of policy to send him to Tungchow, to ask permission of Hu Fah, whom she knew to have fled with the rest. She did not like to give her benefactor the direct no; and the argument that such a weighty matter should not be settled by an old woman, seemed orthodox enough. Off he went in his eagerness, to find, however, what Fung-kiao's mother had not bargained for—that Hu Fah had just returned. The middleman's present being a very heavy one, Hu Fah felt that here was Heaven's compensation for his generosity to the ladies, about whose welfare he had made numerous inquiries. The 'eight characters' [of Fung-kiao's year, month, day and hour of birth] being made out, Wen-teh returned with great exultation, for the betrothal was now legally complete.

"When Fung-kiao heard of it, a scene ensued which

brought out her faithfulness to her Tsin-shing, and also Wen-teh's trueheartedness. Then the maiden retired to her chamber, and refused to eat or drink day after day. She pined away, until one day she ceased to breathe. Her spirit ascended the skies, but the attendants of the Supreme were ordered to return it to her body, as her life-destiny was not yet fulfilled. As consciousness returned, Wen-teh, with all generosity, gave into her hands the dearly-bought document, after which her recovery became rapid, and cheerfulness returned with the glow of health.

"Nothing more being said about the engagement, she thought the matter had been dropped; they thought her friendliness with Wen-teh was a sign of willingness to marry him, and so made preparations for that event. The guests were invited, and the red cloth upon which the young couple were to kneel was spread. Only then did Fung-kiao realise her position. She was brought forth, but stood erect. They remonstrated with her, and at length, seeing no way of escape, no 'star of hope,' but only the kindness of her benefactors, she obeyed the promptings of the attendant women, and went silently through the ceremony. Then saying she was ill, she went to her room, and became once more a voluntary prisoner. Wen-teh could only inquire about her health; she would not look at him.

"Some days passed thus, when she said she had had a dream, in which the spirit of her deceased Tsin-shing appeared to her, asking that a sacrifice should be offered to his memory in mid-river some distance away, after which she might own Wen-teh as her husband. She then wrote a letter, and put it into a box, which she left unlocked.

"They went off in a large house-boat, wherein a feast was spread. Her mother and Wen-teh, wishing to humour her, yielded to her persuasions, and partook freely of the good cheer provided, she herself more sparingly. They then retired to rest, the sacrifice being fixed for the morrow.

"When all was silent, Fung-kiao crept forth, sprang lightly on shore, then walked on in the moonlight until she came to a high-arched bridge over a creek, and taking her farewell of heaven, earth, and her mother, thanking her creators and preservers for unnumbered kindnesses, she bemoaned her lot thus early to die on that lovely, emotion-waking, moonlight night. Then she jumped off the boat into the flowing water.

"The consternation upon Wen-teh's boat some hours after may be imagined. They traced her footprints to the bridge, and wept in anguish. The sacrifice prepared for Tsin-shing was offered for the benefit of her own spirit. This over, they returned, to find a note in her chamber explaining all. It called forth some noble words from Wen-teh. 'My cousin,' he cried, 'why did you do this? Why did you not tell me? I would have given you up after marriage, as I did for a while after betrothal. I would have done anything, or suffered anything, to have saved you from any pain; how much more from this!' Then he broke down completely.

"Fung-kiao was not drowned. Just as she fell into the water, a mandarin's boat was descending the stream, and she was picked up by the boat-hooks of the crew. She was just alive. Restoratives being given her, she slowly came back to the upper world, to find herself upon a boat belonging to a certain official named T'ao, chief mandarin of the præfecture of Shangchow. She was glad to change her name, and became an attendant of the mandarin's daughter. We will leave her in that position.

"The prince had by no means forgotten his promise to his betrothed. But affairs all along had been unsettled; and whenever he broached the matter, his generals urged the plea that State matters must be put first, especially at a time when his loyal soldiers had long been separated from their wives and families. At length, however, he sent a party of trusty men to Tungchow, which he knew to be in the direct line of the enemy's march. The band arrived at Tungchow, to find the city depopulated at the approach of the Emperor's disorderly troops. Hu Fah's house was deserted, but a blind man, who had served them in years past, had been left behind in the general panic. Him they seized and brought before the prince.

"Not knowing whom he was addressing, the blind man told part of the tale already given, adding many a reproach on the faithless young rascal who had been the cause of the misery and disappearance of Fung-kiao and her mother. The attendants drew their swords to silence the slander of their prince, but he restrained them, and gave vent to his woe.

"'Oh, you have a scrap of conscience left, then. I will tell you something more. They are alive, being rescued by a boatman and taken to Lingchow. He had more gratitude than you with your robber bands.' At which the attendants removed the old man, who almost died with terror when he found that he had been reproaching the Imperial son of Kao Chung.

"The young prince was all eagerness to send to Lingchow, but was effectually hindered therefrom, owing to the fact that the general of the opposing forces had enlisted the services of a Taoist magician, who possessed a wondrous talisman by which the city was held under a spell, which, at the decree of Heaven, just stopped short at the lives of the besieged.[1] A consultation was held as to what should be done. Matters were indeed desperate. But one of the prince's officers said there was a counter talisman possessed by a mandarin of Shangchow, who, however, was a staunch adherent of the Empress, and whose son held office near the capital. This did not seem very hopeful; but another general, with much diffidence, put forth a certain plan. He had a recently-deceased nephew, engaged to the daughter of the mandarin of Shangchow. The family had never seen him, nor did they know that he was dead. Now, it happened that the prince was about his age. To remain in Hanyang would be dangerous; to do as he was about to suggest could hardly be more so. Would the prince personate him, gain the confidence of the family, and secure the talisman? The prince was grateful for the suggestion, and fell in with it at once. He managed to escape through the enemy's lines that night, and was soon fairly on his way.

[1] " Ho, call me here the wizard, boy,
    Of dark and subtle skill,
  To agonise, but not destroy,
    To curse, but not to kill."
            PRAED (quoted in *Decisive Battles of the World*, p. 204).

"Arrived at Shangchow, the 'son-in-law' created a favourable impression. The day was fixed for the marriage, and the ceremony had to be gone through, when the bridegroom fell judiciously ill. He had nothing to say to T'ao's daughter, but had plenty of material for meditation, when a glance at her attendant revealed a wonderful likeness to Fung-kiao. Their eyes met for a moment. It was she! But there was no lustre in that look; for was he not married—in spite of all his promises—to another? After some days of continued 'poorliness,' he managed to whisper in her ear that she must trust him in spite of all seeming, also that he would not leave without her this time.

"He was not too ill to be much in conversation with the mandarin T'ao himself, and having felt his way to the subject, asked whether there was not an old talisman in the family. T'ao called his daughter, and told her to bring it out of the treasury. It was exhibited, and its uses explained, and the mandarin's daughter in a fit of anger told her 'invalid husband' to take it back himself. This he did, carefully leaving all the doors unlocked except that in the outer wall. That night the talisman was secured, and one of Li Tan's followers sent off post-haste to Hanyang. 'Now, my lord, fly with us,' the other two said.

"He would not leave his betrothed, however, and so remained a month or so, still 'poorly.' One day he managed, by pleading illness at a feast, to retire and have an interview with the maiden he loved. They both related their adventures, and as he drew near to the close, she asked him wonderingly what manner of man he really was.

"'I am no other than Li Tan, son of the true Empress of Kao Chung,' was the reply. Could it be possible, she wondered, that she was the only beloved of the heir to the Dragon Throne? Her betrothed soon made that clear, and, with promises of undying affection, not unaccompanied with kisses, the two poured out their pent-up emotion.

"A knock at the door! T'ao's daughter was calling.

"Fung-kiao emerged, all blushes, to receive the curses and blows of her mistress. The prince could remain within no longer, and interposed to receive the blows instead.

Hearing the hubbub, the whole household collected. In the thick of the excitement, Fung-kiao dropped her precious gem.

"It was picked up. The device thereon was seen to be the Imperial dragon, the significance of which was not lost upon the mandarin's wife, who went and showed it to her husband. In order to make sure, she hit upon the plan of getting the mandarin to tell his 'son-in-law' that they knew of his fondness for Fung-kiao, and that although he himself would have had no objection to bestow her upon him as a second wife, it was out of the question, for she was already betrothed to Li Tan, son of the Emperor Kao Chung.

"With a smiling face—it was just after the feast—and the blandest tones of voice, the mandarin Tao interviewed his 'son-in-law' in the study. 'My noble son-in-law,' he said, 'you are in love with Fung-kiao, and it would not be difficult for me to bestow her upon you but for a certain reason,' which he gave, adding that he had been looking for an opportunity of sending her, with an adequate bodyguard, to Hanyang to greet her lord.

"Being overcome with such an unexpected speech, what could the prince do but bow his thanks, and say, 'I will not deceive you; I am no other than Li Tan, and will abundantly recompense your kindness some day.'

"Outside the study—'walls have cracks and partitions have ears'—was one of the two remaining attendants, who, hearing the words, glided out in great trepidation, saddled his horse, and flew towards Hanyang.

"Having extorted the confession from the prince, T'ao bowed his apologies for neglect of suitable entertainment, multiplied his expressions of abject contrition, and fixed an auspicious day on which to escort them both. For which Li Tan devoutly thanked him. He then retired, commanded his underlings to secure all the outer doors, and hastened to his wife, saying, 'It is so. He is Li Tan. I could send a messenger to the Empress, who would have him taken alive. But then our daughter will object. If I send him to Hanyang, the lives of the family may be endangered. What do you advise in this dilemma?'

"T'ao's right-hand man and near relative, named Shü-yin, knelt, and urged that the Empress Wu was a usurper, and that the true heir to the throne was his daughter's husband. As Shü-yin was himself in love with Fung-kiao, this plea was not without a touch of loyal self-forgetfulness. But T'ao's daughter interrupted him in somewhat violent language. Shü-yin's mother replied by representing that the mandarin's daughter was now the rightful Empress; would she not on that account decide for the life of the prince?

"'What demon haunts you?' screamed T'ao's daughter. 'He has not made the country his, nor does he care for me. The Empress Wu has the land. Li Tan has just one city and very few soldiers. You would destroy the whole family. Seize him! Deliver him up to the Empress, and get her high reward. Thus say I.'

"'Is that your final decision?' asked her father.

"'What is it to do with me? If you want to annihilate the whole family, let him go.'

"Thus persuaded, T'ao gave orders that the prince should be seized. Hearing which, Li Tan hurried forth to plead for his life. But as he knelt, T'ao's daughter pushed him violently over, crying, 'Don't talk to me! Go to your Fung-kiao.' The underlings rushed forward immediately, 'fierce as wolves and tigers,' and bound the prostrate prince. But someone else rushed forward, and held him fast, crying, 'My husband, I have brought all this upon you!'

"The underlings tried to separate them, but the maiden clung to her lord with superhuman strength. Shü-yin pleaded that if Fung-kiao would not let him go, they need not try and separate the pair. The mandarin T'ao ordered, therefore, that both should be secured in the same wooden cage, and put into the inner prison. He then wrote a despatch to the capital, sending it by two couriers, and when these had gone, ordered all the city gates to be closed.

"With the aid of the counter charm, the troops at Han-yang had utterly routed the enemy, and began to make preparations to bring the prince and his bride back. But just as the bodyguard was starting, a horseman appeared on a jaded steed, gasping out, 'The prince has confessed who he is!'

"Ma Chow was greatly alarmed. 'He is doubtless seized,' he cried; 'perhaps on his way to the capital. Call three hundred more picked men.' And with the speed of wildfire, they galloped on for three days, until they came to a certain fork in the road. 'That leads to the capital. The messengers will pass here.'

"He had hardly spoken when two men galloped up. 'Stop!' cried Ma Chow; 'who are you?'

"'Imperial couriers.'

"'Give up your despatches.'

"'You bold slave, the Imperial despatches are not for you.'

"'The vile usurper! Imperial indeed! Seize them!'

"'It was done, the despatches secured, read, and torn to fragments.'

"'Now choose, you two, death or life!'

"'Pardon us!' cried both men, bowing to the ground.

"The gates of Shangchow were opened to the Imperial couriers, and the whole company rushed in, made their way to the prison, burst it open, and secured the cage.

"It was now the turn of T'ao and his family to plead for their lives. T'ao's daughter alone was deemed beyond pardon and full acquittance, and the prince and his bride were conducted in triumph to the now peaceful city of Hanyang, where, amid general festivities and rejoicings, their marriage was consummated."

Here Nieh Shen-seng ended for the night, saying that there was one episode in the tale which he had purposely omitted, because he thought the story completer without it. He would, however, relate the sequel on the following evening. Which sequel may be condensed into a few paragraphs.

"Several cities fell to the prince, his army being augmented by various contingents (among which may be mentioned the troops who owned for their leader the stalwart Shieh Kang, who had been the indirect cause of the death of

Kao Chung, now a pardoned and loyal subject of Li Tan). The populace around were exceedingly friendly to his rule,

and the Empress thought best to acknowledge Li Tan as a prince of the realm. So the time seemed ripe for his going off to Tungchow to seek out his former friends. He was disguised as a scholar, and his bodyguard as household servants. They were seen by Ma Ti, who treated them very badly, binding and imprisoning them in a garden pavilion, where they were visited by the nurse of Hu Fah's household, whose patience was somewhat tried, for they were purposely dumb. She, however, went and told Ch'eng Tsin and his wife (Fung-kiao's genial cousin). Ch'eng Tsin bought off Tsin-shing for fifty taels, then accompanied him and his attendants to Lingchow, where Fung-kiao's mother was living in sorrow; well cared for, however, by Wen-teh.

"That generous young man, on seeing 'Tsin-shing,' was so affected at the latter's bereavement, and his own unintentional part therein, that he proposed another match—an eligible one—for him. The offer was not accepted.

"The prince's generals, fearing for his safety, sent a strong body of soldiers to Tungchow, and thence to Lingchow. Wen-teh, hearing that Tsin-shing was no other than the prince who ruled over a section of the Empire, prepared for execution, as having been guilty of causing Fung-kiao's death. His mother was first to meet the prince, and begged that in her death the rest of the family might find pardon. Kindly hands raised her from the ground, and kindly lips thanked her. But Wen-teh, knowing nothing of this, rushed forward, bound himself, and, prostrate in the dust, confessed the wrongs he had done, beseeching that, after his death-sentence had been pronounced, his mother might be spared.

"Full of emotion, the prince stooped down, untied his bonds, lifted him up, and told him that Fung-kiao lived as his wedded consort, called him his benefactor, and there and then raised him with the prince's other friends to high office. On Wen-teh's wife—for he was now married—a special title was conferred also. Nor was Lwan-kiao forgotten.

"Hu Fah, his wife and daughter, for whom Fung-kiao had pleaded, were permitted to live, but were fined heavily. The fines were bestowed upon Shii-yin of T'ao's household. Ma Ti and the two nuns were executed, as they richly deserved.

186   A STRING OF CHINESE PEACH-STONES.

"After some years (in A.D. 710), the Empress Wu having died, Prince Li Tan removed to the capital city of Perpetual Peace, and ascended the dragon throne."[1]

[1] He was succeeded by his second son, who, under the title of the Lustrous Emperor, reigned for forty-four years, and is one of the most celebrated sovereigns in Chinese history.

IMPERIAL DRAGON AND PHŒNIX (EMPEROR AND EMPRESS).
From a 16th Century Block of Ink of the same date as that on p. 15.

Chapter IX.

PROBLEMS DOMESTIC AND NATIONAL.

THAT BABY!—A NATIVE DYNASTY AND ITS WOULD-BE
RESTORERS.

"When a tiger or wild bull escapes from his cage, whose is the
fault?"—*Confucian Analects.*

"SPEED the parting year" was the groan of many thousands in Central China as the mud-bespattered, flood-washed, malaria-breathing months dawdled to an end. The Chinese do not quite personate their years. No artist of the times drew a picture of an evil-looking, dirty old man being dragged off to the unseen by the underlings of Hades, assisted in his tardy progress by sundry kicks and coolie-pole urgings. Nor does transmigration apply to the souls of the years, else might the good old days come back again.

Yet the New Year is always, more or less, of an all-renovating deity. "Men at first are radically good," whatever their parentage. And so are the years, affirmed by all the manifold congratulatory phrases and inscriptions. With the New Year the good old times always come back again—in theory. Every door is a door of riches, every hut a palace, every poor man a general or prime minister-elect,—until the year is a month or so old, when the all-renovating deity having fulfilled no one jot or tittle of his life-programme, is ignominiously degraded to the ranks of the commonplace.

But one event needs to be recorded of the otherwise uneventful thirtieth year of the Emperor Tao Kwang (1850), an event, however, which gave a new centre of importance to the home of Nieh Shen-seng, engrossed the attention of his scholars, and influenced as with gentle ripples the surrounding families. One morning, as the youngest scholar, arriving early, was beginning to shout his " Men at first," the pleasing theory was being strongly debated by an infantile voice from within. The more loudly the juvenile affirmed that dogma, the more controversial did that infant become. And for many a day, ay, and in many an otherwise stilly night, formerly dedicate to offerings of midnight oil to classical sanctities, did the teacher, complete as he seemed to be in the four books and five classics, find all his learning inadequate, and all his patience more than tried. The infant—and that infant not a son after all—mocked his scholarship, and asserted her rights to be empress in that empire. Until Mrs. Nieh persuaded her husband to write a few characters upon some narrow slips of red paper, and paste them about the village—

> "Sovereign lords of heaven and earth,
> That young child who came to birth,
> Howleth ever in the night.
> Princely man who passeth here,
> Chant a verse and breathe a prayer,
> Rest her soul till morning light."

In modern days the traveller finds such a slip pasted up on the posts of country inns, and on the once white walls of densely populated alleys in the towns, where " Stick no bills " is hidden up under numberless advertisements. He reads the first few characters, and exclaims, " Strange folk these, even after you know a little of them; some idolatrous nonsense, or a quack advertisement, I suppose." But when the poem is studied and the situation realised, what a touch of nature for all ages; what a link to bind far-distant regions and their denizens together! From the papyrus-fringed home of the inscrutable Sphinx; from the home rendered unendurable by the infantile Diogenes, who must have been an awful child; from the prehistoric home of our own remote progenitors in Aryan times; from the modern palace; from the " summer a dusthole, winter a ditch " slum, the ear of the anthropologist catches the same complaint—the inadequacy of all human efforts to quiet a fractious baby.

In the case before us, the powerful charm was unavailing. No princely man passed that way. Yet there is a satisfaction in having used all possible means. Under which subjective comfort Mrs. Nieh grew well, and her husband was enabled to fall back upon the fundamental doctrine of Heaven's decree. It was ignominious, however, for him to realise that, whereas a magpie's cackling had brought down a fully-qualified celestial to investigate matters, his child's wailings seemed proof against palliatives maternal and consolatory, paternal and classical.

Give it up!

. . . .

1851. Death of the Emperor Tao Kwang (light of truth). Accession of Shien Fung (general plenty). The infant wailed on! Was it from loyalty? The grown-up folks did their best to show the correct amount of sorrow for an emperor they knew nothing about, except as the assumed recipient of their taxes. And having another day of restrictions added to the calendar,  they devoutly wished that Shien Fung would procure the Taoist pill of immortality, and live "a myriad years" at least.

But all men prayed not thus. Lieu came back one day in the autumn from Hanyang to bring the news that a serious rebellion had broken out in the south. "Something will happen" still echoed among the worshippers of the prophet.

As to Nieh himself, it must be recorded that his vocal baby so near was a matter of almost greater moment than a rebellion two or three thousand *li* away. The former was the "present truth" to him. But, like all graduates, he had to go to the county capital annually for examination, and returned with fuller details, which focussed the news into sharp outlines.

The account he brought of its origin is not the one usually

received. It is still quoted, however, in these parts. "A good man down south," he said, "met a thief who was on his way to commit a robbery, and agreed to give him an equivalent for the booty he expected to gain. It was done, and on the man's birthday the robber came among the other guests to congratulate him. A mandarin present seeing this, thought within himself, 'So and So's wealth is not rightly got. He is a friend of robbers.' He wrote a despatch to Peking, and had the good man imprisoned. The robber gang seeing this, broke open the prison, and having defied the law by rescuing him, made him their leader, and being attacked, the rebellion began." [1]

To this Nieh Shen-seng added that this leader of the rebellion had received a wonderful book from the Western barbarians, owing to which he was able to attract men and lead them on. Also that the rebels called themselves Taipings (perfect peace), and proposed to restore the Ming dynasty, and make it a very kingdom of heaven.

These latter facts drew forth his comment that in the *Three Kingdoms* book—that from which he had quoted the story of Ti'ao Hen—there is an historical precedent which they seemed to have followed. It is related in the first volume how that a certain Chang Hoh, afterwards one of the generals of Ts'ao Ts'ao, was walking among the hills gathering medicinal herbs, when he was accosted by an old man leaning on his staff, who called him into a cave and gave him a "Celestial book," called *The Elements of Perfect Peace* (*tai ping*), saying, "You are ordered on the behalf of Heaven to proclaim the doctrines of this book for the renovation of men."

After a word or two more, the mysterious old man disappeared. Hoh studied the book day and night until he was able, it was reputed, to perform various magical feats. He

---

[1] A somewhat similar tale is in print about the rebellion which ended the Ming dynasty. A benevolent man was very generous to the people in a famine year. The mandarin, roused to jealousy by his good name, affirmed that his wealth was not obtained in an honest way, and had him imprisoned. The populace burnt the *yamun*, rescued their benefactor, and carried him off to Li Tsz-ch'eng (of whom more anon), to become that rebel chief's adviser. Perhaps this tale suggested the other.

first called himself the Tai P'ing Taoist, then the Heaven Prince General.[1]

Now everyone has read that book, and the correspondence is very close.

"And the Ming dynasty was a glorious one," said Li. "I have heard Seng-teh say that Ming means lustrous as well as clear."

"Previous to the Ming dynasty," began Nieh Shen-seng, "China had been under Tartar rule for a hundred and fifty years, and longed for emperors of its own."

"Of course," exclaimed Li.

"Are you a Taiping already?" asked Nieh. "One night [in 1368] the abbot of a temple in Kiangsu had a vision.

Origin of the Ming Dynasty.

He was caught up to the northern constellation,[2] and heard the deities there resolving to impart the essential essences of the sun and moon to a certain family. The influences of the Superlative *Yang* [the sun] were to be concentrated in a future emperor; those of the Superlative *Yin* [the moon] were to be incarnate in his consort.

"By and by the wife of a poor man gave birth to a son; the villagers hearing celestial music at the time. The birds echoed the heavenly strains, and there was a halo round the sun.

"The lad grew up to overthrow the Tartar dynasty, and adopted the word formed of the signs for sun and moon combined,—the word Ming. He was succeeded by fifteen other emperors, whose reigns, taken together, make nearly three hundred years [275].

"The Lustrous[3] dynasty, however, was not so prosperous

[1] The last item of similarity was to be added in November 1851, when Hung Sheu-ts'uen assumed the title of Heaven-king. With Nieh's inference (probably never before pointed out in English) the writer fully agrees.

[2] The northern constellation is much quoted in Chinese books. The Taoist *Book of Influence* (heavenward) *and* (earthward) *Response* declares: "There are three august ones, spirits of the northern peck, who, hovering above men's heads, record their sins." The religious use of the northern constellation is an evident development of the Confucian passage already noticed, in which the "peck" is the court, and the surrounding stars the courtiers.

[3]   "Now when with Sol fair Luna doth unite,
     Silver and gold, cheerful the world and bright!"
                                   (*Faust*, Part II. Act i.).

as its name promised that it should be. One year [1459] no rain fell from the sixth to the ninth month, and men tried to devour one another. Later on [1589] the populace in many districts were reduced to eating leather and bark, and died in great numbers. Another year [1609] a great fire destroyed a large portion of Hanyang [our all-important city], and it was followed by a high flood. Some years after [1619] there was a plague of locusts, accompanied by famine. Again, after a long interval, the crops were destroyed by field mice. During the greater part of the dynasty, the times were troublous and anxious. Tartar hordes menaced the land in many parts. And towards the end [1837] there were eight rebel armies ravaging the country. Eventually [1843] a brigand named Chang Shen-tsung, after taking Hupeh, Hunan, and Szchwan, held Hanyang for a year or two, perpetrating the most horrible acts of cruelty and terrorism. Here he was joined by Li Tsz-ch'eng, a blacksmith who had marched towards Peking, and, the gates having been opened by a traitor, had taken it.

<small>Fall of the Ming Dynasty.</small>

"At this time, a certain man living at Tientsin, hearing of what was happening in the capital, was only deterred from setting off at once because it was his aged mother's birthday. She urged him to go at once and save the Emperor, but he pleaded the claims of filial piety. Whereupon she shut herself and all the family up in her apartments and set fire to them, thus removing all encumbrances. Her son went, and was killed, and she has ever since been regarded as of superlative virtue.

"Li Tsz-ch'eng, having been driven out of the capital, eventually came to Hanyang and held rule there. The Manchu conquest of China was completed in the recapture of Hanyang—think of it, our own city! And such was the terror inspired by the ruffians, that we welcomed the Manchus as our deliverers."

"Hanyang ranks next to the capital!" exclaimed Li with pardonable pride.

At this stage Mrs. Nieh called her husband. The baby had been awake for some time without crying, and now emerged with a wondrously placid face.

PROBLEMS DOMESTIC AND NATIONAL. 193

Thus encouraged, Nieh Shen-seng began to relate the story of the last of the Mings. "His reign was full of trouble by reason of the Tartar hordes and internal broils. Li Tsz-ch'eng had reached the gates of the capital. The only trustworthy general was Wu San-Kwei,[1] who was away fighting with the Tartars. Rebellion seemed rife in Peking itself.

The last of the Mings

Prowess of Wu San-kwei

"In this strait, the Emperor resolved to go to a certain temple and entreat the gods to make known his fate by the length of a bamboo slip falling from a vessel. A long slip was to be a good omen; a medium length slip, partial success; a short one, utter ruin.

The Temple Cursed by the Last of the Mings.

"Sacrifices were offered, and the incense lighted, while the Emperor remained on his knees. Amid breathless suspense, the vessel holding the slips was swayed to and fro. One fell to the ground—a short one.

"Snatching it up, the Emperor dashed it on the ground, crying, 'May this temple, built by my ancestors, be evermore

[1] See footnote to Rebel Proclamation, p. 202.

accursed! Henceforth may every suppliant be denied what he entreats, as I have been! Those that come in sorrow, may their sorrow be doubled; in happiness, may that happiness be changed to misery; in hope, may they meet despair; in health, sickness; in the pride of life and strength, death! I, Ch'ung Cheng, the last of the Mings, curse the place!'[1]

"Next morning Ch'ung Cheng and his Empress were found to have hung themselves from a tree branch on a hill near. On the Emperor's person was found a blood-written poem—

> 'My robes are soaked in tears
> (I end my woe-filled years),
> Nought I bequeath but bloody stains,
> These, O ye rebels, your sole gains;
> The false officials seize and slay,
> But spare the people, spare, I pray.'

"The rebels are destroying the idols, I hear. Perhaps this is in revenge for their having forsaken the last of the Mings in his hour of need."

"The Graduate may know everything under heaven without leaving his house," suggested Li, whose ardour for the Mings had now considerably cooled.

But with only occasional rumour, in the place of the daily newspaper, Nieh had to confess himself a mere "frog in a well" as the months went by. The well of classical Chinese undefiled it was, but still a narrow well.

Another year passed. Things were much the same. Threadbare tea-shop stories were patched and did duty again. The schoolboys grew taller, and their books dirtier. "Sister," as the scholars called the now amiable youngster, was nursed and petted, and all but spoiled by everyone except Lieu Fah, whom she hated. If she tumbled in her toddling, there was a general rush of scholars to pick her up. If she cried, there were plenty of proffered sleeves to wipe her eyes. She knew nothing of female degradation in the East, not she. Nor did premonitions of the inevitable foot-binding distress her childish heart. There was another year or so before that should begin. In a word, commend me to

[1] See Stent, *Chinese Legends*, R.As.Soc. N.C. branch, 1872.

a Chinese schoolmaster's toddler (preferably a boy, but, in lieu thereof, a girl such as little Camilla[1]) for an instance of the completest happiness possible to a child of tender years. A trifle less exuberant than the toddlers of Japan, stolid at times compared with the average English specimen, but with a life of freedom which scorns our traditionally orthodox pity, the Chinese youngster of tender years has little cause for complaint, as personal observation soon assures us.

Camilla proved to be precocious. She was the chief talk of the mothers within the village walls. She outshone all the toddlers, as she had outcried all the infants there. Her father had been fondling her — and Chinese fathers can actually do that—one December evening when she had been specially winsome, at a time when ordinary babies, and indeed whole households, are usually asleep; he had just handed her to her mother, and trimmed his rush pith lamp for higher classical study, when a loud knocking was heard at the gate of the village, and a voice shouted,—two voices indeed,— "Open the door! Quick! Open the door!"

The unusual sound aroused the whole village. Everybody lit his or her lantern and hastily emerged. Everybody shouted, "What is the matter?" The dogs barked, and woke all but the most stolid babies; the children commissioned to mind them brought their charges out into the bracing air of night. Everything was chaotic. Even the water buffaloes caught the infection, and began bellowing.

"Noise of firing, and a glare in the sky over by Hankow," was the reply gasped out by the priest-monk and his apprentice from the hill-top.

"Hai Ya! The rebels have come." At which there was a general rush to the respective homes. The babies had gone! but were discovered outside, and carried by general consent to the gate, where the crowd of villagers stopped the way.

In the midst was Nich Shen-seng trying to make his voice heard. He reminded them that the three cities were more than sixty *li* (twenty miles) away, that the "Long-

[1] Her Chinese name was Leu-fei, a classical form of the name of the flower camellia, but she will be known by the more euphonious English name.

haired" (the Taipings did not shave the head) would not know the road, and could hardly molest them till next day at noon.

"To-morrow at noon. They are coming to-morrow!" screamed several mothers. "They are not coming at all." "They are. We shall be killed." "Sixty li." "Go to sleep." First one cry then the other, then all at once, until "Go to sleep" predominated. "Yes, go to sleep," was the general advice to everybody else but those who shouted it.

After a long while the village was quiet but for the occasional bark of a dog, when a general unbarring of heavy wooden doors, whose bars were noisy and whose pivots creaky, together with general cries of "What's that?" proved that the sleep of the villagers was not of the profoundest.

Next morning everybody asked everybody else to mind their door, but as everybody was bound for the hill-top, there was only a decrepid old dame to mind the village gate. She was, happily, very deaf, and had had a night's rest, nor was it possible to get any new idea into her head except that of sitting near the door and waiting till their return. "Till you come," she repeated again and again. She was too old to be surprised at anything.

The whole countryside was evidently aroused, little processions were seen everywhere coming along the winding paths, all bound for the temple peak, from which in the finest weather the Hanyang hill can be just seen. The priest had never had so many guests before. He had now recovered his composure sufficiently to demand that those who wished to worship must first pay for incense, candles, crackers, and yellow paper. Before long, Lieu Fah appeared heavily laden with such commodities—prices duly raised. His father, with an eye to business, had gone off to Tsaitien, ten miles distant, to lay in a large stock.

But the farmers and their families began to realise that as there was nothing to be seen, the present necessity—a pressing one—was morning rice. The husbands began grumbling at their wives for coming, and the villagers reached home, feeling on the whole cantankerous. How different it seemed from yestermorn! Rice over, with its filling, cheering, peace-with-all-the-world influences, how different everything still seemed! And that difference continued day after day, night after night. All was suspense,—aching, tormenting suspense,—filling each hour of the day, and bringing dreams at night which are not enumerated in the *Imperial Almanac*—dreams of hills covered with rebel troops, of lake waters covered with rebel boats, all bearing down upon the sleeper, of hellish shouts, of flashing swords, of shed blood and burnt homes. And each morning came that awful half memory of an undefined something, which gradually focussed itself into: "The rebels are near; they are coming."

No news is to be gathered from the hill-top, and Lieu has been some days away! So we must perforce widen our horizon in order to know what had really happened. The Rebellion, under Hung Shen-ts'uen,[1] had assumed formidable

---

[1] Hung Shen-ts'uen was born in 1813. He visited Canton in 1833, and procured some Christian books from a colporteur. Attempted his degree in 1837, but failing to pass, fell sick, and became subject to "visions." Remaining quiet till 1843, he collected vast crowds by his preaching, and entered into

proportions. The rebels, moving northwards from Kwangshi, had overrun a great part of Hunan, had attacked the capital of that province, but were repulsed by the combined forces of Central China. They then seized the larger craft at the mouth of the Tungting lake, and set sail down the Yangtse. The military officials of Hunan, fearing their return, did not weaken their forces by sending their men to follow in their wake. The rebels landed some distance above Wuchang, marched through a part of the Hanyang county, some miles west of the city, and collected their forces below Hankow, which then had no wall. The rebel soldiers then doubled across the plain.

The only defence Hankow possessed was a half-emptied camp of mud huts, and a few red banners inscribed "Flag of victory." The garrison fled at the first sight of the living cloud. "The few cannot withstand the many." The rebel hosts, with shouts of triumph, came on, seized the banners, tore them to shreds, scrambled over the uneaten morning rice, and having found no one to oppose them, raised their own banner where the biggest of the red Imperial delusions had been, gazed with high glee upon their motto, "Perfect Peace, and the Kingdom of Heaven," and then at the fine view of lofty house-roofs before them. Were some of them but ill-clothed? They soon made up for that deficiency by seizing the loose silken jackets of any fugitives they caught,—for the whole town had either shut up shop and retreated indoors or was engaged in flight. As the captures were chiefly women, the jackets had the effect of making the appearance of the rebels somewhat abnormal. They proved to be human enough, however, to feel hunger like ordinary mortals; and having forced an entry into many of the most promising houses and shops they could find, were regaled with the best cheer such houses could afford. The meal over, trumpet sounds were heard, and, having fallen

The Taking of Hankow.

---

league with two other kindred spirits, who also had "visions" and audiences to listen to the messages thus received. Attempts were made to arrest him in 1850. The Rebellion fully started in the following year, toward the end of which, having captured several cities, the leader styled himself Ti'en Wang, Heaven-king.

PROBLEMS DOMESTIC AND NATIONAL. 199

in, orders were given to cross the Han and take Hanyang.
The Tortoise Hill was undefended. They formed
in line there. A shot or two were fired from the
Hanyang battlements, but it was evidently a case of fire and run.
Numerous pennants decorated the walls, and a big banner here and there, the effect being rather picturesque than martial. It was a mere display of military millinery; which fact not being lost on the

The Taking of Hanyang.

Taipings, they raised a terrific war-whoop and rushed down upon the city. Owing to a certain legend, there is no north gate,[1] and outside each of the gates a deep moat had been dug. Numerous houses encumbered the approaches also. These were set on fire, and the blaze continuing till evening, accounted for the glare seen from the distant hill-top. There were some shots fired from over the gates, stones were hurled, and other such methods used by the besieged; but before the sun went down, the official representatives of the Tartar sovereign had committed suicide,

[1] A poetical name for Hanyang is that of the City of Moonbeams, the lake on the east being called the Moon Lake. By a curious coincidence, this name corresponds exactly to that of the ancient Jericho. Joshua, on taking that city, prophesied that the man who set up its gates should do so with the loss of one of his sons (vi. 26; compare 1 Kings xvi. 34). The legend concerning Hanyang prophesies injury to the daughter of the mandarin who shall build a north gate, which prophecy deals with the assumed history of the family of a mandarin who did so in former days.

their city had fallen a prize to the rebels, who fired volleys at intervals through the night to show that they were proof against any surprises from Wuchang. Thus were the two cities taken on the 23rd December 1852.

The custom of the rebels was to slay all opposers for the first three days, and then to "sheath the sword," and pacify the people. And at this early stage of their progress they kept to their rule with all conscience. So that the citizens, beyond having to provide good dinners, at a short notice, for rowdy bands of men, began to feel that their invaders were not so terrible after all.

The Taiping position, however, was not secure while the great city of Wuchang (whose "long street" is more than three miles long, and whose walls are seven or eight miles in circumference), the capital of Central China, still displayed the Imperial flag. But its turn soon came.

The Taking of Wuchang. The official records state that "the southern rebels attacked the capital of Hunan, so all the available forces of the Empire, with their rations, were collected there. The *Fu Tai* [second literary mandarin], trusting to the soldiers at Yohchow, in Hunan, was not prepared to resist. Hearing that Yohchow had fallen, he was in a great state of trepidation. For want of a better plan, he burnt down the houses outside the [Wuchang] walls. There being no outposts on the Yangtse, the rebels came unannounced. Some Hunan soldiers drove them back to the Red Hill [east of Wuchang, where they made a bonfire of the pagoda erected thereon]. These Hunan soldiers engaged them in many a battle. But as their commander remained in Yohchow, and would not send any help, they could not defeat the rebels.

"Had there been any to join them from within the city, the siege could have been raised, but the *Fu Tai* knew nothing of military matters,[1] and entrusted everything to the

---

[1] That he, being an M.A. or LL.D., writ large, should be expected to be quite adequate to the task of defending a city is evident. The scholar, without leaving his books, is, when that scholar becomes a mandarin, required to know all things under heaven—how to command an army, for instance. O mighty Confucius!

general [just fancy the Lord Mayor-elect entrusting the defence of London to the general!], Swang-fuh [double happiness!], who was ignorant of military tactics also. He could but mass his men like a crowd round a tree. Among the troops there were not wanting those who pleaded to be allowed to prove their bravery against the enemy, but he would not permit them to do so. Thus were their hearts utterly discouraged.

"Eventually the rebels dug a hole under the walls, and entered the city unknown to the besieged."

Here we may leave the official records, noting, however, the fact that the Viceroy's name is conspicuous by its absence. Charitable chronicler! The name he bore, except on his visiting cards, was that of Duffer! He was lazy, grasping, and stupid. In the early morning he aroused himself, and was borne in his fine sedan to the parade ground. He had assumed command; but the troops had hardly assumed the attitude of obedience. He sat in an arm-chair, and gave his orders as to the disposition of the forces. The men looked at him, or, rather, behind him. "Why do you not obey?" he cried, stamping his feet. Why, indeed! They looked again and fled. "Why do you not"— But it now became him to look round. There were the rebels. And there was a sword unsheathed, and, with an exclamation of astonishment, stopped in the middle, his head rolled to the ground.

But an under-mandarin, the Kiang-sha county magistrate, died not thus. Arrayed in his full robes of office, he stood alone and unarmed at his *yamun* gate. The rebels came. He cursed them by heaven and earth. He cursed them by the spirits above and beneath. He prophesied that utter failure would follow their seeming success. He fell, but the rebels would fain have spared a man whose bravery in the hour of death moved them to admiration.

The rest of the officials seemed to have committed suicide. "Their merit and demerit," moralises the chronicler, "about balanced. The more heroic are noted elsewhere"— the brave county magistrate in the popular heart, if not in the records of officialdom. "The rest may be unremembered." Wuchang was taken on the 12th January 1853.

Having taken possession of the hub of the Chinese universe, the Taipings issued a proclamation which read as follows:—

"By Sovereign decree, Viceroy and Governor of the forces, Commander of the cavalry and infantry beneath the skies, Conqueror of the middle and outside kingdoms, Leader and saviour, according to the decree of Heaven above, fulfilling the heart's desire of men beneath, Restorer of ancient possessions, the great and able General Shü [issues this mandate].

Taiping Proclamation.

"It has been said that 'extraordinary deeds everywhere need extraordinary men to do them, men of extraordinary merit,' which is true from of old. Heaven's decree demands man's co-operation. The various realms under heaven belong to all men under heaven, not to any one man, and none but the virtuous shall have their lot therein.

"The last monarch of the Ming dynasty was by no means lost to virtue. The predecessor [of the later sovereigns], Shuin Tsz [1644], was by no means a sacredly virtuous ruler. His Imperial power he received from the hands of violent insurrectionists, whom Wu San-Kwei [1] was powerless to resist. Thus Shuin Tsz the evil-hearted stole the Empire [*lit.* the Imperial vessel] in an underhanded manner, and obtained the earnings of the populace—the 'washed monkey in a man's hat'[2] that he was.

"To this day there have been six generations in possession of the Empire, who have never thought of restoring their stolen property; and, for this two hundred years, who has inquired into the legality of their claim?

"The Tartars have ever proved themselves to be ravenous wolves, violent-hearted, ruling but to the injury of their

---

[1] Already noticed as Chung Ch'eng's one trustworthy general. Hearing that Peking had fallen, he concluded a treaty with the Manchu sovereign, who recaptured Peking in Wu's absence—an unforeseen result of the treaty! Having inaugurated the present dynasty, he loaded Wu with honours, made him ruler over two western provinces, and gave his daughter in marriage to Wu's son. Frequent reminders of both father and son are found in the coins they issued. The reign of his son was short and tragic. After two years, his kingdom being invested by Manchu troops, he committed suicide.

[2] "A horse or ox dressed in a coat" is also a semi-classical phrase.

subjects. They have lately been guilty of tenfold oppression, as will be minutely related for your complete disenchantment.

"To say nothing of times prior to Kia K'ing [1796–1821], it is notable that Tao Kwang [1821–1851] and his son [Shien Fung], each in accord with his own perverse notions, have given office in a most irregular manner, the highest office to the highest bidder. What is the so-called Son of Heaven but a disgraceful rascal? 'Beggars are lost souls,' yet such mandarins regard all capability of feeling shame, regard all economy, as so much 'dust to be swept up.'[1] With aching heart I say it. How can I bear to see men thrown into such deep waters of calamity?

"Happily none can deceive High Heaven, who has sent down an Emperor of the true Ming blood, a man of great determination, who begrudges all time claimed by his bodily needs, a man who has the heart if not [the all-renovating] strength.

"Moreover, Great England, in fulfilment of the desires of Heaven, in accord with the necessities of the times, has come to our help.[2] Truly (as the classics have it) 'the rude barbarian tribes have their princes, and are not as the States of our great land without them.'

"Our endeavours have hitherto been resisted by force, like many other good things are on earth, so that we cannot save the Middle Kingdom in a moment. Our ancestors, however, officials of no mean family, recipients of the highest favours of the Mings from generation to generation, are represented in the person of the present high mandarin general, who dares not but put forth all his efforts to bring back the former state of affairs. He has already taken his second degree [*lit.* plucked a red cassia flower from the topmost branch by the pavilion of the moon], and, seeking office [the gem in the dragon cavern], he entered into official rule three thousand

---

[1] The converse of our "sweeping statements."

[2] The late war would make this lie a terror. Indirectly we did help the Taipings, as they absorbed many of the malcontented militia disbanded after the Anglo-Chinese war. Gordon of course fought for the Imperialists against the Taipings.

li from here. Since which, however, he has suffered many a reverse of fortune [*lit.* fallen into pits, run against dykes], but recognises the fact that such adversities were merely for the perfecting of his abilities, until, emerging from obscurity, he has now attained to high glory.

"In our battles, who can withstand us? When we attack a city, what city does not submit? Nor do we appropriate one article wrongfully, or slay a single man without cause. Leading on the army of the Sovereign, we are as seasonable rain to the thirsty land. And now the south of the Yangtse, together with Cheh-kiang, Hupeh, Hunan, Fukien, and indeed all the other provinces, are held in our embrace. Hearing which, Shien Fung has lost heart [dropped gall-bladder—the seat of courage¹]; receiving which news, his prime minister's soul and spirit have flown.

"Who can devise an adequate plan of action against us? They can but drive the sheep to stop the tigers! Whereat the wise are quietly laughing.

"This proclamation is sent everywhere, that the men of the Middle Kingdom may early make up their minds to come over to us, instead of cherishing thoughts of rebellion and villainy. When our task shall have been accomplished, all may receive the blessings thereof in unspeakable joy.

"The Ming records and the people's complaints show clearly who are right and who are wrong, who ought to depart and who ought to take their place, clearly indeed as the sun and moon [a reference to the sun-moon character Ming].

"If, however, you cast away your former wisdom, you will be involved in the calamities of later days. Resisting heavenly virtue and opposing the interests of the realm, you will be as sons resisting their parents.² Ought such things to be?

"Lo Pin-Wang³ in his memorial ends his appeal thus: 'Pray consider, to whom does the earth really belong?' I would borrow his words, with a present application, and

---

[1] As in Hebrew, see Job xvi. 13.

[2] A reference to Mencius, "From the first birth of mankind till now, never has anyone led children to attack their parents and succeeded in his design."

[3] See footnote, p. 160.

say, 'Pray consider, does not the earth belong to the Mings?'"

The billposters went round with their sheets, leaving a highly-interested crowd behind them wherever one of these extraordinary documents was affixed to a blank wall. Now that they were under Taiping rule, the citizens were naturally curious to know what manner of rule it was likely to be, and what were the "essentials of perfect peace" in the "kingdom of heaven."

"Titles seem to be plentiful. That is well," thought some of the readers of the proclamation. "There may be a chance for me, now that old barriers are being levelled. Aphorisms and virtuous talk. Good again." "He exhorts men," exclaim several with delight.

Why delight? it may be asked. Because in China such phrases as "he is a preacher, he sermonises, he preaches" have a highly honourable significance, and open up pleasing vistas of conscience-ennobling thought. Inexplicable to a Westerner such a state of things, and untranslatable the exclamation of an average Chinaman, as far as the admiration goes—" he exhorts men." Hypocrites or fools! is the Western criticism. Well, perhaps there may be a little of both, but not quite all of either. The Chinaman loves preaching. He also loves history. He loves the two combined. And in every respectable town tea-shop of any size his tastes may be gratified most nights in the year. Having been once, the inevitable "to be continued in our next" at the more exciting parts—which phrase we seem to have imported without acknowledging its native home—urges him to come again.

"'High Heaven and Great England'—weighty arguments! as weighty as any in the universe." "Foreign devils!" exclaims one reader, following the printed "barbarians," but the argument holds all the same. Truth is that which cannot be disproved. It is true. "The forces of heaven and earth are with them. Nay, the general is, to his own showing, a host in himself, a prodigy of scholarship, of adversity-proved determination, and of that valour which can afford to be sarcastic. His peroration is irresistible. We follow it heart and soul. The 'perfect peace' men, restorers of the Chinese dynasty, are the men for us. Yes, they are the men."

"Of course we are!" exclaim several "Longhaired" who have mingled in the crowd. "A good gospel indeed, and we hope you will feed us well while we are here."

Alas! The present practical application of the sermon means that all our ready money is fast going to feed a crowd of ravenous beings from other provinces, who are singularly unlike the "Heaven-king" as far as the relative prominence given to bodily necessities is concerned. It is a good gospel, but what preachers! We may support Buddhism, it is true. It is old-established and respectable, though the priest-beggar in our particular district is neither. But—here comes the crowd again, clamouring for meat and wine. It is always festival with them.

"Yes," cries the leader, "we want meat and wine. We could only get rice and herbs at the monastery at Hanyang, though we killed the old man's pet pigs and chickens, and made him and his apprentices—three hundred of them—eat a morsel raw. What a menagerie there was!"

"You don't mean to say you have killed the animals

there! One of them had the soul of my own grandmother in it. O ancestors protect! O p'u-sah,[1] protect!"

"Ha! ha! ha! I am sorry for your grandmother, but the p'u-sahs protecting, the abominations protecting! That's good. Do you know those eighteen images, the lohans,[2] have promised to help us? Wood and mud idols are no good. Bronze will protect us, and the 'kingdom of heaven' too. But quick, I say, with your wine. Not hot yet! The lohans were heavy, and it was hard work."

"What, have they gone?"

"LOHAN" LIGHTS OF ASIA.

"Yes, why not? Idols are false, but cannons and cash are true. Cannons and cash? Ah, now I feel a bit lively. Bronze idols do protect. Ha! ha! ha! We need them. They come to our help. Aha! What do I see? Your old

---

[1] P'u-sah is the term used throughout the Empire for idols generally. It is cut down from P'u-ti-sa-to, a transliteration of the term Bodhisattva in its Pali form Bodhisatto (T. Watters, Essays on the Chinese Language).

[2] These (eighteen) are generally called Buddha's immediate disciples, but of these only sixteen were disciples of the historical Buddha. The other two are not in all places the same, but Kumārajiva, the translator; and the Military Emperor, 502–550 of the Liang dynasty (already referred to in connection with the thousand character classic and the sympathy of the pines), seem to be popular additions. These lohan images are the "mandarins" of our grandfather's mantelpieces! (T. Watters).

special bronze family idol, ever so old ? Well, it's cost you a lot of incense, candles, and crackers, and has been no use. It will protect you now, when we've altered it a bit. Ha! ha! ha! Here men, a prize! But you, be quick and warm an extra pot of wine for me! I must have a good drink on the strength of this!"

Chapter X.

GODS MANY AND LORDS MANY.

TAOIST MARVELS TERRESTRIAL AND CELESTIAL—THE MAKING OF THE GODS—AN IMPROVEMENT ON NIRVANA—A GREAT STATESMAN DEGRADED INTO A LITTLE GOD—HEAVEN'S DECREE.

"The thousand and myriad gods are all about the same."
Chinese Proverb.

LIEU came back at early dawn after a rather long absence, long indeed to country folk when every day seemed an age. He brought a considerable "stock" with him. It needed two men to carry, and he himself was loaded with etceteras besides. The men were dismissed before anyone saw them. Lieu, indeed, arrived before his young hopeful was awake. Having aroused him, he told his son to be quick and help him in with the box or two. "Heavy!" exclaimed the lad. But a curse stopped any further remark. Once within, however, and the door barred, Lieu's spirits seemed to rise. He unloosened his girdle, and, to his son's surprise, displayed among his garments *a yellow waistcoat trimmed with red*—displayed an inch or so of it, that is. This he hastily covered up again, then, seeing that his son looked curious, told him he had got a few old clothes as security for a debt, but he would kill him if he mentioned it.

Having adjusted his garments in an inner chamber, opening a large box and locking it, and trying the lid, he emerged, undid his lighter package or two, and opened shop.

The news he brought created great consternation, for he dealt in glaring colours and short suggestive sentences. It was not what had happened, however, so much as what might be expected nearer home. The news of temple destruction, for instance, affected the priest by arousing his fears for the safety of the particular temple in which he earned a modest competency. Such fears were partly mollified by the increased custom which the terrors of the villagers brought him. But how long would that last?

As long as Lieu had a candle or cracker or stick of incense, perhaps; for Lieu did his best to arouse the inquirers to the necessity of worship. Indirectly, of course, for it was not his to "exhort men." But he could, by short, tantalising answers, arouse their fears to fever-point. Tsaitien being in imminent danger, he advised them not to go there to inquire. They had better not go out of sight of their homes; the temple peak would form a good watch-tower, and so forth.

Folks came from all the villages to get news, and have a cup of wine, most of them going up the hill with a little yellow paper bundle, until the hillside paths, usually grass-grown, shone out like white serpents.

After a day or two, the news flew from mouth to mouth one afternoon that the "Longhaired" had come—at least a "Longhaired." This the traveller certainly was, and unshaven; but on closer inspection he proved to be nothing more formidable than a Taoist priest-pedlar. The utmost ignorance prevailed as to what the rebels were like, their usual costume and other such details, for Lieu was singularly ignorant and contradictory on these points.

But here was a Taoist who had news to relate. His first business, however, was business. He had come from Hunan, and had had a great sale of charms. He himself bore a charmed life. He had walked through rebel-invested parts apparently unseen, for amid carnage and bloodshed no one had molested him. A truly miraculous power lay in his charms. The special one which could render him unseen he was not at liberty to disclose. Moreover it only operated when danger was near. It had been communicated to his former venerable teacher by the "master of heaven," the Taoist pope himself, who lived away down in Kiangsi, ever so far, whose chair was closely curtained, so that he might not see the ox or sheep or pig from which the folks had been changed, or toward which they tended. He could, by lifting his hand in a particular way, bring thunder and lightning. He had drawn a charmed circle around his province, so that

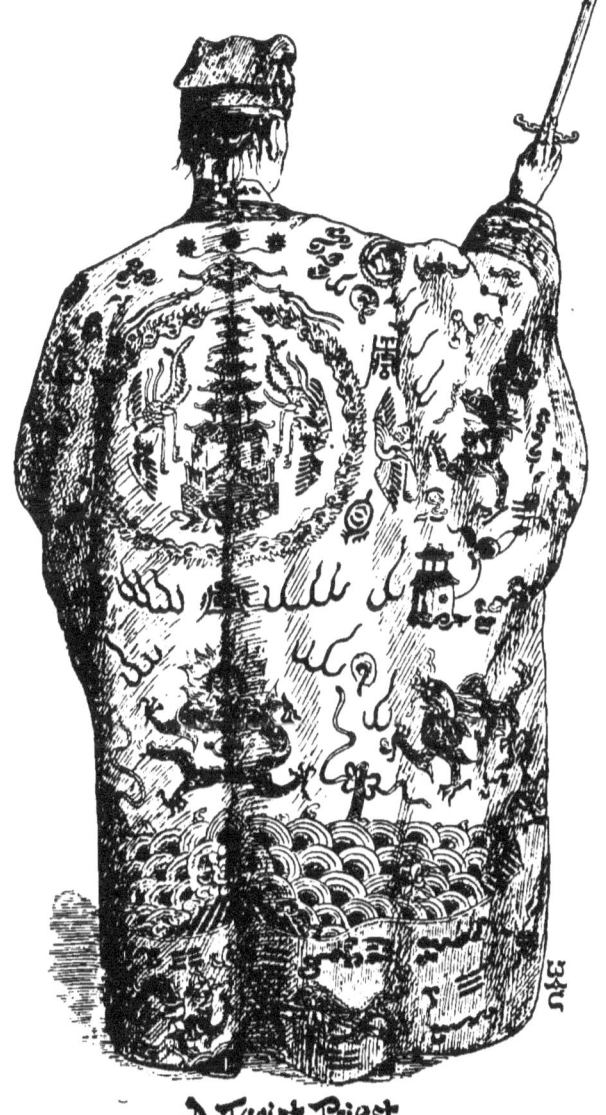

A Taoist Priest.

the rebels dare not enter.[1] They had heard of his powerful

[1] All of which was firmly believed until, when the rebels came, there fled out

seal,—demon-driving and evil-dispelling. He had an impression thereof on his person, with a mystic sign written by the "sacred hand" of the "master of heaven" himself. The paper was old and greasy, but priceless. No, he would never part with it. It had saved his life many a time. "How old do you take me to be? Forty? Well, I am double that, but the same charm that can make me invisible when danger is imminent keeps me at forty. You would like to see it? It is invisible to you, as is my venerable teacher. Don't crowd round the old gentleman. What old gentleman? Why, the one by my side."

"Who? Where?" for the centre of the crowd was filled with children.

"I forgot; I beg pardon. He is invisible to all but me. Do not blame them, venerable sir, they cannot see you."

"Hai Ya!" cried everybody. "An invisible man among us. And that one eighty!" At this the Taoist put his boxes down in the now cleared space, opened a little drawer, and took out a small cone about the size of a walnut. This he fixed on the point of a long needle. He then took a stick of incense from his cap, which no one had noticed to be there before, then a lens from the drawer, and, as the sun was shining, set the incense smouldering. He then rolled up some paper into a spill, dipped it into a little jar of yellow powder, and with the incense set it burning with a green-blue flame, just visible when he shaded it. This he applied to the base of the cone and lit that, then blew out the yellow flame, then jerked the green-blue flame out, quenching the spark after a moment with a theatrical snap of his finger and thumb. But the cone smouldered. It had a hole through the centre, and from that hole proceeded smoke. He lit the blue-green flame spill once more, puffed at the cone, and then set light to the smoke from the apex. This was irresistible. Bewildering wonders culminating in a miracle! Then he kept looking toward his left, where the invisible man was, and carried on a long conversation by the silent motion of his lips, nodding his head in assent at

of the Sacred Palace an ordinary mortal, late Taoist pope and demigod. He was at this particular moment in hiding.

unheard communications, shaking it doubtfully, or looking up to the skies at intervals.

The cone having burnt out, he regained his loquacity. "The 'master of heaven' has summoned my venerable instructor on important business. He is now flying on a crane's back over the sea, but will return soon and let me know."

"Know what?" was the eager enquiry.

"The State affairs of —— " (the dash representing a great deal of silent mouth motion, which ended with a nod). "Oh, that's nothing. It's only a small matter, not worth asking about. I'll tell you something by and by when I have shown you some of my charms. But I must tell you how I got them. I know all that goes on in the palace. My venerable instructor tells me — we are  sworn father and son, you know. Well, in the palace grounds there grow a number of peach trees; not the ordinary sort by any means. They are sacred. Only the master of heaven and his family may eat them. In fact, they feed on them. Then the stones, which are charmed, are given away to those in high favour, to sell to the duly qualified, who carve them into various shapes. My venerable instructor, being employed as confidential messenger, begged a few, pleading that the rebellion would break out, and country children kidnapped unless they were protected—especially little lads about twelve or so; and the master of heaven gave him a hundred or two, with a special efficacy imparted to each. It is the peach-stones that have preserved me in my travels of late. The written charm preserves against accident; these against enemies. They make me nimble. See how I can jump. There now. I could jump much higher, but I won't just now. It is not dignified for a man of eighty. If you have any children that want preserving, now is your opportunity; but if you are secure, I will go off to Tsaitien. My instructor told me just now that it was in great danger."

"So Lieu said!" cried several.

"Lieu? Who is he? The tea-shop keeper? Then you have a tea-shop? I will go there. It is in your village? No, yonder? The keeper must be a bold man, it is so exposed. He came from Tsaitien the other day? Well he did. The fugitives will be flying here in a day or two, if I do not save the town."

"This is not your boy, I suppose?" he said to Li, looking fixedly at Seng-tch.

"Yes, he is," said Mrs. Li. "How much are the charms each?"

"Well, I like the lad, and will sell you a string of them at half the price I could get at Tsaitien. Fifty cash each. There is gold among the rocks in this hill of yours, is there not? They say it is the talk of the rebel camp. What, a temple on the hill-top! Is there a Taoist there? No, only a Buddhist! That is a pity. They are destroying all Buddhist temples, and leaving only the true Chinese ones. Have you heard they have slaughtered the young monks at Hanyang to a man? They spared the old abbot because of his grey hairs. You said the monk on the hill was an old man, did you not? Dead! That is bad. I pity that young man. Well, I must be going. Tsaitien is in danger."

Not before a clamouring crowd asked, entreated to buy; and the crowd increased every moment, for the scene was the hillside, and all the villages were emptying towards the spot. Those who witnessed the early display of magic had spread the news, which grew as it spread. "He can make himself young or old. He can become invisible. He flies on a crane's back. So and so saw him do it all just now." Such were the rumours which spread around; and worn by much excitement, with nerves unstrung by many a wakeful night, there were many to believe it all, and, as a practical application, to buy the peach-stone charms, until eventually they had all gone, and the country folk bid for them one among the other. In the Taoist's hands they had emitted smoke, and so on, and so on. A child was missed by an interested mother, a child with a charm.

"Never mind, he is only invisible for the moment. The charms are too powerful. I will make it all right." And he bid them look up a moment, waved his hands magically, then said, "I have arranged it. You will find him on yonder rock."

They looked at the Taoist. His eyes were closed. But there on the rock was the child.

"Perhaps it is not your child?" he said.

"Yes, it is," she cried. "But how could you know?" she asked, as she returned with a very solid looking toddler, whom she hugged to see if he were real. "Don't let him disappear again; but did you do it?"

"If you doubt it, I can easily do it again for a longer time."

"No!" she screamed, and hugged her babe closer.

"Not till the rebels come. It's all right. Never fear. We grown-up folks can shift for ourselves. It is the children who need protecting."

It was now nearly sundown, and had come over very cloudy and threatening. The hospitable Li, whose son now rejoiced in a whole necklace of peach-stones, invited the wonderful man to stay the night.

"Tsaitien is ten miles off, and it looks like snow," he urged.

"So far as that? I heard it was just beyond the hill yonder."

"No, indeed; nor in that direction."

"Vegetarian, of course?" suggested Li, as he led the Taoist home.

"Of course. Any other food would destroy my remaining charms. I could not protect myself."

A special meal was therefore prepared, during which the visitor gave a somewhat vague account of the rebels and their doings. He never committed himself to anything definite. He had only heard this and that. Moreover he seemed full of other-wordliness, as became a disciple of doctrine (Tao). Being above personal danger, his thoughts seemed to spurn such vulgar details as rebels, and to be absorbed in mystic meditation.

It began to snow, and snow coming within the range of his mental horizon, he brought out from the penetralia of his garments one or two dirty volumes, from which, after some pressure, he read as follows:—

"The silvery pearls are scattered in wild confusion through the air. The heavens are filled with flocks of willow wool. The travellers shake the leaping pear blossom from their sleeves. The thousand twigs bend under a silvery burden. The mountain recluse boils the snow water for tea.

A Snowfall.

"Snow is a treasure. It has sound and colour; it has breath and flavour. Its sound is like the silkworms on the mulberry trees; its breath penetrates the heart and the bones. Its colour is like purest jade. Its taste determines the character of the next year's harvest.

"The first layer is like celestial phœnix feathers;[1] the second like bustard down. The final layers fall like petals of plum blossoms. All waste spaces are filled with them. The rivers alone remain as paths of grey.

"Snow is a revealer of riches and honour, of poverty and low life. The rich pile the charcoal upon the ruddy brazier; within the great doors the flesh of lambs is eaten. The poor have no rice in the kitchen; stoves without fuel. Can it be that a heavenly edict has sent abroad a knife of slaughter?"

This was given in an unctuously sonorous voice, interlarded with interjections and breathings, not to be reproduced even by hint upon paper. This element of Chinese elocution must remain undescribed. A printed Shakespeare even can

---

[1] Herodotus describes snow as showers of feathers, and the phrase of modern sailors, "Mother Carey plucking her goose," may perhaps be a survival of the old German myth which describes the snow as the feathers falling from the bed of the goddess Holda when she shook it in making it.

but give the words. The intonations of the dramatist's most famous exponents die with the actor and the audience.

In lieu of brazier, Li had been blowing into brighter incandescence the scraps of charcoal in a little earthen pot of sawdust, which he handed to his guest, after the recital of the prose poem, to warm his hands. Hot tea followed. Sipping which, the Taoist asked Seng-tch if he had ever heard anything like it.

He had learnt a poem a day or two before. Might the Taoist be favoured with it? Thus encouraged and flattered, the lad repeated the lines—

<small>A Picture of Loneliness.</small>

> "From a thousand hills the birds are all gone,
> The myriad paths no longer footworn.
> But one aged man remains in the cold,
> With coir cape sheltering his shoulders old;
> In his little boat fishing he bends all weary,
> While the snowflakes fall on the river dreary."

This word picture (of twenty characters in the original) having been drawn, and received in silence, the Taoist began turning over the leaves of his book. He had gone off into one of his abstracted states.

"Won't you read us some more?" asked Li. "The snow makes one chilly, and my son interrupted you."

"Ah well, yes, if you like. How would you like to ascend to heaven? My venerable instructor has gone there to report matters. I feel lonely without him. He will not be back till to-morrow morning. I have asked him to make himself visible this time. If he does, you will see him, crane and all. But you might like to know what heaven is like?"

"That we would."

"Well, this is what he saw. I got him to write it down once, and had it printed."

"What, the invisible man on the hill?"

"Yes, the very one. Listen! [Tones and gestures again must be imagined in the above conversation, and the following description of heaven.] Having ascended to the boundary on high, he all at once saw the halls of heaven, where golden light spirted forth its ruddy rainbows in a myriad directions, while the felicitous air breathed out a thousand streams of purple vapour.

<small>The Taoist Heaven.</small>

"The southern gate of heaven was of the deepest emerald glass, glistering and lucent, as if fused in a precious cauldron. On either side were four massive pillars, around which twined pink-bearded dragons, cloud-riding and mist-dispersing. In the midst were two jade bridges, standing whereon were the cloud-aspiring phœnixes, with iridescent plumage and cinnabar-coloured crests, amid glistening beams of ruby sunset light, and emerald vapours, which obscured the starry constellations and the light of day.

"There are thirty-three pavilions in heaven; the cloud-dividing pavilion, the wave-collecting pavilion, the purple sunset pavilion, the pavilion of the sun, the pavilion of the moon, the pavilion of ever-renewed pleasure among them. Each pavilion is ceiled with the teeth of the celestial stag.

"There are seventy-two tiers of palaces, by the pillars of which stand ranks of jade unicorns. There is the star of longevity tower, the star of emolument tower, and the star of happiness tower. At their base are wondrous flowers, which fade not in a thousand thousand years. There is the immortality pill brazier, the eight diagrams brazier, and the water-fire brazier. Between these spring herbs which are verdant and flourishing for a myriad myriad years.

"Within the sacred palaces the robes of the blessed are of rose-coloured silk gauze. Beneath the vermilion throne steps are they whose headgear is like the mallow flower. That temple of living empyrean! The golden dragons crowd through its jade portals. Those sacred towers! The phœnixes leap by the jade-hewn gates, moving in and out along corridors ornate with translucent tracery. Triple colonnades! Quadruple mansions! Ranks upon ranks of dragons and phœnixes soaring hither and thither. And high above all flash beams of purple light. Clear their splendour; brilliant with many a scintillation. A clear clanging sound proceeds from the neck of the magic gourd. On every hand are heard tinklings varied and confused, laminated sounds as of gurgling and dripping, brightly sonorous like those of the jade pendants of courtiers.

"Truly wondrous the sights and sounds of heaven, so rarely known on earth. Golden portals of paradise; silvery courts majestic; purple halls; wondrous flowers, strange herbs fill the jasper realm, far beneath whose audience chambers courses the gemmous hare (the moon, you know); far beneath where they bow before the sacred majesty flies the golden crow (the sun, of course). He who has the felicity to reach the heavenly boundaries will never grovel again in the filthy mud of earth."

Here a dog barked, and the hens cackled, which drew forth the remark that a Taoist philosopher (Hwai Nan-tsz—died B.C. 122) attained to such merit, that when he ascended the skies his chickens and dogs ascended with him.

The household then retired to rest, and probably to dream of invisible men and of heaven. The Taoist, if he dreamt at all, saw visions of a paradise built of copper cash, for his pack was heavy therewith as he rose before dawn to make a soon obliterated snow-track, a remarkably straight one towards Tsaitien.

Instead of an invisible man rendered visible, the formerly visible Taoist, together with a couple of chickens, had disappeared! Had they ascended the skies? Not a footprint of the chickens, and only one human footprint under the eaves!

The story reached the tea-shop, and when alone with his son, Lieu whispered that Tsaitien had been the man's home for half a month, and that he had met the Taoist hawking the peach-stones there at five cash instead of fifty. "But I had my commission some days ago for bringing him here. Good, isn't it?"

"Was the commission an old garment or two?" asked Fah.

"What demon put that into your head! Ah, well," he added, with almost admiration, "you are growing up now. But what would be the use of a garment or two to me?"

"Can't say," and perhaps no one else could then. "But he came from the West, and Tsaitien is eastward. Of course he did, you stupid. I'm disappointed in you." But his face resumed a hideous smile of satisfaction as he said, "It will not do for you to know too much just yet." The garment secret was safe.

Lieu Fah, it may be added, had been withdrawn from school. He had been made to kneel for half an hour for the theft of an ornate ink-slab and a traveller's brass-mounted pen, the latter of which the teacher's father had given to Li for his infant son. Nieh had broken faith! Fah was withdrawn from school. But, as it will be seen, he was now under private tuition.

The villages had enjoyed a more peaceful night than they had known for some time. The Taoist, in lieu of the "immortality pill," had administered a sleeping draught to many. The Chinese farmer is not troubled with nerves as a rule. But with his whole earthly good at stake, and no definite good of any other sort within reach, he may know the miseries of insomnia—so may his wife. It was very much the same a couple of generations back in our own country districts. "The French are coming. Buonaparte is coming!" had something to do with the evolution of "nerves" in many a family. Perhaps the *ergo* of the scares may have been different. "The French have landed. Fight!" seems to be the argument, as witnessed by certain two-edged broadswords served out to the valiant in some country parts. "The Longhaired are coming. Run!" is the phrase still quoted in many a Chinese village. "Run!" but where? First, if the alarm be a sudden one, and there is no immediate danger, run to what apologies for deities there may be. "Incense may be neglected when all is well, but you will have to rush to Buddha's feet in times of necessity." The proverb had been fulfilled in this case.

Having done so, try and find other spiritual aids, which may be combined with the not overtrustworthy help of Buddha. In accord with this the Taoist, living, visible (with friends in the invisible world), vocal and wonder-working, had been almost a heaven-sent prophet. That, at any rate, was the ideal toward which faith was struggling. Doubts there were, but each hid them within his or her breast. Even if the man's ghostly helpers were not of a very heavenly sort, they were strong; and second-grade helpers of superhuman capacity are not to be despised. Did his charms really make that child invisible? You cannot disprove it. Let us take the needed comfort. Then he himself seems to have vanished in an unexplained way. And he could talk. He gave Li a most detailed account of heaven. Again doubts will arise, but do not express them, please.

One man had remained in the background all the while, and was almost avoided by the villagers the next day. He was no other than Nich Shen-seng. But Li and he were such great friends that an evening chat was inevitable. That simple-minded, but, on the whole, worthy farmer felt it to be inevitable; as inevitable as, say, a Westerner's visit to the dentist—and as much to be dreaded; or, to drop all telling but incomplete similes, the communication of one's pet theory to a man with no imagination, a man who knows about everything, and in whose presence one is very young indeed.

Nieh Shen-seng had heard of the Taoist's book. He would not discourse on the various marvels exhibited on the hill. Confucius did not talk of "marvellous things"; why should he commit himself? But the book. To our great disgust he can produce a copy from the shelf. He gives it a slap, merely to shake off the dust, and a puff or two to complete the process, and there it is before us on the table. A description of heaven written by his invisible friend! Why, here it is verbatim, even to the pink-bearded dragons. His friend! Then he must have lived during the reign of the last emperor of the Ming dynasty, he who cursed the temple—a Taoist temple, too. The writer, moreover, instead of being a bachelor Taoist monk (married Taoists there are, " scholars of Tao," laymen of almost equal rank with the "men of Tao"), had two daughters, to the elder of which he gave every cash he could afford on the occasion of her marriage. Her younger sister complaining, he promised her a far better marriage portion if she would only wait in patient faith. The time came, and not a single silver ingot! Instead, a large packet of written paper. " Father's old essays, I suppose. 'One character worth thousands of gold,' and suchlike. All very well, but somewhat provoking when a girl wants 'rouge-money.'[1] Father is a little unpractical nowadays; sits up half the night writing. He is getting old." But the sheets were examined, were sent to the printer, were published; there was a rush for them. Another edition—boards worn out with much use, had to be recut. There's your wedding portion! Happiness—that is plenty of money—ever after! Such was the origin of the Taoist's book. The author might reach his invisible hand across the dynasty toward a Taoist pedlar, unctuous and voluble—yes, and wonder-working, if you like, but—.

[1] Used exactly as our "pin-money."

The hero of the book is a certain Chang Ta'i-Kung (Ta'i-Kung being a posthumous title of honour—" a superlative duke "— in the empire of doctrine), a philosopher who dwelt on the Kwen Lun mountain until he was bidden to descend to earth to provide deities for the populace.

The Maker of the gods.

He found a practical friend who proposed his marriage. Philosophy wedded to matter-of-fact; the ideal baffled by the problem of an empty cupboard and no cabbages for dinner; the future maker of the gods unable to find a sale for dumplings, even at the low figure of half a farthing each. Domestic scenes, not to say squabbles. Matter-of-fact, stupid, but hungry, asking for a bill of divorcement, shouting for it, and eventually getting it, and the opprobrium of all after ages. Philosophy then takes to catching fish, but imagines that a straight, unbaited needle at the end of a rod will induce the wiser denizens of the waters to impale themselves into a region more ideal than water (more oxygen, you know), even if their after history consists of what to the unphilosophical looks very like death-struggles. An inimitable allegory, the wide range of which not even Nich Shen-seng realised as he read the tale.

But wait! "Continued in our next," we find the unsuccessful fisherman discovered by the prince who was afterwards more than deified in the Chinese annals under the title of Literary Monarch, the same that added a fresh string to China's harpsichord. The philosopher is now the counsellor of the ideal prince, next of his martial son. The tyrant of ideal infamy is dethroned, is slain; a new dynasty is inaugurated, and the martial monarch reigns supreme over a populace whose bewilderment of rapture has made Chinese poetry, beginning with the *Book of Odes.* Then the philosopher has leisure to undertake his lifework, and deifies the chief heroes slain in the war—many of them his previous opponents. Hence the reputed birth of Taoism. The deities fill the house, but, in noble self-forgetfulness, the philosopher has omitted to reserve a godship or a standing-place for himself. Hence after ages have found him a place in the cottage window, writing a red slip thereon, readable even by student foreigners. "Chang Ta'i-Kung is here; ye gods, make way"

224 A STRING OF CHINESE PEACH-STONES.

"The very Chang T'ai-Kung who resides in my two windows, and all the rest in the village?" cried Li, whose

spirits had returned, and in whose mind the vulgar difficulty of subdivision into, say, fifty million parts found no place.

"Yes, the very same," acknowledged Nieh, who had

written the red slips for the village, 'remembering to forget' to write one for his own window.

"Then the book is true!" And the Taoist's charms, and everything else! And now the hosts of Longhaired rebels dissolve away, to disclose a vista of gemmous portals, and friendly-disposed, if pink-bearded, dragons.

The scholar remained pensive. He saw that his friend was disposed to draw gigantic deductions from somewhat insignificant premisses. "If it had been an ancient book, a very ancient book, it might be true," he said.

"But is not heaven just as the book describes it?"

"I cannot tell. The Buddhists speak of a Western paradise. I will read a description to you. 'It has a sevenfold row of balustrades, a sevenfold row of silver nets, and a sevenfold row of trees hedging the whole country. In the midst of it are seven precious ponds, whose waters are pure and cool, sweet and agreeable, light and soft, fresh and rich, tranquillising, satisfying, and of fertilising power to the roots of the trees. The bottom of these ponds is covered with golden sand; round about these are pavements of precious stones, and many pavilions built of richly-coloured, transparent jewels. On the surface of the waters there are beautiful lotus flowers floating, each as large as a carriage wheel, displaying the most dazzling colours, and dispensing the most fragrant aroma. There are also beautiful birds there which make delicious, enchanting music, and at every breath of wind the very trees on which these birds are resting join in the chorus, shaking their leaves in trembling accords of sweetest harmony. The silken nets also chime in. But it is all the doing of the miraculous power of O Mi To Fuh, who transforms himself into those birds, and produces those unearthly strains of heavenly music.'"[1]

The Buddhist Heaven for the Chinese.

This was hardly as Chinese as the former description. A heaven minus dragons and phœnixes could hardly be complete. Besides, O Mi To Fuh hardly expresses any personal ideas. The words are a charm to be cut on a stone placed at the fork of country paths, or to be muttered, one for each bead, by

[1] See Eitel's *Buddhism*, pp. 98, 99

monks and recluses, who have nothing to do but accumulate merit, abstain from meat, and perhaps beg, in order that their abstinence may not be total, complete, and final.

Even Buddhism, attempting to supply a long-felt need, was not personal enough in its deities—if the goddess of mercy be omitted for the moment. Taoism deals with deified heroes, which are kept alive and real in the popular mind by the popular tales, delivered nightly in the tea-shops of the towns, and decked out in all possible finery on the boards of the open-air theatre. Tea-shop tales and theatricals, or their equivalents, are no mere luxuries, like a volume of Scott or a historical play. They are necessities in China. Very Chinese they are; but more than that, the human, rather than the Chinese, heart demands a personal comforter and helper in its hour of need. The reality unobtainable, it must have (that is, the heart of the masses must have) some substitute, legendary and impossible it may be, but still a subjective substitute.

What was a man like Li to do? Safety lies in a multitude of counsellors. But here the two chief counsellors give varying advice. Each says, "Follow me," while each moves toward a different place of safety and rest.

"You'd embark in two boats;
Do so if you can!
Off goes one foot to Shanghai,
T'other to Szchwan!"

Such is the rhyming proverb. And now both boats are found to be leaky. What is Li to do? What would you and I do under the circumstances? Call a third. Yes, call a third. Here again the sarcastic philosopher or committee of philosophers who made the Chinese proverbs meets us with the phrase, "Three-legged cat." What is that? A marvel exhibited by the menagerie man? No, an iron tripod used in some kitchens. "Not so, cook," says the carpenter. "A three-legged cat is the triangular, three-pointed bit of iron which, hammered into my bench, gives firmness and rigidity to the board I want to plane." "You are all wrong," laughs the proverb maker. "I have in my

A Three-legged Cat.

mind's eye a metaphorical tripod, a jack of all three religions —a Buddhist-Taoist-Confucianist."

Nieh Shen-seng, however, seems more placid than the rest. Let us, in the person of Li, ask him to communicate a little of his placidity to us.

"I am a Confucianist, and, as the classics say, 'For a man to sacrifice to a spirit which does not belong to him is flattery.' Buddhist spirits do not belong to China. My wife went up the temple hill to pray to the goddess of mercy for a son, and only had a daughter. As to spirits acknowledged from of old in China, we read again that when Confucius was ill, his disciple Tsz-leu asked leave to pray for him. Confucius asked, 'May such a thing be done?' Tsz-leu replied, 'It may. In the prayers it is said, "Prayer may be made to the spirits of the upper and lower worlds."' Confucius replied, 'My praying has been for a long time.'

"On another occasion his disciple Ki-leu asked about serving the spirits of the dead. Confucius said, 'While you are not able to serve men, how can you serve their spirits?' Ki-leu added, 'I venture to ask about death.' He was answered, 'While you do not know life, how can you know about death?'[1]

"He also said, 'Respect the spirits and keep aloof from them.' And again, 'He who offends against heaven has none to whom he can pray.' And again, 'Let the will be set on the path of duty. Let every attainment in what is good be firmly grasped. Let perfect virtue be accorded with.'

"Then the colloquial part of the Sacred Edict of the Emperor Yung Cheng says, 'A perfectly illuminated heart is heaven; a darkened heart is hell'; and 'He who fulfils his duty will obtain the help of the gods.' And in another place it speaks of the absurdity of trying to bribe Buddha with incense, masses, drum-beats, and processions when the heart is depraved.

"A saying frequently quoted by scholars is that 'heaven has heaven-spirits, earth has earth-spirits, man has his man-

---

[1] Very like a Christian echo of this sounds the words of F. W. Maurice. "Shall we know each other in heaven?" it had been asked. "How little we know of each other here!" was the response.

spirit, things have their indwelling sprites.' Tracing up the word 'spirit' in the dictionary compiled in the reign of Kang Shi [1662–1723], we find a quotation from the oldest dictionary in China [about the Christian era], 'The Heavenly Spirit leads forth[1] all things.' I do not know whether this 'Heavenly Spirit' is the same as the 'Sovereign on High' of the classics, but I think so. An ancient passage quoted in the *Golden Mean* says, 'By the ceremonious sacrifices to heaven and earth they served the Sovereign on High.'"

"Then we can do the same," said Li eagerly.

"No; the Sovereign on High can only be worshipped now by the sovereign on earth. That has been the case ever since the Han dynasty, at least. Among the offences of the builder of the great wall and the burner of the classics [Sz Hwang, B.C. 221–209] is noted the fact that before he gained the Empire he prayed to the Sovereign on High. To do that "—

"Well, but," interrupted Li, "I don't see that. Were they emperors who 'served the Ruler on High?'"

"Yes, I believe so."

"But are you sure no others ever did?"

Nieh might well be surprised. Instead of a rather happy-go-lucky farmer before him, he was confronted by searching eyes. The late excitements had seemed to open up a new chamber in Li's easy-going mind. But such a question! Nieh might have adapted the words of Lieu to his young hopeful, and asked, "What higher spirit put that question into your mind?"

In the awkward pause, for Nieh had his button and his reputation to magnify, Li gave vent to another sudden thought. "Nieh Shen-seng, you do what those men did, do what the ancients did. You reverence the classics. You have not 'offended against heaven.' I know the phrase. Seng-teh was humming it over the other day. You pray for us."

What strange thoughts dire necessity had invented! The dullard had woke up and posed the Confucianist.

---

[1] The original seems to be an exact parallel to our word "produce" (*pro* and *duco*), the root meaning of which is retained in mathematics, "producing a line."

GODS MANY AND LORDS MANY. 229

"I dare not; it would be treason; it would be rebellion."
"But to ask that the rebellion would be put down!"
Really the farmer was getting very troublesome. Nieh began turning over the leaves of the classics for want of a reply.
"You need not call Him 'Ruler on High.' Call Him the 'Venerable One of Heaven.' You say it is He who gives us the harvests, and who punished us with the flood. You told me it was stupid to thank the idols for what Heaven had done, and you said that Heaven meant the 'Venerable One of Heaven,' and that He was the same, you thought, as the Ruler on High."

Ay, press him Li! Demand an answer. It is thy right. Thy unsophisticated instincts are right on the main point. Fight it out, even through seeming rebellion. Be violent. Take the kingdom of heaven by force. Oh, to be able to tear off this invisible hat! Seest thou not, my fellow-onlookers, that here is a man battling with all the force of his enfeebled, unused instincts; battling for freedom, for rights, on behalf of which some of our ancestors fought and died, nor died in vain, if thou and I ever learned in our early days the words "my God," not to say those other dearer words. Oh to be visible to him, to be vocal, to put into his mouth, into his heart, the words, "Our Father which art in heaven"!

There are unaroused Lis around the writer; here in a mud-floored, tumble-down Chinese house, their voices sound through the wattle walls, above the pedlars' drums and rattles and discordant street cries in this town of Tsaitien. And when the shops are shut for the night, some will come in, Lis awakened and enlightened, to kneel and breathe the prayer thou used at anyrate to pray once, if thou ever hadst a mother.

The white tie, nay, the human heart, will out. And thy heart too, if it be awake. And the Li who lives next door to you and to me will be brought at least a bit nearer to our Father for our having been neighbours.

"I always used to pray to the 'earth god' when I wanted rain," put in a fellow-villager. Welcome break to the glutinous silence! The crisis is past! "I put up a tablet in the little shrine. Nich Shen-seng wrote it, but the shrine was flooded the other year, and the tablet rotted."

Shrines of the Earth God.

"These shrines," explained the teacher, in a subdued and rather irritated voice (and no one had inquired into their origin in more peaceful times), " are supposed to be the abode of Han Wen-Kung of the T'ang dynasty" (768–824).

The temple on the Nine Recluses Hill-top.

How to avoid the Dentist.

"Yes," said the villager, "one of the many Yangs from which the village took its name. He and his wife are the guardians of the bed. The other day my boy's tooth got loose. It was a bottom one, and he ought to have thrown it over the bed, but he threw it underneath, where upper teeth should be thrown. Will that matter, do you think?"

"My girl's teeth are firm and regular enough," put in another of the Yangs;

Shrine of the Earth-god.

" but then the old woman was very particular to get her to sit on the bed every morning and put her feet regular, the toes against a piece of bamboo. Your woman did not get your boy to do that."

" No, she isn't ' worth cash,' just a potato of a thing."

" But how about Han Wen-Kung?" inquired Li.

"He was an enthusiastic idol-hater."

"Why did he hate other idols?" asked one of the Yangs.

"He was not an idol,"[1] exclaimed Nieh, with some warmth. "He was a statesman and a poet. His letters to his friends are full of the loveliest thoughts. And he wrote a memorial to the Emperor about a supposed bone of Buddha, over which the whole Court went mad. He protested against Buddhism. He brought his paper to an end with three sentences, like three blows on the table [and the action was suited to the word, for the man on whose behalf Nieh had once written the tablet looked as though he might interrupt]—'Man their men, burn their books, house their dwellings.' That means, turn the temples into houses and the monks into laymen. Alas, that such a great man should have been deified into such a miserable little god!"

Han Wen-Kung.

"I worship at the temple on the hill now," said the tablet man, "and if the rebels do not come, I will ask you to write me a tablet—a bigger one—to hang there. That's where the Hanyang mandarins used to pray, and they knew what was what."

"Who is the big idol there?" asked Li. "The 'great king,' I mean, who was he?"

"He was a robber," replied Nieh, "an outlaw, when laws were badly enforced, who stole from the rich to give to the poor. He used to live in these parts. He was the chief among three sworn brothers.[2] When he died, the people, out of gratitude, had a bronze image of him made. Some say they put an arm of his inside, which was cut off in his last fight, and put the image into a new temple on the plain. It was not very efficacious there. But one day an epidemic broke out in a Hanyang

---

[1] In the popular books which describe his essential idolship, he is represented as stopping on the bank of the "heaven river," and drinking a mouthful of its waters. An immortal who could quench his thirst at the milky way ought surely to have been very fully deified!

[2] Compare "Togeder han thise three hir trouthes plight
To live and die each of hem for other,
As though he were his owen boren brother."
CHAUCER'S "Pardonere's Tale."

yamun. This was in the Ming dynasty. A Taoist was called in, who exposed the evil demon and made him visible, invoking the aid of this 'great king' in killing it. So the grateful mandarin erected the temple on the hill-top and had the image carried there. It was badly cast, and broke, but the parts missing—I expect the *yamun* runners stole them—were made up with wood. And for years afterwards the Hanyang officials used to come, with a large train of attendants, and pray for rain, with great success, it is said, feasting afterwards in the old garden, which contains ancestral graves, in the valley on the other side of the hill."

Li, knowing that the teacher never worshipped there, asked, " And what do you trust in ? "

" I trust in fate. It is said, ' Death and life are decreed,' and how can we alter the decree by our prayers ?[1] But I must beg your pardon. I do not say the idols are no use. I should make myself wiser than the mandarins, and even the Emperor, if I did. 'The superior man is catholic, and no partisan.' I am no superior man, but I am catholic, and no partisan."

A few days after this conversation, the villagers were surprised by seeing that the farther peaks of their hill were thick with men. The Longhaired had come!

Nearer, at anyrate; being driven out of the city of Hanyang, they had invested the country to the west. The country folk from the other side had fled to the hill, and were entrenching themselves there. The excitement was getting fearful. Run! but where? Run a mile or two, then run back, with your head aching with maddening bewilderment. What is to be done?

In case the charms should fail, the smaller boys had better be dressed in girls' clothes. The rebels will not want little girls. And so young Seng-teh, who had happily not reached the rapid growing-up period, must appear as little Miss Li. His feet were not very bindable; but country feet are, as a rule, much larger than the highest standards require.

[1] Compare Seneca : " To what end, then, is it, if fate be inexorable, to offer up prayers and sacrifices, any further than to relieve the scruples and weaknesses of sickly minds ? " (Epistle xxv.).

The temple hill was always thick with men now,—not with worshippers, however. The monk there had to chop his own wood and draw his own water now. His apprentice had been withdrawn. The gods had by this time been duly deceived. He did not seem delicate. And the Longhaired were only the other side of the hill.

If we could only alter fate, or get some peace of mind meanwhile!

Chapter XI.

A Taiping Camp.

WOLF CRIES—TRIBUTE SNATCHERS—THE CROUCHING TIGER IN HIS LAIR—TAIPING BIBLE AND DOXOLOGY—AN IDOL FOR A SON.

"There are not two suns in the sky, nor two sovereigns over the people."
MENCIUS.

It is an undoubted fact that cries of "Wolf!" have to be louder and louder each time in order to produce anything like the effect of the first cry. Science will investigate the matter some day, to find in all probability that the initial energy of such a cry must be multiplied by the number of times of its utterance. The effect produced seems to be in inverse ratio to that number of times, modified, of course, by the interval between each cry. At present the subject remains in the region of theory, for neither our (great) grandparents with their "Boney is coming after you if you do not behave yourself," nor the alarmists of the Nine Recluses district with their blood-curdling cry of "The Longhaired are coming," ever quite succeeded in reproducing the initial alarm.

A month had passed, and beyond the emptying of an extra wine jar or two at the tea-shop, and certain social and moral etceteras not fully recognised by the country folk, nothing of vital importance had happened. They were getting used to the near presence of the rebels, which reminds us that we must also include an inverse ratio of distance in the calculations already proposed. In this case "near" meant some miles beyond the hill.

Good digestion and an open-air life will do much for the nerves. But the hands need to be employed. And here it behoves us to record that, in the coldest months,[1] Li hit upon a plan which would help to keep a few out of Lieu's clutches, and would make the village a trifle more secure against the rebels. He had a trench dug all around, and the earth therefrom banked up against the inside of the wall. Though undoubtedly possessed of a great faculty for doing nothing when there is nothing to be done, and sometimes when there is too, the country folk of China are not quite free from the law expressed so concretely in the lines of the redoubtable Dr. Watts, enshrined in the memory of the children of a past generation, which lines, however, with a great deal of the wisdom of the West, do not seem as yet to have found a translator.

As the days grew warmer, there was plenty to do,—rotary pumps to be worked when the rain was delayed; paddy fields, thus flooded, to be ploughed, harrowed, manured, and the vividly green rice (at first closely sown in a little plot) planted out. Even the scholars were called out to help. Nor was the school-less schoolmaster idle. He was found beneath the budding boughs of his silk-suggesting mulberry trees,[2] pulling up rapidly growing vegetables and sowing seeds for more. His dwelling had now both spinning-wheel and loom, his wife spending many an hour throwing the shuttle, while her little daughter was duly diligent in getting in the way; a duty felt by all healthy children to be incumbent on them.

Lieu Fah was busy helping his father to keep his counsel on sundry matters. He was more than ever the bully, and being big-limbed and heavy, he was a terror to such of the boys as had not yet begun to grow up. Seng-teh came in for the largest share of his animosity. He was now a lad

---

[1] "Night is the spare time of the day, the winter of the year."
[2] The rearing of silkworms (at first upon the mulberry boughs—as now in some parts of Honan and Szchwan) is traced to an emperor who lived B.C. 2697; the art of spinning and weaving (cotton), as far as Central China is concerned, to a lady of high rank, who introduced the art B.C. 400.

of thirteen, and, as with many a country lad, showed as yet little promise of future elongation. He was still in girl's clothes, as were several smaller boys. He also wore the necklace of peach-stones. Fah's mildest nickname for him was "All there?"—a never stale joke when one asks the age of a rather small child. It was in no jocular tone, however, that Fah used the word. And the mild phrase was ever wrapped up in somewhat pungent expressions. The chief of these, of course, related to the lad's attire, which, to tell the truth, became him remarkably well, except so far as the "nippit foot and clippit foot" were concerned. As to the peach-stones, Fah did his very best to let out his father's secret—enough of it to prove that Seng-teh's parents were "potatoes." There was therefore no love lost between the youths; and, as bullock-tender, Seng-teh used to wander round the spur of the hill to escape his tormentor.

Here Fah discovered him one day from a distance, and walked toward the spot, busily engaged concocting some new method of mild torture. When a party of Taoists approached from the opposite direction,—a party of ten,—Fah retreated behind a rock upon the hillside and watched the course of events. His sharp eyes detected in one of them the form of the peach-stone vendor. Nor was Seng-teh long in recognising a familiar voice. But what an un-Taoist exclamation it was he heard, "Hallo! a find! here is some beef. All this lot, and only a girl to mind it." And how utterly unorthodox for him and the rest to unloose their girdles and proceed to make halters of them, the swords they had carried at the girdle being held in their hands as they did so.

"Stop!" cried Seng-teh. "Let go! They're mine!" and he tugged at one of the girdle halters with one hand, while he clutched a Taoist sleeve with the other. A small boy in China, as elsewhere, may be victimised by a bully, hypnotised out of his boyish rights, and yet be brave when occasion requires. He struggled, he shouted, he fought, for the exodus of the two chickens had been a subject of Fah's sarcasms. Meanwhile the peach-stone vendor blandly complimented the little girl on her spitefulness.

It was no use resisting, but perhaps they were not quite

dead to argument. "Taoists do not eat meat. You don't, at anyrate"—to the peach-stone pedlar.

"Yes, we do," he said, with his most horrible grimace, "and little girls too when they are obstinate; so not another word. Let go!"

"You said you were a vegetarian once. My father treated you well, and you stole two of his chickens. Where's your conscience?" Then loudly, "Father! father! help!"

"Catch that boy. I know him. There's a big village round the 'tail of the hill'!"

And but for that bit of hill tail, the ox-boy's shouts would have roused its denizens. He ran well, and his long-robed pursuers would not have caught him but for his tripping over the binding braid of one of his feet. Fallen, he still shouted.

Meanwhile, Fah had glided round the hill, possessed of sufficient presence of mind to reserve his own voice until he could whisper the news to his father. His education was progressing.

Seng-teh was gagged, and, as he continued to struggle, his hands were tied behind him, and he was set astride one of the bullocks. The party then made off, with many a glance behind them in the Hanyang direction. Not being pursued, the pedlar became jocular. "Those terrible 'Longhaired'! Even peaceable Taoists have to carry swords nowadays to protect themselves. Here's my charm. D'ye see, girl? Mind you don't feel it. The edge is sharp."

They made their own road, going as straight as possible, avoiding only villages, ponds, and paddy fields. Passing one of these latter, Seng-teh's bullock lost its foothold, and he tumbled over into the mud. Thus adorned, he was replaced on his steed to "dry in the sun." Spring forenoons may be very warm, and when the party had gone on for an hour or so, one of the Taoists took off his robe—to display beneath it a yellow sleeveless jacket trimmed with red, on breast and back of which was a large circular badge inscribed, "Perfect peace. Kingdom of heaven." The rest followed his example. And now Seng-teh began to realise the fact that he had been taken prisoner by the Longhaired.

As they neared a long serrated hill, that of the "Horse Saddle," the lad's gag was removed, and he was told he could shout as loud as he pleased. A turn of the road and a bit of rising ground brought them in view of the camp. The low walls were built of sun-dried brick, and the thatched huts of the same. The largest of these huts was neatly whitewashed; the largest banner waved over it. The camp was empty! But another step or two brought Seng-teh within view of a sort of raised threshing-floor, where knelt a hundred yellow jackets. In their midst, upon a square platform of dried brick, knelt one who was evidently their captain. He was uttering some sentences. He was praying. When all of a sudden the worshippers sprang to their feet, brandished their swords, and with a terrific emphasis, shouted the words, "*Sa Yao!*"

It might well frighten an older youth than the weary, worn-out captive,—the action was so sudden and simultaneous, and the words so unintelligible. Seng-teh guessed that the former sound was kill. But the second was as unknown to him as perhaps it has been to the reader. "Kill the fiends!" were the words of that unearthly yell, all the more unearthly to the terrified youngster because unintelligible. But the long jolting, the constrained position, and the lack of breakfast (eaten early in the country) had brought on a semi-dizziness, in which everything seemed an ugly dream.

"See," said the Taoist, pointing to the camp, "that is heaven, only the dragons wear yellow coats." The "dragons" did indeed crowd through the jade portals (hungry dragons through portals of mud brick) to where, within the immortality pill braziers (iron cooking-pans), they descried the material for the sustenance of their dragonship. Descrying ten bullocks approaching, they raised a shout of triumph, to which the ten cattle-stealers replied with the words, "Tribute! tribute!"

Having reached the camp, the Taoist went up to the captain's hut, and, bowing on one knee, said he had the required particulars, that the country folk, urged by rumours of the valour of the Heaven-king soldiers, had made various entrenchments on and around the Nine Recluses Hill, but that they were very friendly. He had talked them over, and had brought as proof thereof ten fine oxen! On this latter point he dwelt at some length in his voluble manner, urged thereto by sundry doubts as to the way in which the captain would take the presence of the bullock-tender.

Without deigning to reply, the captain went out to see the oxen. "Tribute, sire![1] tribute!" said the men, bowing on one knee.

"Hai Ya! a girl!" was his first exclamation, and that in a stentorian voice. "Who brought her here?"

"Thy Taoist, great official; but she is a boy."

"Come here, you child-stealer!" And the Taoist knelt and knocked his head on the ground. He had calculated on the captain having had his rice before they arrived. Hungry, he was inclined to be fierce.

"He clung to the oxen as we were bringing them away."

"Good; what then?"

"He tried to arouse the other villagers."

"One child against ten men! Go on!"

"We should have been caught."

"Serve *you* right if you had been. And so you have been stirring up trouble yonder. Go! Not you, boy. You come here with me. I am no child-stealer. Do you understand?"

"Yes, sire," said Seng-teh, adopting the term he had heard, and kneeling as he did so.

"You are muddy?"

"Yes, I had a tumble."

"The oxen are tribute?"

"Yes, sire," for he was afraid of committing the ten men, and so followed their phraseology.

"Then why did you resist?"

"Because they were my father's bullocks, and I was minding them." All this in a scared tone of voice, and tremblingly articulated.

[1] The term of address used was literally "Venerable sire," a usual term for an official. To this was sometimes prefixed the word Great. That used by the country folk, however, was "Kingly sire," which expression need not be multiplied throughout the chapter.

"Were they stolen then?"

"They were taken as tribute."

"Clever lad! Have you had your rice? Well, come and have it with me. Take off that girl's jacket. Here, fetch a small-sized coat if you have one. Quick!"

"What's this on your arm?"

"They bound me, great sire; but do not blame them. I struggled."

"The demons. I will bind them."

"Pray don't," said Seng-teh, dropping on his knees again.

"Good boy! Come and have rice."

Thus encouraged, Seng-teh put on the jacket provided, rolled up the superfluous sleeve ends, unplaited his queue, and did it up into a knot, which pleased his patron.

"What's your name?"

"Li Seng-teh. The *seng* of victorious and the *teh* of virtue." This explanation was necessary, for the first sound (according to Hanyang pronunciation) might have been Sacred, Extremely, Abundant, Cautious, Respectful, or Fragmentary according to the character. "A good name, and my surname is Li too. My name in the camp is 'Crouching Tiger.' But I won't eat you. Don't be afraid. Help yourself. Never tasted this before, eh? This is beef. Have as much wine as you like—to-day at anyrate. Never take any? All right, please yourself. It's medicine to me. I am a weak fellow, as the 'mandarin soldiers' know. Ha! ha! ha! This was a 'mandarin camp' once, and I took it. Kind of them to provide houses for us, wasn't it? Do you know this hill? The 'Horse Saddle.'"

"Yes, I know, the hill where Tsz-ki[1] is buried."

"Not far out! Who told you so? Your teacher? Then you can read?"

"Fairly."

"Well, you shall read to me in the evenings. I know a coolie pole character myself, but you shall read to me. Help yourself."

The morning meal over, Captain Li seemed to have

[1] Peh-ya's sympathetic listener.

grown wondrously good-natured, even to the world in general, and asked his young "kinsman," as he called him, how he liked the camp, and the Taipings generally—" not Longhaired, you know, that's a slander, but 'perfect peace men.'"

"Very well," replied the boy, "except perhaps the Taoist."

"Of course, the demon, bringing a bad name upon us. Have you seen him before?"

"Yes, he came round selling charms against—not you, but those he called the "—

"The Longhaired. Out with it. Did he use that word? It's well for him I have had my 'early rice.' He deserted us when we had taken Hankow. He used his coat to rob and intimidate folks. And so he sold charms? What sort?"

"Like these," pulling out the necklace.

"A good joke. The slimy rascal. Don't throw them away. Keep them to remind you of the Taoists and their tricks. Go on."

"He worked some miracles,—made a child invisible, so they said."

"Yourself, I suppose, they will say now. You country folks are easily taken in. But as you have been made invisible, you will stay with me until anyone comes to claim you. Be my son for a while. I had one like you, only not such a scholar. He was killed before my eyes, and his mother insulted and carried off. I was a countryman once down south. Those mandarin soldier demons! They will feel my sword yet. 'Evil has an evil retribution,' though the Buddhists and Taoists do say so. Look yonder. See that hill with the lamp on it, the 'Inverted Cooking-pan' they call it. There's our banner flying. We've given up Hanyang for a while to the 'fiend soldiers,'—the fiends are the idols, you know,—as a cat lets a mouse run off a few feet, or the tiger does a monkey. But the tiger is crouching all the while.

"We have several large camps the other side of the hill, and reinforcements are coming. What will the 'washed monkeys in men's hats' say to that? They can't win. They have no idols to pray to, no wood and mud dummies in men's hats. They will have to pray to paper ones. Their generals are 'paper tigers' themselves. Now read this" (producing a dog-eared book with some of the leaves turned down to mark the favourite passages).

Seng-teh took the book, and read, "I am your High Lord, the Imperial Sovereign on High; ye shall not make any 'death-deserving thing,' nor graven nor moulded thing, nor set up a spirit image, nor erect a stone tablet in your land, to bow down and worship. I am your Imperial Sovereign on High."

"Don't you quite understand it? Well, it is a Sacred Book,[1] and tells men not to make idols nor worship them. So

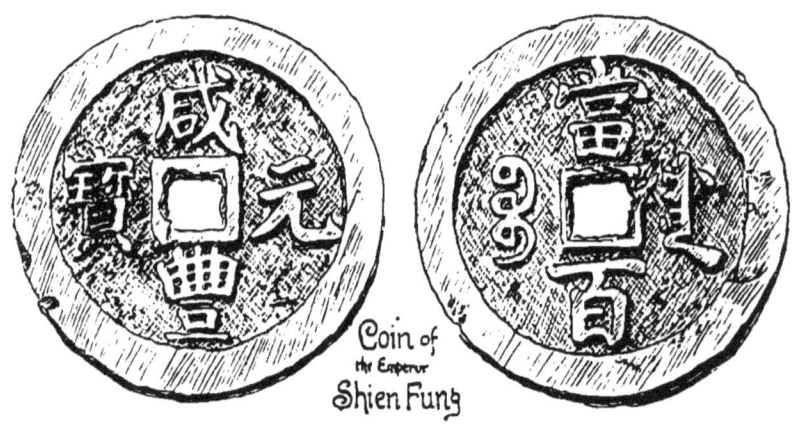

Coin of the Emperor Shien Fung

we melt down the bronze ones into cannon and cash, d'ye see? Look here at this big cash [producing one about two inches in diameter]. This means that even the monkey on the throne is short of copper. A cash is worth its weight in copper, you know. But this is marked on the back with two Manchu characters and in Chinese 'value 100.' Turn it over and you have 'Shien Fung original treasure.' Do you know what the name Shien Fung means?"

"General plenty," said Seng-teh.

"Everybody thought so when they gave it to him. But just split up the characters, and you have man 人, one 一, and weapon 戈, instead of universal; and two lords 主 主 on

[1] Seng-teh had been reading no other book than that of Leviticus (xxvi. 1) in the Taiping Bible.

a mountain 山 with beancurd 豆 underneath. Listen. I'll sing it to you," and in the usual heaven-aspiring, earth-dropping nasal drawl, he whined out—

> "See, every man has a halberd in hand.
> Two rival rulers the mountains demand.
> Founded on beancurd, how can the realm stand?"

It was a strange coincidence—the Chinese call it a prophecy—that the very auspicious characters chosen for the Emperor Shien Fung (1851–1862) should afford such awkward results on dissection. Such dissection can only be illustrated by our anagrams. "Napoleon," for instance, was discovered by an enraptured people to contain the words, *Napoleon, on, olcon, leon, eon, apoleon, poleon*,[1] "Napoleon, being the lion of his people, was marching on destroying the cities." "Victoria, England's Queen," as all true Britons ought to know, "governs a nice quiet land."

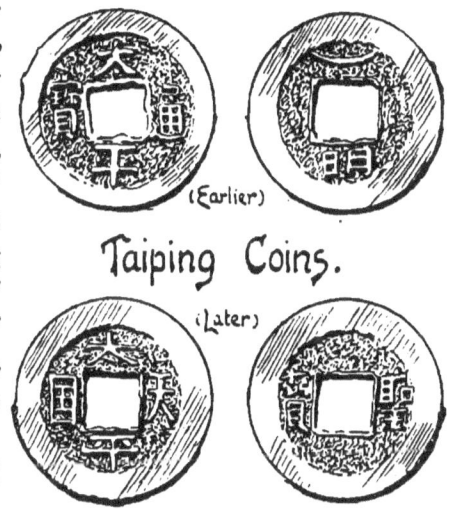

Taiping Coins.

"There is no resisting of Heaven's decree," continued the captain; "even the characters on the coins bear witness to it. Now, look at these coins; are they not bright and new? They are ours. Here is the first kind the Heaven-king issued. "Perfect peace, current treasure," on the face, and a moon-mark made by the Heaven-king's thumb-nail[2] on the back, which is"—

"The sun and moon, Ming," put in Seng-teh.

[1] Quoted by Rev. A. Smith in another connection.
[2] If this indeed be the origin of the moon-mark on the back of the earliest Taiping coins, the Heaven-king was following a precedent of 1130 years before. The story is that Yang Kwei-fei, the all-powerful favourite of the "Lustrous Emperor," Li Tan's second son, had a coin mould offered for her inspection, and left the mark of her thumb-nail on the wax. Coins thus marked during that reign are still current.

"Right you are! Now, this one, see what you make of this?"

"'Perfect peace, Heaven what?' Is that kingdom?"

"Yes, of course."

"But it is not written the ordinary way."

"No," laughed the captain. "The ordinary character for kingdom has a 'perhaps' inside the enclosure. Ordinary kingdoms don't last. Ours will. It has a 'king' inside the enclosure. Now, the other side?"

"Sacred treasure."

"Right again, because the Heaven-king rules on behalf of heaven."

"Then is this the *Celestial Book* which our teacher told us that the Heaven-king had given him by an old man in a cave?"

"I don't know about any old man in a cave; but this is part of the *Celestial Book*, sure enough. There are a lot of volumes. Some have a bit of commentary. This was the earliest. I have only this one volume, worse luck. It came from the West. Wonderful place the West. Now read on over here."

Seng-teh read the words: "I will destroy your stagings and trees, cut down your sun images, casting your corpses upon the corpses of your false gods, and in my heart reject you. And I will destroy your cities [that they become] a wilderness, and will sweep into desolation your sacred places, and not receive your smoking incense."

"There! we are preaching that to the enemy. You have heard about the Hanyang monastery? Very good. Well we are destroying all the 'mud-moulded and wood-carved things.' But we like bronze better. I am a great fellow for bronze. It was bronze that lifted me from the ranks— Well, what is it?" This latter in a stentorian voice to a soldier who stood in the doorway.

"Drums and gongs in the camp yonder."

"Silence all!"—a veritable tiger roar. "How can one hear with that racket going on? All right. Only drilling. You do the same." Then softly to Seng-teh, "Don't you think I can shout?" None but the totally deaf would have denied it. The lad had already replied with a very decided start at the first " opening of the mouth."

Seng-teh was left in charge of the camp, with instructions not to steal a certain bronze cannon, a special pet of the captain's, and from between the battlements he had a good view of the performance. The men filed out of the camp and fell into line on what had been the prayer-ground. Trumpets sounded. Orders were given. Drums and gongs began to complicate matters. Marches and counter-marches were performed. Flags and banners waved and wheeled in very great number. (In later days the most terrible thing about many a camp of red-jacketed coolies is the bunting displayed. A camp of ten small huts has been known to display as many as eighteen large flags besides a number of small pennants.) The flags were triangular, red with a white scolloped edge. They had mostly been taken from the enemy and altered to suit Taiping requirements. The red meant victory, the white the alternative—death, as the captain explained afterwards.

After the other manœuvres, several of the soldiers took up long bamboo poles and shook them about with many a contortion, thrusting at imaginary enemies until each was tired out; then others took up the poles and repeated the performance, the drums beating all the while. Then came exercises with swords; defiant (though very theatrical) attitudes were assumed. No powder was wasted, and Seng-teh noted that, besides the captain's pet cannon, there were only a few smaller ones of iron, taking a ball of an inch and a half diameter, heaps of which, roughly cast in iron, lay on either side.

The captain came back calling for refreshments, which proved to consist almost entirely of wine warmed in a pewter pot. " Now for the history of my pet cannon," he said. " We came up to a city in Hunan, and found there on the walls eighteen soldiers holding banners. We shot and shot, until the flags were torn to ribbons. But the men would not die. They did not fire upon us, but just stood there. We stormed the walls, I led, and what do you think we found ? They were bronze *lohans*. The ' small

Idols guarding a City.

gall-bladder babies' had hid, and left the *lohans* to guard the walls. We had lost a lot of ammunition, for the images were dressed up in red, to imitate soldiers, and the smoke prevented us from seeing whether the first eighteen had fallen, and others taken their places or not. The 'babies' ran out of the opposite gate, and the *lohans* went into the melting-pot, to come out much improved for their hot bath. This is half of one of them.

"I like you. You must call me father. Say it. That's right. Now go outside and fetch me some more wine."

The lad did as he was bid, shouting, "Cook! the great official wants some wine warmed, and be quick about it."

"That's the tune. 'Great official' sounded well. 'Some,' not 'more,' was well put. And the hurrying up put the button on the cap. You will make a general some day. You must have one cup."

It was taken with much coughing.

At length it seemed to be nearing the time for afternoon rice, for the captain had begun to fire volley upon volley at the Taoist and his nine fellow-robbers. A distant trumpet sound interrupted him. It was a wonder he heard it. The trumpeters of his own camp took up their very brazen-sounding instruments and blew a like blast.

At this the men arranged their apparel, one or two letting down the hair to do it up in a neater knot. And, smartening themselves up generally, proceeded to file out of the camp towards the flat piece of ground.

The captain having adjusted his attire and taken his last look in the glass, told Seng-teh to bring the yellow-covered Sacred Book, and prepare to read the chapter he had glanced over in the morning. "Put plenty of voice into it. Then we shall sing, then I pray, and then we shout. You heard us this morning."

Yes, the lad had certainly heard, but had hardly connected the war-whoop with worship. He was now to assist in the ceremony, if not in the practical application of the whole. The men had already formed themselves into a hollow square, facing the raised earthen platform. To say that the country boy did not feel the awful power of the eyes which every-

A TAIPING CAMP. 247

where confronted him would be to make him more than
human. His heart beat rather wildly as he found himself
within the square. But the captain having given an un-

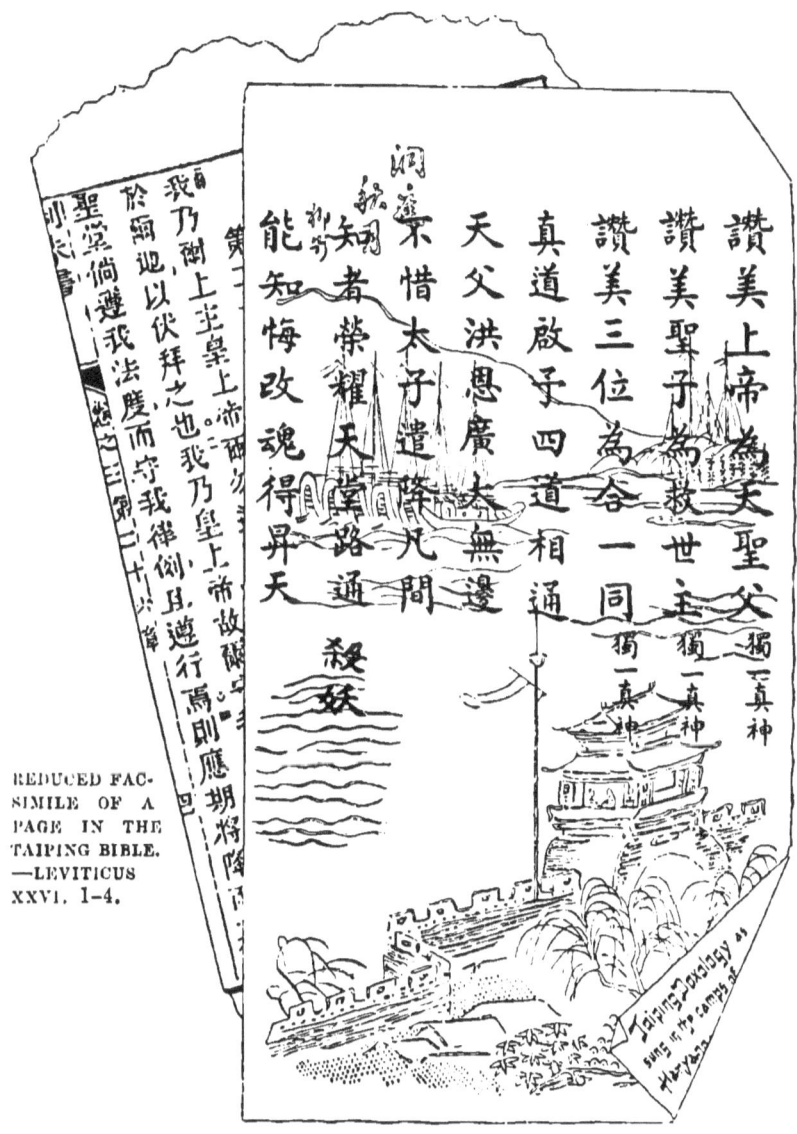

REDUCED FAC-
SIMILE OF A
PAGE IN THE
TAIPING BIBLE.
—LEVITICUS
XXVI. 1-4.

necessary order for silence, said, "My adopted son will read
out of the Sacred Book," and with growing clearness he read
in childish treble Leviticus xxvi. One thought crossed his
mind: "The Taoist would not listen to my poem the other

night. He has to listen now to words about his idols as well as those of the Buddhists." But he kept his eye upon the book in case he should see the man in question. He felt all the more afraid of him now he had been the innocent cause of his disgrace. The chapter over, understood perhaps by few, the soldiers, with noisy vociferation, sang—

The Early Doxology of the Taipings.

"Praise God, the Holy Father of Heaven—the only true Spirit.
Praise the Holy Son, the Saviour of the world—the only true Spirit.
Praise the Three Persons, united in one—the only true Spirit.
The truth is proclaimed to us, the way is everywhere open.
The Heavenly Father's flood-like grace, immense and illimitable,
Spared not the Imperial Son, but sent Him down to mortal regions;
When men know this glory, the Heavenly road is open.
When men repent, their spirit shall ascend to Heaven."

Then all knelt, at first in silence, until Captain Li read a prayer out of a well-worn book. It was addressed to "The Heavenly Sire" and to the "Holy Mother."[1] He prayed for pardon in the words, "We sinners pray the Father to forgive us our sins." The last sentence was, "We obey the Heavenly decree to slaughter the fiends."

Then all sprang to their feet, brandished their swords, and shouted, "Kill the fiends!" And so the worship ended.

The captain returned in silence to the camp, Seng-teh walking with him, and the men following in a somewhat irregular manner. The worship seemed to have a temper-subduing effect upon Seng-teh's patron, as far as little things are concerned, but seemed to fill him with a very rage against unrighteousness. Hungry, he was irritable; having prayed, his irritations seemed swallowed up in a consuming passion against idols and their priestly or official worshippers. He hurled an anathema glance against the Taoist as he turned to

[1] The phrase "Holy Mother" marks the beginning of unchristian importations into the Taiping phraseology, for it does not refer to Mary, though perhaps suggested by Roman Catholic usage. The being thus addressed is supposed to be God's wife! Already in other camps the hymn had become corrupted, the titles of the rebel leaders being blasphemously substituted for the Divine names. Eventually, the Christian element was ousted by such blasphemy.

find him smiling during the reading, and it would have been bad for him had the captain lingered.

"Well done, my son!" he exclaimed as they reached his hut. "But no thanks to the slimy fellow who brought you. Have you another father? Well, try and forget him until he comes to claim you. Where shall I go to claim my son, my own boy? He has 'ascended to heaven.' He was a good lad. The cursed fiends! You are my son to-day. Well done, I say." And as the meal was being brought in, he produced from a box a sheet of decorated letter paper on which was written the hymn they had just sung. "Take yonder pen and write two characters underneath, the two words, 'Kill [the] fiends.' There now, it is complete. And if you have to go, never you bow down to them. Promise me."

"I promise," said Seng-teh fervently, for he had been impressed with the service, and had taken colour from his surroundings.

The captain began by handling his chopsticks in a somewhat fierce manner. "The literary mandarins," he said, when his mouth was free enough for articulation, "are 'turbid eggs promoted eight steps'; the military mandarins are just paper tigers, or rather dogs. 'Draw a tiger badly, and you have a dog.' Paper dogs who worship wood and mud. We will see that they have no bronze to worship. Bronze is meant for cash. Well, they all worship that.

"But I will tell you a tale about idol gods. There was once a man who went off to the O Mei mountain, a celebrated **An Idol Apprentice.** place in Szchwan for temples. He went in order to learn how to lead a lazy life, with plenty to eat and to spend, and so apprenticed himself to one of the great idols of the place, who told him to carry water for the temple for a year.

"The year over, the idol told him he must work yet another year. Now, what the man ought to have done was to have got a fellow-apprentice. The proverb says, 'One monk, two buckets of water [he carries two, you know]: two monks, one bucket of water [they carry a pail between them]; three monks, no water at all [each leaves it to the other.)' He carried for a second year and a third, then refused to do so any more.

"'What! after only three years? Such folk as you must go on for thirty, before their store of merit is complete.' At which he realised that the idol was making game of him. He then pleaded that he was short of cash.

"'Well, take the two handles of the temple doors and go!'

"'What use are they?'

"'Oh, the first is called, After-this-never-pay-your-debts, and the second, Never-pay-at-all. Thus you will be able to get on without work.' He declined the rings.

"'Well, then, I will give you my bookshelves.'"

"'What good are they? I cannot read, and do not mean to learn.'

"Oh, they are called the Library of Lies; the books will teach you how to deceive.'

"The man turned away in disgust, but the idol called out after him, 'Go to the god of riches, and ask him for help.'

"He accordingly went, and was encouraged by seeing an ingot of silver in the idol's hand. But the reply was disappointing. 'Yes, I have an ingot here, but it is like you. It is worthless and empty, and will only be firm [or stiff] when you are firm [or stiffened] in death.'

"Baffled here, he was recommended to go and appeal to the door god[1] pictures. 'They are gaily clothed enough,—a sure sign of wealth. Ask them for money.' But the two pictures replied that their clothing was only paint, and suggested that he should go and supplicate the god of literary honours. 'He is standing on one leg, as if leaping for joy. No doubt he is well off.'

"The man went, but was met with the reply, 'I happy?

---

[1] The door god pictures represent two brothers of old time, who had the power of summoning all the ghosts before them under a certain peach tree, binding those who had wrought evil with withes of reed and giving them as food to tigers. So in old time the officials on the last night of the year had their figures cut on peach wood mounted on reeds, and painted the likeness of a tiger on the doorways as a talisman against evil (see Mayers). The tiger head still survives on all official buildings, the reeds at the doorways of houses in the fifth month festival and the door god pictures at the new year. The Romans had their gods of doors and thresholds, Forculus and Limentinus.

I well off? The rascally idol-makers have forgotten to give me my other leg. You may consider yourself lucky to possess two. Get along with you.'

"He then went to beseech the deified tortoise and snake, but had not time to get out even the word 'lend' when the tortoise popped in its head, and the snake glided off.

"Baffled all round, he returned to his master, who said, 'Lazy fellows like you will be always in want to the very end.'

"That's just the thing, to the 'very bottom.' Good, isn't it?" And both laughed heartily.

Next morning Seng-teh was up betimes, his "father" still snoring like an amateur thunder god. He opened the door, and went softly out, looking about him. He was challenged by the sentinel in what seemed to him a harsh tone of voice. "They are jealous of me," was the thought; but the momentary semi-submission changed to an attitude more worthy of his standing. "The high official wants a cup of tea," he replied, and repeated the same in a louder tone at the door of the cook's quarters.

The man emerged with a yawn, rubbed his eyes, took up his flint and steel, and with a few blows ignited the paper spill held close to the stone, puffed that into a flame (a simple operation to all but foreigners), set light to a bundle of dried grass with a few twigs of wood above, which proved to be damp, and had therefore to be encouraged into ignition by vigorous fanning from beneath with a worn circular palm leaf fan. The red unglazed kettle was one of those in which the flame is allowed to come up through a tube in the midst of the water,—an early Chinese ancestor of our modern tubular boiler,—and very soon the water was near boiling.

With regard to boiling water, as in many other things, the Chinese motto is "Not far out," as every resident knows. Moreover, the modern cook holds his pet doctrine concerning the after history of that water. Once having boiled, it is ever regarded as boiling water. There is unconscious science in the matter, however. Pond water not raised to boiling point has been proved to be harmful,—the Chinaman hardly ever drinks cold water,—but once having boiled, it is regarded (not by our modern sewage commissioners and water analysts but) by the Chinese as drinkable. Seng-teh took the large covered cup in his hand, and entered, to find the captain sitting up and (under the influence of the "bedding demon," through whom comes any early "crossness") delivering his soul in an irritated tone of voice, which changed at once as he saw the tea.

"That's right, my son; you have been well trained. 'Filial piety is the head of all the virtues.' The lazy rascals never bring tea till I swear at them. Now tell the cook to bring three hot sugar cakes." This being done, he added, "These are scald-the-back cakes, do you know? Never heard of it? Well, when a man bites hard, the melted sugar inside runs on to his coat at the elbow, then he lifts his elbow to lick it off. Ohoo! The sugar has run down his back. Take one and try." The directions being followed, and the desired result obtained, due commendations resulted.

<small>Scald-the-back Cakes</small>

The captain had hardly dressed, that is, arranged the garments in which he had slept, when a soldier came to say that a countryman besought the favour of an audience. A man was seen approaching the door, where he fell upon his face. His clothing was poor, and his head tied up with a black cloth, a sign of illness.

"What is it?" roared the captain.

"Kingly official," wept the man, at the sound of whose voice Seng-teh exclaimed, "Father!"

"Is that you?" gasped the suppliant.

The captain looked from one to the other and said, "Stand aside, guards. Get up, man, and come in."

Without moving, the man related that he was a poor man, and that he once had four sons, but the three elder ones had been killed at Hanyang by the honourable Taipings. "They ought not to have resisted heavenly virtue, but they did, and died for it. I have only this one lad left."

"Is that so, boy?" asked the captain.

"It is," replied Seng-teh, for Chinese filial piety often forbids a son to be more truthful than his parent.

"Then you had better let him stay and help the cause of

heavenly virtue. We are mild as children toward country folk, but it is death to resist us. Hit us, and we will strike back."

"Alas, I am so often poorly, and times are so hard."

"Were the ten oxen yours?"

"I respectfully present them; but give me back my son, my only remaining son."

"You are generous, being so poor; but Seng-teh is my adopted son, and I will teach him to tell the truth."

"He is indeed my only son."

"I believe that. And I believe you like him. I will not keep more than one of the oxen, and I will give him up —my own son was slaughtered by the demons, you know— I will give him up upon one condition."

"A thousand conditions, kingly official."

"The condition is, that you speak the truth. Can you do that?"

"Of course."

"I believe that's a lie like the rest of your tale. Very poor country folk don't dress up their *little girls* in good clothes while they go in rags. Nor do they buy whole necklaces of peach-stone charms. Charms indeed! As though we were blind devils," and he pulled Seng-teh's string of peach-stones from under his jacket. "You see I make him wear them to help him believe in Taoists and idols. I know how much you gave for them. I know they were carved in T'saitien by a rascally chicken-stealer—chicken-stealer, I repeat, and general thief, who sold his yellow coat to another thief, that he too might bring disgrace upon us by his robberies. I know everything. Now, what is the name of your tea-shop keeper?"

Li hesitated a moment, and said, "Lieu Fuh-t'ang."

"Truth after due compulsion. There's no deceiving me. And I know that a certain Li Sung-sen is the richest man of those parts. Do you know him?"

"A myriad pardons, kingly official, but not rich. Taxes and floods!"

"Yes, taxes paid to the wood and mud worshippers, potatoes in mandarin hats; and floods sent as a retribution from heaven. And we come to your help, and your sons resist heavenly virtue, and get killed. How many of them? Ah, you may well be silent. You don't deceive the Crouching Tiger; that's my name, I can see in the dark. I can roar, and I can show my claws when needed. But stand up, man; a father should not kneel while his son stands. You meant well, only such things won't do in the kingdom of heaven. I only want to frighten deceivers into trustworthy men. You are right at heart, and your son does you credit. Do you want him? Well, I am no child-stealer or bullock-stealer either. We are friends with all who will be friends, and the country folk like us and send us tribute. Come outside a minute. Look, there are the fishing-boats on the lake and the farmers in their fields. Ask them how they like us.[1] Now come in and sit down. Pardon my roughness. You tried to disguise your condition, and I dealt with you accordingly. Seng-teh, call for tea."

All was politeness at once. Li's suspicions were disarmed, and he spoke out his thanks for the kindness his son had evidently received.

"What idol do you worship?" asked the captain at length. "I used to worship them once."

"I have not worshipped any lately; our village teacher does not believe in them."

"Sensible man! but what does he worship?"

"I do not know. He believes in Heaven's decree."

"So do we. But we worship too. You will see us. We worship the Sovereign on High [the term translated God in the hymn of the Taipings]. But don't you worship the big idol on the hill-top? You know who he was, I suppose. A robber, I hear. Is that not so?"

"Yes," said Li, "but one who stole from the rich to give to the poor."

"Then if I had lived in his time, they would have made a god of me, which I shouldn't like. I'd rather be a captain here. But what is he made of?"

"His body is more than half bronze, but the image was

---

[1] Such a question put nowadays to the old men elicits but one answer, "They were *very* good to us when they first came, *very* good."

old and was broken in moving. Anyhow the rest of him is of wood."

"Call the Taoist!" roared the captain. He was brought, and with head hung down was thrust into the official's quarters. "Bow down, you rascal," and the Taoist fell on his knees. "What is the big idol on the Nine Recluses Hill made of?"

"I have heard, great official, that he is bronze. He is big enough for several cannon."

"Who said I needed cannon? Now, if that bit of bronze is not here by to-morrow morning to be cast into cash, I will brand you as a spy. Another word and your head shall fall! Go! Look after that wretch"—to the soldiers. "No, call him back. You will have to conduct a party there this morning and fetch it."

"Great official," cried the man in real terror, "it can only be brought by water, and I only know the 'dry road.' The lakes wind about so."

"And I wouldn't trust you. But if it is not forthcoming"— The sentence was ended with a suggestive wave of the hand. "Go. Now I want thirty volunteers."

While they were being collected, the captain said, "Your 'great king' as you call him, would have been a Taiping if he were alive; and it is only fair that he should be allowed to help us to save the people now. Don't you think so?"

Li thought it best to reply, "Yes."

"Will you lead the party? When you return, your son will go back with you, and all ten bullocks, if you like. Nine? Well, then, nine."

The thirty having presented themselves, the captain said, "On the Nine Recluses Hill is a temple, and in it a large idol made of bronze, that is, part of it. My friend here, Seng-teh's father, will be your guide. Take two large boats with sails, and bring it back to-night. Don't rouse the country folk. Don't bring a bad name upon us. The idol, nothing else. Death to the fiends!" The last words accompanied by a blow which smashed the top of the tea-poy near. When they had retired, he said to Li, "My tiger cubs will be mild as lambs unless they are attacked. But if the country folk attempt violence, they will show their teeth in self-defence. You understand?"

Just then the trumpets sounded for morning worship. Seng-teh explained the ceremony to his father, and told him they were indeed going to worship the Sovereign on High.

"May I come too?" he inquired. The undertaking before him seemed to need some help. He hardly liked the thought of it. But his son; he must have his son.

He had a place appointed him at an angle of the square, where he devoutly wished he had come in more respectable attire. He had been over-persuaded by a neighbour or two against his better judgment. His heart leaped as he saw and heard his boy read so well, standing beside the captain, who had thoroughly gained his respect. He had never seen more than one or two persons worship idols at once, and the silence of the men during the reading, and especially the silence when kneeling, impressed him. Nor had the singing grated on his ears. It had seemed sublime. It was in praise of the Sovereign on High. He wished he had known the words. Perhaps Seng-teh would teach him. But Nieh Shen-seng, what would he say? The captain, however, began to repeat the customary prayer. Li did not grasp it all. Nor was he prepared for the sudden climax.

The morning meal was really a happy time. His son was there before his eyes, and the captain was genial. "There is just one thing I like about one idol of China.

The Forbearance of the Thunderer.

The thunder god never interferes with a man's rice. Even if he determines to strike the unfilial, he always allows the man to empty his bowl first." Then the subject of country alarmists came up, and what harm they did to the "cause of heaven." Li, however, promised to do his best to make matters right in his neighbourhood. He assented almost cheerfully to the arrangement that Seng-teh should stay behind till he came back, and went off with the thirty men, who had turned their coats inside out so as not to needlessly alarm the villagers. The blue lining would not look suspicious at a distance. Their hair was done up in a knot at the back instead of on the top, which would look more like the country fashion. But each carried a muzzle-loading gun and a sword. " Only," as the captain commanded in his parting words, " for self-defence. Bring back the idol. That will be good. Bring it back without firing a shot. That will be better still."

It was a merry party. Three soldiers rowed in each boat, the rest helped with their swords, and as there was hardly any wind, they whistled in hope of coaxing the breeze (a general custom). Once fairly started, they struck up a ditty chanted by the youngsters in those parts, beginning, " Our black hen lays white eggs." Then " *Keh keh ta* "—to represent the cackling of the bird—" *Yih ko tan* " (one " piecee " egg) from the right. Then " *Keh keh ta* " in unison, and " *Liang ko tan* " from the left, and so on up the numbers, with increasing difficulty to the tongue, and loud laughter at the mistakes made.

Li had resolved not to take the party all the way to his native village by water, but to land them on the other side of the hill, so that they might proceed without much observation, and that he himself should not be seen by Lieu and company. What slight forebodings he had were being dispelled by the high spirits of the party, with whom he already felt very much at home, though every stroke of the oars was bringing nearer to his home the once-dreaded " Longhaired."

Chapter XII.

The Longhaired have Come!

TEA-SHOP AND HILL-TOP—A TUSSLE WITH THE TAIPINGS—
NO NEED FOR HIRED MOURNERS.

"Our endeavours have hitherto been resisted by force, like many other good things are on earth."—*From a Taiping Proclamation.*

The anxiety caused by Seng-teh's disappearance may be imagined. On his father's own feelings previous to his starting for the camp to try and recover him, we need not dwell. They belong to our past tense. But here was material for a very big wolf cry, taken up indeed by the whole countryside. No one had seen the wolf, for Lieu, on receipt of the news his son brought, bound him on oath not to tell, and, to prevent him breaking his oath, kept him under his eye the whole morning. So that a search party did not start until the cattle-stealers had taken oxen and ox-boy a long way on their journey. The oxen had been seen from afar, and ten men, also a small figure upon one of the beasts. So the case became clear at length.

Lieu received the news as news, but had already matured his plans, which consisted in stirring up the country folk to an armed resistance, should another band of rebels appear. In order to further this, he would "stand treat" that day. He could not afford to receive "Longhaired" visitors, with the Taoist for leader, and perhaps a transmogrified *yamun* runner or two in the band. He knew well enough that the country folk had little to fear, and that Seng-teh would

THE LONGHAIRED HAVE COME! 259

probably be released. He knew that cattle-stealing was not a general custom among the Taipings, but it did not suit his purpose to whitewash those he had already done his best to blacken into incarnate demons.

Arrayed in a respectable coat, and wearing a silk hat too, he harangued the crowds who assembled. The wine helped

his words down, and those who filled his tea-shop were mostly at his beck and call.

That night he and his son were busy burying sundry ingots of silver and various "black goods" (stolen property), which had accumulated in various boxes kept locked, and even nailed up, in his own inner room. The fact was, that in his journeys to Hanyang he had formed the acquaintance of a nest of robbers. Hence his extreme hospitality, and, behind the scenes, his generosity to the tax-collectors when they came. They were more or less in his secrets.

Our system of setting an honest policeman or detective to capture thieves has never found favour in China. It is a thankless task. Has not our own Milton declared that—

Set a Thief to Catch a Thief.

> "Neither man nor angel can discern
> Hypocrisy, the only evil that walks
> Invisible, except to God alone"?

That being so, argue the Chinese, who, without such a definite statement of the case, have a big volume of experience from which to quote, the only alternative is to set those most versed in hypocrisy, the friends of robber hypocrites, rather than men chosen from the generality, to catch the robbers. So in this mundane universe (the Empire of China) rascals are set to catch rascals, and in the lower world (moulded after the pattern of China) demons are set to catch demons. Just as our spectroscopists have proved that the composition of the heavenly bodies is very similar to that of earth, so the Chinese, through dark spectacles and dream-glasses, have proved to their own satisfaction that the spirit world is constructed upon the model of the Middle Kingdom, with its mandarins open to bribery, and their underlings carefully balancing their gains with their pains, with a definite price for every hundred blows, and the certain apprehension of the offender when no more money is forthcoming. The machinery is marvellously complete. Every criminal is known. Granted sufficient force to work the machinery, every criminal is caught. What better system could the gods devise?

As rebel soldiers, the underlings could not easily be bought off; and the Taoist—an actual fact—that very morning had surely known that his yellow coat would enable the man to whom he had sold it to indulge in his thievish propensities.

But at length the gains from that source were, with the rest, hidden underground, and if the country folk would only resist, no rebel need come near. In the morning, therefore, he sent round to the villages saying that the Taoist had proved to be a spy, that it was he who had led a band of "Longhaired" to take away Li's cattle, his son, and perhaps the man himself; and that they might be expected any moment with a larger band to commit worse atrocities. He advised them, therefore, to have a heap of fuel in readiness, so as to be lit whenever they should see a suspicious looking party approaching. Then perhaps they had better run to his shop, and make it a rallying place. He had a few ironshod coolie poles which might be useful, but they had better bring their own. The advice was taken by the folks on both sides of the hill, and on each peak a heap of fuel was collected, so as to warn the whole neighbourhood. Signal fires had been in use from ancient days. They would revive the custom to-day, if needed. So that before noon everything was in readiness, even to the wine so generously supplied by Lieu to all comers.

Alone on the highest peak of the hill, in the now solitary temple, the feelings of the priest-monk were not enviable. He had for long been subject to nervous terrors. He missed his little apprentice. He was not a thoughtful man, and he had in former times been well content to vegetate on the hill-top between the excitements of an occasional visitor. He had learned to pass many an hour with hardly any thought, certainly without any mental exercise. The art of thinking about nothing at all seems easily learned by many a man of his class. Buddhism has idealised it into a virtue; in this case such virtue seemed to be the path of nature. No tastes, no pursuits, no particular business, no anxieties; a paradise of negation was his in recent days. But now, his young helper removed, for his parents feared the rebels more than the gods, he had to do everything for himself; and after the recent excitements, he began to talk to himself, and found himself to be bad company. The wheel of doctrine was a phrase, a mere phrase known to him; a revolving wheel of terror was now the fact of his mental life. The customers had fallen off, and even the visitors of late. But now the startling news of the "Longhaired" having penetrated to the very foot of the hill, set the wheel revolving at a frightful speed. His days were misery, his nights dream-haunted; an alarming state of things to a man used to vegetating on, in full hopes, too, of continuing to pass his life in that happily negative state.

It did not occur to him to pray to the many idols over which he had charge. He rang the bell, beat the drum, and lit the incense night and morning—that was all. "I never worship idols," said one of his class in later years. "Why are you here, shaven and shorn?" was the inquiry. "A man must live," was the all-sufficient reply.

Yes, a man must live, but how can he continue to do so with any, even of the most negative, comfort; with the idol-destroying, and, if report be true, priest-slaying Longhaired within sight? Their flag it was upon the Horse Saddle Hill, and to-day they might be expected. It could not be. The temple was as solitary as ever. Bees and butterflies hovered as usual. The copse around the temple was vocal with the most peaceful warblings and twitterings. But what meant that heap of fuel prepared at the command of the messenger who came with the dawn? And what meant the layman jacket and trousers he had bought of Lieu? And what meant his beating heart and throbbing temples? Anon he found himself standing before an old weather-worn red stone grave tablet, which he had at his leisure chipped away to something like thinness. It covered an old rabbit-hole, which, at the first alarm, he had hollowed out until it was large enough to secrete a man. The grave stone served to cover the entrance.

From between the trees he looked out over the familiar landscape, but what was that he saw? A column of smoke! And in front of it, coming straight for the hill, a band of men whose step seemed to savour of the camp. They passed another village, and, as they left it behind, another column rose. Was he dreaming? No, it seemed real, and with palpitating heart he clutched his beads and passed them through his fingers. He had often done that mechanically when visitors were in sight. Now, for the first time in his life, he breathed a fervent, a feverish *O-Mi-To-Fuh*,[1] as each bead slipped by.

[1] The Chinese transliteration of the Sanscrit word Amitâ (Buddha), which is part of Amitâbas and Amitâyus, the names of the Buddha who presides over

THE LONGHAIRED HAVE COME! 263

But his waking nightmare was interrupted by a voice which startled him into action, "The Longhaired have come! Quick! Light your fire!" Having said which the man disappeared as suddenly as he came.

He hurried up to the temple platform and saw the country folk on the inner side of the hill hurrying toward its base. He guessed it was toward the Yang Family Pavilion; but that village was out of sight by reason of an intervening peak, over which he saw the messenger of a moment back hurrying as if for dear life. He grew dizzy. His head swam. He

the Western Paradise. For a transliterated untranslated Christian term compare our Hallelujah.

managed with difficulty to take off his priest's garb and put on the ordinary jacket and drawers. He could not find his flint and steel, but at length broke off a piece from the spiral of smoking incense, and with trembling hands applied it to a spill. He could hardly puff it into flame. It was lit at last. And there by the stove was the pot of oil, with the help of which his vegetables were usually cooked. When would he have his next meal, he wondered?

He hurried out, and nearly stumbled in his haste, emptied the pot of oil upon the heap, blew up the spill once more with some difficulty, and set the twigs on fire. Then a scared look all round. More fires, the band of Longhaired evidently at the foot of the hill, perhaps to appear over yon peak before he had reached his hiding-place. A sound behind him! It was only several birds taking flight together as the breeze blew the smoke over to their tree. He thought *they* had come. Was he still free to hide? It seemed so. And he managed to squeeze himself into the enlarged rabbit-hole, and to adjust the grave stone. But his heart-beats sounded to him like the thud, thud of an army of Longhaired doubling along in search of him. His beads were wet and clammy, but they were passing between his fingers and thumb at such a rate that the hard skin was like to be worn thin. The hand that held them was getting cramped. But there! A sound which forced them into greater speed. The silent *O-Mi-To-Fus* became an audible moan. It was only a rabbit trying to find its home. There would be louder sounds in a few moments.

There were sounds of firing! A bang, then another, then several together. Confused shouts were heard, shouts from voices which seemed familiar. And above the confusion rose the words, "The 'mandarin soldiers' are coming. Death to the Longhaired." The tramping of feet came nearer; it seemed to shake the hill. A general rush, and, as the heavy feet passed, more shouts, "The 'mandarin soldiers' are coming. Death to the Longhaired."

The temple was invested, but it was by the villagers. The sounds of firing became more evident, the bangs more irregular but louder; it was but a ruse. The artillery consisted of Lieu's loud squibs, such as are used at weddings. An excellent ruse; for see, the thirty Longhaired stood at bay upon a small protuberance just below the temple. And in their midst was Li,—Li who had brought them there,— trying to make his voice heard. They hated the Longhaired, but, filled with wine as most of them were, they now hated Li still more. The native who acts as guide to a "foreign devil" is often regarded as a more hateful, because "traitor," devil himself.

Li kept vociferating, and they shouting, " The 'mandarin soldiers' are coming," but that cry seemed to lose its novelty. Why did not the Imperialists come? Because the loud banging squibs were nearly all gone. The three hundred villagers would have to fight. The Longhaired waited with provoking calmness for either the Imperialists to arrive or for them to begin the fight.

The bangs ceased. The cry was now for a moment, "The Imperialists have come!" and every head turned round. But no signs of them to the eyes of the thirty men yonder, and no explanation of their waste of powder and shot.

Again Li tried to make himself heard. He waved his hand in signs for them to go back. "Go back? What? And let the Longhaired capture the temple, to swoop down upon us at any time." Li had been all along a traitor in disguise. He was trying to save his land at the price of theirs. They showered a volley of curses upon him. See if he will gesticulate now! A slight movement among the Longhaired. They were loading. Each man picks up a stone—the largest to be found. One has been thrown. It has not gone far enough. Another has fallen at the feet of one of the rebels, who turns to Li, and says, what those of the temple cannot hear, "You bear us witness, we are attacked." The lambs are beginning to turn very tiger cubs. They came up the hill in high spirits. They are beginning to feel enraged.

No need to appeal to Li for witness; an ironshod coolie pole comes flying down like a boomerang. The point has wounded Li. No use to ask him to bear witness. He is insensible. He is bleeding. At the sight of blood, and the gyrating coolie poles, and the great stones, which now fell thick and fast, the order is given to "Fire!" and then "Charge!"

Thirty muskets discharge their contents. Several villagers fall, the rest flee into the temple, for the path down the hill is narrow and exposed. The front porch of the temple is set on fire for protection. There is a large courtyard behind. "Seize a burning brand, each of you. The Longhaired have come." They had scaled the steep rock. They are at the door. They cannot enter. It is burning. But they can fire through the flames. To right and left, every man of you. Over the parapet, those who dare, and attack them from the side. A hundred leap down, not without a tumble or two. They are up on their feet. A coolie pole poised as a spear is thrown. A Longhaired falls. Now rush on and engage them at close quarters, ye hundred or more. Break down the shrubs and belabour them with your poles. They are too close to fire. A butt end against ten coolie poles. A general struggle, now forward, now backward, now by the signal fire. Wrestling and struggling, and several fall over on to the embers. Then up again, coolie poles and butt ends, stones from behind, which wound several villagers. All is confusion, curses, and death-blows.

But the Longhaired have taken the temple, fifteen or more of them. They fire. Several fall. Charge them, throw your poles and stones. They fire again. Run for your lives. The fugitives are stopped by reinforcement from farther villages; a band has entered the temple from behind. One or two more Longhaired fall. Fire, ye Longhaired, and flee through the blazing porch; clamber down the rocks. The rising ground is reached. One of the men has fallen upon Li. Up again. He is dying; leave him there, and back all that are left of us to the camp. The sun is low in the West. The fight has taken some hours. There are only ten of us left. The "Crouching Tiger" will roar!

The copse was flaming. The villagers must try and save the main part of the temple by cutting down the trees near, and by bringing buckets of water up from the well, a hundred yards down the hill, to throw it over the exposed woodwork.

The gilded face of the "great king" shone out with a diabolical smile as it reflected the glare. It was otherwise nearly dark. The twilight is short in these parts. And now the temple lanterns were taken down, fitted with the candles kept on the table before the large idol, and the wounded were attended to, the Longhaired beheaded with their own swords, the rest carried home on easily detatched temple door shutters. As the last man was leaving the temple, he turned to the idol and cried, "You mean wretch, after all we have spent on you, not to protect us." And no one criticised the utterance.

The voices and footsteps having died away, the priest thought he might emerge. His hands were badly blistered, for a burning branch had fallen upon the thin slab. His long terror had made him unconscious of a little pain. He crept along by the light of the still incandescent timbers and that of the pale moon, to find what had once been his home a very desolation. Happily his rice was in a jar at the back. He burnt his hands further to get the cooking-pan out from the embers in the front. There was plenty of fuel, and he soon had his rice, without vegetables, and only the big black pan for bowl.

As the minished party of villagers reached the foot of the hill, the present need, after the wounded had been carried home, was coffins for the rest. Lieu had been busy removing them out of Li's house. Li had brought the Longhaired there, and so the coffins were common property. The two best, however, Lieu had carried to his own house in case of emergency.

The consternation in the various hamlets over the missing ones can only be realised by those who have lived in China during times of excitement—or perhaps epidemic. Our grief is comparatively silent. Chinese grief is blatant. We may hardly know when anyone has died next door. In China the whole neighbourhood hears the awful wailings. Weddings are so noisy that all the neighbours are forced to rejoice with them that do rejoice. A death in one's street at night, with its screams and cries and doleful wailings, forces all but the soundest sleepers to weep with those that weep. Those hopeless, heartrending wailings! Dante, had he visited

China, might have left behind him yet more realistic pictures of despair. The whole family of survivors seem to descend into Hades with their lost, their ever lost one.

Li's wife seemed distracted. Her boy gone, her husband killed, killed by the villagers, and called a traitor by the very men he had once helped.

"He may not be dead," suggested Nieh Shen-seng.

"They have not brought him back," moaned the distressed woman, who, however, had just enough hope to prevent her from beginning to wail like the rest. In attending to the other wounded men, no one had thought of Li. But Nieh soon had three volunteers helping him to carry a smaller door, taken out of its sockets, from Li's house, and, bidding the poor woman refrain her tears, they started up the hill. Reaching the partly-ruined temple, they could find no one there. They shouted for the priest-monk, who presently answered from among the blackened stumps of the trees. He had retreated to his rabbit-hole again, half-dead with a fresh scare. They lifted up their lanterns to look at him, and his pate, with its stubble of some days, was white. He looked an old man. "I sat in the temple," he gasped, "after a mouthful of dry rice, when a figure entered covered with a yellow cloak, and when it neared me it roared like a tiger. I started to my feet. It began to elongate. The cloak began to rise ever so high. I fainted away. When I had come to, I found myself on the ground. There was nothing to be seen, but the roar was in my ears. I ran outside and hid in the copse. I have been there a long time. It has seemed years. And the sins of former days have been coming up to torment me. I was not a good lad before I came here. I ran away to a temple when my sins were found out. I paid the old priest to shave me and to brand my head.[1] I had stolen some silver from my father. It was either running away or swallowing opium. My father said he would kill me, and he meant it. I ran away with some of the priest's clothes, ran by night and rested by day, for three or four nights. Then I came here. It was a demon. It was a wronged spirit."

The four men could not but pity the shivering object before them, with his early whitened hair. Nieh quoted from Han Wen-Kung, saying, "Truly has it been said that 'when anyone rebels against heaven or man, or goes wrong in any way, . . . the demon becomes visible through something possessing form, and makes use of that which has sound in order to bring retribution.' Ghosts and demons are the reproaches of a troubled conscience.[2] But do you know where Li is?"

The answer being in the negative, they turned to go, when the priest called out, "The bronze incense altar has gone, and two of the small bronze idols."

"This is no demon," said Nieh, "but one who knows the temple. How big was the form you saw?"

"Not quite a full-grown man; but I could not see distinctly."

"Well, let us look for Li."

"Can I come too?"

They found him after some time. There was no road straight down, and they had to go round. He was still alive,

---

[1] This baptism of fire is performed in the monasteries at stated times upon the heads of the now initiated candidates, by means of several sticks of incense being fixed with paste of incense powder upon their bald pates. The paste being dry, the sticks are lit, the future priest-monk clenching his teeth, and muttering, then crying, O-Mi-To-Fuh, as the ignited stick shortens to the skin. Thus branded the man may claim a meal and a night's lodging in any temple in the Empire.

[2] Compare Lucretius:—
"... the guilty soul presents
These dreadful shapes, and still itself torments."

but weak from loss of blood. He seemed as though he would hardly last till he got home. But, entering the door, they gave him some wine. His wound bled afresh. He had just strength enough to say, "The best one."

"The best what?"

"Wood,"[1] was the reply, the last word the man uttered.

And now his wife began to wail. "My heaven," she cried, "My sister," with all the possible words for loss and despair.

In moments of intensest anguish, national and even racial distinctions are generally levelled, yet in Li's last words he proclaimed himself a Chinaman. His words are easily explained. Not so the cry "My sister" when a widow mourns. Yet the custom is universal, at anyrate in Central China. Some quote a curious legend to the effect that in very ancient times all the inhabitants of the Empire (or the world) were killed with the exception of two sisters, who by Heaven's decree became husband and wife. Others explain the expression as being the only available term of relationship possible. The word "husband" must not be mentioned, for he is gone for ever. Still less appropriate is his name, seldom or never used by the middle-aged during life. He has always been called "father." He is not a parent, nor an elder or younger brother, but he is dear. The word "sister," therefore, is the (unexplainable) term used.

Nieh Shen-seng wept too, but quietly, and tried to comfort her with the words, "Weep not, he cannot rise again. The water is spilt on the earth.[2] It is Heaven's decree. We cannot resist it." Poor comfort that. He felt it to be so, but it was all he had to give.

The best coffin? They had all gone! Perhaps it was already full. No; Lieu had been seen to take it away. It was recovered with great difficulty and many reproaches. There was no peace to be kept now. Nieh, however, was calm. Lieu was furious in his demonstrations.

---

[1] Here are two Chinese characteristics, the desire for a good coffin, and the avoidance of ill-sounding words. "Wood" is a frequent word in China for coffin, as "tree" seems to have been in Judæa for cross (Acts v. 30).

[2] Compare 2 Sam. xiv. 14.

THE LONGHAIRED HAVE COME! 271

There were many burials that night on the hillside. In one we may perhaps be mourners. The wine had gone off, and Li's good deeds were not all forgotten. Bearers were found ; a lantern-carrier and a gong-beater volunteered their services. Nieh wrote a few characters upon a slip of paper, a charm at the top, and the words, "Virtuous friend deceased, Li Sung-sen, senior brother's spiritual person," underneath, and repeating once more, " Weep not, he cannot rise again,"

the little procession started to bury the farmer by the side of his worthy father. Nieh himself was sorely in need of comfort.

There were one or two burials within Lieu's closed doors too. Into the hole were put an incense brazier and two bronze idols.

With early dawn he anticipated Nieh by begging his pardon for any thoughtless words, and asking whether Mrs. Li wanted to sell her husband's fields. He was prepared to give ten thousand cash an acre for the best fields (a Chinese acre is one-sixth that of England. The price in these parts for average land is fifteen thousand). With this offer Nieh thought best to close. The widow was too distracted to say yea or nay. He also sold his own house and vegetable garden. He knew he was being swindled, but then the Long-haired would surely return unless unforeseen events transpired. After early morning rice, Nieh gathered together his more portable belongings, and, with the price of the sales and his own scanty earnings, took boat for the four of them across the lake to the tongue of land towards the east, where his wife's brother lived.

Chapter XIII.

SUFFERING BY DEPUTY.

ANXIOUS FOR THE FRAY—-SPIRITS ALCOHOLIC AND DEMONAICAL —THE ART OF SUBSTITUTION.

"O locust god! O locust god divine,
Eat all my neighbour's crops, but don't eat mine."
Chinese Proverb.

IT was an eventful day in the camp of the Taipings. About noon a horseman came from the Inverted Pan Hill to say that they were crowded out with reinforcements from Hunan, who had retired before Cheng Kwoh-fan's soldiers, to strengthen the hands of their comrades in the more central station. The messenger brought a dispatch from the general to the effect that Captain Li was to move further inland, about half a day's journey, and to construct a camp capable of holding double the number of his own men. They had not yet retaken Hanyang, the messenger added, but were in high hopes of doing so with the aid of this newly-arrived contingent.

All was soon bustle and preparation. Ammunition and stores of rice were carried down to the boats, with Captain Li's pet cannon and various other appurtenances of private or general property. There were no tents to strike, but instead bundles of spades, hatchets, and mattocks, received as tribute from the blacksmiths of Hankow, were carried down the slope to the lake. With these they could construct fresh huts.

"It is time we were out of this lukewarm place," said the captain at afternoon rice. "Life without fighting is like food cooked without oil and salt.[1] I wish it had been nearer Hanyang instead of further out."

"You really like fighting, father?"

"Like it? I love it! It is my element. I belong to the Mings, and before the first emperor of that dynasty gained the throne, a dangerous enterprise was proposed. The soldiers were in high spirits, and the officers so eager for the fray that two of the generals

An Historical Duel.

fought a duel to decide which should lead the vanguard and have the first onset. I belong to the Mings. And so did your ancestors two hundred years back. But I expect they were farmers, who did not know the taste of blood."

"One of my ancestors," replied Seng-teh, "was a general under a later Ming emperor. He is buried in a fine tomb, with attendants and horses and lions and elephants in pairs to guard the place, and a sculptured archway with two pillars in front."

"What do they guard the place against, you young Taoist?"

"Oh, that is just a saying. I do not expect there are

---

[1] A lad was once asked what was meant by "daily food" in the Lord's prayer. His reply began with oil, salt, rice, etc. A poverty-stricken household is described as having no oil and salt.

any goblins about that hill. But it is said[1] that not far from our hill there is one from which a great deal of copper was once mined, and that, as is usually the case on hills containing much metal, various sprites appear, now in the form of chickens, now of children."

"Are the lions alive?" asked the captain, laughing.

"They are made of stone. But there are strange stories about one of them, which most folks believe. A great deal of rice in the ear having disappeared, the theft was traced to one of these beasts. Some say they are cats, but cats do not eat uncooked rice. Some say it was one of the horses. At anyrate one of them was the robber, and a Taoist"—

"Taoists again," roared the captain. "Remember your peach-stones, but go on. Go on, I say."

"Well, a Taoist was called, who hit the lion or horse a blow with a knife, and a lot of blood gushed out. Since then no rice has been stolen."

"Good; very good. Have you ever seen a son-slaying conjurer? because I have. There are two ways of doing it. One is to plunge a long knife into him under the ribs, the other is to hack at his neck with a kitchen chopper. And quite a lot of blood spurts out—out of the handle, don't you see? It is hollow and filled with red stain, and the blade is made of cardboard —renewed, of course, each time.

<small>Child-Slaying Conjurers.</small>

"But your ancestor must have been a big man to have such a fine grave. You should have a silver-mounted thumb-ring when you talk about him, then you can elevate your thumb [the acted superlative] and display the ring, don't you see? like the swells do. But where is the grave? Beyond the Nine Recluses Hill, I guess, and not far off. You folks stick to one place from generation to generation. Suppose you point it out to me to-morrow?"

<small>One use of the Thumb-ring.</small>

Seng-teh was visibly alarmed at the last sentence. The

---

[1] To this day, by such men as Chinese B.A.'s. We must remember, however, that our words cobalt (cobold) and nickel (the original of which survives in the slang phrase Old Nick) both refer to goblins infesting the mines whence these metals are procured. The "little men" legend in our own land is not yet defunct amongst miners.

captain was all very well where he was, but a camp hard by his home! The thought was not a pleasant one.

"Why, what's the matter with the child? Don't stop eating. Here, take a cup of wine. Your face is an unlucky colour. Cannot be helped, my son. We shall hurt no one who does not hurt us. And it is Heaven's decree. Ah, well, I am as hard-hearted and tough as one of your stone lions. But I used to be a child once myself."

"More wine!" he shouted. "I should like to have a set of cups made out of the big bronze idol. There will be plenty left. I do drink a little, although nothing much to be complimented upon. I am not so far gone as a great wine-bibber of old days, who directed that after he had 'ascended to heaven' his dust should be made into wine-cups. He was always full of wine on earth, you see.

<small>The Will of a Wine-bibber.</small>

"But I will tell you a tale about wine-drinking. I had it read to me once out of a virtuous book. A stupid *yamun* underling was once taking a rascally Buddhist monk to prison. As he started with his prisoner, he was afraid of forgetting his things and his errand, so he began mumbling, 'Bundle, umbrella, cangue, warrant, monk, and myself!' At every two or three steps he repeated the list, until the monk, seeing the sort of man he had to deal with, treated him at an inn on the way until he was so drunk that he wanted to sit down by the wayside and sleep. When he had gone off, the monk took off his cangue, shaved the man's head, put the wooden collar upon him, and fled. On coming to, the man exclaimed, 'Let me wait until I have counted everything. Let me see. Bundle and umbrella are here.' Then feeling his neck, he cried, 'And the cangue, too; and here beside me is the warrant.' Then half-scared, 'Hai Ya! I don't see the monk,' but, rubbing his itching pate, he gleefully added, 'The monk is still here. But where am I? Bundle, umbrella, cangue, warrant, monk, but where am I? Bundle, umbrella,'"—

<small>A Temperance Tale</small>

"Please, sir, we have been up the hill, and no trace of the boats. They cannot be back till after dark now."

"Bring in the Taoist. His face shall itch!"

He was brought. He pleaded in vain for a few hours' grace. He could not control events.

"You are a magician!" roared the captain, none the less terribly because at first in sarcasm. "You have charmed the idol. You have made it invisible with your peach-stones. You have stuck your greasy paper on its back. Who was it deserted, and made us out to be a set of demons, to be kept back only by your charms? Who was it abused the hospitality given? Who was it stole the chickens? Who was it stole the oxen and the child? You unspeakable wretch! We might have had the bronze in a day or two, without any trouble, but for you!

"Seng-teh! Write me four good-sized characters, 'Perfect peace, kingdom of heaven,' and be sure you write kingdom without a 'perhaps' in it; write king instead, a king within the four seas.

"Good! Now to work, as near this as you can, my cubs." And spite of the man's abject pleadings and protests, two men took a needle each and scratched the characters on the Taoist's cheeks. "Rub the ink well into the scratches, my son. I like this. But if any of my cubs have fallen, we may have to erase the characters with a sword. Rub in the ink, plenty of it. Now, you wash your face before to-morrow evening if you dare, and you will have no head to wash afterwards! It's a shame to put such good characters upon such a face. I wonder the needle went through the skin. It is so thick.[1] You won't keep your head upon your shoulders long. I am a prophet. Now say your thanks."[2]

The Taoist knocked his head upon the ground, and said, "Many thanks, great official."

"Taoists are scamps," he added, when the man had gone.
Demon Scare Demon. "There is a story of a seller of pictures— portraits of a celebrated Taoist—going along the street, when a woman asked the vendor, 'What use are they

---

[1] A thick-skinned face answers to our "brazen-face."

[2] It is customary for a criminal to thank the mandarin for his fatherly chastisement. Compare the incident of Caligula sentencing Canius Junicus to death. "Do not flatter yourself. I have given orders to put you to death." "I thank your most gracious majesty for it," replied Canius (Seneca).

for sticking about the house? The door gods have swords and hatchets, and so frighten demons away. These portraits have good-natured faces.' Her husband replied, 'Yes, but the man's deeds were all the more frightful and villainous. Buy one.'

"That is it. They frighten the demons with their villainies. They act like the images stuck upon house-roofs, or like the mirrors over doors. The demon comes and sees his face in the glass, or the ugly image on the roof, and flies in terror. I give them credit for that.

"And the Buddhist monks with their subscription books for their temple,—their own private 'five-viscera temple,' as everybody knows. Have you ever heard of the monk who went into the country with his mass-book and a pair of small cymbals? A tiger met him. The monk clashed his cymbals in his face, and he swallowed them. Having nothing left besides, the monk threw his mass-book at the beast, who ran off to his den.

Give! Give!

"The little cubs asked if he had brought anything for them to eat. 'No,' he replied, 'but I am glad to have got home without paying anything.'

"'Without paying anything, father?'

"'Yes, my sons. I met a monk, and only swallowed a couple of thin cymbals, when he brought out his subscription book! I had to run hard, or he would have got a donation out of me.'"

Seng-teh laughed, but with a pale face.

"Don't fret, my child. The idol is heavy and the way is long. I expect the hill is steep too. We Taiping folks are peaceable enough. And the people will soon get to know us. There was once a blind man crossing a plank bridge over a dry stream. His foot slipped. He caught hold of the boards with his hands, crying, 'What shall I do? I shall surely be drowned.' A passer-by told him there was nothing to fear if he jumped down. But he still hung there, shouting his throat dry. By and by his hands gave way. He dropped a foot on to dry ground. Then he laughed, saying, 'What a fool I was to hang on there

Drop the Heart.

so long.' Yes, the folk's hearts are suspended now, but they will soon 'drop them.' "[1]

The lad, however, could not get rid of his forebodings. And though the captain did not confess it, he was not so hopeful about the safe return of the party as he was about his own future victories, and the triumph of their cause. His recent exhilaration had had a flavour of hot wine about it.

The hours went by, and the second watch sounded, when Captain Li announced his intention of going to sleep.

"You take a spell of night watching, if you feel like it. It's part of a soldier's duties, you know. But you had better lie down at the fourth watch, whether you sleep or not. They say, 'One sleepless night, ten unpeaceful days.' That is how we fight so well, I suppose. But you are not quite 'one of the trade' yet. If you like, you may read up that Sacred Book, so as to get the characters off like a string of crackers. It will give you influence among the men."

It was a strange night for Seng-tch. Book in hand, he started at every unusual sound. Between the loud snorings of the captain were heard the stamping of his two horses near, the pacing up and down of the sentries, the click of the dice tossed about in a rice bowl, and sundry sounds from the party in charge of the boats, where they were evidently carousing. Then the distant bark of village dogs, the croaking of the young frogs, and an occasional hoot of an owl or two seemed but to intensify the silence—silence which could only be broken by his father's voice. He felt terribly lonely. He wanted his mother. He felt inclined to cry for her, as many an older countryman of his does right on to the days of hoary hairs, when in deep sorrow or intense pain. He was susceptible to education; he had taken kindly to his surroundings. That education had progressed by leaps and strides during the long period of forty hours since he entered the camp. An educated man is one whose instincts of adaptation to various

---

[1] This latter and very frequent phrase, to "let the heart drop" or go, is, of course, the converse of the "suspense" quoted by the Chinese, as well as ourselves. Other halves of the circle are found. We speak of "light and trifling." The Chinese (as the Hebrews, Ps. iii. 3, "glory," and in many other places) use "heavy" in the sense of (sedate and) "honourable."

environments, literary or circumstantial, have been drawn out into exercise. No true education, however, makes us forget our mother. The "our" is not English or Chinese; it is universal. Seng-teh's education was progressing. But he wanted his mother. The night was awfully weird and desolate to him. He had never been from home on a wakeful night before. Where was home now?

He went out at last and looked about; the moon of seven days old was just setting over the waters beyond which his father had led the party. Outside the camp the barely-definable landscape seemed provokingly calm. Within the enclosure the dismantled camp looked desolate enough. The bats wheeled overhead. They were lucky, no doubt. Not to his child-heart on that dreary night, however.

The fourth watch was sounded upon the drum, and the silence which followed seemed as real a thing as the drum roll. But what was that? Surely two musket shots. The sentinel had heard them. "Call the captain," he said. Seng-teh called the cook.

With hot tea in hand the lad approached the sleeping officer. His heart beat wildly as he awoke him. The "Crouching Tiger" was indeed roused. He seemed inclined to spring upon everyone and everything. "Send fifty men to meet them. It is the party coming back by land. Something has happened, and," he hissed through his teeth, "something more will happen soon."

The few minutes which the fifty took to get into marching order he called a "good half-day."[1] They started fully armed, the lesser half carrying torches (of worn-out bamboo rope). After proceeding some miles toward the west, they found ten comrades more or less mud-bespattered and bedraggled, who explained that the moon going down, they had got stuck in a paddy field. Moreover, three or four were wounded, and the rest had had to carry them by turns. Then came the story already known to the reader.

The news roused the captain to a pitch of almost uncon-

---

[1] It is an unsolved problem in Chinese mathematics as to how many "good half-days" may be contained in twelve hours. There may at least be three or four times as many "half-days" as quarters in an orange.

trollable fury. He fired off his excessive feelings by platoons and volleys. As yet it was all blank cartridge. It would be otherwise by and by.

"Very likely dead," was the news which stunned Seng-teh. He could not realise it. Coming after the stirring events of the past days and the night watching, it benumbed and dazed him. But close at hand was the fact of the captain's rage. It both aroused and restrained him. He had to adapt himself to the paradoxical environment. His education was progressing.

With earliest daylight, a large contingent was seen emerging from between the low hills toward the east. Both morning worship and the morning rice must be finished before they arrived. The chapter of Leviticus read by Seng-teh, though fluently rendered, could hardly have been understood, even as far as the phrases went, by anyone present. The book was not in mandarin colloquial, as are those in use in the various places of worship now. But there is a certain mysterious awfulness in a series of unexplained sounds, as the Buddhists know well as they recite their half-Sanscrit masses. In the modern treaty ports, the "foreign" police have found that "foreign" orders will often make loiterers and obstructionists "move on" with greater readiness than Chinese phrases would. The uncouthness of the sounds arrests the ear; there is a superiority about them which may argue superior force. The Sacred Book of the Taipings was all the more sacred because mysterious and unexplained, and the definite commands which they found therein were all the more forcible as coming from undefined clouds of spiritual mystery. The moral of the whole was gathered up in their customary shout, and this morning, reduced in numbers though they were, that shout came forth from martial throats with more terrible emphasis than ever.

Then followed a hurried meal, and the firing of a triple salute from the bronze cannon, now mounted on Captain Li's boat. Mutual greetings were exchanged in military fashion. The newly-arrived commander took possession of his quarters, and sent half his men to escort the retiring captain to the shores of the lake. The fleet consisted chiefly of "sanpans" (a word used at the ports for small ferryboats, but in Central China belonging properly to small gunboats for thirteen men, with a little house at the stern for the commander [which house is removed in action], and a small iron cannon at the bows). These had been captured from the Imperialists, and dragged over a then muddy track from the river to the Moon lake, which washes the foot of the Tortoise Hill, then rowed an hour's journey further over the long chain of lakes which occupies such a large area in the county of Hanyang.

Besides the "sanpans," there were three or four larger sail boats, dignified, rather glorified, like the rest with banners. Sails were hoisted, parting assurances of good luck exchanged, and the hundred men on shore fired a parting volley.

It was one of the loveliest of spring days, and in Central China the weather can be so bland and bright in the spring and autumn as to suggest the impossibility of such things as sudden "fierce winds" and thunderstorms. Fair weather and the delights of spring may but mock the mourner and irritate the already enraged. But Seng-tch was a mere child in years, and the difference between a day on the lakes and the cramped-up life of the camp began to tell upon Captain Li also. He was at anyrate mollified into silence, and Seng-tch raised to a sense of importance in which any forthcoming tragedy had a not agonising part. If his mother and the school teacher, yes, and the schoolmaster's little daughter, as well as his wife, had gone away, as probably they had, he did not care much what happened to the rest, especially to Lieu and company.

"Your village is on the farther side of the hill, is it not?"

"Yes," replied the lad with a sudden start.

"We shall not encamp there. It will be on the Han-yang side."

"Has the captain spent his internal ammunition?" anxiously wondered Seng-teh.

"I am your father now."

"Yes, father."

They were soon in familiar waters; the lake only washes the farther side of the hill. "Your village is one of a group, I suppose?"

"Yes, father."

"Which is it?"

Seng-teh replied by pointing out a cluster of hamlets half a mile distant from his rather isolated village. He was but a Chinese lad.

"Well, it cannot be helped. We must pass along there to get behind the hill. Your father is dead, I expect. Whom have you to care for but me now?"

"My mother," said Seng-teh with a rather forced sob.

"We don't harm women, and I will do nothing to your teacher. He was not among them, I guess."

Did the captain contemplate a wholesale massacre?

As they neared the shores, the blackened remnants of what had once been boats met the captain's eyes. They had been brought there, and then, on second thoughts, burnt. There before them, too, was a column of smoke, and there on one of the hill peaks a large fire. The rowers were urged on to their utmost speed. The captain leaped on shore, crying, "Follow me all, except three men for each boat." They made straight for the first village, snatched many a fire-brand from the bonfire, and the village was soon in flames. "Now for the next, my cubs. Remember the twenty." And another and another hamlet were given to the flames.

"Now for the hill-top." It was that farthest from the temple. The encampment was empty but for dogs, pigs, and chickens. "Kill them all," roared the captain. "Now let us reconnoitre."

"Yonder," said Seng-teh, trying to appease him, "is the garden where the Hanyang mandarins [" Monkeys, you mean. Go on."] used to feast after praying for rain."

"The trees will do for fuel, but yon's the spot," pointing to a rather wild place a little way up the hill. "Why did not the country folk make a camp for us there? Bring a flag. No longer staff than that? Cut down the tallest of yonder pines. And some of you go down and seize all the oxen and pigs and poultry around those villages," pointing to the blazing hamlets.

The orders were obeyed in wondrously quick time, and the flag of the Taipings waved over one of the peaks of the hill of the Nine Recluses.

The new camp did not take many days to make, and on taking possession thereof the captain gave a feast to all,—with plenty of meat,—while corresponding festivities were celebrated in the hill-top camp, and by the crews on the boats, who remained there to intimidate any evil-disposed natives by the firing-off of a cannon at sunrise and sunset.

The Longhaired having come, Lieu impressed upon his associates the desirability of sending up a conciliatory deputation to the rebel camp. The proposal was scouted at first; but, as usual, he talked his customers over—half-hypnotised them perhaps into his way of thinking; and, moreover, he was going with them himself. Twenty would be enough; and at length the twenty were gathered together for a preparatory drink.

They proceeded to the camp with sundry presents of oxen and other live stock which had belonged to deceased villagers whose widows and orphans had fled. To these Lieu added a box of tobacco. He had also nobly undertaken the onerous task of interviewing the captain.

Seng-teh was duly astonished to see the evil-faced man enter—all the more evil-looking because smiling.

"Who is that man? You seem to know him?"

"Lieu Fuh-t'ang of the tea-shop—which was burnt the other day."

The man looked up from his knees with a glance of sincerest admiration and fervent gratitude at the latter clause.

"How dare you appear before the Crouching Tiger? Bind him."

"I come to apologise, kingly official."

"With empty words?"

"No, I have brought twenty men, who beseech the kingly official to take their lives in atonement for the blood some of them shed the other day in their ignorance."

"You are one of them. Unsheath your swords, guards!"

"Not so," cried Lieu; "I have brought twenty besides. It was I who told them of your honourable cause, and persuaded them to atone for their resistance of heavenly virtue."

"And you?"

"I have brought a small present of beef and other meat for your acceptance."

"It is well for you that I have dined. I know you, and so does the Taoist. Fetch him in. Give them a hundred thanks each. Do not trouble about breaking the skin. The full hundred [1] mind."

The two men had to crawl up on their knees, and thank the official for his kindly correction. The face of one of them presented a strange picture of black and red. He was permitted to wash it. "And wash off the marks of the blows too, if you can."

"Fetch in the twenty. I lost twenty tiger cubs the other day. You killed them."

"No, kingly official," they cried in chorus. "We are from other villages."

"From Kwangtung province, or Szchwan, or perhaps Chihli! Now choose between being decapitated or becoming Taiping soldiers, with the sacred characters tattooed upon your cheeks. Death or life?"

"We plead to live, kingly official." And the tattooing

[1] The usual custom is eight for every ten.

was proceeded with, the Taoist this time being made to rub in the ink. "I wouldn't have that man Lieu. He may go. But if he does not bring us tribute every third day, not only meat, but wine and general stores, we will seek him out and cut him up piecemeal [the extreme punishment of the Chinese penal code]. Do you hear, guards?" And Lieu being unbound, limped out.

They were destined to remain in the camp of the Nine Recluses Hill for some months. Seng-teh early gained the news of Nieh's escape, with his own mother, to the "lip" of land (Chinese lips are often the most prominent part of the profile) called after the Tung family. It is an isthmus of a mile or two in length, out of the beaten tracks, and the fine trees, so like those in an English park, which grow there still, mark it out as one of the few places in the Hanyang county left unshorn by either the Longhaired or the Imperialists.

Happily for the country the crops that year, and indeed of the two succeeding years, were unusually good. That is, in Hupeh.

"Because we have destroyed so many idols," explained the captain, who, however, now that he was on the spot, was feeling the force of the "any-day-will-do" argument with regard to a particular idol.

Around Nanking, however,—the natives said through the wrath of their injured deities,—there was a sore famine. Many were reduced to killing and eating their children, and of selling their grown-up daughters for slaves.

Moreover, certain traders, not always attached to the rebel camps, though acting in their name, used to reduce the number of mouths to be fed by seizing the best-looking damsels and shipping them, huddled up in the holds of small boats, to the central stations. This horrible trade increased during the years of civil war. One or two such girls, who have survived into wrinkled old women (Chinese women often age early), have heartrending tales to tell a sympathetic lady who inquires into their history. Two such have been boat-rowers upon the Moon lake at Hanyang, the rough boatman giving up a fare now and then to the Nanking ladies. A young girl tenderly brought up ending her days as a boat-rower! "My husband is old and ill," says one, "but he has been a good husband to me." "You are very poor?" "Yes, but happy." "Do you remember the days of the Long-haired?" "Ah, do I not! Sin's penalty, sir. Sin's penalty" (that is, sin in a former state of existence). Further than this an Englishman does not inquire. His wife may.

In the ninth month (October 1853) the Taipings re-captured Hanyang, which event was celebrated with great festivities in the Nine Recluses camps. And what was also to the point, some boat-loads of ammunition and several iron cannon were brought thither.

During the feast, Seng-teh related how that on the twentieth of the month there was a curious custom among the country folk near the Inverted Pan Hill. By the roadside was a heap of stones, known by the name of "Old Dame Han's grave." The word Han might be the ordinary surname of that sound, but, as his teacher had once said, it was probably the character for "chilly" (which would make

The Chinese Jack Frost.

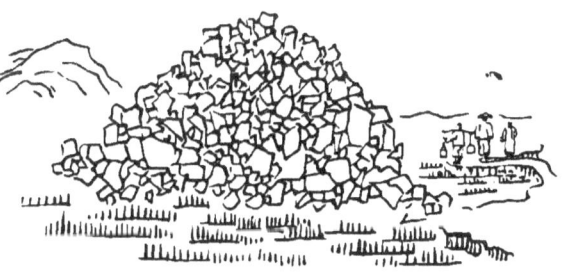

Dame Han correspond to our Jack Frost). The passers-by threw a stone on the "grave," crying, "Old Dame Han, Old Dame Han, don't come across the Yangtse!" meaning, "Let them have a cold winter there, if you like, but don't bring your frost here." If the day be fine, they predict a severe winter; if wet and windy, the reverse.

The tenth month opened with the news that the Imperialists were massing their troops to attempt the recapture of Hanyang. Reinforcements were arriving from the western provinces. Cheng Kwoh-fan still held Hunan. Messengers came and went between the various Taiping camps daily. A battle was imminent. It was fought. Captain Li was well-nigh furious at his marching orders coming too late. The battle was a sudden one, and disastrous to the Taipings. The camps inland were soon overcrowded with the defeated. Hankow and Hanyang now displayed the Imperial flag, and for five *li* out, as far as the "Five-*li* Mound," an ancient signal station (similar mounds being possessed by many a city), the Imperialists held their own. The main body of the Taipings had fallen back upon Hwangchow,[1] fifty miles down the Yangtse. Perhaps they would come back and turn the tide of battle once more.

One or two Imperialist spies had been captured by Li's men, and their severed heads made into ghastly adornments of the camp, being hung by the queues upon pine poles. Other heads were hung up by their long unplaited hair upon other poles erected upon the "Five-*li* Mound," it was said.

Meanwhile Seng-teh, who had begun to grow up, was getting used to camp life, and could look upon ghastly heads dangling in the moonlight even without a shudder. The thoughts of a possibly impending battle flushed rather than blanched his cheeks. He had made some progress in his drill, had become a fair marksman, had gained muscle at anyrate. He could ride a horse as easily as he had ridden the water buffaloes of former days. Captain Li had given him one of his two horses.

"There was a little recreation among us country boys once," he said to the captain. "You bay is shallow during some months of the year." It was a good many feet deep just then, but Seng-teh's geography was purposely confused. "We used to sit astride our buffaloes until we came to the brink, then see who could stand up and ride thus upon their backs while they half-waded, half-swam across on their way home."

"This water buffalo," replied the captain, pointing to Seng-teh's horse, "can both wade and swim in blood, as you will soon see. Stick to him then, my lad; he wades on to victory."

They were very much attached to one another, the captain and his "son." But Seng-teh could not quite

[1] Which, like Hanyang, used to be a little kingdom some centuries B.C.

forget his father's untimely death, nor his widowed mother, the teacher and his family.

Early one morning before sunrise, drums and gongs sounded from the lake. A large fleet of Imperial sanpans had come up in the moonlight. Captain Li's crews resisted them as best they could. A boat-load of combustibles which they sent with set sail into the midst of the enemy did considerable damage, but their own boats were soon seized to make up for losses, and the lake shores grew red with blood.

There was desperate fighting on the hill-top, but after an hour's struggle that position was taken, and now the battle raged around the main camp. To the overpowering numbers of the enemy were added the advantages of the hill-slope. Captain Li fought desperately. He was a match for ten men near at hand; not proof, however, against a well-aimed bullet from above. He fell. His men fled, and Seng-teh among them. He, however, on horseback, soon distanced his pursuers, and made off by a circuitous route towards the teacher's and his mother's new home.

Chapter XJV.

AN OLD, OLD STORY IN A NEW EDITION.

ELIGIBLE AND YOUNG—ANCIENT AND MODERN AUTHORITIES MATRIMONIAL—WHERE DID PIGTAILS COME FROM?—AND THE NUMBER SEVEN?

"The seven emotions are Joy, Anger, Grief, Fear, Love, Hatred, Desire."

A REBEL on horseback, though a young one, was sufficient to strike terror to the hearts of the country folk. And soon a chorus of voices was heard before and behind him, shouting the once familiar cry, "The Longhaired are coming!" a cry which carried with it no merely subjective terror as the months went by. The Taipings were degenerating. Was it that, being everywhere "resisted," they everywhere sought revenge? Or was it from the fact that their ranks were being swelled by the members of secret societies and rascals generally? Perhaps from both causes. There were few men of the Captain Li stamp in command. And with his death, Seng-teh's sole reason for attachment to their ranks had ceased. How many an ardent votary of a "cause" is but attached to a particular man therein! The "cause" is often the man. The Taipings, to Seng-teh, had meant Captain Li. Now they were almost the "Longhaired" again. At anyrate, for personal safety, he must throw away his yellow coat. Reaching a quiet spot, he dismounted, took a large stone, wrapped it up in his jacket, and threw it into a pond hard by. He then did up his hair at the back of the head, so as more to resemble the country folk. Henceforth the cries his appearance raised were merely, "A horseman! Can't the horse gallop!" "A horseman" was seen from the "Tung Family Lip" long before he arrived there. The horse might perhaps swim through blood, but the lake waters were deep, and ran far inland. He had to go a few miles yet. It seemed a long way round. All the better. The place was more secure.

Once round the sharp angle, he began to wonder whether he should have to ask at every cottage he came to as to the whereabouts of his friends. This would involve tedious replies to cross-questioning. Everybody would want to know everything about him, and he was tired out. By the wayside, however, was a little tea-shop, whose jovial looking proprietor looked the opposite of his early antipathy, Fah's father. He stopped there and inquired.

"Mrs. Li from the Yang Family Pavilion is not far off. She is yonder. See!"

Seng-teh but saw some grave mounds.

"That new one is hers."

The lad fainted.

When he came to, he was lying in a strange room. His side was very painful. He had been slightly wounded, though he had not known it at the time. He had but noticed a little blood upon his lower garments. He thought it had been a splash from someone else. His education had been progressing.

But who was this bending over him? "Nieh Shen-seng!" Yes, and his wife too, and a little girl. The horrible dreams he had been having were only dreams.

"You have been speaking 'dream words,' my lad." He had been raving all the afternoon and night, and was still very feverish. "Kill the fiends," had been a frequent cry. But the words "father," "mother," and words of early childhood predominated.

"Don't cry," said a little voice; "that's father, and that's mother."

"This is your home now," said Mrs. Nieh in a kindly tone of voice.

As the days went by and the fever began to abate, he

was favoured with somewhat lengthy communications from the little damsel of three and a half years old. Chinese children, as we have already noted, are often far from being deficient in sweetness. Their affection may be ardent at an early age. They readily attach themselves to anyone in whom they have confidence, even to a foreigner—who is not a foreigner, but Mr. So and So, to them. And little Camilla was decidedly winsome. The sick boy thought so at anyrate.

He would cry every now and then. Chinese boys may really love their parents. But each time, when his little friend was near, she would do her best to comfort him.

"Why do you cry?" she asked one day.

"Because I have no father and mother."

"I have," cried little Camilla; "that's father, and that's mother."

"And you always have been a second father to me, Nieh Shen-seng."

"You were always a bright scholar, Seng-teh."

At this stage Mrs. Nieh whispered something to her husband, who nodded assent. Then she added aloud, "Would you like to call Nieh Shen-seng your father?" And the little maiden clambered over him, put her cheek against his, and said, "That's father, and that's mother." Seng-teh put his arms around her, and said, "According to the Shen-seng's high grace let it be so," a sentence which happily sounded less pompous in the original, but which the importance of the occasion called forth. Nieh Shen-seng said nothing, but fetched—a razor, which he applied to the front-half of Seng-teh's head, to the great alarm of the little maiden. The operation being continued, the child began to cry, and could only be comforted by him for whom her tenderest sympathies had been thus drawn out. She had always objected to have her own head touched with the razor (for little girls come under the law of the barber for some years, that their front hair may grow the better). But here her old playmate was being killed. "Charles I.," said a bright little English scholar once, "had his head decapitated." Her father was at anyrate decapitating Seng-teh's head. She

AN OLD, OLD STORY IN A NEW EDITION.

took up the severed locks, and said, as though to comfort them, "What pain! what pain!" Then, "Don't cry," partly to herself, partly to the locks of hair, partly to him who had lost them.

"Come!" said Seng-teh, holding out his arms. Again the little maiden clambered over him, and he kissed away her tears.

One of his hands being at length free, Nieh Shen-seng struck it with his open palm,[1] and clasped it for a moment, saying, "We will dispense with other ceremonies, but I will go and write out the eight characters."

The "eight characters" having been brought, Seng-teh could not but gather the bedding around him, sit up, and make a deep bow to his future father and mother in law. On the other doings the reader must not generalise. Chinese engagements are not usually concluded by means of a razor, a kiss, and a striking of hands.

After a few days he was to be found fully clothed, though with the invalid's black cloth bound round his temples, sitting up to partake of an engagement feast. He claimed to be the provider, for the silver from the sale of his father's lands was now his.

While the table was being prepared, however, a horse was heard outside rattling its bells.[2] It had been brought in from "grass."

"What's that?" cried the little maiden. Her betrothed took her out to see, when she stroked the horse, and rattled the bells to her heart's content. Thus we see that engagement was followed by courtship.

On being brought in, she pointed to the musket which had been left leaning up in a corner.

---

[1] Prov. vi. 1, xvii. 18, xxii. 26. Hand-striking is a frequent mode of settling a contract (as that of suretyship). The holding of hands (*Julius Cæsar*, Act 1, scene iii.) may have been a transition between the ancient hand-striking and our modern hand-shake. It is still in use as a letter phrase indicative of close sympathy.

[2] It is usual to have twenty or thirty "bells" suspended from the horse's neck. These help to clear the way in crowded streets. The "bells," of globular form, are usually ornamented with a tiger head and the Chinese character for longevity. Compare Zech. xiv. 20.

"Hai Ya! It is loaded; I forgot. Had I not better fire it off?"

Nieh Shen-seng thought he had better do so. "But tell the folks not to be alarmed. It looks a terrible thing." The scholar had only seen the primitive duck guns, which have a long barrel. There is a little hole near the stock through which some of the powder is shaken on to a flat piece of iron. The trigger holds an ignited piece of loosely-twisted rope. Such guns, the ancestors, however, of our modern rifles,[1] do not look very terrible.

Seng-teh gave the child to her father, and shouldered his gun. Just then a flock of rooks were flying over at some height. The young marksman happened to hit one of them.

"What a tremendous bang!" exclaimed the folks from the nearest village (Nieh Shen-seng's house was somewhat isolated).

"You are a second Li Tan," smiled Nieh Shen-seng, when he had recovered from the shock.

"Give me my Fung-kiao," he replied. But the young empress-elect disdained to come. She cried, "Go! go! I don't like you."

"Then I shan't like you either." Thus we see that the courtship of these young folks was interrupted by the orthodox lovers' tiff. "After all," as the Chinese of to-day often remark, "'middle and outside' are very much alike."

---

[1] "The Chinese were before us in all our inventions—printing, artillery, aerostation [!], chloroform [!]. Only, the discovery, which in Europe at once takes life and birth, and becomes a prodigy and a wonder, remains a chrysalis in China. . . . China is a museum of embryos" (Victor Hugo).

"Exactly the same," another is sure to reply. "Not a bit of difference."

In this case the reader's feelings must be harrowed by the recital of the fact that the estrangement, with all its bitter recriminations, continued until Seng-teh's betrothed was bundled off to bed in the early evening. She yielded next day on receiving the present of a paper horse, made by her betrothed. But these are after-words, as the tale-books say.

Nieh's brother-in-law was the chief guest at the afternoon feast. He was irrepressible as ever. The bowls having been emptied, and his sister being engaged in vain attempts to get her daughter off to sleep, he exclaimed, "Nieh Shen-seng, could you not read the classics to her? That would send her off if anything would." Are not East and West exactly alike? The joke is quite Chinese.

International Sleeping-draught.

By way of congratulation, another guest observed that " An eighteen-*lohan* daughter is not to be compared to a lame son."

" Not as *lohans* go," replied the brother-in-law. " But the proverb for Seng-teh is, ' A man may be ten years older than his wife, but she may not be one year older than he.'"

Nieh Shen-seng tried to wedge in a classical reference to the effect that, even were the difference greater, it might still be a good marriage. "*The Book of Changes* says, ' When the withered willow brings forth tares,[1] it is as an old man obtaining a [young] wife,'—in no wise disadvantageous. He may hope for sons. ' But when the withered willow puts forth flowers, it is like an old woman gaining a [young] husband.' In that case "—

Discrepancy of Age not always a Disadvantage.

" I once heard a story," interrupted the irrepressible, " of a bride who was a trifle more than a year older than her husband. There was a youth who had been adopted in early childhood, and, of course, had taken his adopted father's name. He wanted a wife, and hired a go-between. ' Ten matchmakers, nine liars.' The engagement was completed and the marriage

A Man must not Marry his ... Mother.

[1] The word, thus literally translated, is explained in the *Imperial Dictionary* by a word which usually refers to " grain in seed that bends down in an easy,

day fixed. The ceremony was performed, and the bride taken into her chamber, when she started at the sight of a cabinet once familiar to her. She asked her husband his child-name, at the sound of which she might well be startled. It was she who had given it to him. He was her own son. She had been left a widow at the age of seventeen, had married again, and, after some years, had lost her second husband."

"Hai Ya! Did that really happen?"

"I have heard so. But I will tell you something which I saw with my own eyes at Tsaitien. I often go there, you know. It makes all the difference being this side of the lake. I saw it with my own eyes, mind—on a stage. Ha! ha! ha!

"There were two friends in adversity who consulted how they could escape therefrom. And what was their adversity? The old woman! So they agreed to go upon a trading expedition. Li Kai-tai, no relative of Seng-teh's or mine either, was the name of one; Sen Tin-hwa that of the other."[2]

Hen-pecked.[1]

"The latter went home, and, with many a conciliatory smile, acquainted his lady of his intention. 'You are going off because you are afraid I shall make you kneel down again.'

"'N-not s-so! I-I-I w-w-wish to g-g-go and d-do b-b-business, and b-b-bring you a whole l-l-lot of m-m-money.'

"'Nonsense. Kneel down at once.'

"'Oh, please'—

"'Kneel down.'"

"Li Kai-tai, his 'sympathetic friend' [with a nod to Nieh

graceful manner." If that explanation were pressed, we might find here a marvellous anticipation of the modern botanical explanation of the two sorts of willow catkins. (The mysterious book in question was old in the days of Confucius.) But while this explanation cannot be fully disproved, the internal evidence points to new shoots from the old root.

[1] "The hen-bird announcing the morning" is the Chinese phrase.
[2] The chivalrous Englishman is often bothered by Chinese crowds insisting that in our land men are the slaves of women. The best reply seems to be: "There is a country where such is often the case, but it is not my humble land." "No?" "No; it is the great country where a certain Li Kai-tai and his friend Sen Tin-hwa used to live. Its inhabitants 'fear the old woman' greatly." General collapse and aching sides!

Shen-seng] arrived at the door, which had been closed, pushed it open and entered. 'How is this?'

"'I am l-looking for a c-cash which I have d-dropped.'

"'Never mind the cash. Get up.'

"At that moment the 'old woman' came in, and asked what business the man had to come interfering. He said he had come as mediator for his friend. 'What! a sheep-faced[1] man like you!"

"At this stage Li-Kai-tai's wife came in. He stammered frightfully, fearing greatly. She ordered him to kneel down too. The two wives then retired to consult as to what to do next.

"'Now or never!' cried one of the victims, and both ran off to appeal to the mandarin. They beat the drum[2] at the *yamun* door, for their case was urgent. The mandarin emerged, and asked what had happened.'

"'The old woman,' they pleaded.

"'Whose?' gasped the magistrate in trepidation.

"He sent for the two women, but before he had time to question them, his own wife appeared. He turned pale with fear, and addressed her most deferentially.

"'Why did you not call me before?' she screamed out. 'I mean to judge this matter. What is your complaint, my good women?'

"'Disobedient husbands, great lady.'

"'A hundred blows each! Now, carry your wives home on your backs, and learn to be submissive in future. And you! If you were not an official, I would order you a hundred blows too. Carry me in on your back, and be more submissive hereafter.'"

Mrs. Nieh came in just then, but the laughter was so loud that she had to run back to see if her little girl had awakened. Chinese babies, however, are not over-sensitive to sound when once asleep.

[1] The expression used was, "Look upon my face," an Old Testament as well as a Chinese idiom.
[2] There is a drum kept at the doors of *yamuns* for cases of emergency. It is seldom used, the underlings guarding it too well. Hearing it, the mandarin must come out as he is.

"Better luck to you, Seng-teh. You have the advantage of age," laughed the irrepressible. Nieh Shen-seng then related the somewhat familiar [1] legend of the wife of Chwang-tsz, the Taoist sage. It may be given in a condensed form. Chwang-tsz (cir. B.C. 330), whose writings rose to high repute in the reign of the Lustrous Emperor (son of the historical Li Tan), was out walking by a certain hill, where he saw a woman fanning the grave. He inquired the reason of the strange procedure. She answered that her husband, who was buried there, had ordered her not to quit his grave until the clay was dry. As she wished to go home as soon as possible, she was fanning it to accelerate the tardy process of drying. The philosopher fanned it dry at once with his magical fan, returned home, and related the story to his wife, who vehemently condemned the widow's scanty respect for the dead.

Fanning the Grave.

After a while, Chwang-tsz was taken ill and died. His widow had promised that she would never marry again, but she soon became enamoured of a young man who introduced himself as one of the deceased philosopher's pupils. They were soon betrothed, but he fell ill with cholic, and in reply to her solicitous inquiries, said that there was only one efficacious remedy for him, namely, the brains of a newly-deceased man. She went, therefore, to her husband's coffin, and opened it with a hatchet, when, to her great alarm, he rose up alive and well. The "disciple" had been the product of his magical powers. She fled and hung

---

[1] It appeared in Goldsmith's *Citizen of the World*, 1763 ; in Davis's *Chinese*, 1845 ; and has been retold by R. K. Douglas in his *Chinese Stories*, 1893. An interesting parallel to the latter part is found in *German Popular Stories* (Chatto & Windus, 1892), pp. 126-27, where, instead of a philosopher, we find an old fox. The climax is thus told :—

"'Now, Pussy dear, open windows and doors,
And bid all our friends at our wedding to meet ;
And as for this nasty old master of ours,
Throw him out of the window, Puss, into the street.'

But when the wedding-feast was all ready, up sprung the old gentleman on a sudden, and, taking a club, drove the whole company, together with Mrs. Fox, out of doors." The fox in this old tale has nine tails, to which the Chinese have a curious parallel in the saying, "He is like a nine-tailed fox, bad to provoke."

AN OLD, OLD STORY IN A NEW EDITION. 299

herself for shame. On which the philosopher began drumming upon a

basin, and gave vent to his feelings by singing a song beginning—

"Alas! earth's joys are empty all;
From open flowers the petals fall.
She dead, I must her bury;
I dead, she sure would marry."

"There are many memorial arches in Hanyang," continued Nieh, "erected in honour of virtuous widows, who were the opposite of all this.[1] The rebels may destroy the temples, except those of the Sacred Sage, but it would be a myriad pities if they were to destroy these. As to my child, it will be with her as with a young bride of the T'ang dynasty, whose husband was banished indefinitely. She tied her hair with string, and covered it with white silk, on which she made her husband write, 'No hand but my lord's shall undo this.' After twenty years he came back and found the silken seal unbroken. So when our general comes back in triumph, he will find his bride faithfully waiting for him."

"Seng-teh, ever virtuous and ever victorious!" cried the brother-in-law.

"I do not dare. But you really wish me to be a 'mandarin soldier'?"

"Yes, a 'heaven soldier.' Only thus will you be a filial son. Instead of the 'hut by the grave,' yours must be the 'opposing ramparts.'"

"What hut by the grave?" asked one of the guests.

"The neighbouring county to Hanyang on the north-east is Hiaokan," replied the scholar. "'Filial Influence,' you know. It originally had another name, but a certain filial son built a hut beside his father's grave, and remained there without shaving or washing for three years, subsisting upon the food which the benevolent brought him. When the time had expired, he was escorted to the city in great state. The ordinary city gate was not honourable enough for him.[2] The wall had to be broken down. He was feasted by the mandarin, and the name of the county was changed to 'Filial Influence.'

The City of Filial Influence.

---

[1] Compare the phrase "widows indeed," and the case of Anna, Luke ii. In the *Adventures of Hatim Tai* (from the Persian), the traveller, after witnessing a suttee-burning in India, observes, "Yet, in my opinion, the best proof of constancy would be to live single after the husband's death. This would be an ordeal more trying than even the flames of the funeral pile." Strangely enough, the motto on Chinese memorial arches is "fiery woman," *i.e.* heroine.

[2] Compare Psalm xxiv. 7 and 9. Also the reception given to the winners of the Olympian games. "At their return home, they rode in a triumphal chariot into the city, the walls being broken down to give them entrance" (Potter).

AN OLD, OLD STORY IN A NEW EDITION.

Hearing which, certain 'wandering-hand-leisure-lovers' took to building huts on their fathers' graves in many places. One of these having been invited by the unwilling mandarin, was noticed to use his chopsticks with his left hand. 'Is that your filial piety?' exclaimed the mandarin. 'Did your parents teach you a left-handed doctrine?' In which phrase, I need hardly remind you, the word 'left,' as in some ancient usages, has a bad meaning. Eventually the Emperor Kang Shi

issued an edict against these hyper-filial practices. You therefore are absolved from such an observance."

"I hear he has been over-filial in another direction," broke in the unmitigated, the "taste" of whose witticisms must be explained as being the Chinese word for flavour. "Taste" is the word applied to condiments, to food with plenty of salt or pepper, or to a bowl of capsicums. Is the anecdote pungent? Never mind from whence the pungency comes. Does the remark tickle the case-hardened mental palate of the man who makes it? It is in good "taste" as far as he is concerned. Which was exemplified in a very mild way by what followed. "I hear he has been over-filial in another direction; he remained unshaven for more than forty-nine days."

This playing about with the one sacred subject of a Chinese orphan's mind, and the sarcastic reference to his rebel days, stung the lad to the quick. We fight over the word "liar." In China the filial fight over the word "unfilial."

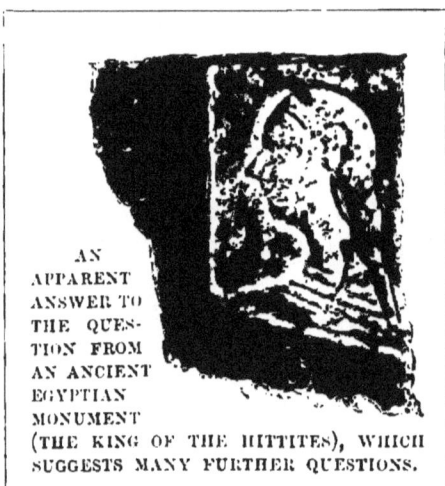

AN APPARENT ANSWER TO THE QUESTION FROM AN ANCIENT EGYPTIAN MONUMENT (THE KING OF THE HITTITES), WHICH SUGGESTS MANY FURTHER QUESTIONS.

"I ask you, Where did the shaven head and the queue come from? Our ancestors two hundred years back knew nothing of it."

"You young rebel!" retorted Seng-teh's uncle, whose playful manner had suddenly changed, like that of a playful pussy who smells a rat. "You young rebel! The man who won't apply the razor to his forehead ought to have a bigger knife applied to his neck.[1] That's all I have to say to you."

"Seng-teh's unshaven days are over," said Nieh Shen-seng calmly, by way of restoring the peace.

"Then he is not like the Literary Emperor of the Han dynasty, of whom you were telling us the other day," blurted out the brother-in-law, determined to fight, even if it were from the Longhaired camp. "'He nursed his mother for three years without closing his eyes or unloosing his girdle,' and of course without shaving."

"Don't be irreverent!" exclaimed Nieh Shen-seng. "You are a regular 'heaven-net, earth-gauze' man. You would catch men however they move."

"I am three years your senior, Shu-k'ing."

---

[1] The dogmatism of this reply is more than matched by that of Sir William Fairfax to his little daughter, the afterwards accomplished Mary Somerville. She had expressed a wish that Englishmen would discard pigtails, when the fierce old Tory, who viewed those appendages as the very insignia of loyalty to church and king, thundered out with an oath, "When a man cuts off his queue, his head should go with it."

It was now Seng-teh's time to be peacemaker. "I know the reason of the three years' mourning. It is given in the *Analects*: 'It is not till a child is three years old that it is allowed to leave the arms of his parents' [his betrothed had only been weaned a few months back]; but what is the reason of the seven times seven days of—unshaven head?"

"I cannot tell. But in the commentary on an obscure passage in the *Book of Changes*, that very old classic which Confucius venerated so as to wish he had fifty years more to give to its study, it is said, 'In the tenth month,' the winter solstice, 'the *Yang* [masculine or solar] principle emerges, and is completely embodied in a month's time. At the fifth month the *Yin* principle [female principle, exemplified in the moon, but here rather the deprivation of the Yang] emerges, and after seven periods'—six [lunar] months and a portion—'the *Yang* principle returns. There is also a revolution every seven days.'

<small>The Sabbatic Number Seven.</small>

"Then in the works of the Taoist sage Chwang-tsz, just mentioned, it is said, 'The lord of the southern seas [*Yang*] and the lord of the northern seas [*Yin*] often met in the domains of the lord of the centre, whose name is Chaos, who always treated them handsomely. Whereupon they agreed together that in return they would find some means of benefitting him, saying, "Every man has seven openings, the two organs of sight, two of hearing, one of taste, and one of smell. Chaos alone has none. Let us try and pierce some for him." So the first day they succeeded in piercing the first hole [*i.e.* gave light to him]; but by the time seven days had elapsed, Chaos died.'[1] Nine, however, is the Taoist perfect number, formed of three times three. Thus they speak of the nine-storied heavens.[2] Seven is not elsewhere quoted by them."

Nieh Shen-seng being now on his mettle for superiority

---

[1] This looks like a survival of Genesis i. with its "Let there be light" as the first fiat which led to the ultimate "death of Chaos."

[2] One is almost tempted to find a parallel to this in Milton's "ninefold harmony" of the spheres. That, however, is a probable reference to a Grecian lyre of nine strings. The Taoist expression will be seen to be a reduplicated parallel to the "third heaven," quoted by St. Paul.

of knowledge, which makes a man the real senior of another, turned up the *Imperial Dictionary*, and read, "'The number seven comes from the seven stars of the northern constellation,' but, according to another authority, 'from the sun, moon, and the five elements,—metal, wood, water, fire, and earth.'[1] It is also said that in ancient times the statesmen, on receiving hereditary titles, made a sevenfold obeisance. It also speaks of the three-seven herb, which has three leaves on one side and seven on the other; but the proper name of that medicinal herb may be 'mountain varnish,' the same sounds as three and seven.

"Seven seems to be the Buddhist perfect number. Thus, in the winter, at the Hanyang monastery, they have a ceremony called the 'Sevenfold race,' where men and women run round a pole to the sound of masses for seven days—to get rid of their sins, it is said. The correct time for masses for the dead is seven days, and the correct number of priests is seven. In some parts, too, seven garments must be worn by the bride on her wedding-day. In other parts, I have heard, every seventh day is unlucky."[2]

Seng-teh chimed in with the remark that, following their Sacred Book, the "Longhaired" observed every seventh day in a distinctive fashion. That book, they say, came from the West, but it is not Buddhist.

"Curious," said Nich Shen-seng. "We cannot, however, accept them as our teachers. The classics are all-sufficient."

"On this point?" wickedly inquired his brother-in-law.

---

[1] St. Augustine is not very lucid upon the intrinsic properties of the number seven. He says: "Let this be a sufficient admonition, that three is the first number wholly odd, and four wholly even, and the two make seven, which is therefore oftentimes taken for all" (*City of God*, xi. xxxi.).

[2] Every seventh day is marked on the Amoy almanacs as *Mi er* (or occult day). The sound probably represents the old Persian *Mihr*, a name of the sun or sun god. This would make it literally Sunday, with which day (and not the Jewish Sabbath) the day corresponds. The day is said to have been thus marked from time immemorial. The fact that it is not marked on the Peking almanacs would seem to argue that it did not arise from Jesuit influence. It is always placed on that part of the page which contains the day unlucky for doing work. In the course of ages the "Sunday" may have been accidentally moved one day forward. In Corea, the same day is called by the name "day of great light" (*Notes and Queries of China and Japan.*—T. Watters).

AN OLD, OLD STORY IN A NEW EDITION.

"The character for West has always a good meaning," continued the scholar, not deigning to notice the remark. "But they are insurrectionists. How do they observe the day?"

"By having meat and wine."

"It is their eating day,"[1] said the brother-in-law with a pun (*to eat* and *seven* being the same sounds). "That's it. What more need be said? I am going."

Thus the conversation after the betrothal feast ended.

---

[1] A French writer, puzzled to discover the pleasures of the English Sabbath, has called our Sunday, *jour qu'on distingue par un* pudding!" (Bulwer Lytton, *England and the English*, p. 177).

Chapter XV.

IMPERIAL POP-GUNS.

A GOLDEN OX IN COMMAND—SACRED STONES—INTERRUPTED MEDITATIONS—THE FATES, AND HOW AN OFFICER MADE FRIENDS WITH THEM.

"Soldiers, military affairs are your occupation. Be thoroughly versed in firing, riding, archery, and drill: keep perfect rank."—*Sacred Edict.*

WITH the next day came the news that the Imperialists had encamped at Soho (river of the So family), a town nearer to Seng-teh's birthplace than was his present residence; seldom visited, however, by the inhabitants of the Yang Family Pavilion, in consequence of a former lawsuit between them and one of the chief clans there.

Wishing his "son-in-law" to become a "heaven soldier" as soon as possible, Nieh Shen-seng took him and his horse across about a mile of lake, then by a road a few miles further, and gained an interview with the commander, Yang Ch'ang-sz (*Ch'ang*, as in Wuchang, means splendour; *Sz* is the name of a classical river). Their conversation was most entertaining to the two parties concerned. Each bedizened the other with polite phrases. A verbatim report, even if possible in the grossly ordinary words of our unideal language, would be voted very tedious by the reader. From such tedium, therefore, he shall be magnanimously spared.

This commander being related to all the known and unknown generals of the day, Seng-teh's fortune was made, his horse accepted as a present, and the youth decked out in a red coat with a broad blue border. He would rise in the ranks under the commander's special smile.

Commander Yang's forces consisted of sanpan crews. "Sanpan" must be retained. One cannot say gunboats. That would be too big a name. Pop-gun boats would be irreverent. Yang we may call a naval officer, though he had never been to sea, nor had his fleet. He would have been very sick, and his boats would have overturned with the first big wave.

But in China there is a strange correspondence between the produce of fresh water and salt. The only difference, the Chinese say, is that salt-water fish are found ready salted, whereas their's are not. A hundred miles north-west of Hanyang is a city called Tehngan (virtuous peace), where are broad sands, as of a beach. When the river is low, a pony might go four or five miles in a straight line over these sands with a little wading, disturbing with his hoofs such things as cockle and mussel shells, and innumerable white stones from which our seaside children strike phosphorescent fire. Shrimpers' boats are seen there, and an occasional sea-gull flies overhead on the stormier days, 800 miles from the sea. The city of Virtuous Peace was soon to be visited by the naval officer Yang and his fleet.

At present he was at Soho. The So river has long since run dry. Perhaps it never existed. *Ho* may after all be *hu* (lake). Yang was a very different man from Li, as Seng-teh soon learned. In person he was inclined to be corpulent; in disposition, though very bland on occasion, he was somewhat treacherous and cruel. His men did not like him. He was more Chinese than Li, more of a scholar, with many of the scholar's bad points. He was a literary B.A., but had "sold his books and bought a sword," as a seal of his —not the big official seal—indicated. When Nieh had gone, he appointed Seng-teh his place upon one of the sanpans, and remained invisible, except from a distance, for ever after.

The country folk had suffered far more from his presence during a week or so than those nearer the Nine Recluses Hill had done in several months from the "Longhaired." He was rapacious and covetous. He preferred silver to oxen; he demanded both. His men nicknamed him the "Golden Ox," from the name of a hill they had passed in entering the lake from a canal just above Tsaitien.

The rebels having now invested part of Tehngan, and there being none of the "vermin" to exterminate in the immediate neighbourhood, and hardly an ox worth having from the impoverished country folk, he ordered his fleet to emerge through the canal into the Han. The day was auspicious in weather as in Imperial foresight, and it was a brave sight to see his war galleys going single file along the narrow canal. In the latter part, where the current is rapid, they had to use boat-hooks. Many of the boats "bumped," and some got stuck in the mud by the kilns which adorn the eastern bank. The left bank, a Tsaitien man informed our young hero, presented a remarkable sight in the second month (seen at its best in our early April). There were nearly three miles of rape in flower, yellow and scented, and very tall (five or six English feet high).

At length the boats emerged into the Han. They had then twenty miles to go along the winding river to Shinkeu (the "New Canal"). Here they left the Han. The canal was narrow, and the water pouring down from the lake at a furious rate. The boats were towed. They made slow progress. Yang was dyspeptic and volubly cantankerous.

The lake reached and passed, the "Celestial Maiden" Hill of Hauchwan being in sight on the left, they anchored for the night at a small town which Yang did his best to wipe clean. His opium had run short. That of the place, he said, was not worth smoking. It produced no exhilaration. And the very opposite of exhilarated did the naval officer prove to be. Seng-teh, hearing his voice from afar, thought there were compensations in his own lot.

The next night found them at Kehmatan (frog pond), where even the frogs had died of starvation, so Yang remarked. His men meanwhile enjoyed the bread (a coarser edition of that of our farmhouses) which is characteristic of the place.

It was found that the water was too shallow higher up the "Præfectural River" for even the smallest boats to go with anything more than the speed of a tortoise. It

IMPERIAL POP-GUNS. 309

was a matter of wading and pushing for them. A fleet drawing a couple of feet of water would be out of the question.

They must therefore march overland a distance of twenty-six miles, and leave their cannon behind. This was done, and at the sight of the Imperialists the rebels retreated farther north. So that Yang gained a decisive victory. Is it not recorded in the official books of the Præfecture to this day? After a few feasts within the walls of the city of Virtuous Peace, the houses of which were very low, suggestive of the previous dynasty, but the fare in the winter months consisting of mutton, boned and sold with the crackling on, hares, and game, besides the inevitable year-in-year-out chicken and pork, Commander Yang retired on horseback—Seng-teh's horse, as it was a good one—to the "Frog Pool" of deceased frogs aforesaid.

Here he heard that Hanchwan (streams of Han) was invested by the rebels. The fleet therefore set sail for that county city. They anchored at night hard by the tomb of one of Confucius' disciples, not quoted, however, in the *Analects*. Here, with good opium from Tehngan,—Yang preferred that to the wine beloved of Li,—he had a quiet evening in company with the "Sacred Sage" and his disciples.

In the early morning one of the boat crews—it happened to be that one in which Seng-teh was found—was sent to the city to reconnoitre. They were dressed in garments contributed on compulsion by the country folk in the village near. "Yon's the 'Tiger copse,'" said one of those who acted as guide. "There is a golden rabbit under the ground somewhere, but we have not yet found it. Are any of you Mohammedans,[1] for I have heard they can see into the earth?"

They approached the city, with hoes over their shoulders,

---

[1] "In the Tang dynasty, on the occasion of the opening of trade with foreign ships, the Mohammedan King Mahomet sent his mother's brother from Western countries to China to trade. He built a tomb and monastery. . . . Soon after the monastery was completed, he died, and was buried in the tomb, in accordance with his intention" (from a Chinese work, quoted by Dr. Edkins).

to make them as countrified as possible. They halted before a bit of rock, where their guide sat down. "Do you know the history of this?" he inquired. "This indentation was made by the god of war, when he sat here. Here on the left is the dent made by his foot. Here on the right the place where he rested his famous sword. But it needed sharpening, and so one of his two 'brothers,' the present god of pork butchers, sharpened it upon this bit of rock behind. See, it is flat and red. On the thirteenth day of the ninth month the mandarins come out, light incense, and knock their heads on the ground before it.[1] If the weather is damp, it emits blood on that day, and we have a good harvest."

A native of Hanchwan came running along from the city. What news? The rebels are retiring, as there is a large Imperialist force coming down the Han. News had been brought by messengers who have come across the country by road, which saves seven miles, you know,—sixty-three instead of seventy. (He gave the distance in *li*.) They have not gone yet, but are making preparations to go.

Which news was duly reported to Commander Yang. At sunset, moreover, the Imperialists seemed to have arrived and entered the evacuated city. A little later, a countryman came to say that he had fled from a certain Hwang Kwei-keu (kneeling dog), a violent man of those parts, who had joined the rebels, and that they intended, thus strengthened in numbers, to attempt a night surprise. He was afraid to take the news to the city, for they had spies who knew him.

The captain of Seng-teh's boat having related the news, that youth volunteered. He could go dressed as a country boy. This being reported to Yang, Seng-teh was authorised to do so. He sallied forth, therefore, in the pale moonlight along the paths which the morning's expedition had rendered familiar. The "Celestial Maiden" Hill was already dark with men! The enemy was rallying there out of sight of the city. So he changed his course and went round. The nearest gate was the "Joy Gate," as he had learned, but he would go by a circuitous route to the other side of the city, where the outlook was over frequently flooded flats. The

[1] This custom is still annually observed.

sense of importance repaid him for the peril of the expedition. His rain hat and grass cloak, moreover, and his youth seemed to him a great protection.

At length, following the walls, he came to the east gate,

nearest the river. It was shut. He hammered with his fists at the iron-studded door. A sleepy voice answered from within. The words "benighted country lad" proved to be ineffectual.

"But the rebels are near."

"That they are not. They know better. They are farther off."

"I will give you a hundred cash—three hundred."

That proved a key to the massive though somewhat worm-eaten and badly-plated doors. They were unbarred.

"My cash!"

"The way to the military mandarin's *yamun*?"

"Stop!"

But the country lad had fled amid a hail of curses upon his ancestors, near and remote. The streets were clear, the inhabitants were enjoying the first night's rest they had dared to take for some time, effectually protected from weak-minded burglars by the night watchman, who was certainly making a brave noise with his piece of hollow bamboo and his gong.

To this functionary Seng-teh attached himself, after the former had recovered from his shock at seeing anyone about. "The way to the military mandarin's *yamun*?"

"Why?"

"Never mind why. Important business."

"You are a burglar." But the burglar had fled, to accost another night watchman (his tom-toming of course being a guide to his whereabouts), from whom, after letting out his errand, he obtained the desired information, the watchman accompanying him by way of protection, and also to claim the honour of bringing the news.

They hammered at the *yamun* doors, but how could an official doorkeeper, still less the higher custodians of the inner portals, through whom alone access could be obtained to the unspeakably great one,—how could even the lowest of the series be expected to attend to a country lad's cry? He hammered and hammered, and, from within, the doorkeeper cursed and cursed. "You would beat all the paint off the door gods, would you?" You being a euphemism for the exact titles of address employed. Yes, Seng-teh would have done that if the doors could thus be opened.

The watchman called out "Burglars," that being his official cry. The country boy called out "Rebels, conspiracy, night surprise," and the like, until his throat was dry. When their tone of voice changed. "What is that?"

The moon was beclouded, and there was a glare in the sky toward the west. "It is our boats. Quick! In the name of the Emperor, open the door; the rebels are upon us."

Sounds of firing confirming it, the doorkeeper arose, saw the glare, beat the emergency drum, and fired off one of the petards kept for salutes. Then, keeping the outer door closed, he hammered at the inner one, claiming the news to be the result of his wakefulness.

The noise from outside grew louder. A glare was seen within the city. "They have forced the Gate of Joy," said the watchman. "Come with me." They ran round to the north gate, and aroused the sleepy gatekeeper. He would not let them out, but went and aroused the little company of red-coats in the guardhouse near. He had made the discovery of the invasion all by himself. They thanked him, for they ought to have had one at least on watch. They roused their demisemi-captain, and told what they, with their unaided sentinelship, had discovered.

Guided by the watchman, Seng-teh found himself upon a point in the low wall from which it was easy to descend. The bricks were much worn, and a girdle eased the operation wonderfully.

"I was once chased by a burglar," the man began; but looking round, and thinking he saw pursuers in the present tense, made off in among the vegetable gardens, where there were plenty of trees, also of ill-odorous tanks, as Seng-teh nearly proved. Then on, over a plank bridge to the river bank, where lay the boats that had come down the Han that day.

They were challenged by the now aroused crews, whom Seng-teh might have aroused before if he had known their location. The watchman struck his bamboo in the characteristic way, and thus narrowly prevented himself being shot as a rebel. Still on for a hundred or two yards to the "Superlative [-ly anything you like] Pavilion." This, if the folk would admit them, would form a watch-tower, and, for the present, a place of safety. Being admitted at length, they ascended the staircase, aroused a few friends of the keeper, who were being accommodated for the night in the sanctum sanctorum of the god of literary emolument, spite of his chronic attitude of "just about to kick out." Is it to prevent any accidents that the idol-cutters generally leave the uplifted leg unfinished? An idol with only one leg would hardly seem to be a worthy object of adoration for even the most "catholic and no partisan" scholar. But we are fiddling while Rome is burning. Moreover, no scholar, however learnedly Confucian, worships his one-and-a-half-legged " Literary Splendour" image when there are rebels within a quarter of a mile of him. He uses both his own legs then.

The sleepers being aroused, came out on the balcony, saw a glare, heard reports of firearms and the mingled noise of a city where everyone was shouting or screaming, and where fierce fighting was going on in every main street,—and fled to their country homes, leaving the two alone.

Commander Yang, who was not going to be deprived of his night solace for any Imperial contingent, however welcome, for any " Kneeling Dog," however savage, had, after Seng-teh's departure, come out on deck to body forth once more to his now illuminated soul the forms of the disciples, one of whom was buried on the low hill before him. Under such artistic use of the imagination, the tablets were no longer mere stone. The whole seventy-two of the sage's immediate followers were there, standing or sitting around the philosopher. So real was the vision, that he was hardly surprised to see a head peeping over the upper wall of the tomb, then another and another. It was part of his dream, or, if objective, a countryman or two engaged in the truly Confucian "investigation of things," which, as everyone who has read the classics knows, is determined to be the source of "complete knowledge," "complete knowledge" the forerunner of "sincere thoughts," "sincere thoughts" the forerunners of "rectified hearts," "rectified hearts" of the "cultivation of the person," "cultivation of the person" of "regulated families," "regulated families" of "rightly-governed kingdoms," "rightly-governed kingdoms" of a "tranquil and happy empire"—"all under heaven." "All under heaven tranquil and happy." "Yes, this is good opium. Hope to get some more when I dine to-morrow with the other commander. Most fortunate our meeting, though he is no schol"—

"Bang!"

"Bang! bang!" And Commander Yang has gone to meditate elsewhere. His men, many of whom have been smoking opium also,[1] are now aroused to a death-struggle. They drive back the enemy, they leap on shore, when some more of the enemy leap into the boats with torches lit from smouldering spills, and the name of Confucius' immediate disciple grows lustrous in the flares of the burning fleet. But the rebels, or rather the country folk who have joined them, are chased to the city walls and in through the open gates, where, after scaling the wall, their comrades have well-nigh captured the city. Here a burning house reveals the red blood pools, and the ghastly heap of the dead red-coats, or those in the civilian's blue. All around are groans, cries, shrieks of agony, forming a compound yell.

Once within the city, the pursued turn round and receive their pursuers upon the points of fixed bayonets, or hurl iron-shod coolie poles at them, spear fashion. The heap of red-coats grows higher and higher. It serves as a rampart, but over that gory heap the enemy comes in a wild charge. Back, all of you, to the Gate of Joy! It is reached! It is shut! The living mass presses against it. Some are crushed in the struggle. That gate will not be opened again to-night. Break through yon house to the right! Up on the walls, now down, however impossible the leap! See, there is a pile of bodies beneath to lessen the drop. Now for the river! All is lost. The "Kneeling Dog" reigns monarch of the "Streams of Han."

. . . . .

As the year closed (February 1854) Seng-teh might

[1] "As to the soldiers, it is quite notorious that the regulars at the commencement of the Taiping Rebellion were so demoralised and emasculated with opium that it was lucky that they had strength enough left in them to run away with!" (V. P. Suvoong, M.D., B.D.).

have been seen as one of a group of sanpan soldiers, clad in red jackets with broad green adornments, squatting or reclining on deck, hard by Tsaitien. His comrades had even grown tired of gambling, and now tale-telling was the order of the day, the subject being the approaching New Year.

Our New Year is sometimes represented as a new-born babe in the arms of Father Time. That latter personage is unknown in China. His only parallel is the star of longevity, represented as a very high-browed old man, of senility so extreme that he has passed the days of second childhood, and has returned down the evolution scale to stop at the restful climax of happy vegetation. He is but connected with the New Year by contrast. This infant, though not definitely represented as such, is, as the reader has gathered from a previous chapter, the embodiment of super-infantile sensitiveness.

A breath of unlucky phraseology, and he is disfigured for life. But which are lucky and which unlucky words seems to be an open question, if the following tale, related on Seng-teh's boat, be true:—

"One of the underlings of a *yamun*, on the last night of a year, left his hat on an empty coffin he had extorted from a dealer. In the early morning, the mandarin went out as usual to worship the god of riches. 'Where's my hat?' exclaimed the *yamun* runner when the time came for him to accompany his official master. 'On the coffin' [*kwan ts'ai*], replied his wife, to his great horror. He would surely need the coffin that year. But snatching up his hat, he had to go out without relieving his pent-up feelings. He was only just in time.

<small>Punning Propensities of the Fates.</small>

"That year he prospered wonderfully. The word *kwan*

had meant *official* recognition, and *ts'ai* riches. [The gods had given him the benefit of the pun.]

"A comrade of his, hearing of his good luck, resolved to try the experiment. 'Where's my hat?' he cried as the moment came. 'On the "longevity chest"' [*seu ch'i*], replied his well-instructed wife. But that year he did nothing but *receive* the *anger* of his master."

This tale was received with forced approbation, for after the very mottled fortunes of the past year, and the many risings in country parts, all the lucky words in the language seemed to have some punning interpretation which meant calamity. The Imperial designation, as we have seen, under its apparent good luck, meant the distractions of the Rebellion. This might be welcome to soldiers. But the Chinese soldier, not being quite a patriot, fights with some hope of a name, or even promotion to office. What use would office be, when, as with Commander Yang, even an evening's calm meant death; or riches, when the rebels were attracting all the daring thieves from the various counties?

The first tidings the New Year brought was to the effect that the rebels had retaken Wuchang, Hanyang, and Hankow. "There had been a great battle by Hwangchow, fifty miles down the Yangtse. It had been fought during a snowstorm. The Imperialist general, after fighting desperately, had killed himself, and many of his officers had done the same. The Admiral T'ang had held the Yangtse, but the *Fu Tai* [second mandarin of the province] took away his men, and he drowned himself. The *Fu Tai* fled for shame and poisoned himself.

"The new *Fu Tai*, knowing that his men could not hold Wuchang by reason of the snowstorm stopping the ingress of rations, led them forth in flight from the city, and was beheaded as a traitor."[1] Were such things encouraging to the already defeated troops of the Hanyang county?

The little fleet in which Seng-teh now found himself had orders to remain at Tsaitien; and remain there they did for the year. The chief events of the twelve months took place on land. So that they themselves were only soldiers by apparel and sympathy.

[1] Wuchang official records.

IMPERIAL POP-GUNS. 319

A large contingent came down from Szchwan to retake Hanyang. These "yellow-turbaned" troops were, like their commander, of splendid physique, and possessed of that form of subjective bravery which underrates the powers of the enemy. A great battle was fought at the foot of the Inverted Pan Hill, which ended in great heaps of white bones, scattered along the road, from Dame Han's grave to the lake. The rebels' position was so strong that no one dare bury them. Among the bleaching bones, as the weeks went by, were still to be seen bits of yellow cloth, which had once been turbans. The bones had once been Szchwan braves.

So matters dragged on till the eighth month, when Cheng

Kwoh-fan with his Hunan men defeated the rebels, and retook the three cities.

"Time flies like an arrow, days and months like a shuttle," as the Chinese say in lieu of our row of stars, and it was now the New Year (March 1855). This month again was marked by a repetition of the bad luck of the previous first month. The rebels came back again and retook the three cities. No, the news was not quite accurate. They had attacked Wuchang, but had been driven back.

Wuchang possessed a new *Fu Tai* named Hu Lin-yi, of

both literary and military talents, who was destined to make a name in both departments. His own city being intact, he was wont to sit upon the end of the Serpent Hill, under the shadow of the Yellow Crane Tower, and, with the two cities in sight,—the stolen goods in view,—to devise some plan for their recapture. His most trustworthy officer was a certain Pao Ts'ao, some years his junior, but possessed of a high hereditary title. Fired by the sight of the enemy's fleet, the boats of which had once been Imperialist, he gathered together all available boats for a battle. They met in mid-Yangtse, Hu Lin-yi looking on. Pao Ts'ao felt that not only his eyes, but the eyes of all future readers of the official records, together with the eyes of the Imperial Court, were upon him. Alas! Eleven of his fourteen men were shot down before his eyes, the crews of the other boats suffering in a corresponding manner. He turned and fled. He landed and entered the city. "It is no use!" he said to Hu Lin-yi.

[margin: Hu Lin-Yi and Pao Ts'ao.]

"Not with such cowards as you to lead."

"What? A coward not to go on fighting when eleven out of fourteen had fallen?"

"Yes, a coward. Give him forty blows."

Was the *Fu Tai* in earnest? He was. His hand sought his cheek. He began to smile. That was enough. Hu Lin-yi had a peculiar birthmark upon his left cheek. When thoroughly enraged, he would smile strangely, and in extreme cases scratch the mark with his long nails. That meant the death-warrant of someone or other.

The lictor was just in time. Grasping the red staff used as part of the apparatus of court-martial, he belaboured the prostrate form of the young viscount.

The thirty-two blows (8 = 10) having been given, the officer jumped to his feet and confronted his judge. "Look here, Hu Lin-yi"—he actually used his name and thumped the table as he did so—"Look here, if I do not gain a victory by this time to-morrow, not my fist, but my severed head shall be bumped on this table."

Who could resist such a speech! "He has called the *Fu Tai* by name!" ran through the ranks. And there were plenty of volunteers. It was to be the same small fleet of sanpans as that which was so severely thrashed an hour before. But orders were sent forth to collect a few dozen cotton-wool-lined *pei wos* (quilts, blankets, sheets, and even "beds" in one) in which the Chinese sleep. "Was it a grim joke after all?" No; P'ao Ts'ao had all his wits about him. After sundown these *pei wos* were taken to the river's bank and thoroughly soaked in water, then put tent-wise over the little gunboats.[1]

It was now dark but for the rebel lights across the Yangtse. Guided thereby, the bedding-protected boats rowed across, were seen, were met, were fired upon, and returned the fire from musket barrels put through holes in the bedding. It mattered not where the men fired, the enemy was all around. The Imperialist shots took effect. The little cannon at the bows opened up a way through the broken line. Now, all sail up! There is a fair breeze. The thickest part of the enemy's fleet is left behind. They can hardly fire with any conscience, for their own men are encamped on the bank behind the daring P'ao Ts'ao. Down with your sails, ye Imperialists! Up the steps of the landing-place before you. A little more fighting, and the rebels' guns are captured, and are now turned against the mass of ferryboats into which the rebels retreat. Hankow is won! Hu Lin-yi will smile in another way now. He will prepare a feast, and, with many an apology, will prophesy endless honours for the man he had beaten but a few hours ago.

[1] "A double curtain of fishing-nets around the boats proved effectual against the bullets of the opium smugglers around Macao" (E. Molloy).
During the siege of Paris, and especially at the time of the Commune, mattresses were put up at the windows as a protection against bullets.

Chapter XVI.

THE MART OF CENTRAL CHINA.

HERO-WORSHIP—EXCHANGE NO ROBBERY—DRAGONS OF WATER AND FIRE—SHOPKEEPERS AND SHARPERS.

"Beat your gong, your candles vend;
Each one to his trade attend."—*Chinese Proverb*.

IT was the sixth month (July 1855) before the little fleet stationed at Tsaitien had orders to sail down to Hankow, a great event in the history of the lad of fifteen and a half years, in whose career, by this time, I hope, we may feel some interest. Hankow is to country lads of these parts what London is to many a farmer's son in our own land. Perhaps the name is decked in even more iridescent radiance than is our own great lonely city. It is a panorama of never-wearying sights. It is the place *par excellence* for wondrous tales.

With something like enthusiasm, therefore, Seng-teh beheld the forests of masts, and what were to him gorgeous and massive structures which lined the left bank of the Han, as his boat glided down with the current. They anchored by the landing-stage called *Wu Seng Miao*, the temple of the Military Sacred One, otherwise the Imperial Kwan, the god of war. Having seen the indented resting-place of this once human worthy outside the walls of Hanchwan, Seng-teh, though true to his promise to Captain Li with regard to the non-worship of idols, to which he was helped by the admonition of his peach-stones, could not but be interested in this famous personage.

THE MART OF CENTRAL CHINA.   323

He had read in the *Annals of the Three Kingdoms*

how that Kwan Yu (second century A.D.) was joined at the
The God outset by the virtuous Lieu Pei, afterwards
of War. emperor, and the impetuous Chang Fei, enshrined
to this day in the hearts of pork butchers the wide Empire

over; how that these three had sworn an oath of brotherhood, which was sacredly kept as the years went by.[1]

The virtues of Kwan Yu seem to have been chiefly those of heroism, loyalty, and probity. On one occasion the trusty warrior had conducted two captured ladies to a place of safety, outside which, lantern in hand, he stood sentinel the livelong night. He was evidently a man to be respected, all the more because of the lawless times in which he lived.

From the demisemi-lieutenant (with whom Seng-teh was in high favour) he heard the following account of how this hero came to be deified. "The Emperor Kien Lung [1736-1796] gave out one morning that, as he sat on his throne in the dawning light,[2] he saw a man standing before him with a drawn sword in his hand. Asking his name, he was answered, 'I am the second of the sworn brethren.' On looking at the sword again, he found it to be that so often depicted by artists, and so minutely described in the Annals. It was over a hundred pounds in weight, and was called the 'sombre dragon,' the 'reclining moon,' and, when well worn, the 'saw of glittering frost.' Answering as it did to this description, its bearer could be none other than Kwan Yu of antiquity.

His Deification.

"'Where is the third brother?' inquired the Emperor. 'In Yiyang,' was the reply. On making inquiries, it was found that Yiyang was a small town in Hunan [of less rank than Tsaitien], and that its little mandarin was named Chang Pei. This coincidence confirming the Emperor in the truth of his vision, Chang Pei was sent for. He, poor man, was so terrified by the Imperial summons that he inhaled gold leaf and died. The Emperor then gave out that he himself was no other than the Lieu Pei of old time [and therefore, by reason of a few years seniority, Kwan Yu's superior]. This being allowed by the courtiers, he decreed that the Imperial Kwan should everywhere receive divine honours."

Half-way down Hankow from the God of War Gate is a

---

[1] The traditional portraits of these three worthies have already appeared hovering over the Hanchwan rock.

[2] All Chinese officials have to be early risers. Morning calls are paid at 6 A.M. The Emperor is supposed to rise much earlier still.

bend in the Han, where the Emperor Kien Lung, a great traveller, was once entertained, hence its name, the Imperial Reception. Passing the spot one day, the lieutenant told Seng-teh that Kien Lung was a very Chinaman and no Manchu. The previous Emperor had a daughter, and sent for a certain statesman who was rejoicing over the birth of a son, commanding him to bring the babe for the Imperial benediction. The infant was taken into the inner apartments, and exchanged for the new princess. The minister did not find it out until the bundle of silk wraps was undone. He dare not expostulate. "The Emperor Kien Lung," added the narrator of this legend, "wanted to restore the Ming dress [Mose in Egitto], but his foster-mother forbade him, as those in power would not scruple to kill the man who should thus stoop to raise his countrymen. Thus, you see, except for Manchu mothers, we have a native dynasty after all."

Kien Lung not a Manchu.

That bend in the river was decked in roseate hues at once. To the mind of the appreciative lad, who had only known Tsaitien, and who had only once paid a hurried visit to two real Chinese cities, the one a literally sleepy place, the other a 'sleepy city' in a state of nightmare, Hankow was a marvellous place, full of bewilderingly busy life. Moreover, his first sight of it was through the glorifying glasses of historical legend. Everything seemed broad and large to him. Let us try and look at the great mart through his eyes, though they be child eyes. Every country lad feels very young when he comes to Hankow.

There is more in this standpoint than we may at first imagine. It is not quite parallel to that of the artist who subjected the Hill of the Nine Recluses to a form of idealisation which must be described as poetic untruth. It is true artistic vision, it is " breadth." Our old masters drew a figure or a landscape as no modern artist could draw either, though he had the same models before him. The eyes of the old masters were child eyes. Hence the "breadth" of their pictures. We may analyse their pictures and speak of skilful massing of lights and shades. But the "breadth" is unexplained. It is but the child's standpoint. The old masters bid us look at men and things, scriptural and classical, through their child eyes.

The modern visitor enters the Han from the Yangtse. He has breakfasted at the "Concession," with its massively rigid piles of stuccoed bricks; he sees a "bit of a creek," a creek, he is informed, which runs considerably over a thousand miles inland. A river, then, with a conglomerate mass of junks, and a row of tumbledown houses behind them on the dirty banks. Bustle, noise, a swarming mass of heathendom, and a reeking mass of dirt—such is his analysis. He has not seen Hankow.

But let him live in some country place long enough to catch its spirit, then when the dreariness becomes well-nigh appalling let him come down the Han in company with a brightly intelligent country lad, all eyes and ears and memory. He may then, through his sympathies, catch a glimpse of Hankow.

"What a wonderful variety of boats!" "Yes, even a boatman can hardly tell all their names."

"What wonderful houses and tea-shops!" "Yes, and wonderful tales connected with some of them, and more wonderful ones connected with the temples. There is the Sen Family Temple[1] yonder, behind that landing-place. Would you care to hear the tale? There was once a mandarin at Ichang [a thousand or so *li* up the Yangtse] whose father gave into his son's hands a number of silver ingots [fifty-three ounces each] to take to his native place. Fearing the youth would get into mischief at Hankow, the father covered the silver with molten tin, and called them ingots of tin. The young man reached Hankow, and wishing to see a bit of life, determined to sell his tin. The tinsmith having found out the secret, bought up the whole boat-load at 200 cash a catty [say, 6d. per lb.]. Before long the young scapegrace had spent all, and died in want. The enriched tinsmith soon after had an infant son. He had some forebodings that the spirit of the deceased prodigal had entered the babe. The child cried and cried until something was

Marginal note: History of the Ancient Sen Family Temple.

[1] It is the only bit of older Hankow which yet remains.

smashed, when it smiled. Thus it grew up. Its only pleasure was in destruction and waste.

"When grown up, the lad was challenged to spend three hundred taels [ounces of silver] at a meal. This he accomplished by procuring a number of peacocks' hearts and livers.

"Could he spend three thousand taels in a forenoon? 'Yes,' he said, and invested the sum in gold leaf, which he threw away leaf by leaf from the Yellow Crane Tower of Wuchang. It was splendid sport to see the crowd on shore and the concourse of boatmen scrambling for the gold leaf.

"After some years, the tinsmith died of grief, previously turning his remaining wealth into three hundred and sixty houses and the erection of the Sen Family Temple. His only stipulation with the tenants was that they should provide food and sleeve-money for his son for a year. The son having spent all his ready money, thought there must be some cause for their generosity. Discovering the houses to be his, he sold them all, but after two years died on the river bank a beggar without a cash."

Reaching the mouth of the Han, they threw the grappling-irons on shore at the "Dragon King Temple" landing-place, where Pao Ts'ao had forced an entrance a few months back. It is a busy spot. "Mandarin ferryboats," capable of holding as many as forty passengers, are coming and going between Hankow and Wuchang. The sunlit city of Wuchang, with its famous Yellow Crane Tower on the end of the Serpent Hill above the ancient battlements, seemed well-nigh Imperial to young Li. Behind that tower the temple walls seemed to open and display the sculptured effigy, in a reclining attitude, of the famous poet of the wine-cup, Li Ta'i-peh.[1] Seng-tch was no wine-drinker; few country lads of these parts are addicted to the cup. Instead, he seemed filled with the artistic new wine, under whose influences all pictures worth the name are painted. To while away the long hours at Tsaitien he had done many a drawing; rough and improbable the results might be, but truly appreciated by his comrades in a land where every house has its picture.

There was nothing doing to-day, so he would draw Wuchang. But here he felt the disadvantage of his low standpoint; that drawback which has forced upon Chinese artists their downward perspective. Every picture is drawn from a hill literally or metaphorically. Victor Hugo speaks of aerostation being known of old to the Chinese! This may well surprise the resident, but at anyrate each artist has his mental balloon. In some cases he soars above his own head to include himself in the picture. Chinese perspective is a necessity in a land of flat, but hill-surrounded cities.

At sunset the lieutenant went ashore " to see a relative." The rest of the men began the tale-telling so characteristic of Chinese evenings; characteristic, indeed, when Hankow supports so many professional tale-tellers.

"The deity of yon temple once [à la Kien Lung] wanted to see the world. Hovering over a pool, he thought that a bath in its cool waters would be delicious, so he changed him-

---

[1] Ta'i-peh (extremely white) is the name of the star Venus, of which this celebrated poet (699-762) was said to be the incarnation. At a very early age Li Ta'i-peh gave signs of remarkable talent and of a remarkable capacity for wine. Later on, "his penmarks agitated the elements; his poems moved the gods to tears." He came to the front in the Court of the Lustrous Emperor (second son of the historical Li Tan) owing to his deciphering an insulting message sent from "abroad." Here he triumphed over some statesmen who had previously snubbed him; one had to rub his ink, another to take off his boots for him. He was not too cautious in his witticisms, however, and offended the Emperor's chief favourite (Mistress Yang Kwei-fei, noticed further on), and was banished. The rest of his life was marked by much wandering and more wine-drinking. But in the years of his disgrace he produced the poems which have gained him high celebrity, and which have idealised the wine-cup too.

self back into a carp. The result was delightful, until he
The Dragon King. found himself hooked up by a fisherman on to the bank. His spirit flew straightway to the Taoist 'Sovereign on High' [a name stolen from the classics], and demanded a redress of grievances. The Supreme Deity merely remarked that fishermen would catch fish; and if he

valued his dragonship so lightly as to return to the carp condition, he must expect to be caught."[1]

"I know a more 'tasty' story than that," said another man. "There were once two youths living in adjoining huts
A Chinese Fairy Tale. on the same hill, whereon was a cave haunted by sprites, who used to come forth and help themselves to the crops, and were even said to carry men away to

[1] "Rain-cloud dragons are by no means creatures of a pond."

the cavern. One day a girl's shoe dropped down at the door of one of the huts. The lad, named Wang Er, who lived there, picked it up, and saw that it belonged to no mean damsel. Before long, Imperial proclamations were issued, promising high office to the man who should bring back a missing princess. The shoe must belong to her; and, having consulted with his friend, Wang Er set off with him to explore the goblin cave.

"They let themselves down by a rope, and wandered ten *li* in semi-darkness, when they came to a stone door, whereon was written, 'None but Wang Er can open me.' At the approach of the wondering youth, the door opened of itself, and there was the princess inside, whose sorrow now turned to gratitude. When they had reached the mouth of the cave, Wang Er suggested that his friend should should first ascend, then draw up the princess, letting down the rope for him to follow. Which latter the false friend omitted to do, spite of the princess' expostulations.

"When Wang Er realised that they had gone, and that there was no means of exit for him, he was duly distressed and terrified. He would fall a prey to the goblins. They would eat his mother up too, perhaps,—and he was a filial son. But he determined to explore the vast cave, to see if there was no other way of egress. Having walked a long distance, he came to an opening where was a lake glistening in the sunlight. A bridge spanned a narrow part of it, and beyond the bridge was a large house, its roof supported by tall pillars. As he crossed the bridge, he heard his name called, and, looking all around, saw a huge dragon coiled around one of the pillars.

"'Wang Er, come and unloose me!' it cried. 'I daren't: you will surely devour me,' was the discreet reply. 'I will not. Do fetch a bucket of water, and throw it over me. I am the son of the Dragon King, and will reward you for it.'

"Wang Er did as he was requested, and the dragon glided down, to transform itself into a handsome young prince. 'It was I who flew off with the Emperor's daughter, and was condemned by a certain goddess to be glued to the pillar by the solidified froth from my mouth. I cannot sufficiently reward you, but request the favour of your company to my home. Shut your eyes!' And the two flew off to the seabeach, where they plunged into the briny depths, to find a beautiful causeway, on either side of which were lobster-soldiers and crab-officers, the Imperial guards of the Dragon King. They were soon greeted by great fishes, who, with many marks of respect, hailed the return of their lost prince. The palace doors flew open, and they beheld the mighty monarch himself. To whom the prince related his escapade and its sequel, with loud praises for his deliverer.

"Tea being brought, Wang Er was entertained as an Imperial guest. 'We will banquet to-night,' said the Dragon King, 'to celebrate this auspicious occasion.' But the hour came, and no visible preparation. When the monarch said, 'Bring my magical teapot.' And it was brought. 'I want three men,' he said to it. The lid opened, and out came the three men, who commenced to spread the feast. 'Now, some dancers!' And out tripped four beautiful maidens, who sang and danced in a most graceful manner during the sumptuous feast. 'Let us have theatricals. Also a royal salute.' Guns boomed, and a stage and players in gorgeous costumes appeared.

"This over, the King promised Wang Er anything he would like to ask. Who with much diffidence suggested the magical teapot. Even this was not denied him, on the rescued prince's comparisons of the relative value of sons and teapots.

"The prince then accompanied Wang Er along the ranks of lobster-guard and crab-officers, until they reached the shore, and then the hill where Wang Er lived, where the grateful prince left him.

"'Why have you been so long, my boy?' asked the mother through her tears. 'I have been wailing for you. And your friend has been made a great official.' 'Has he! Well, we must have something to eat.' 'Alas! I have only a cash or so to spare; buy the maximum of rice and the minimum of extras.' 'No, mother; we will reverse the poor man's saying to-day!' and, taking his teapot in hand, he cried, 'A feast for mother and me.' And to the old dame's unspeakable amazement, the feast was spread in a trice! Then he related his adventures.

"On the morrow he called for carpenters, and they came; for silver, and ingot after ingot came tumbling out. Timber and stone were bought, and the house was eventually completed. When Wang Er's 'friend,' happening to be in the neighbourhood, thought he would like to give zest to his higher position by coming to see his old home.

"He was met with deserved reproaches, but was equal to the occasion. 'The Emperor sent urgent messages,' he said, 'and I could not wait for you. But you, too, have fared well.'

"The trustful Wang Er explained the cause, and exhibited the magical teapot. His 'friend' seized it, but the pot fell, and was broken. At this the false friend fled.

"Wang Er was stung by this heartless treachery, but learned a needed lesson on the subject of over-trustfulness. He gathered up the fragments, when they united! Off he went post-haste to the capital with his treasure. The Emperor was so pleased therewith that he gave him the highest literary degree possible" (called *Chwang yuen*).

"*Chwang yuen* cake, two cash a square," cried a dealer on a boat at the sound of the words. "Who wants *chwang yuen* cake?" The amused audience invested in a few squares, treating the tale-teller to the largest share for his tale.

At the moment, the "lieutenant" came on board, and ordered the boat to proceed up to *Wu Seng Miao*.

There was no moon, and they had some trouble in finding a place for the grappling-iron. Several boats had to make way, the boatmen well-nigh swearing at the representatives of their national army. It was like turning out of bed in an inn to accommodate more honourable guests. The weather was sultry and tiring, too, and they had been rowing all day, they said.

When a sudden outburst of fire from the bank seemed to presage a general launching forth. Above the thirty-feet flames,

A Chinese Fire.

rolled up great volumes of luminous smoke, and down came the fiery rain of sparks. It was the work of an instant. Gongs were beaten; the water-carriers formed into line. Very primitive "fire dragons" arrived with their bands of lantern-bearers. They could but save the neighbouring block of buildings. All was livid flame, until the crackling roofs fell in with a crash upon the burning timbers. Seng-teh had seen one of the sights of Hankow,—a sight, he said, he would never forget.

Next day, a dreary space remained, whereon were erected mat huts; for the dearest friend of a burnt-out man will not receive him for three days. "He has sparks about him." A strange form of latent heat! He is an unlucky man, punished

by the fire god. Whom the neighbours seek to please by celebrating his preserving kindness ("I am not as other men are") in thanksgiving masses. At such times a pole is erected on the spot, surmounted by a paper crane, and flying a pennant, at the top of which is written a powerful charm heading a column of characters, "Imperial heaven, golden gate, the gemmous emperor, the great, heavenly, adorable, mysterious, exalted Sovereign on High." Such flattery ought to disarm any deified Chinaman! On this occasion a man was burnt to death, and in the early morning the charred fragments of his body were collected, placed in a coffin, and a Taoist ("scholar," not in this case a priest) performed a dreary mass over the remains.

At morning rice one of the soldiers volunteered the statement that near his home a house of the value of a hundred strings of cash was burnt. The neighbours subscribed, and spent a hundred and twenty strings upon masses and theatricals, the burnt-out man not getting a single cash.

"Yes, he did, though. It was a big one, three feet across." A soldier began to laugh. "He carried it for three days." Another burst out laughing. "It was square." Several more joined in.

"Nonsense," cried Seng-teh: but with the rest he nearly choked himself. It was, of course, a cangue, worn for three days by the "fire head." Forty blows are given as well. If the owner of the house where the fire originates be a man of some position, he hires a substitute. A gong-beater is heard going about the street offering four or five thousand cash—say a hundred cash a blow—for any such substitute.

After morning meal, Seng-teh asked permission to go on shore. "Mind you are not robbed. Hankow is noted for sharpers, and you look an honest lad. Privates, however, are greater sharpers still. But bring me a pound of the best tobacco."

"How much am I to give for it?"

"Did I not say you were honest [simple]? You are raw. Go into a shop and ask for it. Tell them the Longhaired are fond of smoking, and may be here in a day or two. They are afraid of them by this time. But you have a conscience. Here, take this card of mine."

"And bring us a pound too," whispered the others.

He had never been in a real street before, so wide! He measured it. It was fully twenty feet in some places. And there before him was an interminable avenue of delight, decked with signboards, horizontal and vertical, with charac-

ters emblazoned thereon in all the colours of the rainbow, besides black and gold. He was dazzled, entranced.

"I am glad to see you," exclaimed a well-dressed man. "Come and have a cup of tea, or wine, which you prefer. Who would have thought of seeing you here? What wind blew you hither? You do not know me? Impossible! I was your father's great friend years ago. Your honourable surname is surely"—

"Wang."

"Exactly. I thought I could not be mistaken."

"And my name is Hwui-keu, the *hwui* of wise and the *keu* of dog." At which the man retreated, crestfallen. "So young and so countrified," he exclaimed *sotto voce*.

Thus encouraged, Seng-teh began to feel "free of the city." Seeing a little crowd before him, he found the object of their contemplation to be a slice of pork dangling from a string. The problem was to guess the exact weight. Several paid a cash or two, and tried their skill; but the shopkeeper, who acted as referee, declared them to be somewhat out.

Pasted on a blank wall he saw an appeal to the benevolent to spare the life of frogs. Their harmlessness, the pleasing character of their music, and, above all, their essential likeness in form to children, were the arguments used, the latter point being demonstrated by an illustration. Hankow, then, was so secure now, that, being perfectly safe ourselves, we may concentrate some of our energies on saving the frogs. A little further on was a "hand of the realm," as his calico signboard declared. "Every prescription powerful" was written underneath. He had a long bladder in his hand. It was filled with water, but contained a pellet which rose to the top every time he inverted it. A man who could do that could surely heal any disease whatever. But Seng-teh was in perfect health.

He might fall ill at some future time, as another physician, squatting on the ground, assured his little crowd that they would. Under such distressing circumstances they would rue the day when they passed him by without a purchase. He had a large tortoise-shell to exhibit, also a skull or two of some unknown beast, a discarded snake-skin, some rather large snake-bones, and a dried crocodile three feet long. Who could resist such a display! In his hand he had a very brown bone, from which he was rasping some dust. The packets contained the same all-powerful tonic, for the bone was from that all-powerful king of beasts, the tiger. He had also a bit of tiger-skin underneath the packets, the contents of which would all but bring dead men to life again. He was once at the point of death himself; and so forth.

Stalls of ironware, of brass incense braziers, of song-books, of fancy goods, of fruit, with baskets of fish, and tubs from which the fish could be bought alive, helped to reduce the excessive width of the street. Chair-bearers elbowed their way through the crowds, and barrow-men swore when they met other barrow-men coming in opposite directions. Water-carriers, filth-carriers, carriers of cash, men with huge bundles of rush-pith for lamp-wicks balanced on their shoulders; beggars, Buddhist, Taoist, lay; merchants, coolies, gentry, ragamuffins, men on horseback, frost-bitten cripples, who dragged themselves along on the pavements, greybeards and *gamin*, made up the strange medley of life beneath those gorgeous or neatly ornate signboards. Here, too, was a sight to awaken a train of thought, a Taoist pedlar selling peach-stone charms,—the crowds neither impressed nor irritated thereby. Seng-teh would have liked to have seized him by the hair. But he had gone the other side of a portable restaurant. Sellers of silk thread, with little drum rattles; sellers of rice sugar, with their sonorous dangling bells; braziers, with their series of brass clappers let loose, then caught in the hand with a clang; whistle sellers, giving proof of their musical abilities; blind fiddlers, with their violins rendered fully audible by reason of a snake-skin stretched over a wide bamboo tube; criers of small cash for large (six for one); criers of everything tasty, from "oil-fried rice-crust" (caked in the pan), to "Blood, blood, pig's blood," helped to make up the general chorus of sound.

The only possible way in which a newly-arrived Westerner could idealise all this would be in Mrs. Browning's words—

"O earth, so full of dreary noises!
O men, with wailing in your voices!"

Or with the author of *Bitter-Sweet*—

"I scanned the signs, the long and curious signs,
And wondered who invented them, and if
Their owners knew how strange they were."

Or with Shakespeare—

"The rankest compound of villainous smell that ever offended nostril."

Happily the Chinese sense of smell is as undeveloped as is the outward and visible sign thereof.

But to Seng-teh the main street of Hankow was the very ideal of "bustling excitement," which words form the countryman's definition of happiness. A block in the street ahead, for the excitement had risen to fighting point, an excitement even for those bred and born in Hankow. Shouts, struggles, queue-catchings, and separation by peace-makers—such are Chinese fights.

The block recalled Seng-teh to the remembrance of his errand. He had not examined the numerous open shop-fronts to see if there were any signs of tobacco therein. He would keep his eyes open for that commodity, glancing at sign-boards and wares.

Flour and dumpling vendor, coir matting, face powder, skin-covered boxes, blacksmith, straw hats, dye works, engraver, cords and cottons, carpenters and coffin makers, basket ware, idols, lime dealer, silver bracelets, beancurd, flowers for ladies' hair, spectacles, coolie poles, buttons, barber's shop, scroll mounting, balances, combs, umbrellas, embroidered silk, medicines, oiled boots, curiosity shop, second-hand clothes, copper dealer, fans, oilshop, silk hats, colours, leather-seller, cotton-wool dealer, scissors, pewter worker, leather, vermicelli, cracker, cloth dealers, salted ducks, stockings, opium, ink and pens, cloth boots, tea-shop, paper houses and horses for funerals, pawnshop, wine-shop, incense, porcelain, edible sea-weed, coal, chopsticks, and so on, with various repetitions and modifications, all described as old-established warehouses, which they might be for what he knew, but without tobacco for sale. At last! He entered, and showed the card, giving an unauthorised apology. The two pounds were quickly weighed out; and he returned with loosened jacket, for it was hot, and most of the folks about wore no jackets at all. He would have liked a fan, but felt nervous.

"Back again already! We didn't expect you till to-morrow at the very earliest. With that card you might have tasted all the myriad happinesses!"

"If you are as victorious as virtuous," exclaimed the lieutenant, "you will be able to inflict forty blows upon Hu Lin-yi himself. Remember me when you are supreme general, won't you? But were you taken in?"

The episode with the well-dressed "friend" having been related, the lieutenant banged the table, struck his hands, and well-nigh danced. "Not so raw after all." And the clap of thunderous laughter which followed reverberated again and again from his comrades outside the little palace on the stern.

In a few moments all was bubble and puff from the circle of water-pipe smokers. "In my parts," said one of the men, who always located his tales, "there was once a man who complained to his master that he had not enough tobacco to smoke. 'I am out in the paddy fields up to my knees in mud, planting out rice or working rotary pumps from morning till night, and when I come home I am at everyone's beck and call.' 'Well, will an ounce a day do?' 'Oh, make it more than that!' And on his constant complaining, it was made more and more, until it was over a pound a day. At last he came to his master asking for an old teapot.

<small>A little more Tobacco.</small>

"'What for?' 'To fill with tobacco and smoke from the spout!'"

Sharpers, however, were the topic of the day. And many a tale was told upon this inexhaustible subject. From these a selection will suffice.

"A comely-looking woman accosted a man from Tsaitien, and asked him to accompany her outside the 'mart.' She recollected his face, she said, and she was otherwise friendless there. He did not disabuse her mind, and went with her. They had not gone far, however, when their conversation was interrupted with cries of 'Stop, you wife-stealer!' 'Please, I am a good woman,' whined the

<small>Sharpers.</small>

female.[1] But the male was beaten so, that he thought best to drop the thousand cash he carried and run. 'Easily got! Easily got!' exclaimed the *two* sharpers, and, after a change of apparel on the part of the 'female,' the two males went back to spend part of their gains in a wine-shop."

"Not bad," said the man of location, "but I know a better tale. A friend of mine was in Hankow with only about a hundred cash. He managed to borrow some gay silk clothes, such as are worn by the wealthy, and entered a pipe-shop. He had previously invested a few cash in a little of the finest tobacco. He asked to see the best water-pipes they made, selected the handsomest, and asked for a boy to carry it to his boat. He was passing through Hankow on his way to a high official post, and suchlike. Before leaving, he put in some of the tobacco, was handed a spill with all due politeness, and so 'used' the pipe. He next went to a hat-shop, and selected a mandarin's hat with a high-grade button, and had a shopboy to carry that behind him also. Thus equipped, he went into a bank, and asked to look at their silver. He would have to change a great deal of cash eventually. Might he test one of the ingots [fifty-three ounces], leaving his attendants till he either returned the silver or sent coolies with the cash? Certainly. But—you guess the rest. A friend of mine. I could give you his name."

Seng-teh asked whether the tiger-bone sellers were swindlers in a small way.

"Yes, they are only ox-bones dyed," replied another; "but I know a tale of a famous pill-seller in Hankow."

"I know," cried the locator; "it is Yeh, near the Sen Family Temple. His pills once brought a dead man to life again."[2]

"No, it was not. This man's pills were made by an idol

---

[1] The Chinese, though not noted for chivalrous speech, have at least common justice sufficient to call men "males." Can it be that the onesided speech of some Englishmen is a survival of grossest barbarism, when there were neither "ladies" nor "women," but human animals in place of wives? If so, we need hardly continue to emphasise the fact!

[2] This celebrated family of pillmakers still carry on a great business, aided by this legend.

he had in the back of his shop. A pill appeared in the palm of the image twice a day, in the presence of the customer. The price was a thousand cash, and he generally sold both. His signboard was inscribed, 'Production mysterious; efficacy marvellous,' and he soon had a big name. A gentleman, who was in the medicine line himself, tried might and main to find out the secret of this wonderful pill. He waited his time, and at last got so friendly with the pillman as to invite him out with him over the Hanyang lake and across the Yangtse. He promised to bear all expenses. He had a magic purse, he said, which kept him supplied with a hundred cash whenever he wanted. They had some refreshment at the shop within yon archway on the Hanyang side, after crossing the river. The hundred cash was still unbroken! Then they took a boat to the Plum Hill on the Moon lake, went up into the Buddhist temple there, and had tea and sweetmeats. Still the hundred cash was unbroken! He produced it from his inner girdle after lifting his robe. It was tied up on a straw. They returned to the foot of the Tortoise Hill. He paid the boatman, still taking the coppers from the unbroken hundred. They walked along the Tortoise Hill and crossed the Yangtse. Still that hundred cash came whenever he wanted to pay anything. They had refreshments at the Yellow Crane Tower, with the same result. The pillman wanted to pay at least for crossing the Yangtse to the Dragon King Temple. 'By no means,' his friend replied; 'it costs me nothing.' The pillman, of course, asked him in, and over the tea and tobacco they agreed to exchange secrets. The pillman took him behind the image and showed him a little mechanism, which he could work from behind the counter. By pressing his foot, a pill emerged each time through a hole in the idol's palm. 'Now for your secret!' 'Here it is,' said the other, producing a girdle with seven purses all alike slung upon it. 'Put a hundred cash in each, and shift it round each time. Simple, is it not?' The pillman moved to another town."

The roars of appreciative laughter may be taken for granted, but the locality man once had a friend in the country who could look very simple and talk very broad. He came into Hankow one day with a couple of little knobs of silver in his hand, and a bag with some lead imitations of such knobs over his shoulder. He was met by a splendidly-dressed sharper, who took stock of him, and accosted him politely. The countryman confided with him as to how he had come by the money; said he was a stranger in Hankow, but wanted to buy some things, if he could only find out where the good shops were. He was horribly afraid of sharpers. Would the benevolent gentleman kindly direct him? The "benevolent gentleman" told him that all the good shops were below *Wu Seng Miao*, which was three *li* distant. He had only just gone one *li*. Moreover, the gentleman would go with him; his own business was not important, and really the sharpers were very cunning. So they went on, the countryman—"I could give you his name" —rattling his two knobs in his hand. His benefactor treated him to some wine, then they continued their way, until the countryman felt sleepy; the wine being strong and his load heavy. He must sit down. Did his friend know of any secluded court? One was soon found, with bricks piled against one of the walls. Might he take hold of his friend's sleeve, for he was nearly asleep? He would know then if his friend rose. Then he went off into loud snoring. The townsman quietly slipped out of three silk jackets, took the bag, and ran. As did the countryman in the other direction with his silken booty.

"That was a good tale about your relative you told to so-and-so," said one of the men, who had not yet contributed anything beyond the inevitable laughter.

"Which relative?"

"That B.A., you know."

"Yes it was. He was a clever man"; but the speaker had just the slightest suspicion of hesitancy in his manner, and just a slight start when the tale-teller began by saying: "He was a putter-through of *yamun* cases, and for excessive cheating was sent to the lower regions to receive fitting retribution. The King of Hades having enumerated his vile deeds, commanded two demons to take a certain amount of oil and boil him in it."

Here the locator tried to interrupt, but the narrator continued: "On his way to the cauldron he said to them, 'I am very thin, you know. Why use all that oil? Half will be plenty. I know you are fond of oil; keep the rest yourselves.' They accordingly appropriated half the prescribed quantity. Whereupon the lawyer said that he had an important communication to make to the King of Hades, and they could come with him, if they liked, to see that he did not escape.

"Being ushered into the presence of his judge, he asked if offences such as those for which he was condemned were never practised in Hades itself. The question called forth an emphatic denial. 'But,' urged he, 'I know better. How much oil did you order these demons to take to boil me wherewith? Just so. Now look in the cauldron, and then in the private apartments of these demons.'

"The King of Hades did so; and feeling that the lawyer was too clever a man to be anything but dangerous down below,—he had even threatened to appeal to the [Taoist] Supreme if he were not released immediately,—sent him back to the upper world."

The locator had no more stories to tell. He had been caught by a sharper, and that sharper an innocent-looking comrade.

When the lieutenant came on board next morning, he said that their little fleet had been ordered back to Tsaitien. The *Fu Tai*, Hu Lin-yi, had come down from Kingken (a town twenty miles up the Yangtse), was engaging the rebels there, and wanted all possible assistance.

When they arrived in the afternoon they found that the battle had been fought and won. Tsaitien is itself on a flat piece of plain. To the east is a piece of water, and further eastward a range of hills. The rebels came down from these hills, and tried to wade through the apparently shallow water, there being only a narrow path over a bridge. While they were floundering in the mud, Hu Lin-yi, with great promptness, had his boats dragged over a bit of land, and drove the rebels back with heavy losses. His nickname hitherto had been "The Runaway," for, spite of his rough treatment of

Pao Ts'ao, he had retreated in the one battle he had previously fought. Here he was, doubtless, largely assisted by volunteers from the town's-people; but his name must be changed to Leopard now. (Both sounds have to be represented by the letters *pao*, but in the former nickname the word has an explosive aspirate on the *p*.)

The rebels having retreated afar, the little fleet, after remaining a few days at Tsaitien, was ordered down to

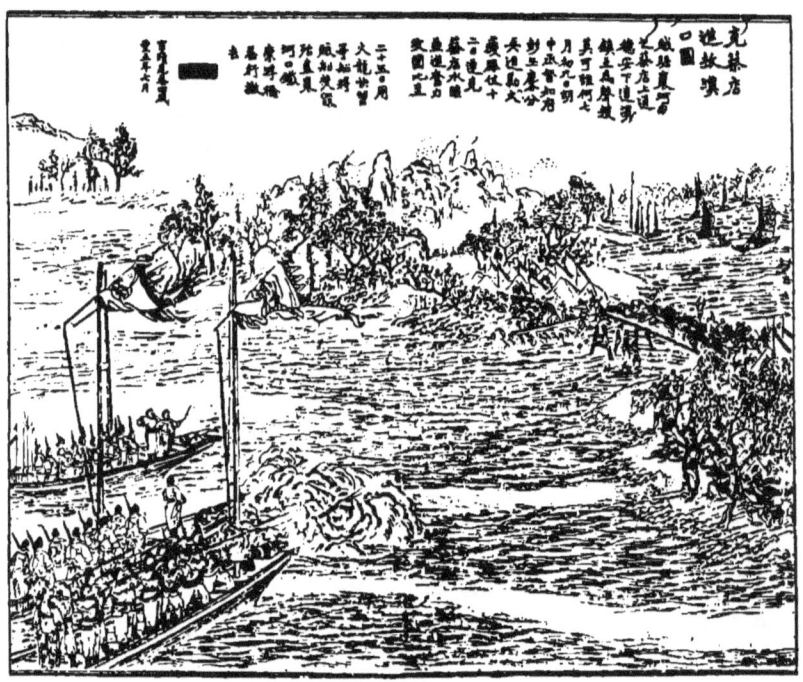

Hankow on the afternoon of the seventeeth. By that time Hu Lin-yi had returned to the Yangtse.

"Hankow once more!" exclaimed the lieutenant, "though I hear the folks there had a scare as they saw the rebels row down in their stolen boats. I hope there are one or two folks left. On New Year's Day, the shut shops are bearable, but in midsummer!"—

The current was swift, and in two hours they were once more at *Wu Seng Miao*. The place looked quite normal, though, from the rapid current, the boats anchored there were rather fewer than before.

It was now time for rice, an after-dinner smoke, and tale-telling. (The lieutenant was on shore.) This time the subject was good mandarins. One of the men sang the praises of "Tsao, Clear as Heaven,"[1] the name by which that virtuous ruler of Hanyang, so much beloved for his generosity in the year of the great flood, is still known. "The folks of Hankow and Hanyang," said the soldier, "are so fond of him that they hold monthly processions in his honour. I wonder how the other mandarins like it?"

"He is now away in the east," said the locator; "and one day, as he was out walking in plain clothes, he saw a countryman—a friend of mine—who seemed to be in distress. His speech was that of Hanyang, whereupon the gentleman asked him what sort of mandarins they had now. He replied that the less said the better; he did not want to discuss the 'long and short' of such fellows. 'But we once had a real good mandarin. During the flood year, the populace pulled the chair of the præfectural mandarin to pieces, and then when the county mandarin, "Clear as Heaven," came along they knelt before him. He was a good mandarin.'

"'I am he,' at which words my friend went down upon his knees. He took him back to his *yamun* and gave him sufficient for his journey home. I could tell you the man's name."

"He was not a B.A., I suppose," said the man of the oil talc. "I have it! He was the country sharper with the lead-knob bag! Did he manage to steal much while he was in the porch of 'Clear as Heaven's' *yamun*?"

A volley of curses followed; for though it is a brave thing to claim as acquaintances or relatives clever folk who shine out as superior to their fellows in a zigzag form of wisdom, whose reward is gain, it is another thing in China when the sharper is a "bare-stick" lawyer, the hated of men; it is another thing when the sharper is brought face to face, even in the thoughts, with a man like "Heavenly Clearness," the beloved mandarin of 1849, whose memory, strengthened by contrast, has meant public processions, and of whom the old folks still speak with watery eye. And an ex-rebel soldier sitting

[1] See pp. 132-134.

upon a bench in the evening exclaims, "A hundred or two like him in office, and there would have been no rebellion, but "— the old soldier has a Sacred Book in his hand, one of the later volumes—" real perfect peace, and the real kingdom of heaven. God bless him!" which conversation we could locate if we were thus minded.

Chapter XVII.

FOUR MILES OF FLAME.

"Dense smoke encaged the corner-stones of earth;
Black vapours locked the utmost bounds of heaven.
The gathering clouds enlivened the fierce flames,
Till flaring crimson mocked the sunset sky.
The winds become the fire's attendant troops;
The flaming general straight his orders gives;
Urged by his might, they go their deadly way.
Oh, furious, roaring blaze borne on the blast!
Oh, blast of terror on to victory led!
The pass of heaven is reached, is forced, is won!
The gates of earth succumb to raging flames!
The whirling, glittering snakes dart everywhere.
Ah! who can flee his awful doom?"
From *The Making of the Gods*.

ON this same seventeenth day of the seventh month in the fifth year of the Emperor whose national designation was "General Prosperity," there had been a battle at Hwangchow, fifty miles down the Yangtse. It began in the early morning. Both sides lost heavily, but in the end the rebels gave way, and were chased by a band of three hundred of the militia southwards toward Hankow. At dark the pursued had reached Yanglo, twenty miles from the central cities. They seized the boats anchored there, slaughtered the boatmen, and having a fair wind and almost a full, though at times cloud-covered moon, set sail up the Yangtse. It would be hopeless for them, weary with the battle, the flight, and not a few wounds, to attempt to take Hankow by martial force. They were in doubt as to the strength of the garrison. It probably outnumbered them. (It did not, as it happened, the forces being elsewhere.) They had at least evaded their pursuers, and might find some opportunity for revenge. Hankow had played fast-and-loose with them, had treated them well when they took the place, had treated the "mandarin soldiers" better when they had retaken the mart.

A plan was suggested. It was adopted. There were eighteen volunteers who, as they neared Hankow, divested themselves of their upper garments, smeared their faces, chests, and arms with blood—there was plenty available in one or other of the boats,—let loose their long hair, brought it round to the front, held a sword wrapped therein between their teeth, and having gathered together in the foremost boat, waited with smoking spill in one hand and a couple of bamboo-rope torches in the other. The night was getting more and more clouded. The fifth watch was being sounded on the Imperialist drums as these horrible looking demi-demons arranged their goals in various points of the now familiar streets.

The outpost camp passed, they leaped on shore, each going in his appointed direction. There was no wall.

. . . .

It had been a merry evening on Seng-teh's boat. The little disagreement had been settled by the locator going on shore to secure a supply of wine, which having cost him nothing, he the more freely distributed. The lieutenant was on shore, as also the semi-officials of the other boats, who had found the days at Tsaitien long and the nights insipid. So the rest had a merry time. Seng-teh, though not an abstainer, was rallied on his meagre abilities at imbibing. In polite circles there is quite a gamut of compliments in use on the subject of a man's ability to drink wine, and a corresponding gamut of humble disclaimers. No such compliments fell to the lot of the sturdy lad of fifteen and a half, but he could tell a tale or two by this time.

It was the fourth watch before there was anything like quiet, and then the shouts were but exchanged for thunderous snores. Seng-teh, being still sober, was to watch for the remainder of the night. The custom is for two men to divide the night between them. His boat being the chief one in the little fleet, it fell to his lot when he heard the drum beats from the central station to take up the two sticks, and pass the sound on to those higher up the river, to the night watchmen, and the wakeful public generally. Having done so, he felt very sleepy. He must lie down. Everything was still, but a lamp here and there flickering in the high wind, and the cry of "Blood, blood" (pig's blood), which sounded well-nigh demoniacal,—what customers do these night hawkers get? —proclaimed that there was a busy town near, with its more than half a million inhabitants. The lantern on the bows all but blotted out the outline of the houses. He would read until daylight. The volume was one of the *Making of the Gods*, which he used to read to the lieutenant. The Taoist's description of heaven was now familiar, and the various poems and descriptive pieces he was learning by heart. The piece for to-night was the description of a fire, in which a sprite was exposed and consumed. It seemed too fine for the occasion, but poets are wont to deal in hyperbole. "Dense smoke encaged," "Dense smoke encaged the corner-stones of earth," he repeated to himself several times, until he was interrupted by a shout, then another. Something was happening on shore. He tried to arouse the sleepers. They but swore, and turned over, snoring again. But the shouts increased. Then a light appeared far away to the right hand. It seemed to spread toward the centre. A man ran along the bank, crying, "Demons!" He was a night watchman, only proof against distant thieves.

"Stand!" shouted Seng-teh. "What is it?"

"Demons with torches. Hundreds of them!" cried the man, and ran on.

The glare became unmistakable; more fugitives with the same tale; more efforts on the lad's part to waken the sleepers, until, the shouts on shore increasing, he took up his drumsticks and belaboured the hands of one or two. He was cursed, he was seized. Everyone seemed to strike out at once. "Demons!" he shouted amid his struggles; then he changed to "The Longhaired are upon us."

At this familiar cry some began to rouse themselves and yawn. They let him go. He seized a petard or two, and fired it outside. General cries of muffled voices, "What is it?" More shouts on shore, and the glare, which had now reached the spot opposite to him; no, it extended farther to the west. "Demons! Long-haired! Fire!" was shouted, was screamed, was yelled on shore. "They are near. They have taken *Wu Seng Miao*. I heard their guns. Run!"

It was not glare now, it was flame. Huge tongues of flame shot up above the houses, lighting up the figures of men and women bold enough to go up for a moment on to the wooden lofts above the roofs. The upper story of *Wu Seng Miao* gateway, where only an old Vegetarian's tiny lamp is to be seen as a rule, was full of fire-lit faces. Luminous smoke rolled overhead, carried by the high wind afar. It rained sparks. The heat was unbearable. The summer's night was becoming hot as an oven.

A splash! It was a man leaping on to a boat: no, ten men had made the leap, one had fallen. His body was whirled on by the rapid current. His cries were unheard in the general roar. Down the steep bank came men, women, and children, bearers of boxes and bundles and babies; they fell in a heap on the boats or into the water. The bows were nearly sinking. "Quick! unloose the chains! Let the grappling irons go. Clear the way, all of you," and a dozen were pushed into the water, to cling upon the boat-sides until they dropped, carried down with the rest. The river was thick with bodies. "Bring a hatchet." The chain will not be undone. Hew away at the block which holds it. Harder! Faster! See that great mass of humanity tumbling down the bank. Only just in time. They would have swamped us. It is light as day. To the oars every one of you; shake off the clinging hands. Off! Across the river. Push this boat and that with your hooks; never mind the men who cling there. Curse and rave, but push—row! The river is half-blocked. See, a boat has overturned! Look at that mass of boats above! The river is narrowed here. There will be a fatal block in a moment. Row for your lives! Blocked it is, but we are in the front. Look out! That great salt junk is overturning. Out of the way of the mast. Our comrades' boat is snapped in two. There are demons in the current. The oars bend, they break. Use your poles and broken oars. We must get across. Hands off. We must live. Splash, splash! Shrieks! Curses! But we have reached the other side. "Save life, save life!" Who can save a hundred? The cries are lost in the roar of the fire, the crackling of slates, and the terrific yell of ten thousand in death agonies. The kingdom of hell has come. It is pandemonium on earth.

> "The red tyrannous fire
> Mounts up in the dark,
> Ever redder and higher."

To stay there on the boat is to be scorched. There are no Casibianca legends here, and no commander to give orders. Every man for himself. Struggle for dear life. See the boats have caught. Clamber up the bank as the others do. They fall, dragged down by clinging hands. Over the shifting mass. Up again. The water has but cooled you. There is a blank space. Press in. Just in time—on dry land with a chance of life if you outrun the thick rain of sparks.

The path led from a small temple to the god of boatmen, —already on fire,—to the "Ancient Bell Tower," on the "Moon Lake Causeway." It was well for Seng-teh that he had had a bit of tolerably clear road, for the latter path was one mass of fugitives, unable to proceed by reason of a block by the bell-tower archway. In a densely crowded road, an archway narrowing it by one-half may stop all progress. The crowd forms one compact mass too wide for the gateway.

Happily, the youth was on the outside, and could go round, wading through a swamp on the left. On the right, many were drowned in the lake. But he must join the main path farther on, as part of the lake waters come through a bridge, and it is too deep to wade there. But there was another dense crowd by the bridge, those on the outside being jammed against the granite posts and the connecting poles. Among them was a man dressed in silks whose head was bleeding. His voice was heard above the general din, shouting, "A thousand cash for a boat!" Then "Two thousand," then, finally, "An ingot of silver." But the boats had gone. The pole gave way, and, with many others, he fell into the water.

Under one of the buttresses was a man with a boat-hook, with which he caught hold of the garments of the wealthy man, who, grasping his bundle, laid hold of the outstretched pole. The holder thereof seized the bundle, then calmly shook off the man, nay, pushed him under with the hook, and held him there. Was it a dream? The man's face seemed familiar. It looked like that of Lieu! Seng-teh now for the first time discovered that he had his musket with him. He had snatched it up mechanically as he sprang from the boat. He had loaded it at the first alarm. An irresistible impulse made him point it at the dark form under the bridge, but it was wet. Some folks from the archway came crowding up. It was hopeless for him to try and ascend where so many were being pushed over. One thing remained, he could wade round the bit of lake on the left. But, reaching drier ground, he stumbled and swooned away.

A spark upon his cheek proved a speedy restorative, and he came to himself, to notice that the Tortoise Hill was not far off. Limping along dry land, wading through swamp, he reached the foot, with just enough energy left to clamber half-way up the rocky sides. Here he found two masses of rock which almost met at the top. Into this cavern-like recess he crawled, held his musket mechanically, and sat down. His head was bleeding, and he was very faint. The horrid glare before him seemed part of a hideous nightmare. But he was out of the range of the sparks.

Before long, however, the ground seemed to shake. The rebels had taken the hill from the other side, had fired a volley, which he felt rather than heard, and had struck his musket from his hand. Such was the dream which passed through his bewildered mind in an instant of time. His last moment had come! He had escaped the flames but to perish by a sword-thrust. His whole life rushed before him. Lieu and his son, the teacher and his wife, their marriage, then little Camilla, his father and mother. He began to cry, "My mother! my mother!" But the dark mass before him had gone. It was not a band of rebels. It was a large boulder loosened by the pressure of the crowd on the hill-top,

which had come rolling down, falling full force upon the two pieces of rock under which he had been sitting. Poised there an instant, it had fallen upon his gun-barrel, and, crushing that, had gone crashing down toward the swamp far beneath. He realised what had happened now.

It was unlikely that another such boulder would follow suit, but the lad's nerves were shaken, and, picking up his shattered musket with soldierly instinct, he clambered up higher. He could not be dreaming now. There were undoubted sounds of firing. If his ears deceived him, his eyes did not. There was a general stampede along the ridge of the hill. Getting nearer, he heard the cry, " The Longhaired ! The Longhaired ! "

The fugitives did not seem to be pursued, though the firing continued. He was unable to run, and seemed not to care now whether he died or not. He would scramble up to the top and see what had happened. He had to rest very frequently, and each time he sank to the ground there was *that sight* before him. It was as real when he tried to shut his eyes and turn away, as when he looked in that direction. Four miles of towering flame ! The wooden-framed dwellings of six hundred thousand, among them those whom he had seen bustling along the crowded street under the gay signboards ! That sharper, where was he ? Where was the Taoist pedlar,—not his Taoist, whom he saw shot through the back when the Imperialists came, but that other Taoist ? Well, it could not be helped. But those busy shops with their shopmen and customers ? It could not be. He was in the street again. No, he was alone near the hill-top on that awfully sultry night. "Dense smoke encaged—encaged the corner-stones of earth." Had the writer of the lines seen a city on fire ? Four miles of flame !

But he must struggle up to the top. When he had done so, he found that the firing was from the Hanyang walls. It was a cannonade. Yes, there was a double row of yellow jackets returning the fire from behind earthworks below that blazing mass a quarter of a mile off. What was that mass ? The temple, of course. Seven temples, he remembered. See, a shot aimed too high has hit one of them, and carried off with it blazing beams and a fiery shower of ignited stuff down over the steep sides of the rock.

The scene at the end of the hill seemed to be absorbed in

the wider facts of that terrible night. There is a point beyond which the already dazed brain ceases to receive further shock, and he sat looking on, like an overtired spectator at a theatre. He seemed to be going off into a stupor.

Time passed unheeded. It might have been half-an-hour, it might have been two hours, but he realised by and by that the firing had ceased, and that there was a form before him, squatting down upon its heels, with an evil smile on its face.

"Hallo! you mandarin soldier, are you dead like the rest? Alive? Well, look yonder. A fine sight, is it not, better than a bonfire of paper houses?"

Was it a demon or a man? It was a young man. His voice was unmistakable. It was Lieu Fah.

He raised himself, and pointed his musket at the figure. That was enough. It disappeared with a shriek. It crouched behind a gravestone, then ran, then crouched behind another, then ran again. Until half-way down the hill it was stopped by a man who raised himself from the ground. He had a yellow sleeveless jacket on, clearly discernible in the glare. He hurriedly took it off, and his under coat too, put it on again, and the blue jacket with sleeves over it. The younger of the two pointed with the finger up to the hill-top. Sengteh pointed his musket at them, and both ran off, bearing what seemed to be heavy burdens.

He was alone again. The glare seemed to increase, for the further horizon could now be defined. The temples were still blazing, and on the left was that awful glare. Whence came the increasing light? Look, over Wuchang yonder there is a great red ball of fire! What new wonder was that? It was the rising sun.

Chapter XVIII.

Imperialists to the Front.

CASABIANCA — PENG THE IRON STRIKER — STORMING A CITY WALL—REWARDS OF VALOUR—IMPERIALIST PROCLAMATION.

"The deep blue sea has become a mulberry plantation."
Chinese Saying (Met. Great Changes).

WITH the dawn came the habitual sense of having to get up and begin to do something. Seng-teh had been used to rise at dawn as far back as he could remember. He felt the force of long habit. It was as a strong undercurrent. Part of him seemed more or less sensible of his present surroundings. But the mechanical seemed to predominate for the moment. He rose to his feet, rubbed his eyes, and stretched, then looking away to the west he saw the strange landscape. He was not at home then, nor—it took a moment or two to come—on the small gunboat. Yet there were the hills once familiar to him at one time. When was it? In the Taiping camp? But they seemed reversed. They were. The Inverted Pan Hill was towards the left now. Yes, he was the other side of them. He was alone on the Tortoise Hill. He felt alone. Every morning hitherto had brought with it something to do, and someone to speak to, or someone to command him. It is a rare thing to be ever alone in China. He felt lonesome indeed. His head pained him. He instinctively undid his cloth girdle, tore off a piece and tied it round his temples, feeling as he did so that his hair was clotted together with dried blood. Yes, he remembered, his head had been bleeding. He felt poorly and terribly lonely. He began to wail, "My mother, my mother!" This was not strange. Many a grown man had died during the night with those words as his death-cry.

They suggested the old home. Where was that home now? Yonder lakes showing out dark and slaty against the sky to the south-west looked home-like. Yes, they connected with that of his early home. He would go thither. That side of the hill was not so steep as the other. The home-like stretch of water attracted him. There was a broad path. It was a continuation of the Moon Lake Causeway. It led to Hanyang. He would cross it and walk straight to the home-suggesting lakes. It was all grave mounds, down the hill, across the paved path, and on the other side. All grave mounds, and not a human being to be seen. Was everybody buried? No, that was absurd. He recalled the burning town. There it was, though the flames were lower and less luminous now, and black places appeared, from which there ascended smoke rather than flame.

He staggered as he walked. Was he drunk? His head seemed to swim. No, he was faint and hungry. It had been mostly drinking last night, and last night seemed ages off. He had at least lived whole years since then. He felt well-nigh old. But still he caught himself wailing, "My mother!" He came to a house at last. It was empty. He entered. A cat looked at him and began to mew. It was something to see even an animal. It ran away. He went into the kitchen. There was the cooking-pan, and close by in a jar was the rice. There were bundles of dried grass, and on a little shelf the piece of black flint and the bit of steel. More for the sake of something to do, than for any definable reason, he struck a light, lit a fire of dried grass, put the rice on, and sat down to watch the cooking. He seemed to feel that someone owed him a breakfast. Had he not suffered enough and excited himself enough in the night? At anyrate there was no one to dispute his right. He ate the rice without any vegetables, and felt a strange sort of virtue in doing so. He felt strengthened. He could go on now.

From the rising ground on which he stood he could see

that the path he had made for himself ran parallel to a canal which was a continuation of the Moon lake. He would follow that water; perhaps it connected with the larger lakes. Before him on the left was a high bank, partly artificial, for there were earthwork turrets all along the inner bend of the canal. On the right bank were some low houses, but no sign of inhabitants. Keeping up on the rising ground past a few cottages, he reached the earthworks. There was no one there. Round to the left he found what was evidently the West Gate bridge of Hanyang. There seemed to be a gentle flow of water from the other side. He soon found himself standing upon the bridge, and noted that a deserted street ended there at an archway. On the other side the road forked. The water beneath was probably from the Yangtse. He wanted the lakes, and the left-hand road seemed promising. The houses were few, and he soon emerged to find a rather fine building in an enclosure before him among the trees. This was the celebrated Hanyang monastery. On its left was a little red-painted structure, where the old priests were cremated. On the right was the Hanyang camp, on a low hill.

The monastery enclosure seemed to be full of old or sick folks. In their flight of the night before, the fugitives, unable to take them all the way, had by common consent found privilege of sanctuary for them there. Part of the enclosure had usually been given up to the nourishment into longevity of sundry animals, which, having an abnormal number of toes, claws, spots, and the like, had been thus proved to be deceased progenitors of the donors. These had been slaughtered at the rebels' first onset, and the fact that the place had been the scene of rebel carousals more than once did not add to the comfort of its present terrified inmates. Seng-tch was loaded with questions as he approached, as to the chances of their safety.

But a voice from the camp made him turn his steps thither. It was that of a hunchback on crutches, who looked a beggar, authoritative nevertheless. The Imperialist flag still flew from the central flagstaff. The hunchback was indeed a lay representative of the Imperial forces of Central

China. He was almost a Casabianca. He was remaining there in the camp, "whence all but he had fled." He did not flee, for the simple reason that the soldiers on retiring had secured the gates, and told him to give orders to any able-bodied man he saw to make all speed toward the lakes, where "they could be saved."

He prevailed upon Seng-teh to let him out, then pointed out the way with his crutch. From the canal there was a smooth wet track going off to the south. He was to follow that. Beyond some paddy fields he now saw gangs of men engaged in pulling boats along over the uneven ground.

As he neared the place, he heard a voice shouting, "The General Peng will decapitate you." It was not addressed to him, however. The boats were chiefly sanpans from Upper Hankow, as he afterwards learned. At the first alarm their commander had ordered the crews to drag them over the south bank, which was low there, into the Moon lake. Having done so, most of the men had fled. So pressed men were now needed to aid what soldiers remained to get them into broader waters. On each boat was a gong-beater as at a launch, and at each stroke of the gong the men answered with a shout and a tug, loud cursing from the commander filling up all gaps. The name of "The General Peng" was used to add emphasis thereto. Seng-teh had not been in Hankow long enough to realise its terrible force.

"You are young," cried a red jacket; "take my place and beat this gong, or the rebels will be upon us." The lad did as he was bid, but had to sit down for faintness. "You lazy rascal, Peng will have your head off," cried a voice. He stood up against the mast with his gong, but fell over as the boat gave a lurch in passing over a grave. Seeing which, the gong-beater tied him up. "I had rather have been burnt alive," said a man loud enough for Seng-teh to hear, "than fall into the hands of " Peng the Iron-Striker." Who was this awful Peng, the lad inquired; but no one answered.

The name had not been given without a cause. General Peng seemed to be a blacksmith's hammer incarnate, whose blows often fell upon his own men. The Chinese would say he was the incarnate hammer-wielding thunder god. He seems to have been a veritable Dracon. Every offence is said to have been punished with death. Like Judge Jeffreys, he never seemed to relish his food so well as when several heads had fallen. He seemed to feed on life-blood, only the pork was what the South Sea Islanders used formerly to call "long pig." At anyrate he was a terrible disciplinarian, the very sound of whose name for many a year made folk at a distance shrug their shoulders; those a little nearer exclaim "Hai Ya!" with unwonted emphasis; and those nearer still to brace up their energies as for a forlorn-hope expedition, or cower, or flee, according to their respective states of mind.

It seemed a "good half-day" before the boats had all reached a little canal which forms a sort of terminus for passengers to the water-washed villages on the shores of that long chain of lakes. So irregular are those lakes in outline that a couple of sanpan fleets might play hide-and-seek for some time therein. No signs of "Peng the Iron Striker." "He is round that bluff," said a redcoat in charge of a boat which had evidently been on the lake all the time. The last of the boats having reached the open, the same man shouted, "The General Peng will only have 'blue clothes.' Strict orders." At this, one or two hands clutched at Seng-teh's red jacket. They would rather not enlist under Peng. The youth in the red coat was tied up, however, and the jacket would not come off.

"Come along, all you. Let that child alone, you folks there. I have orders to shoot anyone who goes off," and the crew pointed their muskets at the crowd. "What of the redcoats?" asked one of the boldest of "blue-clothed." They would be shot as deserters if the General Peng found them. "And we shall shoot them as deserters if they run away now." This, in Chinese phraseology, was indeed putting them "between two difficulties." "We must not stay, we must not go," cried one of them. "What are we to do?" "Take four of the boats to Kingkow [Golden Mouth] up yonder, sixty *li*, and join the fleet there." This was at least feasible.

The north wind had abated somewhat, but was still a fair

breeze; and nothing loth to get out of the clutches of the "Iron Striker," the redcoats—none of Seng-tch's comrades among them, he found—set sail for the most northern part of the broad lake. The calm seemed delicious to all. Whether they had been hoaxed into exertion or not, they did not know. Probably the authoritative man thought to accumulate a little merit, and curry favour with the indomitable Peng, who, it seems, did treat well those he fancied, as long as they fulfilled his ideal.

"No need to hurry. Yonder is a village, and the tiles are smoking" (the roof with its loosely-laid tiles is one great chimney in Chinese cottages). "We can get some rice there." And so they did after the country folk had recovered from their scare. The rest of the journey by water was still more delightful to bruised and battered men, flame-hunted by night, and Peng-terrified at dawn. The track, too, was smoother and muddy, and they had the pleasure of afternoon rice with their new comrades by the Dragon King Temple at the foot of the "Hill of the Great Host," opposite the town called "Golden Mouth."

A despatch arrived from the General Peng ordering all the boats to go down by night to Kiukiang (160 miles down), while he kept the rebels in check in the immediate neighbourhood. It was a somewhat risky expedition, as the rebels had now made the Hanyang hill their rendezvous, and there was of course a moon. But the current was rapid, and there was no fiercely contrary wind. They chose the Wuchang side, and having safely passed the Tortoise Hill, with its rebel watch fires, found that Hankow was still burning in some parts. The rest was a stretch of glowing or blackened débris, in the midst of which they seemed to see one building standing erect. It was the Sen Family Temple, a warning to dishonest tinsmiths and prodigal sons.

The couple or so of days on the river, with the favourable current and general breeziness, restored health and cheerfulness to the party. The greater half of the men in Seng-tch's contingent were land soldiers from the Hanyang camp, and were ordered on arrival at Kiukiang (*lit.* nine rivers), and he among them, to march inland and join the main body of Imperialists, who were doing their best to dislodge the rebels from one or two cities they had captured.

An Imperalist general named Kwan was marching on to Raochow, the præfectural capital of the district in which were the Imperial potteries. They were to join him. On the evening of the second day's march they met fugitives from that city, who informed them that, being unable to hold it, the rebels had set it on fire in various places and retreated therefrom in the night.[1] They had gone, chased by the Imperialists in the direction of Feuliang, the county capital of the pottery district, a walled city only twenty miles distant from that important centre,—a mart comparable to Hankow in size, and supplying perhaps the greater half of the pottery in use in the eighteen provinces. Toward this Feuliang, therefore, the contingent turned their steps. It was on the fourth morning that they joined the forces of the General Kwan encamped outside the walls of the city. The rebels did not seem inclined to show fight. They doubtless had plenty of provisions, but seemed short of ammunition. That had gone in the flames of Raochow.

"The city must be stormed on the morrow," were the orders. Ladders were constructed, swords sharpened, and all the available ammunition served out. In the early dawn the rebel flags were flying as before, and the city gates shut, but there was no sign of life. The sentinels were probably on the lookout, though themselves unseen. The houses outside the city walls had been burnt by the rebels, so the space between the camp and the prize to be attempted was more open, and the besiegers more exposed.

"Ten ounces of silver to the man who first scales the walls!" At which a comely youth seized one end of a ladder and began dragging it by himself. The other end was seized. The walls were still clear. Other ladders followed, and the men behind doubled on. First to start, first to arrive. The ladder was placed in position, and almost over the back of the other bearer Seng-teh clambered up. It had been a sudden impulse. He had acted upon it. His left hand was on the battlement. The ladder was too short. He looked

[1] The walls are still in ruins.

down for a moment to see how to place a foot on the top of one of the poles. In that moment he felt something descend upon his hand slashing away two of his fingers; the ladder slipped, and he fell senseless into the mud below.

Meanwhile another ladder and another were planted in other places, the storming parties being driven back with stones, butt ends, boiling water, oil, and even molten lead, and fell in heaps below. But a band of Imperialists had doubled round the walls, entered it from the other side, cut a "blood road" to one of the gates, opened it, and let in the

main body of their comrades, until after a desperate struggle the city was taken, and there were only half the number of Longhaired to escape; the rest had been entrapped into a corner and shot down wholesale. Part of the city had been fired, but the flames were brought under. The wounded were now attended to. One of the men who had marched up with our hero from Kiukiang went in search of him, and found the lad just alive, but badly shaken and weak with loss of blood. He was carried with others to the temple of the god of war, whom the general claimed as an ancestor, and his hand attended to.

Next day the general came with his under-officers to see the wounded, presented Seng-teh with the promised reward, and spoke highly of his bravery; several others who had distinguished themselves receiving like presents. These were trebled in a day or two by a deputation from the potteries, which had been in imminent danger. The destruction of the works at the end of the Ming dynasty was an often-quoted tradition, and, relieved from present fear, the kilnowners could afford to be generous. Of course the General Kwan received the lion's share. It was he who gained the victory, but a few of the braver privates were not forgotten.

When the regiment left for Kiukiang, Seng-teh was in a fever, and could not go with them. A well-to-do man, however, who had been present at the prize distribution, offered to take care of him. To his house he was accordingly removed, but grew worse, and began to wander at nights. It was midsummer, and seemed terribly hot. His ravings had to do with the burning of Hankow, and with the earlier scares in his own home.

His benefactor called in the best medical help the city afforded, under which—or, was it in spite of which?—he slowly recovered. His patience seemed to win the hearts of the household. He had a keen sense of their kindness. In his convalescence they provided such luxuries as chicken broth, pork gravy, and even shark fins and pigeon eggs, to say nothing of rather sour peaches and pickled onions, which helped him according to the relative nourishment and digestibility of each. They treated him as though he were a son.

On his full convalescence, his host said one day, " I had a relative who was killed in the recent battle, and his house was burnt. He has a daughter about your age. Are you engaged ? " Seng-teh replied that he was. " She is doubtless killed by now, and here is a home for you. The rebels will not come here again. They want the cities on the Yangtse. A provincial capital or two are more than a crockery shop, however big. We are three hundred *li* from Kiukiang by the nearest road, and nearly five hundred by water. [Distance seems greater in China, where travelling is so slow.] They made a mistake in coming here. They will not do so again, unless they gain the whole country. Take my advice; here is a home for you. I have heard that Hanyang is burnt clean, all but the walls. You said you lived in that countryside. She is dead by now. Take my advice. Have we not treated you well?"

Seng-teh had tried to put in a word, as the long lecture—of which the above sentences are but notes—was delivered. He was stopped each time by "Listen to me." But at last he exclaimed, "She is a little child"— (There are no tenses in Chinese.)

"Yes, of course; I see you are wise. Engaged when babies, I expect. You folks in that part always are. I had a relative who went up to Hanyang once. Well, they have run away from the rebels. Dead, I expect. If not, you are, you know; you would have been but for me. She thinks you are dead; you think her dead. She is dead. Here is a home for you, a good family, and some means of living. Many a young military graduate would jump at the chance. And a mere soldier of the ranks! But I have taken a fancy to you. All right; it shall be so."

"When I was ill"—

"Exactly so; don't mention it. I took you into my house and tended to you and fed you up." And so on, and so on.

"I was only engaged two years ago; and I like the girl."

"Like her? How do you know? 'Ten matchmakers, nine liars.'"

"I have seen her; she was with me when I was ill before."

"Very improper; not at all respectable."

"She was three and a half."

"Ha, ha! A mere baby. Here is one your own age. Speak. I ought to command. Do you take my advice?"

"I cannot."

"Then don't expect to see me again. You are well now. You can go and find out her grave as soon as you like."

"I will go to-morrow morning."

"Go."

A little later on, came in the mistress of the house. "I am sorry you have 'sinned against' my husband. He is very angry about it. To 'forget kindness and reject righteousness' is a bad thing. We thought better of you."

The lad could not but weep his disclaimers; he felt it all. But there was the kindness of his teacher to be remembered, and right to be maintained in that direction.

What was he going to do? "Join the army again," he replied.

"But you are too weak for the journey, still more for the fighting. Will you not take our advice? I can talk my husband round."

"Do not blame me; I cannot."

"Then I have a plan. You can draw. My little boy is delighted with those pictures you did for him. Why not go off to the potteries? You can take a barrow; and I will try and get my husband to write a letter of introduction. He knows several kilnowners there. Your betrothed is a teacher's daughter?"

"A B.A., my father's best friend. He buried him when he was killed by the rebels, and took my mother to a place of safety, and buried her too when she died."

"That makes a difference. I will manage it."

"They nursed me through an illness—not such a long one as this. I have been a trouble to you"— And he burst into tears again.

"Don't cry like that, my child; it shall be done. A graduate, father and mother, filial son. I'll make up a tale."

Next morning saw our hero with a small but weighty bundle sitting upon a barrow, *en route* for the potteries. The good wife had arranged it, and there was something about "filial son" and "brave soldier" in the letter he carried. And his left hand would help to make identification complete. That evening he had found lodgings in the house of a quiet old woman, after gaining an introduction to his benefactor's friend, from whom he received the name of an artist, under whom he could learn. Walking through the streets of the busy mart next day, as he returned from a visit to the artist

IMPERIALISTS TO THE FRONT. 367

in question, he saw the following proclamation was posted about :—

CHENG KWOH-FAN.

A Proclamation of Cheng Kwoh-fan.
"The Imperial Minister of the Board of Ceremonies, Cheng [Kwoh-fan], issues this proclamation concerning the putting down of the rebellion :—

"The turbulent rebels, Hung Sheu-ts'uen and Yang Sheu-chu'ng have now been in revolt for five years, wreaking their malignity upon some millions of the populace; devastating the cities and towns of more than five thousand square *li*; oppressing the people indiscriminately; robbing them to the last straw; seizing them for captives; tearing off their garments . . . and beheading all who will not surrender their last ounce of silver. For a double handful of rice their male captives are forced to do battle for them, to excavate under city walls, and the like. For a single palmful of rice their female prisoners are made to stand guard upon city walls as night-sentinels, or to carry loads of rice and coal. If any of these will not unbind their feet, they chop them off [thus being comparable to the Chinese Nero Chow (B.C. 1154–1122), a human vivisectionist], and exhibit them as a warning to others. If a boatman refuses to carry them upon any secret expedition, he is killed, and his body exposed, to terrify the rest into submission.

"These southern rebels live lives of luxury. They are great in their own eyes, and regard the populace of the three-citied Yangtse and the Double Lake District as less than so many dogs, pigs, and sheep. Being thus overbearing and implacable, all flesh hearing thereof must feel compassion for those oppressed by them.

"From the ancient days of Yao and Shuin[1] each generation of ages has upheld the far-reaching doctrines which magnify the relations of emperor and statesman, of honourable and humble, of old and young, fixed and irreversible as the position of the members in the body. But these southern rebels, borrowing the ways of the barbarian tribes, and the religion of the 'Lord of Heaven,'[2] depose sovereigns and degrade officials, their 'officials' calling every man 'brother' and every woman 'sister.'

"The farmer may not plough, but must still pay taxes; for, say they, his fields are the fields of the same 'Lord of

---

[1] The two model emperors of ancient Chinese history and literature. The filial piety of the latter was so great that in his younger days elephants used to plough and wild birds weed for him.

[2] The term adopted by the Roman Catholics, and afterwards by some others, for the Divine name, which term, however, is not the one used by the Taipings. That was "Sovereign on High."

Heaven.' The merchant may not trade, but yet must pay them; his wares, forsooth, are the property of the Heaven-king [Hung Sheu-ts'uen]. The scholar must not study the Confucian classics any more, but instead must follow the words of Jesus in the New Testament, treating all the morality taught in China for thousands of years as so much 'swept-up dust.'

"Never until these latter days have such things been—no, not from the days of creation. At such unorthodox teachings, our Confucius and Mencius must be weeping bitterly in hades. Shall any scholar, then, or any able to read, fold his arms in his sleeves and sit in peace?

"From of old, men of highest virtue have been deified to bear rule in hades, holding official posts there corresponding to those on earth. Yet these rebels, in their fierce violence, reverence not such deities.

"Li Tsz-ch'eng,[1] arriving at Confucius' birthplace, did not desecrate the sacred temple. Chang Shen-tsung [a rebel of the same time, cir. 1644] worshipped the god of literary emolument. Not so those southern rebels. They burn the temples of the sages, destroy the Confucian tablets, scattering their fragments on the ground. In every city they come to, they first burn the temples, with their remembrances of good statesmen, even of the majestic god of war, and the ruler of the eastern purgatory. They defile their courts, and hew to pieces their bodies. Thus they treat Buddhist, Taoist, and local deities, and the shrines of the earth spirits. There is no temple they do not burn, no image they do not destroy. The deities are enraged, they will cool their anger[2] [in their destruction].

"Having received the decree of the Son of Heaven, the present leader of fifty thousand troops on land or water swears that 'even in his sleep he cherishes his burning

---

[1] See p. 192 on the fall of the Mings. Added to Li Tsz-Ch'eng's other enormities, he destroyed the potteries.

[2] The phrase is literally "snow their anger," anger being regarded as both hot and red. Compare a corresponding expression in Isa. i. 18. Curiously enough the above phrase occurs in both classical and mandarin versions of v. 24, "I will ease me of mine adversaries."

wrath.' He will prove his courage by destroying the turbulent rebels, by saving the captured boats, and by rescuing the intimidated captives, urged thereto by his indignant loyalty to the true sovereign, and from pent-up anguish at the denial of the relations proclaimed by Confucius and Mencius, the massacre of myriads of the populace, and the indignities cast upon the higher and lower deities. This proclamation is accordingly issued that all may be acquainted therewith.

"Should there be loyal and brave men anywhere, let them gather others likeminded to join in this righteous war, and break up the nest of rebels. Such sympathisers in our cause shall receive the rations they deserve. Should there be superior men who hold the orthodox tenets, and hate those of the 'Lord of Heaven,' being stirred up to rage on behalf of our doctrines, they shall have the reception due to honourable guests. Should there be benevolent men who will subscribe toward the expenses of the army—those who give sums up to a thousand taels shall be rewarded with degrees; those who give more than a thousand taels shall be recommended to the Emperor for high office. Should there be any among the rebels who will behead their leaders and give up their cities to us, they shall be rewarded with official posts in the Imperial army. Should there be any for long intimidated [by the insurgents], whose hair has grown, but who will throw down their weapons and submit, they shall be reprieved, and shall have means given them to enable them to return home!

"During the Han and T'ang dynasties, rebels were as thick as down, the emperors living dissolute lives, and thus being unable to maintain peace. But our present Emperor is full of anxious energy, reverencing heaven and compassionating the people, not extorting overmuch in taxes, not forcing the populace to enlist. Each reign, indeed, has been characterised by generosity and benevolence.

"The rebels will assuredly be exterminated sooner or later, as even the simple may know. If any, therefore, who have been intimidated by the rebels are willing to continue on as their followers, helping them to withstand the Imperial

IMPERIALISTS TO THE FRONT. 371

soldiers, they will lose their all when the great army comes, their costliest possessions being burnt with fire. I shall be able to make no distinctions then.

"My virtue may be poor, my strength small; my only claim is that of loyalty and fidelity to my post as commander of the army. Such loyalty and fidelity is witnessed to by the sun and moon above, by the deities and demons beneath, by the waters of the long Yangtse, and by the shades of the heroic and faithful. All know my heart, all hear my words. This proclamation, therefore, wherever it goes, is as binding as an Imperial edict."

After reading this with mingled feelings, Seng-teh turned aside to notice that a young man, a little older than he, of rather thin, prominent features and hair which curled where it escaped the queue, had been scanning his face.

"You have been to see Kang Shenseng the artist? I was once his pupil; let us be friends."

Chapter XIX.

Art and Artists.

PICTURES ANCIENT AND MARVELLOUS — TEXTS FOR ALL TIMES — FORTUNE AND FORTUNE-TELLERS — FRIENDSHIP AND FAITH — A PANACEA FOR ALL WOES.

"There was once a recluse who, when he was merry, painted the plum blossom, when sad, the bamboo."—*Mustard Seed Garden.*

"I HEAR you can draw," said Kang Shenseng to his new apprentice.

"Miserable daubs, I assure you," replied Seng-teh.

"It is usual for me to receive a fee; but having heard of your bravery, the kilnowner who recommended you to me has made that right for the first six months."

"I do not dare."

"Can you read? That is good. Then I recommend you to buy the *Mustard Seed Garden*, and study it well."

Seng-teh bought the book, paid a small sum for punctuating it to a poor scholar whom his new friend recommended to him (he was of the same surname, and indeed wore the same hat and boots, as it happened), gave a feast to his fellow-apprentices and one former scholar, and so commenced his studies.

<small>An Art Treatise.</small>

The volumes in question were first published in the year 1680. The plates had evidently suffered much from the recutting and recutting of the boards, but the type was unaltered, and contained much that might interest even a Western reader.

The compiler described himself as an invalid, who, being debarred from the contemplation of the finer landscapes of the Empire, was wont to while away the weary hours in company with his collection of pictures. He had once gone on a pilgrimage to visit the great artists of the day, but had been met with frowning glances and haughty scorn. Under such tyrannous monopoly he at first felt discouraged, but eventually resolved to publish his collection of paintings, supplemented, as they were, by those of an æsthetic friend.

When Seng-teh had learnt off the preface by rote, and had had its meaning explained by his new teacher,—for the style, like the standpoint of the artist, was far above the level of the street,—he asked whether the writer was merely "talking politeness," or whether that was likely to be an authentic history of the production of the book.

Kang Shenseng took the latter view. Art had been in a flourishing condition once, as he would gather from the canons laid down by various ancient artists in that book. The greater part of the painters nowadays were on the wrong side of those rules. They expressed a lost ideal. The old days were better in every way.

That evening Seng-teh's new friend looked in, and the question was referred to him.

"Not a bit of it," he replied. "Every preface is either a string of phrases in praise of the author, which he has paid a man to write, or else a string of humble talk by the man himself if he is so proud that no one will write for him. He can at least gain the praise of the reader for his politeness."

"But do you not think that the old days were better?"

"No, not a bit. We cannot draw figures that look so real that one 'seems to hear them cough.' Yes, the old days were better! That is nothing. There was an ancient painter who lived, I guess, before the days of Pan Ku,—he, you know, who hewed out heaven and earth with his hammer and chisel; perhaps it was Pan Ku's younger brother,—who painted chrysanthemums so well that at the proper season they emitted perfume. Then there was another who painted a dragon on a wall, all

Realism in Ancient Art.

but the eyes. The admiring crowd pointed out the omission. He took up his brush and added the required dots, when the dragon went soaring away. That's what the scholars tell us as sober truth.[1] It is part of their trade. They deal in curios. They are curiosity shopkeepers, and half their trade is to tell lies. Printed books are frauds. Everything in print is half a lie, and the biggest liars are the writers of the prefaces. Painting is in a better state than ever, and so is the art of drawing lying pictures with characters."

This kind of talk was perfectly strange to Seng-teh. It was so unorthodox; and yet the speaker was fluent and brilliant in his remarks, more so than anyone he had known before. He could not follow him altogether, but felt unable to answer the arguments put before him; and though he had not quite liked the face of young Tai (that was his surname) at first sight, yet he felt grateful to him for his interest, and for the enlivened evenings which their intercourse promised.

It was certainly a great advantage for Seng-teh to be under a man like Kang Shenseng. He was a genial man of somewhat more than fifty. In wealthier days, before his father came to grief over the failure of a bank, he had bought a B.A. as a help toward future office,[2] but being reduced in circumstances, he supported himself by painting scrolls and teaching pupils. Apart from such as he, the beginner would have had to have started at coarse work and slovenly style decoration of the very cheapest wares, work which would have rendered it almost impossible for the novice to have risen to anything like conscientious painting afterwards.

The days were at first divided between making copies of the designs most in vogue and the study of the *Mustard Seed Garden*. The preface being mastered, the following paragraphs were learnt off, explained, and enlarged upon:—

" Excellence does not consist in multiplicity of detail, nor

---

[1] "Ned Bagshaw of Chr. Ch. 1652, shewed me somewhere in *Nicophorus Gregoras* that ye picture of St. George's horse on a wall neighed on some occasion " (Aubrey's *Gentilisme and Judaisme*. Quoted in *Mythland*, p. 31).

[2] Such officials are generally sneered at by the *literati* as "stinking of brass."

ART AND ARTISTS. 375

in bare simplicity; difficulty is not art, nor is ease; non-accordance with rules does not ensure an artistic style, and with overmuch method the result may be highly inartistic.

Ancient Canons of Art.

"First give rigid attention to all rules, then follow your genius and break away from them. Work without brush-marks [*lit.* ' bury your pen in a grave']; let harshness give place to smoothness [*lit.* ' rub down the iron into mire']. Give ten days to a piece of water and five to a rock, and you will thus be able to paint the finest landscapes in the Empire. Study a myriad books; travel a myriad miles. If you want to work without rules, first follow every rule;[1] if to paint with ease, first take pains; if you would have a slight and simple style, first study all the multitudinous details." Which remarks are quoted by an ancient artist of unknown date.

The commentator adds: " In using your brush, it is better even to be immature than cramped, better to be audacious than for your work to savour of the market-place. If cramped, your work will be wanting in life; the market-place is full of vulgarity, and vulgarity must have no place in Art. To drive away vulgarity, there is no other plan than much study. As the literary style rises within you, the vapours of vulgarity will descend and vanish.

"The student must make up his mind and choose a definite school of painters for his model until he is practised in that style, his hand answering to his thoughts. He may then turn aside to other and various styles. Then he must melt and recast the whole of his gains from various schools, and form a school of his own. The more eventual variety the better; but at the outset, the more undivided his studies the better."

Then follows a quotation from another artist, also of unknown date. " When a picture seems to be alive with motion and breath, as though of heavenly creation, it may be called a

[1] Compare the words of the philosopher Yen: " In practising the rules of propriety, a natural ease is to be prized. . . . Yet if one knowing how such ease should be prized, manifests it without regulating it by the rules of propriety, this likewise is not to be done " (*Analects*, Legge).

work of Genius. When the touches are something above the ordinary, and the washes are in accord with good taste, a fertility of motive controlling the whole, it may be called a work of Excellence. When there is correctness of form, and a general observance of rules, the result may be called a work of Ability."

Another ancient artist adds a fourth classification, which he calls "the easy style." The authority first quoted says that a certain artist ". . . did not draw real mountain peaks, but what he did were far more artistic than real ones. Was it not so with Li T'ai-peh's poems and compositions? Another celebrated votary of the wine-cup, after a drinking bout, picked up a worn-out writing-brush and painted a woman leaning against a tree, making blots on her cheeks, but with more effect than all the powder and rouge in the world could produce.

"Writing and painting may both be classed under the head of penmanship. . . . If one studies the poems of a certain scholar [whose name is given] and the essays of another [equally famous], one will be in touch with the immortals [*lit.* having an immortal maiden scratching the itching places —of the artistic world]. If one's poems and compositions or paintings are out of touch with the world, better cut off one's arm, for what use is it?"

Another ancient authority says, "Govern your brush, let not your brush govern you." After which the artist first quoted adds a few words on the subject of ink. "Old ink should be used on old paper, for old-style paintings. There is no flash and fire in old ink. . . . If it be used on new satin or on gilt fans, it will not be so suitable as new ink, lacking its lustre. Not that the old is not better, but because new paper and satin do not harmonise with it. One might as well bring a recluse clad in the costume of the ancients, away from his abode in the recesses of the hills, and set him in a guest-hall, amid the glitter of men newly made honourable, or those who have suddenly leaped into a fortune. Would there not be laughing in the sleeves! Old ink, then, must be kept for old paper, new ink for new satin and gilt paper."

The subject of colour is thus treated: "Literature no less than landscape has its colouring. Sz-Ma Tsz-ch'eng [a great historian of ancient China, cir. B.C. 163–85] took in hand the various records of bygone days, with their resplendent old tints, and so produced his masterpiece. Eloquence, too, has its colouring. Two celebrated orators [names given] could make out black to be white and white to be black. The tongue of one of them is like an 'ocean path,' the abode of sea monsters. You may be a good man, but without colour who will make any mark in the world? A colourless man is a useless man.

"With the breath of the four seasons in one's breast, one will be able to create on paper. The five colours well applied enlighten the world." From which brilliant generalisations the author descends to the practical, and says: "Sandstone, red, and indigo are the standard colours for landscape painters. They are the hosts. Other colours are like aristocratic guests bowing and retiring. . . . In the military world some rush like tigers into the battle, but the general remains behind in his tent, directing the events of the day. Some colours are my soldiers of the ranks."

The orthodox discussion of these tenets was followed in the evenings by the unorthodox generalisations of young Tai. He had the peculiarity of never remembering what he had said on the previous night, but being reminded thereof, he went off again in the same strain.

"'Chrysanthemums and dragons,' yes, I remember. Have you heard of the painted cat which caught mice? Well, I will tell you the tale." He accordingly related the following between the mouthfuls of the supper which Seng-teh began to provide as an institution. "There was once a fortune-teller who used to sit near the gate of a large *yamun*. He had the reputation of being a man of great ability and accuracy, and the high mandarin at whose door he sat believed in him thoroughly.[1]

Dick Whittington in the Far East.

[1] A much-patronised fortune-teller of Wuchang used to affirm that the then *Fu Tai* of Hupeh, a brother of Cheng Kwoh-fan, once consulted him about a petition he had drawn up, asking whether it would gain the Imperial favour

"A young water coolie of the place once asked him to tell his fortune well, and offered him eight hundred cash for the job. He had forgotten his 'eight characters' [year, month, day, and hour of birth], but having received such a sum, the fortune-teller agreed to find eight propitious characters for him. From these he prophesied that there was a princedom in store for him. The coolie took the paper, but soon afterwards dropped it.

"The mandarin being very particular about reverencing written paper, had his bearers pick up a piece lying on the street before them, read it, and found that there was a high destiny awaiting the young coolie. He had him called in, offered to support him, set him to study, and eventually gave him his daughter in marriage.

"The fortunate young man, however, was in the habit of exclaiming, 'Worth eight hundred cash! Well worth eight hundred cash!' the meaning of which he would not divulge to his wife. One day, however, the exclamation having been made in the mandarin's presence, he had to confess that it referred to the somewhat manipulated document the fortune-teller gave him. At this the enraged mandarin tried to make his daughter give up her husband. She refused, and he put them into a rudderless boat on the sea. The boat drifted on until it stranded at length on a rocky island which was strewn with remarkable stones.

"These they gathered till the boat could hold no more, then set sail again, reaching a certain land where was a large city. The faithful wife left her husband in charge of the boat, went on shore, and soon found a large curio shop, the wares of which attracted her attention, especially a painting of a cat which hung from the wall. This so struck her fancy, that she returned to exhort her husband to try and procure it. A crowd followed her, and collected around the boat, jabbering in some unknown tongue.

"After inspecting the cargo, the inhabitants of this foreign realm seemed evidently to be asking the price. In-

or not. His reply was that it had better not be sent until the tenth month, which was a polite way of expressing his want of confidence in its success. It was sent, contrary to his advice, and brought the sender into disgrace.

structed by his wife, the man held up five fingers, which at length was rightly interpreted to mean five hundred ounces of silver. Further signs were made to show that the picture of the cat must be given in. It was done, and they set sail again.

"Fortune brought them eventually to a city upon the shores of China, from whence the former water-carrier proceeded home with his wife, but they were treated very shabbily, being put into a stable. Here, however, they learnt that they had no ordinary 'treasure' in their picture; and after a while, proclamations were posted everywhere to say that the Emperor was troubled by the ravages of an enormous rat, which had killed many a cat. He offered high rewards to the man who would rid the palace of the insufferable pest. Hearing of which, the wife advised her husband to go off to the capital with his picture. He did so, gaining an Imperial interview. Having fixed the scroll upon the wall, he watched beside it at night. The rat proceeded forth as of old, but the cat leaped from the scroll and killed it. Whereupon the Emperor made the man a prince of the realm. A good tale is it not?"

"Is it at all true, do you think?"

"True? Who said it was? Nothing is true nowadays. I don't believe in anything—except myself, and your suppers."

"What about fortune-tellers? I cannot say I believe in them, but I should like to know whether my friends are alive."

"Well, ask them then. There is a noted fortune-teller in Feuliang. He does a brisk trade at examination time, and some of his predictions are sure to come true. He knows men at a glance, and has bundles of characters which can be dissected in either of two ways. But countrymen are his best customers. They look upon him as a prophet. He takes in every item of a man's dress, you see, and notices what he is carrying. Perhaps the man's boots are dusty. This looks as though the man has walked some distance over a dry road. If the dust is thicker in front than behind, he guesses that the countryman has come against the wind, and so on.

"The man may be grasping a prescription. He gathers from

<small>Fortune-tellers' Methods.</small>

this that there is sickness in the house. By many a sign which you, and perhaps I, might neglect, he obtains an important clue, makes a shrewd guess or two, gets the man's cash, and a big name into the bargain. He has also a number of slips on which is written, 'Last night at such-and-such an inn I dreamt I should meet you.' 'You are from so-and-so, I believe.' If I were not a pottery painter, I should be a fortune-teller myself."

Seng-teh had the uncomfortable feeling that he too had been read. But his friend was good company, and he would be lonesome otherwise.

"Well, be a fortune-teller for the moment, and tell me where my friends are," he said with a forced laugh. The reply was in a sentence of five characters, which is comparable to those uttered by the ancient oracles. It might mean "your father is alive, your mother dead," or "your mother died before your father," or "your father died before your mother." Seng-teh, not knowing the trick, undertsood it in the latter way. "How did you know?" he asked.

"Never mind; I am right you see."

"My parents are both dead, as you say, but the folks I refer to are my teacher and his little daughter."

"Fled."

"You are sure? But are they alive?"

"Yes"; which would of course be the most pleasant answer to give.

"But you do not believe in fortune-tellers, or in anything."

"I believe in myself. And in you too. Let me tell you a tale of two good friends. You know the proverb, 'It is the long road that determines the strength of the horse.' Well, let us call the friends Leu Yao [long road] and Ma Lih [horse strength]. The words *Leu* and *Ma* happen to be surnames, you know. Leu Yao was a young man of considerable means. Ma Lih went in for gambling, and was often in difficulties, from which his generous friend helped him out several times. He at length followed his friend's advice, and reformed, passed his examinations, and became a mandarin. Leu Yao, how-

A Tale of Two Friends.

ever, had bad luck, lost all his relatives except his mother, and was so reduced in means that he had to live in a mat hut. Hearing of his friend's good fortune, he determined to go and visit him, a journey of some hundreds of *li*. He left all the cash he had with his mother, and begged his way to his friend's *yamun*. Ma Lih received him heartily, but took no notice of his tale of sorrow, merely bidding him to eat, drink, and be merry.

"At last he became angry at his friend's disregard of his mother, and said he must return. He asked for two thousand cash. Would he not like a horse as well? his friend suggested. But he only gave him a lame donkey. He went off cut to the heart. Ma Lih then ordered one of his retainers to mount a fine horse, overtake Leu Yao, and offer him both the horse and three hundred taels, blaming Ma Lih when he had heard his tale. This he did, and exchanged beasts, for he said he did not live far off, and wanted to do some good deeds. Leu Yao thanked him profusely, and galloped away home.

"Arriving at the place where his hut used to be, he found a fine house. He did not know where his mother was. She was within, living in great comfort. Ma Lih had sent swift messengers to order its erection directly he saw his old friend. Then Leu Yao knew the heart of his friend. I like taking folks in like that. My friends are very wealthy. True friends are scarce. You are one. I am a queer fellow, but you will know me by and by."

Yet Seng-teh's friend never asked him back. His discourse was scholarly and perhaps his tale might be true. At anyrate, he was certainly good company.

The first day of the month came round, and Kang Shenseng duly lighted three sticks of incense and two candles in front of the god of riches image on his "mantelpiece." Having bowed before it, he told Seng-teh he might worship it, if he liked. It was as good as any. Seng-teh replied by pulling up from the collar of his garment his string of peach-stones, which he still wore. It was a charm, after all, against any tyranny on the subject of idol worship, for though the faith of the idol worshipper may not be great, the word "custom" is a terribly tyrannical word. Having told his tale up to his father's death, emphasising the part of the Taoist in it all, his art teacher seemed content for him to be "godless." "But you should worship your ancestors. That is a good old custom, you know. It is filial."

That evening the matter was referred to his friend. "I believe in idols? Not I. I am as good as any dead man was, and far better than wood and mud images. Have you heard of the man who apprenticed himself to the great idol of the O Mei Hill in Szchwan?"

Seng-teh had, and felt he had scored a point. On being asked where he heard it, he confessed it was in the Taiping camp.

"Taiping, you rebel; you mean Longhaired."

In Seng-teh's mind, Captain Li hardly belonged to the Longhaired. He was a Taiping to him. And to turn off the conversation, he asked about the proclamation he was reading when he first saw his friend. He could not understand the term "Lord of Heaven." He had never heard it in the—Longhaired camp.

Young Tai's reply consisted in the information that there was a "Lord of Heaven" hall in a village not far off, that the morrow was their worship day, as he knew from one of their "religion eaters." He asked Seng-teh to take a holiday and come with him. "It is great fun."

Seng-teh asked his friend to morning meal, during which he explained that the Sacred Book of the Longhaired was called the Old Covenant, and that the proclamation referred to the New, which he could not understand.

Reaching the cottage, they entered, to find five or six ill-clad men having a morning meal.[1] "We are selfish," said the man at the head of the table.

"Oh, please, please!" they replied (*chin-chin*, the usual reply to the usual phrase).

"We had our meal at home before we came," said Tai in a rather sarcastic manner. The man at the head of the table seemed to feel it, but said, "Sit down, please," and he

[1] The writer does not commit himself to any undue generalisations in this description, but draws one particular place from the life.

handed them the water-pipe, while they proceeded with their meal.

Seng-teh, looking about him, saw that the central picture represented what he at first took to be the goddess of mercy bringing a child to earth. He asked whether it was not so.

The men looked at him to see whether he was in earnest, then made the "ten sign" (a cross) upon their chests, and said, "By no means." Seng-teh apologised for his mistake, still looking at the picture. The "penmanship" was strange.

"It is printed," said his friend, which a closer examination proved to be the case. Under it was the Imperial Tablet inscribed "Sacred Edict." Three sticks of incense were burning before both, and two candles were lit.

"May we see your Sacred Book?"

"Yes, with pleasure," and the man handed Seng-teh a volume called *Lo Ma* (Roman) *Prayer Classic*. The characters were familiar, but they would not go together.

"Have you any book called the New Covenant?" he asked.

"No," was the reply, "our spiritual father has it." This phrase Seng-teh knew to be a polite name for a præfectural mandarin, and thus did not take it to refer to a foreign priest.

"Do you not read it? It speaks about the Lord of Heaven."

"Yes it does, but it is heresy to read it. It is rebellion."

"Then the Longhaired did not learn of you."

Again the man looked; then seeing him to be in earnest, made the "ten character" sign, and said, "By no means."

"Have you heard of anyone called Yesu [Jesus]?"

"Heard!" they all exclaimed, laid down their chopsticks, and made the same sign again.

"But the book which speaks of him," said young Tai, sarcastically, "is, you say, a bad book."

"These are reviling words," exclaimed the man at the head of the table. "Have I been wanting in politeness to you?"

Seng-teh rose to go, apologising to the company, and

pulling his friend away. He was more bewildered than ever.

But the remembrances of the camp and the peach-stones recalled his friends, and, being left alone, he wrote a letter to Nieh Shen-seng and sent it off. He felt lonely again, and home-sick. When would the reply come, he wondered.

This matter was referred to young Tai. "Don't believe in home-sickness," he said. "I like to come in here, and you like me to come; but if I were a recluse on the top of one of your nine peaks,—with a little secret in my possession, of course,—I should never feel lonely."

The reference to Seng-teh's early home did not improve matters, and the flippant manner of young Tai, refreshing when directed against mere orthodoxy, was somewhat obnoxious in connection with feelings with which he could have no sympathy.[1] "What is your secret? Is it private, like that of gilding in the potteries?

"Well, we are friends, and I will tell you a tale. Many years ago, a young scholar, who had taken his first degree, went up to the capital to take the next. He stopped at an inn some distance from Peking, where he found an accomplished maiden who was able to converse with him upon his own subjects. Her father had given her leave to reject any suitor she did not like, and had promised not to sell her to any moneyed man she knew nothing about. She was therefore 'unspoken.' Mutual affection sprang up between the two, and the young scholar vowed that when he had taken his degree he would return in the eighth month and make her his bride. He proceeded to Peking, and was fortunate enough to get not only the hoped-

Origin of the Poppy.

---

[1] In the travels of the Buddhist monk Fah Hien (4th or 5th century), who spent fifteen years wandering through the "Buddhist kingdoms," it is related that "Several years had now elapsed since Fa Hien left the land of Han; the men with whom he had been in intercourse had all been of regions strange to him; his eyes had not rested on an old familiar river, plant, or tree; . . . no face or shadow was now with him but his own, and a constant sadness was in his heart. Suddenly one day, when by the side of a gigantic image of jade, he saw a merchant presenting as his offering a fan of white silk [presumably a Chinese fan], and the tears of sorrow involuntarily filled his eyes and fell down" (see Legge's trans., p. 103).

for degree, but also the office of county magistrate. At this he was so elated as to forget the maiden and his promise. He returned home another way.

"She, however, as the time went by, began to get anxious and poorly. In the tenth month, receiving no news, she sickened and died. Two months later the young mandarin received an Imperial summons, and proceeded to the capital again. He went by the same road as he had gone before, and stopped at the same inn. The landlord felt highly honoured to see a county mandarin come up to his door, but soon recognised his guest of the previous summer. 'Where is my bride?' asked the mandarin. 'Alas, great official, she loved you so much as to pine away and die when you did not return.' They went together to her grave. It was evening; he desired to be left alone, shed many bitter tears, and being very weary, fell asleep. In his dreams the maiden appeared to him, saying, ' Our connection [*yin yuen*] is broken, but on waking you will find an herb which will help to console you. It is a medicine for sorrow, and an elixir for all woe.'

"He awoke, and found a plant he had never seen before, nor was there any reference to it in the herbal treatises he had brought with him. He carefully dug it up, potted it, and by and by found out the soothing properties of its juice. From the words of the maiden he called it the[1] *yin sheu* flower" (the former word is a pun upon the first word she used; the latter, is that of budding, which occurs in the Chinese for "B.A.," budding talent).

"And have you that flower?"

"I have its dried juice; or, what is better, I have foreign opium."

---

[1] This character *yin* in the name of the poppy as generally written means jar; the second character, from the T'ang dynasty onwards, is always *seu* of millet, from the resemblance of a poppy head to a millet jar. The above tale, though (formerly) current at the potteries, does not seem to be in print.

The poppy is mentioned by Homer as a garden flower, its juice by Hippocrates. Virgil speaks of the "lethean poppy." Pliny and Dioscorides also mention it in the same connection. The poppy seems to have been introduced into China by the Arabs in the eighth century A.D. (Dr. Edkins, Historical Note on the Poppy in China, 1889, reprinted in the official Blue-book 1894).

Chapter XX.

How to become a Demigod.

Fiery ordeals—wine—opium—immortal rabbits, and medicines which immortalise.

"It is the long road that determines the strength of the horse."
Chinese Proverb.

Next day, Kang Shenseng referred again to the subject of idols, and asked Seng-teh whether he had noticed two temples in the streets, the names of which he gave. He would tell the story thereof. "At the end of the Ming dynasty great havoc was caused at the potteries by the insurgents, and all the kilns were destroyed. Nor as time grew quieter were there any found who could build fresh ones after the old pattern. An old man and his daughter drew out a design for a kiln which was to be twenty feet high. It did not answer, however. Several alterations failed to improve it,—the pottery was either broken or unevenly burned. The maiden then suggested that the door should be made her own height, with two breast-high indentations for watching the fire, and other apertures for ventilation underneath. This was done, and perfection was nearly attained.

The Legend of the "Fire Goddess."

"On the second trial, she went on top to see if she could discover the reason of the remaining defects, was overpowered by the charcoal fumes, and fell in. The kiln then answered perfectly, and that form has been adopted ever since. The maiden was deified, and her temple called by the name of the Fire Goddess."

"Do you know that the packers at the potteries get better rice served out to them than the artists? In ancient times the masters gave their employés common rice alike. On one occasion, it being worse than usual, the whole body of pottery workers went to complain to the mandarin of Feuliang. They are great on trade unions here, you know.[1] To offend one man is to offend all, and many mandarins are afraid of them. But this man, hearing of their coming, procured a helmet and greaves of iron, which he said he would make red-hot, and if any out of the three classes of workmen—artists, clay workers, and packers—would put them on for a moment, his fellows should henceforth have the finest rice procurable. He evidently thought such a challenge would put a stop to their complainings.

[sidenote: The Martyr to the Cause of Rice.]

"They, however, requested him to heat the articles. This done, one of the packers stepped forward, and, calling upon his friends to cherish his memory, took up the greaves, put them on his legs, lifted the red-hot helmet on to his head, and fell down dead.

"The amazed mandarin ordered that the packers should have the finest rice procurable, and that if any faulty rice was found in their bowls by an inspector appointed to call every seven days, their employer should provide a day's theatricals, and give them three loads [3 cwt.] of rice [which regulation holds good to the present day]. One of the pottery painters, hearing of this, ventured to try. He took up the helmet, but let it slip just as he had raised it to his head. He died, and the mandarin, commending his daring, said that the artists should always have medium quality rice provided for them. Of the clay workers, none was found daring enough to make the experiment.

"The deceased packer was deified, and a temple erected to his memory, with a tablet therein, on which were recorded his doings. You should go and see it."

---

[1] The trade unions of the Middle Ages "may not inaptly be compared to the then military organisation of the country; as so many industrial regiments quartered in every town." Here, at the potteries of Kiangsi, those trade unions have more than once become a formidable, if disorderly, military force, to the terror of the mandarins.

That evening these legends were submitted to young Tai for criticism. He seemed less sarcastic than usual, and maintained that they were true. "Here are the kilns and the rice for proof," he said. "I can only get medium quality rice, and even the Imperial artists get the same. I hope to get in among that set in a few months' time with the help of opium. If they ever deify me, I hope they will give me that. It must be dull sitting in a temple year after year, with only incense to smell."

To Seng-teh the deification seemed as likely as the opium for the deified. His friend seemed to read his thoughts,—they were expressed in his face,—and said, "Not at all. Have you not heard that in some temples opium is regularly given to the idols? I have heard it was in Hankow. The chief of the monks gave out that he had a dream, in which the idols told him that if they had opium given them, they would answer all prayers. The news spread, and a great opium-smoker came, smeared a large quantity on the lips of the idols, and offered his prayer for riches. Not long after, his elder brother died, and he came into his property. A young man prayed for his father's recovery, and he recovered. A young woman prayed for a son, and by and by had one. They each gave a tablet. Then the suppliants came in crowds."

Opium for the Gods.

"Yes, I heard that; and I also heard that the mandarin came round in the fourth watch of the night, and found the priests smoking, and several nuns singing to them. Then he went back, returned at daylight, seized the monks and a large pot of opium, and was near upon smashing the idols."

"Mandarins are fools," replied Tai. "You are always trying to spoil all my best stories. Opium for artists, I say, and for idols too."

"And monks?"

"Yes; and monks too. They live lonely lives. The best monk China ever had was a great wine-drinker. Opium is better than wine."

A picture of Captain Li and Commander Yang came up in Seng-teh's mind. But he merely asked to hear about the monk referred to. "You can get the book for yourself.

HOW TO BECOME A DEMIGOD. 389

The making of a priest-monk.

The Drunken Demigod.

There's too much in it to tell at one sitting, and it is only about wine. Well, as you have asked, there was a temple not far from the capital somewhere in the Sung dynasty [in the reign which began 960 and ended 976 A.D.], and one snowy night the monks were all startled by a loud noise like that of thunder. They went searching about, and found that one of the bronze *lohans* had tumbled over on to the ground. The old abbot told them it meant that one of them had come to earth. That night a child was born in a wealthy house. The old abbot went and claimed him for Buddha, and then died.

"The lad was brought up very well, always had a leaning towards Buddhism, but did not think of becoming a monk until both his parents had died, when he went off on a pilgrimage to find the two abbots, whom the old man had named just before he died. He found one of them at last, and asked him to shave his head. The abbot, seeing he had been brought up in luxury, demurred at first, but at last yielded, and so, while the rest of the monks were tinkling and drumming, and whatnot, his hair was cut off. Then he had a very bad time sitting still on the bench. He tumbled off twice and was beaten. He had a bad time with the food too.

"At last he appealed to the abbot, who hit him with his palm and woke up the *lohan* in him. He rushed away, and ever afterwards behaved as a madman. He had a great liking for wine, and when well drunk did wonders. You see, wine reveals the man's nature. If he is a beast, the beast comes out. If he is a *lohan*, that comes out too.

"One day the temple wanted repairing. This was the second temple. They could not endure him at the first. Well, they made him take the subscription book. Three thousand strings of cash were needed. He promised it in three days, if he had wine enough. He rushed out, and threw down the book in the *yamun* of a high official named Mao, then went back and played the fool. But the Empress had a dream in which she saw a *lohan*, who commanded her to send three thousand strings of cash to a certain temple. He told her she would find the address by inquiring of the statesman Mao. She did so, and went in person. There was a to-do.

"She then ordered all the monks to pass before her, that she might identify the *lohan*. When his turn came, he told her he was only a poor madman who could turn a somer-

HOW TO BECOME A DEMIGOD

sault, which, to the scandal of all present, he did there and then. The Empress, however, said it meant a son for her. A somersault in Buddhism, you know, means a new birth. She wanted to thank the demigod, but he had gone, and the rest of the monks only found the madman after some days playing with some children among the lotus flowers.

"This is only one adventure. That man could do anything when he was drunk enough, for intoxication reveals a man's real nature, you see. But opium is better; it *makes* a man a demigod. It is a solace, but much more. Am I not eloquent? It is opium. Have I not a lively imagination? It is opium. Can I not criticise the ancients? It is opium. Am I not lifted above the world, past or present? It is opium. Is not my standpoint that of the immortals? It is opium. Can I not draw well; can I not invent; am I not going on the Imperial staff? It is opium.

"Look here. You and I are friends. I come in rather late because I have my opium first. Why not get a set; and if you don't want it yourself, entertain a friend with it. Or I will bring my set here; but then I want it at home. You will get one. That will be grand; a pipe at both places; so I can come in here soon after work, unless you would like to come round to see me. I have not asked you before. No offence, I hope? I am tired of the place, and like to get out of it at night. The *fung shui* of this house seems better. Well, let us go out and get the things at once. I can lend you some money. You have some? That is good. Be independent. The shops are shut, but there is always a little window place open in the door. The shops shut early. There have been rowdy folks in these streets before now. All night trade is done through those little windows."

They returned after a while with the complete set. "It

is rather late to-night," said young Tai, "and I will get back. You go to rest early. I will not disturb you further," and he was gone.

And Seng-teh was left alone with his new set of utensils

and a small pot of the wonderful dark-brown stuff which was the making of his friend. His landlady came in soon after. She had been out at a neighbour's, having such a confab as old women in China and elsewhere love. She asked whether he was going out again, and on his replying in the negative, she bolted the outer door, and retired for the night.

HOW TO BECOME A DEMIGOD.

Seng-teh, however, could hardly be expected to retire without just trying a little of the opium. He would investigate things in a truly Confucian manner. Already he felt himself a philosopher by anticipation. It seemed strange, and yet very interesting, to use the various utensils. He took his first puff, then another, then put a little more opium into the bowl of the "pipe." Yes, his mind was being enlarged. His past history, wherever he took it up, seemed to grow broad and large. He did not know how interesting it had been. The old familiar landscape took fresh lines. Nieh Shen-seng's entertaining evenings at home grew in fascination. He rose above his troubles. His camp-life was glorified. The burning of Hankow grew into a sublime spectacle. His scaling the wall was a deed which deserved immortality. Then he took up his brush-pen, and looked around; the very room seemed to enlarge. He found a sheet of paper, and drew a design for the appeal for white rice, and the martyrdom of the packer. He excelled himself. It was a masterpiece. He was now in the true region of art. He was among the Immortals. Was it all in his drawing, he wondered, or was the eye itself under a spell? Perhaps both. If it was mostly subjective, all customers ought to be smokers. But on comparing it with his other laborious work, it was found to be far more excellent. He was now an art critic. The old masters were fools. Let them pass before him as the monks passed before the Empress. He would denounce them each one. "You fool, to pride yourself on your work. Call your pictures poems? They are wretched fly-crawlings. Next man. You rascal! You have imposed on the world long enough, with your empty name. I denounce you. Your fame is a stolen one. You are a thief and a robber. I condemn you."

These last words being uttered aloud, the old landlady appeared. "Are there burglars in the house?" she asked. Seng-teh laughed heartily. He was mad, she thought, and told him so. He laughed the more.

"It is opium," she said.

"Of course it is," he replied; "any fool might know that."

She retired a moment and came back with a little book.

"Look here, my child; this was given me to-night. I was to give it to you in case you had begun to smoke opium. You have begun. I could not have believed it. Let me exhort you. It is a bad habit. It is ruin. I cannot have you smoking in my house. Read this. It will tell you how bad opium is."

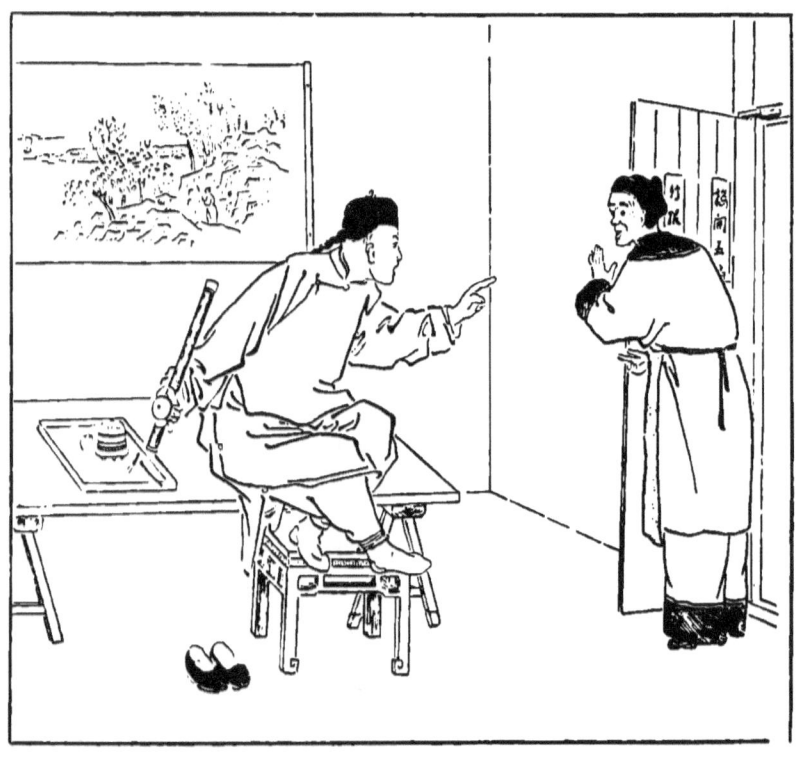

Seng-tch took the book, and found that such words as "poison," "delusion," "dissipation," "evil," and "ruin," were plentifully scattered up and down its pages. Then he turned to the end and read: "The superior man embraces virtue, the mean man embraces [or wishes to own] the *land.*" There was evidently a pun here. The sentence in the *Analects* meant worldly possessions, but the writer evidently meant opium, the common name for which is "mud." Confucius could not have meant that. It was wrong to twist classical words for the condemnation of those who smoked. It made the smoker out to be a "mean man." It was an insult upon himself, upon Seng-teh, who had done a deed which ought to place him among the national heroes.

"It is true" said the old woman; "opium is a thing of hell. It is poison. I cannot see you ruined in my house. I never had opium smoked here before. It will bring a bad name upon me. It will ruin you."

"What do old women know about it? This book was written by your elder sister."

"My elder sister? I never had one. My mother" —

"By your aunt then!"

"She never learnt to write."

"She got someone to write it for her."

"Did she? I must ask her to-morrow. I had a long chat with her this evening about her chickens and pigs. She never said a word to me about it, though she hates the poison herself. She is a clever woman. Last year" —

"The old potato!"

"No, she is not! She is a clever woman. Last year" —

"You, I mean, you old potato."

"There now! To be abused in my own house! It is all because of that opium. You never talked like that before. I cannot bear it! You must give up smoking, or I cannot have you here."

"I will go elsewhere to-morrow morning."

Seng-teh did not sleep that night. He must have another pipe to help him to get over his insult. He had been insulted in print. He had been insulted by an old "potato" of a landlady. Next morning he would go. And he did. Leaving the money due to the old woman on the table, he called a coolie at dawn, and went round to his friend's quarters, to receive a cordial greeting. There were two to laugh now. But Tai's laugh seemed rather forced. There was a nervousness about him, which did its best to hide itself under jerky sentences and explosive guffaws. His early morning self was hardly that of the evening. It was like the hopping and fluttering of a bird whose wing has been broken, rather than the soaring flight. He looked ten years older. The room, too, looked poverty-stricken and bare, whereas any young man of artistic instincts who has lived in any one room for some years will, in China as elsewhere, generally have some traces of such instincts visible upon the walls. There will be a curio found on such and such a stall, a scroll from such and such a dealer; and although Tai had spoken of his lodging in a depreciating manner, Seng-teh was hardly prepared for a picture of extreme want. Tai explained that he used to have the walls covered with paintings, but he had got above them now, and liked to form his own pictures mentally, unhindered by scrolls.

The question of breakfast came up. There was only a handful of rice in the house. "Shall I go out and buy some vegetables?" "Yes, do. Have you cash, or shall I get you some? I ought to pay when you come here. Never mind. Just as you like. Ha! ha! ha!" The laugh seemed almost sepulchral. It recalled the smile of Lieu of the tea shop, but it was very different. That was a thin mask over the face of a rascal. There was something like despair in this. Seng-teh had never had to buy his own vegetables before. At home and in the camp they had been provided. Here the old lady had always procured them for him, giving him all possible variety.

Breakfast was an ill-concealed failure. When it was over, Seng-teh wanted to hurry away to Kang Shenseng. His friend said he would like to see the apparatus bought the previous night. If it was not all right, he would change anything that was faulty. "It has been used."

"Of course, I remember. You are sensible, and the old woman a fool. She might have known that you would have resented any 'demon words' just then. And you called her a potato. Ha! ha! ha! So she is. Now let us see. Yes, they seem to be all right. And they were cheap too. You would have had to give half as much again for them. But I am 'in the trade.' Leave them out. I will see after them."

The evening found the two friends together again. The evening meal, like that of the morning, was provided by Seng-teh. The other paid him in apologies. Now for the opium. Seng-teh opened his little pot. It was empty. "A thousand pardons. I had a friend come to see me just after you went.

He must have emptied it. I have just a little in my pot. Shall I get some more? Well, if *you* will, it will be kind of you. Friends should not stand on ceremony. Ha! ha! ha!"

They smoked together, and a change came over the aspect of affairs. The room did not seem so bare. Seng-teh had misjudged his friend after all. And Tai's conversation was entertaining, decidedly so. Nor was he himself wanting in repartee. Opium was the elixir of life, the genuine pill of perpetual youth of the Taoists, he was now forced to own, which was the prelude to some banter.

"I thought you did not believe in Taoists?"

"Not in their charms, unless opium be one."

"If it is, and it is, you believe in them?"

"Don't bother me. I believe in opium."

"Yes, Western opium; opium from the Western barbarians."

"The Western barbarians gave the Taipings their Sacred Book. I used to read it in the camp. I was younger then, but the men used to reverence me, and then the cry of 'Kill the fiends.' You should have heard that!"

"And seen the burning of Hankow?"

"Yes, and seen that. It was an awfully grand sight."

"You young rebel! I don't like to have rebels in my house; I am a good subject. Ha! ha! ha!" This time the laugh sounded hearty enough, but there was a sting in it. Things seemed larger and grander now to Seng-teh. But sarcasm seemed larger too. His friend was almost insulting. "I do not know that it was the Longhaired who set Hankow on fire. I expect it was the Imperialists, who were unable to withstand them."

"But their Sacred Book told them to destroy the cities of the idol worshippers. You told me so once. It is a bad book."

"It is not."

"Was the burning of Hankow a good deed? I have you there. You are a young rebel; your hair is longer than I thought. Ha! ha! ha!"

"Am I a friend to the rebels? Look here at my left hand! I scaled the wall. I was the first to do it."

"But you believe in the rebels all the same."

Seng-teh's left fist came down with some force on the bed frame. "Stop it, I say!"

"You stop it! I thought to have a quiet evening, and you are a regular young tiger all at once. 'A tiger cub,' I believe is the phrase, and your captain is the 'Crouching Tiger,' is he not? Tell me if I am wrong. Only don't smash the furniture."

Seng-teh rose and made a motion as if to go. "Look here. Captain Li was a hero, a very god of war. And are not many of the mandarins scoundrels, and their underlings worse scoundrels still? And the Longhaired had right on their side at first. Many of the Imperialist captains oppressed the people far more than they did. But the Longhaired were joined by a number of secret society vagabonds,—the 'Kneeling Dog' at Hanchwan, for instance. And so it was elsewhere. When the wind blows hard upon the waters of my lake at home, the waves wash up all sorts of muck and floating weed, and as they dash against the shore they are brown and dirty. The mandarins are the wind, and the dregs of the people the muck, and thus we have the dirty waves."

"Well put! Well put! You are better than a Sacred Edict preacher. It is all opium. Lie down again and finish your pipe. The Longhaired were bent on destroying the potteries, as Li Tsz-cheng did at the end of the Ming dynasty,—bent on taking away my trade and my opium. Which I can smoke in peace now, thanks to heroic Imperialists like you. You don't say you have had enough. Hand me your box. I have only just begun."

"I have had several hundredths of an ounce."

"A few hundredths! That is nothing. I take three-tenths a day now. All the artists in the potteries smoke, some more than that. Did you know that Kang Shenseng was a big smoker? He is; so are sensible men, especially those on the Imperial staff."

"Yes," said Seng-teh, as a sudden thought struck him. "I suppose you will get rich then. You deserve it. All success to you. They pay you badly at present."

"Yes, a miserable two hundred cash a day. I live on private means."

HOW TO BECOME A DEMIGOD.

Seng-teh looked thoughtful for a minute. Tai's opium was swallowing up all his wages. He was spending all he received. And glancing round the bare room, he guessed rightly that private means meant the pawnshop, and, yes, it must be so—himself.

"What is the matter?" asked his friend, as he tried to read his face.

"I find I have left a jacket with the old woman. She was washing it. I must go round and see about it." And he went out.

Arrived at the old woman's house, he found her with red eyes bemoaning her fate. The jacket was a fiction. He asked her whether she had that book she showed him last night.

"No; your friend came for it this morning."

"What? Tai? What did he want with it?"

"It was his. It was he who gave it to me the night before He met me outside and told me you were beginning to smoke; told me that it was a bad habit, and he did not like to see you ruined as he was; told me to tell you I could not allow smoking in my house. I told him I could not afford to give you up. He said you would not go, that you liked me, and so on. And now you have gone."

It was a plot, then. Tai had guessed he would take it badly. "She might have known that you would have resented any 'demon words' just then." He saw it all. Tai was in difficulties. He had pawned himself clean. His clothing was old and scanty. He needed someone to come and live with him. Tai had hardly spent a cash upon him hitherto. Seng-teh had paid up all along. Yes, he saw it all now. "I will be back to-morrow morning," he said. "I apologise for any rudeness. To-morrow morning without fail, never fear."

Seng-teh went back with well-acted cheerfulness. He had the under-garment on all the while. He was sorry he ran away. Would his friend have more opium? all he had, if he liked. "Let us have a happy evening. Tell us a tale," and so forth. He had heard that emperors smoked opium; was it not so?

"Yes, Tao Kwang was a smoker. It was smoke which

helped him to compose his anti-opium edict, which he wrote with his own hand. He sent villainous spies all over the land, who used to get on the tops of houses in the dead of night and scent out their victims. And many a high mandarin and rich merchant was ferreted out from his most concealed apartments, to be executed like common malefactors. Opium-smoking flourished nevertheless. The Emperor was a smoker.[1]

"And that anti-opium tract the old potato showed you, it was written by an old smoker named Wu. I knew him." Seng-teh had also heard of him. He had come trying to borrow money of him soon after his arrival. He was a friend of Kang Shenseng, he said.

"It is all false. Did I not say that books were lies? Anti-opium books are. I believe in opium, as you said just now."

Before his friend had aroused next morning, Seng-teh's things had all been removed to the old woman's house, and he went to work after his morning meal. That evening Tai came in, apologised for any insults he had uttered the previous night, and said one of his rich relations was going to be married in Feuliang. Could his friend lend him a thousand cash, or, say, two thousand, as his relative was well-to-do, and he wanted to make him a suitable present?

Seng-teh "lent" him a thousand; and next evening Tai came in with a wadded jacket, which he had needed badly. His private means had arrived, he said. Which Seng-teh understood, and did not press him for repayment. Tai's hopes were high as regards the Imperial staff.

And in a few days they were fulfilled. He was now among that favoured number, but did not offer to refund the loan. Perhaps he would do so by and by. He brought one or two cheap luxuries with him to add to the supper.

After a month or so he came as usual, but shivering with the cold. He said it was a touch of ague. An uncle of his had died at Kiukiang. Would Seng-teh lend him five thousand

---

[1] This paragraph seems to be substantially true. Tao Kwang's opium-smoking rests on good authority, and the villainous conduct of the spies is confessed in a proclamation by the Viceroy of Hupeh, issued 15th March 1839.

cash? Also, as he did not seem to smoke now, would he let him have his smoking apparatus?

Seng-teh gave him a thousand and the apparatus, wishing him a good journey and a speedy return. Next day Tai had gone. He had little luggage to take with him, and had forgotten to pay for his lodging. Sundry other little bills came in to Seng-teh. The creditors said Tai had assured them that Seng-teh had been in debt to him, and had promised to pay them to make matters square.

This Seng-teh refused to do, telling them it was a falsehood. They grumbled at him and cursed young Tai, but having no claim upon our hero, went their way.

The next thing Seng-teh heard was that his former friend, after being unsuccessful in the Imperial works, spoiling a vase or two, had been seen in the streets of Feuliang, sitting at a stall for the sale of anti-opium pills (containing opium). Later on came the story that he was found to be his own best customer, swallowing a number a day, and that he had gone elsewhere.

"There is a rabbit in his crockery shop," observed one of Seng-teh's fellow-pupils. "You have not heard the tale? *A Rabbit in a Crockery Shop.* Where were you brought up? No wonder he took you in. It is one of the stock stage plays of China. A man named So T'ai-sz got rich and opened ten crockery shops in Peking.

"Two of the Immortals had a grudge against him, and consulted how they might do him harm. One of them at length determined to take the form of a rabbit, which the other was to try and sell to So. He went past the house, and attracted the man's attention by saying that the rabbit was very expensive indeed. He could not sell it for less than fifty taels. 'What is there precious about it?' asked So, and he took the rabbit in his hand, and began to stroke it. It was certainly a fine creature. But the fine creature darted off, and he after it.

"The rabbit made straight for one of his crockery shops. 'Throw the crockery at it if you cannot get it in any other way,' cried So. It eluded the chase until the greater part of the crockery was smashed. Then it made for the next shop, and so on, until the stock of the whole ten was broken."

"An appropriate tale," said Seng-tch; "but how is the rabbit represented on the stage?"

"By a man, of course.[1] But the opium-curing pills remind me of a better tale. That is also a play. You ought to see it acted. A doctor enters, saying, 'Four generations of ancestors have practised medicine. I can go to all the five points of the compass and accumulate wealth.' A knock at the door. 'Who is there?' 'It is I, one of your former patients.' 'What? Have you not taken my medicine?' 'Yes.' 'Aha! I made sure it was your ghost. I am afraid of ghosts.' 'Your medicine made me well.' 'You don't say so?' 'Yes indeed, and I have come, doctor, to ask you to go and see a student, a relative of mine, who is ill.'

The Physician in Farce.

"'All right, I am ready.' 'Which way shall we go?' 'Oh, please don't go by the main street. I attended a man who had fever there a little while ago. I gave him the "five yellows," a big dose, and he was cold at once, as cold as any one might wish. Yet they were not satisfied! I cannot go by the main street.' 'Well, we can go by the back street.' 'No, no. There was a man there taken with violent spasms. I gave him a good dose of arsenic. His spasms ceased immediately. Then they wanted to summon me as being

---

[1] The origin of the Chinese stage is traced to the Lustrous Emperor, son of Li Tan, who is said to have visited the palace of the moon over a bridge formed from a staff thrown towards the heavens. Arrived there, beautiful maidens were seen singing and dancing. The Emperor, on his return, taught their movements to some youths of the palace, who were called "the disciples of the pear garden." All the women's parts are personated by men on the orthodox Chinese stage. It is only in low tea-shop recitals that women are found singing theatrical ditties. The real plays (followed by farces as above) are not very numerous. They are all semi-historical. *Peh-ya and his Sympathetic Friend* is one. The Christian objection to the Chinese stage lies in the fact that many of the heroes represented have been deified, so that they are a form of idolatry. Actors, though well paid, are not allowed to compete for degrees to the third generation. St. Augustine tells us that "the Greeks think they have good reason to honour these players, seeing they must honour them that require these plays: the Romans, on the other side, are so far from gracing them, that they will not allow them a place in a Plebeian tribe, much less in the Court of Senate" (*City of God*, ii. xiii.).

HOW TO BECOME A DEMIGOD.

the cause of his death. I could never bear that. My reputation would suffer. Matters were smoothed over by my taking the funeral into my own hands. I could not imagine how I was to provide a coffin, but at length remembered an old medicine cupboard of my father's. I cut off its legs and made a box for the corpse. As to bearers, there were four of us, myself, wife, son, and daughter-in-law, and we carried the box between us. As we went along, I sang, "It cannot be helped, it cannot be helped, it cannot be help-ed." To which my wife added, "You heal a man, and heal him to death, and I am thus involv-ed." My son continued, "To heal him to death, and such a fat man! How can we fat men carry?" My son's wife chimed in, "In future then, see only thin men, they're easier far to bury."'

"There's a lot more about curing a hunchback by laying him on a city gate with the other gate on top of him, and five huge dyer's stones [3 cwt. each] on the top of that, for forty-nine days. But where were you brought up? I suppose you have only studied the classics."

Seng-teh did not feel inclined to substitute that fellow-student for his former friend Tai.

Chapter XXI.

Changing Scenes.

OUR POTTERY PAINTER RETURNS HOME—MEETING A FOREIGNER, AN ADMIRAL, AND OTHERS.

"Many will adorn brocade with embroidered flowers,
But who sends charcoal [to the poor] in a snowstorm?"
A Chinese Saying.

ACCORDING to the Chinese, the potter's art dates very far back indeed. It is said that it had its rise in the reign of the **Pottery an Ancient Art in China.** Yellow Emperor (B.C. 2697–2597). An evidence of the antiquity of Chinese pottery, and also of an early trade with Egypt, is furnished by the discovery of small Chinese vases in ancient Egyptian tombs. The inscription on one of these is still readable. The characters are, "Flower-opening, seventh year."

This vase is supposed to belong to the latter end of the eighteenth (Egyptian) dynasty. Chinese porcelain had been imported into the West by the Arabs in the thirteenth century, was known in Italy in 1330, and was imported into France as early as 1370.

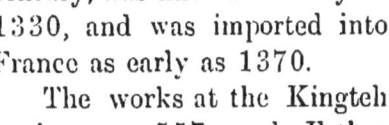
CHINESE VASES FOUND IN EGYPTIAN TOMBS.

The works at the Kingteh mart were already flourishing in A.D. 557, and Father Entrecolles stated that in 1712 there were no less than three thousand kilns in operation. It is said that there are eighteen renowned potteries in the Empire, but the Kingteh mart has long since ousted its rival at Nanking The Chinese diet (as that of the Romanised Britons [1]) has, from

1. Quarrying. 2. The pounding mill. 3. Further pounding in a trough.
4. Kneading by buffaloes. 5. The potter's wheel. 6. The kilns.

the earliest days, consisted for the most part of well-cooked food, in which broths, stews, and pulpy messes have prevailed. Thus the culinary art has stimulated that of the potter.

The word *kaolin* is pure Chinese, and comes to us from the

[1] See *Life of Wedgwood*, pp. 11, 12.

Kingteh mart. It is simply "high peak," the name of the hill from which that kind of clay is obtained. *Petung-tse* is simply "white lumps of clay." The preceding Chinese drawings (published in an English form in 1854) represent the various processes through which it passes.

At the end of six months, Seng-teh began his pottery painting by making drawings of the graceful Chinese orchid upon the already-glazed bowls in ordinary ink mixed with a little alkali. These were afterwards immersed in a colour which burns to a brick red. During the firing the black ink would be burnt off, leaving a design of white flowers upon a red ground. This method of grounding intricate patterns is characteristic of Chinese porcelain.

After further tuition he went on to higher and more remunerative work, drawing butterflies and gold-fish, landscapes and flowers, and eventually historical scenes. These were at first coloured by another painter, but Seng-teh soon learned to colour his own drawings. In all cases the ready-glazed ware is used as the basis.

Thus he went on, year in year out, slowly and steadily rising. His wages were ample for his needs, and his habits were simple. He avoided opium, and was not much given to wine. He continued to write "home" at every great festival,

Throne of the Heaven-king.

but received no answer. Perhaps his letters had not reached Hanyang. There was no orthodox post office. The young

CHANGING SCENES. 407

lady once offered to him was now the mother of several children, he heard. Where was his betrothed?

The Rebellion had long since been put down in Central China by Hu Lin-yi, Peng the Iron Striker, Cheng Kwoh-fan, and, according to popular report, the god of war, the Imperial Kwan himself, who had come down from the skies in a bodily form to assist his orthodox votaries against the idol haters.[1] But from some more reliable sources Seng-teh heard that the "Western barbarians" quoted by the rebels in their proclamation, had had something to do with their final defeat.

End of the Taiping Rebellion.

Would he ever see Hanyang again, he wondered. His longings for home were stirred up by the fact that some of his own wares had gone to the long since rebuilt mart of Hankow. At length he found an artist who was familiar with the process of engraving on china, afterwards rubbing an oily form of ink into the lines to make them more evident. To this man he accordingly resorted in the evenings, and became his pupil. When proficient, he might with the savings of some years open a small shop in Hankow itself; and if he could not construct a kiln, might at least practise his art of pottery engraving. It was not so showy as painting, and more laborious, but the pictures looked very well, to those who could appreciate fine art. The added work, however, began to tell upon him, and in the winter of the fifth year of Tu'ng Tsz (1866–67) he began to have attacks of ague.

Loneliness

Though he had hitherto resisted the consolations of opium, he soon found he had not the requisite degree of cheerfulness to draw, even

[1] In consideration of the above fact (!), which is quoted to this day, the Emperor Shien Fung (in 1855) published a decree in which he commanded

when the fits were not upon him. His letters were unanswered, and he grew very low-spirited. He must smoke. He bought the apparatus and began. It helped him. It seemed to bring him new life, but he felt more depressed than ever between whiles, though as yet the insufferable craving was unknown. He had avoided this by taking the pipe at irregular intervals.

One day there came a letter. Yes, a letter for him; from Hanyang too. It was couched in high style, describing itself as "an inch of mulberry bark,"[1] and said that "the great official Nieh" had a post up north with copious emolument, that the breath of his essays had pierced the northern constellation, and that the classical style of his poems had caused some excitement among the Immortals. This wonderful production bore the name of Seng-teh's "uncle," who "just knew a whole coolie-basket of characters—the size of an eastern melon" (the largest pumpkin in China). He had evidently hired a scribe to write for him, and that literary individual had evidently proved to his own satisfaction that quite a number of classical phrases might be deftly strung together on one small sheet of variegated paper. That they were mostly phrases, Seng-teh knew, but the "official post with copious emolument," though gratifying to a former scholar of a mandarin, was hardly the bread the hungry "son-in-law" required. "Up north," too, was a somewhat wide term. He, however, wrote at once, enclosing a letter to Nieh Shen-seng, promising his "uncle" an adequate reward if he would find out the address, and forward the letter. His spirits had risen. The ague fit had been postponed by the excitement caused by the letter, but now he grew melancholy once more. He had heard enough to unsettle him for work, but no message from Nieh Shen-seng himself, and no word about his betrothed. She must now be about seventeen, if alive. How comely she would look! And he? That careworn, ague-

---

that the same divine honours which were paid to Confucius be paid to Kwan, the god of war. General Gordon, who came on the scene in 1863, and who put an end to the rebellion (in Eastern China), has not been heard of in the central provinces.

[1] A certain species of mulberry bark being made into paper.

thinned face haunted him every time he looked in the glass. He waited a month. That was time to get some reply from a place not much over two hundred miles away. It did not come, and his ague increased. Opium gave him no relief. He just dragged himself about the room with his head tied up. He felt tempted not to smoke but to swallow a bolus of opium, and so end his misery.

But one day a barrow-man told him that some real foreign ague medicine was to be obtained at Kiukiang. A friend of his had been healed. He determined to set off. At least he would die a few *li* nearer home. In packing up his things he took the precaution of filling a new trunk with stones and distributing his earnings in two old boxes among his clothes. He called a barrow, telling the two barrow-men to take special care of the new box. Which they did, for having arrived at Kiukiang, they almost threw him and his two old boxes down upon the new foreign embankment, then ran off with the heavy chest.

A man resembling a soldier in dress came up and ordered him to move on. But he could not stir. He was shaking from head to foot. A crowd of coolies soon collected. When a native was seen approaching with a bundle of books under his arm, crying, " Virtuous books, exhorting men to break off opium, half given, half sold, fifteen cash. Books exhorting to repentance, all half given, half sold."

" Here comes the foreign religion cater; go with him to the foreign devil. He has medicine." And a coolie threw down his pole, caught Seng-teh in his arms, and went off with him, while another coolie followed behind with his boxes and bedding. They took the whole to a native house near, laid their burdens, human and otherwise, down in the porch, and commenced clamouring for their cash.

" Have you cash ? " asked the bookseller.

" Yes," feebly answered the ague-stricken man. " I will give it you by and by."

There was more wrangling than ever among the coolies as the bookseller counted out some cash by fives and gave them to the bearers.

" All this way, and only these coppers ! You have got

rich on foreign dollars; the foreign devil should pay us in silver too."

The altercation grew noisier and noisier, until a foreigner emerged from the interior. "Here comes the eye-scooper!" was the cry, and the crowd took to their heels.

Seng-teh looked up bewildered, to see a strange and kindly face bent over him. The man had no queue! His hair was short and yellow! And such a moustache!

"Who is this, and where is he from?" asked the foreigner in strange accents.

"A sick man, sir. I found him on the embankment, and the coolies brought him here to be cured."

The foreigner felt Seng-teh's pulse, and went into an inner apartment to bring out a liquid in a glass—the first glass in the hands of the first foreigner Seng-teh had seen.

"Drink it up. It is very bitter; but never mind. It will do you good."

Seng-teh actually understood what he said, but was too amazed to reply.

"Have you any friends here?"

"No, foreign devil."

"Foreign Shenseng, you mean," said the bookseller.

"I beg pardon. Foreign Shenseng, I know no one here. I am from the potteries. The barrow-men dropped me here and ran off with my new box. I am dying."

"No, you will not die. We will soon make you better. Cheer up. I can find you an empty room for a few days." Then the two carried him in, undid his bedding, arranged it, and laid him upon it, with his boxes by his side. The foreigner brought in one, and the bookseller the other! Seng-teh looked up from them to the wall and read upon a red scroll, "Our Father which art in heaven," then felt giddy and remembered no more.

Some days passed, and he was able to walk about. One evening he heard some voices, singing, "Praise the Sovereign on High, the root of a myriad happiness" (the doxology).

It reminded him of the old days in the camp. He entered the room from whence the sound came, and saw four or five natives kneeling down, and the foreigner with them.

They arose slowly at last. He almost expected to hear them shout, "Kill the fiends!" but instead, they came round him and said they were glad to see he was better. It seemed stranger than the first day at the camp. What was he to them? Cups of tea and the water-pipe were handed round; and as he began to feel at home, he proceeded, in reply to inquiries, to relate his history. "Praise the Sovereign on High," they exclaimed, when he had finished. But they were not Longhaired. The foreigner certainly was not. He asked if they had a book called *Li-wei-ki* (Leviticus). Yes, they had. And there, in easier style, almost colloquial, Seng-teh read the chapters most familiar to him in the Taiping camp.

After a few more days, he found to his surprise that there was nothing to pay except for his rice. "We don't want you to be a 'religion eater,'" was the explanation. "But I do pray the Sovereign on High to lead you. He will do so."

He left at last with a letter of introduction to a friend of the foreigner in Hankow, and invested the greater part of his savings in a well-selected stock of porcelain. In his boxes, too, he had one or two specimens of engraved cups, teapots, and the like, also his tools. He took his passage upon a boat laden with eggs, as he feared robbers upon those wonderful and terrible foreign steamers.

They reached Wusueh by moonlight when he was asleep. But his sleep was broken by an altercation between the boatman and the official at the lower customs station, whose voice did not seem quite unfamiliar to him. He looked through a crack in the side of the boat apartment, and, by the light of a lantern held aloft by the representative of Imperial authority, he recognised Lieu Fah. There was no mistaking that face. It had but grown like its father. He did not go out to greet him, but stood listening.

The boatman pleaded that he had no money. Would the honourable customs official take the required sum in eggs?

"Yes," was the reply, "at the rate of one cash apiece."

"They are four cash, sir, and I can get five for them in Hankow," protested the man. He would let them go at three, but not for less. The customs officer told his men to seize the quantity he said would represent the required percentage at one cash each, quoting, as he did so, the name of the terrible Peng, who decapitated smugglers.

The discussion aroused the occupants of the boats anchored hard by, from one of which a short, oldish man emerged. He gently asked the cause of the dispute, and heard the noisy tale from both sides. "Then," said he, "you ought to give back three-fourths of the eggs. The country price is four cash."

"Who are you, old-head?"

"I am a traveller who loves justice."

"A customs-defrauding son of a demon; son of a dog demon."

Whereat the old man called a couple or so of men from his boat.

"Return three-fourths of the eggs," he cried.

"Hands off, you potato," shouted the minister of the law, as he clutched hold of the men's sleeves.

"Our orders must be obeyed," said one, and he jerked himself free, to fall over on to the eggs in the customs boat.

"Give me a hundred more!" shouted the customs man, and he seized the egg-vendor by the queue.

"No," cried the short old man; "return them all." Whereupon the extortioner began to beat the boatman. The old man interposed, and received a blow. He jumped with excitement. "Seize this dog!" he shouted.

CHANGING SCENES. 413

Ten men rushed forth and seized the bully, who cried "Pirates," and cursed vigorously.

"Bring out the lanterns." And two large globe-like lanterns were brought out. Fah was dragged by the queue on to the old man's boat, vociferating maledictions on the "old thief's" ancestors. But when the lanterns were lit, the inscription thereon was no other than "Admiral of

A peep at Wusueh from the Yangtse side.

the long Yangtse, Peng."

"Now apologise, dog, or I will have you cut up piecemeal." The wretched man knocked his head on the boards with a resounding thud, he trembled, he screamed for mercy, he sobbed, he talked about a poor old mother. To whom Peng transferred the epithets he had just before hurled at his own ancestry.

"Do your work." And one of the men divested himself

of a blue jacket, to display a red one underneath, rolled up his sleeves, and unsheathed a broad-bladed, long-handled sword. Two others held the condemned man by the queue.

"Let go!" Which Fah understood to mean pardon. "A thousand, myriad thanks." But the words were interrupted with, "Kneel upright." Then, "Kill!"

The blade flashed through the gloom, and the man's head fell. In an instant the executioner held it up, and Peng called out, "Count eight hundred cash, and give it to him."[1] The corpse was then kicked overboard, the deck mopped clean, and the head taken on shore to be hung up on the little gateway of Wusueh, as a warning to defrauders in general.

Then suddenly calmed down, Peng said to the now kneeling egg-seller, "Take back four-fifths of your eggs. The rest are to be given to my men to reward them for their conduct."

"Sire," cried another voice, "I have some porcelain on board. May your soldiers take the required amount?"

"Who are you? Where do you come from?"

"I'm a pottery painter going up to Hankow. I was once an Imperialist soldier under the General Kwan. I was present at the taking of Feuliang."

"You are a deserter, then?"

"No, Sire. I was the first to scale the wall, and lost two fingers of my left hand. Then I was ill, and turned pottery painter."

"Have you had any reward?"

"Yes, at the time. I merely wanted to pay what was due."

"Let me see your pottery. Have you anything of your own doing?"

Seng-teh replied that he had some engraved cups of his own workmanship, and went off to get one. He selected a covered cup with the design of the "empty city stratagem,"

---

[1] On behalf of the eight virtues, filial piety, (younger) brotherliness, loyalty, faithfulness, propriety, righteousness, frugality, and modesty (or "shamefastness"), which the decapitated man has denied. A frequent term of abuse is "Forgetter of eight," which, inked upon walls, refers to a special form of utter depravity.

CHANGING SCENES. 415

in which a general, unable to withstand the formidable hosts of the enemy, had the city gates opened, and played the harpsichord on the battlements, while a man swept the path underneath.

He knelt and presented it with both hands. The Admiral had never seen that kind of work before, and the design was, of course, appropriate. "It must have taken some time," he said almost kindly. It had taken four days, Seng-teh said.

"I will take it. Give him twenty taels."

"Not a cash, Sire."

"Twenty taels. I reward virtue as well as punish vice."

It was given.

"Now set sail," and the egg-seller's boat procceded up the river.

"Hai Ya!" shouted the boatmen when they were well on their way. "What do you think of that? Terrible man that Peng. He killed his own son for smoking opium. That was putting his household right, you see. Then he complained to the Emperor of a viceroy—a viceroy, mind you—who was a smoker and did not do his work, and he had to go.[1] And

---

[1] The execution of Peng's own son is quoted to this day among the semi-official class. It may not be true. The degrading of a viceroy is a fact, however. It was only on the death of Peng, about 1890, that he was restored to office. Peng himself was eventually caught in the practice which he so con-

a 'mean man' of a customs officer oppresses the populace, and abuses a quiet old man, then, *Whtt!* off goes his head!"

"Yes, he has entered the jar!"

"What jar?"

"That is a proverbial expression referring to an official of old time who was a great extortioner. The Emperor sent an under-official to call upon him, and bade him relate the supposititious case of a mandarin guilty of certain grave offences, inquiring what should be done to him. 'For such rascality,' was the reply, 'hanging is too good. Let a great jar of oil be prepared, and boil him alive in it.' 'Will your Excellency be pleased to enter the jar?' exclaimed the Imperial messenger."

Thou art the Man.

"Good! Rascals in office are the worst rascals. But you seem to know 'The Iron Striker.' Were you afraid he would smell out your pottery?"

"I never saw him before, though I was very nearly doing so one day. But I promised the foreign doctor at Kiukiang I would keep a clear conscience in my business."

"What, that straight-legged? That eye-scooper? What does he know about conscience?"

To this Seng-teh replied that foreigners' knees were jointed after all; that he had seen the foreigner kneel down and get up without the aid of a stick. The boatman urged that it was foreign magic. Their knees had no joints, and when they lay down at night they had to get a native to pull them up in the morning; that in their own land there was always one man in each mandarin's house who slept leaning against the wall, and thus was able to pull them up from their beds. If he tumbled over? Well, it was death to him, and the night watchman was called in to assist the foreigners out of the horizontal into the vertical position. All of which is still quoted in some parts.

Foreigners all Straight-legged.

---

demned. Being afflicted with cholic, a native doctor made him up some pills containing opium, and he soon became under the spell of the craving. According to other accounts, opium was mixed in his tobacco, which was the earliest form of opium-taking in China, and explains why the Chinese smoke rather than swallow.

On the next count, Seng-teh hardly hoped for success. He could only make his protest. So firmly rooted was the notion that foreign medicines owe their efficacy to the eyes, brains, etc., of infants, that now, twenty-odd years afterwards, it is supposed that owing to the Hunan placards of the early months of 1891 reviving the old notion, nine-tenths of the Chinese still believe it; and, as an overwhelming evidence of such belief, may be quoted the fact that in June 1891 the waters over which the egg-boat was then gliding were lit by the lurid glare of burning mission-houses in the fatal Wusueh riot, which arose simply and solely from the report that some infants in coolie baskets (on their way to a Roman Catholic foundling home at Kiukiang) were being taken there to be dissected into medicine. Kiukiang was far off, those (W.M.S.) premises were nearer, and hence burning houses, insulted ladies barely escaping with their lives, and two murders.

<small>The Origin of their wonderful Medicines.</small>

Seng-teh turned the conversation by asking whether the rebels had ravaged that countryside. Have they not! Nearly every one of the hills inland has the remains of an encampment around the top, some of the hills on the other side of the Yangtse too. But twenty-six miles inland at Kwangchi there is a high hill famous for its leaping-stone. Filial sons and others go there in pilgrimage, kneel and worship at intervals as they ascend the hill; worship at the " First heaven gate " archway, then at the " Second heaven gate," then at the " Third heaven gate," and finally at the temples on the top, behind which is a jutting piece of rock. Here they stand a moment, then with an obeisance throw themselves over into the chasm hundreds of feet below.

A little further they came in sight of the " Split Hill." The water looked calm enough in the moonlight, but the boatman said it was a terrible place for sudden storms, the wind rushing down between the range of hills on either side,[1] to the upsetting of many a boat. On the top of one of

---

[1] The state of things there is a very close parallel to what happens on the Lake of Genesareth: " Storms of wind rush wildly through the deep . . . gorges which descend from the north and north-east, and are not only violent, but sudden" (W. Thompson, *The Land and the Book*).

the hills were ancient altars to the god of the winds, whose worship exists now only as a tradition, and in the characteristic whistle of boatmen when they want a fair breeze.

As the boat proceeded a little further, the boatman pointed out the tomb of the boatman's god, Yang Sz, by whose temple Seng-teh had scrambled on shore at the burning of Hankow.

Towards morning they reached Kichow, famous for its "dragon snakes" (cobras), and, previous to the Rebellion, for its enormous bronze image of Buddha, said to have contained gold, broken up but not wholly carried away by the rebels.[1]

Later on in the day they came to Hwangszkang (yellow stone streams), in the hills of which there were iron and coal (since worked by the Viceroy under foreign supervision). One of these hills was said to have opened suddenly a year or two before, to reveal a whole arsenal of rusty weapons and blackened rice. How long it had remained there, no one knew. The place where the ancient chain was thrown across the Yangtse was pointed out. The wind continued favourable, and the moon was bright enough for night travelling. The boatman had rested by day, leaving the craft in charge of his son.

Passing Wuchang county city (fifty miles below the provincial capital), Seng-teh was aroused to have a look at the ancient city of Hwangchow, so often the rendezvous of the rebels.

At evening on the second day they reached Yanglo, where the boat stopped for the night. Here were rocks of red sandstone worn by the water into curious shapes. In the recesses of these rocks, the boatman said, there were thousands

[1] The writer had a piece of the eye of this image submitted him for analysis. The gold seemed to be a mere tradition.

of tiny mussel shells, the waters retiring too early in the autumn for them to develop.

Here Seng-teh went on shore to have a chat in a tea-shop. The conversation was on the subject of a much-beloved graduate called "Lieu the Good," who lived in the country not far off. He had been writing a book recording the virtues and vices of contemporary men of note. But a day or two before, he had taken too much wine, and had cursed his uncle. On sobering down, he was so filled with contrition that he determined never to write a bad word about anyone else, and forthwith burned half of the work he had had in hand for years. He there and then made a vow never to touch a drop of wine again. And from his determined character the folks said they knew he would keep his word. He never worshipped idols. He called them "wood and mud," and said they were dead men at best. Nor did he worship ancestors even. He said that following a good example was the best and only ancestral worship. He also exhorted his sons not to burn cash paper or incense or fire a single cracker when he should die. He had not done so when his old father died. Yet he was not a "foreign religion eater," and certainly not one of the rebels.[1] Seng-teh was emboldened by this conversation to exhibit his peach-stone necklace and to tell its history, and they had an interesting time, he and the tea-shop frequenters.

Among these were several barrow-men[2] from Peking, the high road striking off from the Yangtse there. One man had done the journey some tens of times. Another had borne many an M.A. in a sedan to the capital, and had brought back several *Han Lin* (the highest degree), one or two of which returned to take office.

A boat cut in two with an inscription thereon, stuck upright on shore, told that the Admiral Peng had once visited the place, and convicted some boatmen of smuggling. Their heads had been severed and exposed at the time.

Next morning the wind was high and contrary. The

---

[1] This story of "Lieu the Good" seems to be perfectly true.
[2] There are no "cany waggons light" in Central China. The barrows are heavily built of tough wood, and have no sails.

water flowed rapidly too. The boatman made his son go on shore and tow. It was midday before they passed the "Green Hill," where lived a noted man of great strength, who in a drunken fit had chopped up several idols. The boat proceeded on slowly, and the sun had just set as the journey was over and they found themselves nearing the now rebuilt mart of Hankow.

Chapter XXII.

Father and Daughter.

"If a father will not be a father, a daughter must still be a daughter."
Chinese Saying.

WHERE was Nieh Shen-seng all this time? On the evening that Hankow was burnt, his wife had retired early. He was sitting up reading by the light of a rush pith-lamp, looking every now and then toward his wife's chamber. He did not study far into the night as a rule, but this was a special occasion.

At the fifth watch the dogs began to bark, and wooden bolts to be withdrawn. Soon the cry was "Fire! Fire!" and there were answering shouts of "Where? Where?" Every man was soon outside, and there over the north peak of the Hill of the Nine Recluses was a glare which seemed to turn night into day. Nieh had caught up his book in his hurry, and could see to read the characters. The north-east walls of the cottages were bathed in rose-coloured light. "The rebels are upon us!" screamed the women. "Run!"

Nieh went back to see his wife, and tried to comfort her. He was answered by wild laughter interspersed with groans. He watched by her side, going out every now and then to look at the ever-increasing glare, and as the vivid red paled before the dawn, he was a widower.

That evening two coffins were carried out of his house, one of them a tiny box of rough boards. They were interred together in a field hard by.

A few days later the rebel flag was seen flying on one of the peaks of the Nine Recluses Hill, and Nieh, having converted all his wife's landed property and his own few belongings into silver, set off with his little daughter round the tongue of land and along the west road. He might meet some friends of his grandfather at Fancheng,[1] and perchance learn something of his relatives farther north in the province of Honan. He had a barrow for his little girl, bedding, and boxes. He himself could walk.

The journey took the greater half of a month, as they dare not go the direct route. As it was, they more than once saw rebel watch-fires in the distance. Arrived at Fancheng, he told his tale to the county mandarin, who introduced him to an old resident. This former friend of his father engaged him as teacher to his grandchildren, who, as in the ideal Chinese home, all reside near.

Here he was well content to remain year after year, and but for his daughter's future, and his own still cherished hopes of an official post, might have lived and died at Fancheng. The old-style Chinaman clings to a locality like a limpet to a rock. Detach him from one locality, and he clings to another when once fairly settled there. The scholar does not like to "leave his house," and probably the pleasing assurance that he may "understand all things under heaven" without doing so, was a little self-satisfying concoction of a sedentary scholar. Moreover, as the years passed, Nieh Shen-seng developed a chronic cough, for which a friend recommended opium. This was undoubtedly of soothing influence at first; but, as usual, this celebrated doctor required his fee,—a heavy one, the submission of the man's will. The "craving" came, and its demands became more and more pressing. The opium habit made him less inclined than ever to break up his home. But his daughter needed a home too. Seng-teh was probably dead. He had not died out of her heart, however. She just remembered him, and her father had often spoken about his promising young scholar, who was to have been a military mandarin some day. As she grew up she spent many an hour of her secluded life dreaming of the brave young officer. She was sure he was brave, and she

[1] Fancheng is 413 miles from Hanyang. It is in North Hupeh, to the north of which province is Honan.

knew him to have been handsome; as a child she had thought him perfectly handsome. And such considerations have some weight with Chinese maidens after all. Then, though the paper horsie had long since died a natural death, she had a picture he had drawn for her—an ideal picture of the Nine Recluses Hill, idealised on lines not generally adopted even by Chinese artists. The colours were gorgeous. They had fascinated the little girl, and the little girl's heart endured within the maiden. Seng-teh was a good scholar, but why did he not write? He did not know their address perhaps, but then his uncle did. And he surely would seek that uncle out if he were alive. Was Seng-teh alive? or, terrible thought, was he married? She would rather he were dead, she thought, for then he would belong to no one else. She had no one else to care for beside her father, and she did care for the hero of her dreams, whether he were dead or alive— unless he were married; then her feelings would be reversed.

Very diffidently one day her father broached the subject of some offers he had had for her hand. In reply, she burst into tears, and said he did not care for her. He assured her that such words were a proof of his care. She replied by quoting Fung-kiao. "I do not want any Wen-teh," she said; "I want my Li Tan."

"Is that final?"

"It is, father." And so the subject dropped. But the years went by, filled with study and embroidery and filial offices; but still went by, until the *Imperial Almanac* marked "Tung Tsz, sixth year," was received from the *yamun*. New Year's festivities came, and anon her eighteenth birthday. About which time the father of one of Nieh Shenseng's pupils had received a post as under-mandarin at Hanyang.[1] Here was a break in their monotonous existence, and Camilla did her utmost to persuade her somewhat immobile father to go down to Hanyang with him. At last, after much pressure, he made up his mind.

[1] The ancestral graves were in Honan, and thus he was qualified (after taking his degree there) for a post in Hupeh. No scholar must become mandarin in his native province, for fear of collusion with his relatives and friends.

But the expectant mandarin was taken ill with fever, and could not go for a month or so. This unsettled Nieh once more. It was Heaven's decree that he should stay where he was. Did Heaven's decree extend to herself, Camilla wondered. Something within her, which she was fain to call Heaven's decree, pulled in the direction of Hanyang. She said nothing about it to her father, unless her pale cheeks spoke to him. No, he did not seem to notice them. It was always his cough, and his opium, and his depression of spirits. He seemed wrapped up in self now.

She made bold, however, to converse with the expectant mandarin one day when she had gained an audience. Would he try and hold Nieh Shen-seng to his former decision? The mandarin-elect said he would, and gave her a look which made her blush. He would insist on her going down, and, of course, her father too. He would find a place for him, and do his best to make her happy. Then, to his wife, after Camilla had gone, "The old smoker will be past his work in a year; we must get him off; everyone says so." Then to himself, "She is a nice girl, and I could do with a second wife. She would not be expensive either."

He almost commanded Nieh to go with him. He would find him a place. Nieh should be his own secretary, until he was on the way to office himself. "Heaven's decree" evidently pointed to Hanyang now, and for Hanyang they started.

Hardly had they done so, when the note enclosed to Seng-teh's "uncle" arrived. The "uncle" had not hurried, and, of course, its recipients would hardly be guilty of a more unseemly haste than that displayed by a countryman. So they kept it by them "till opportunity occurred" to send it to their brother in Hanyang.

In China, speed is regarded by common consent to be in inverse ratio to the importance of those who undertake any business at all. Coolies run, the populace walk, the scholar sways himself majestically along, the gentleman rides in a chair,—the delay in getting chair coolies often compensating for the vulgar speed at which they carry folk; and even then it is they who move, while the gentleman sits as unmoved as an amateur idol. Mandarins are never in a hurry to put any matter through, and the Son of heaven—"the all-patient heaven"—takes at least six months to realise that anything has to be done—at least Shien Fung did in matters connected with the Rebellion.

So that when the letter did reach the *yamun* at Hanyang, the mandarin, not being very gratified at being mistaken for a postman, laid the note by, and forgot it altogether. But, as the Chinese tale-books say, "these are after-words."

On the sixth day, the current being favourable, they reached Tsaitien. There were large buildings upon the north bank. These, Nieh Shen-seng explained to his daughter, were oil-presses, the last they would see. "There are none in Hankow, and never will be." "Why?" "Because the *fung shui* professors say Hankow is of the raft construction, and any such hammering as oil-presses require would cause the ground to collapse."[1]

<small>A Bit of Fung Shui.</small>

"But the hammer is horizontal, you told me once. How could that cause the ground to sink? Do you believe it? It cannot be true."

"If you believe it is, it is; if you believe it is not, it is not," interrupted the expectant mandarin, with a smirk upon his face. He had not heard the full question; but, as that is the stock answer to all questions of faith, he felt it to be an apt quotation. Then turning to Nieh Shen-seng, he said, "Is it not time you smoked a little? Early sorrows. Familiar scenes. Harrowing memories, you know."

Nieh Shen-seng thought he would not. The journey had done him good, and with the old neigbourhood not far off, his old self seemed to return. Not altogether pleasantly, however. The face he once used to see in the glass seemed to loom out before him like that of a schoolmaster confronting a truant-playing scholar who had disgraced himself. "You are myself," he seemed to say; "why rebuke me thus?" "You are not I," seemed to come the reply; "why are you not?" "I am Nieh the graduate." "Yes, you still bear your father's surname, and the degree is yours, but where is the 'superior

---

[1] *N.B.*—Some boarded floors of Chinese schools in Hankow are remarkably springy. Can it be from the use of the rod there? *Fung shui* professors, please explain!

man' that men thought they saw in you? You have degenerated, and you know it."

Camilla would have retreated had she had the opportunity, but she replied, with just a trace of sarcasm in her tone, that they had been talking about the oil-presses. "Yes, of course. About 'thanking the girl,' I suppose. No?
<small>Thanking the Girl.</small> Never heard of it? Well, there was a wealthy old man, owner of one of these presses, who was returning from Hankow by boat after an unusually good piece of business. Wishing to go on shore for a while, he did so, but was caught in a heavy rainstorm, and the only dwelling near was a small mat hut, toward which he made his way. There was only a young girl at home, that is [here he smiled], a young girl of eighteen. She invited him in, brought him tea and tobacco, and had him dry his outer garments before the fire of reeds which she lit to prepare refreshments for him. These, though frugal, she served up with great politeness. Such hospitality so affected the old man that he asked her to bow before him, and become his adopted daughter, which she did. He then asked her whether she was 'spoken' or not. She said she had been as a child, but the boy had died [when he was about fifteen]. He said he would find a good husband for her; and, on returning, not only did so, but made the young couple a present of silver sufficient to buy forty [Chinese] acres of land, and to build a house.

"The place, some thirty li from here, is called 'Thank the Girl' still. When I first heard it, I thought it meant 'chase the girl.' It is the same sound, you know. Just think of it, 'chase the girl,' how comical!" Camilla, however, did not seem to appreciate the comicality very much. And, casting an inquiring glance or two at her, he retired, to leave her blushing deeply.

"That hill on the right," said Nieh Shen-seng, without looking up, "that hill with the curious notch in the centre," —then a pause—"is called the City Wall Hill, from its appearance." Here he paused again, and seemed absorbed in reverie. "That hill, father?" "Yes, of course, that hill is said to sink three-tenths of an inch every year, three-tenths of an inch"—another pause—"three-tenths of an inch, of course, but it is probably the mud rising at the yearly flood time—the yearly flood time."

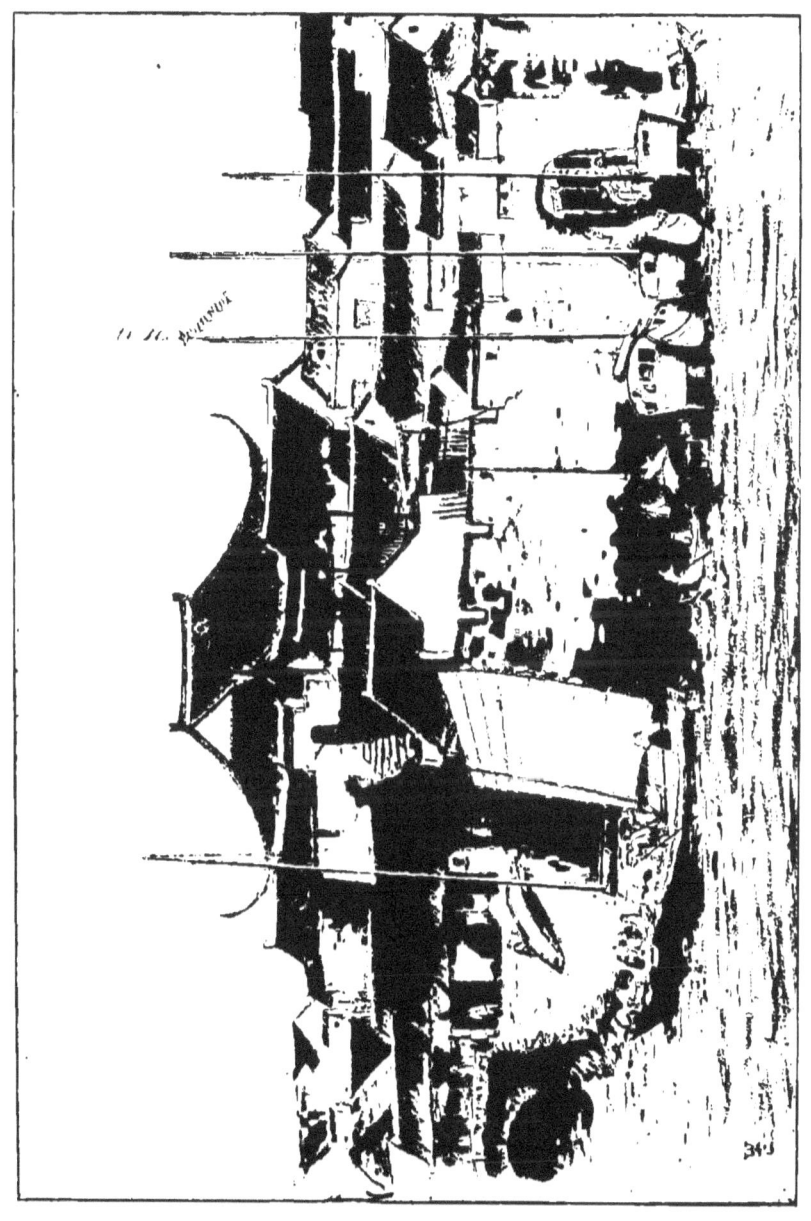

"Are you poorly, father?"
"No, my child, only sad. Fetch. me, yes, fetch me my

opium pipe. No, don't yet. We are now on a line with your birthplace. The hill is out of sight, as is the nearer Horse Saddle Hill of Peh-ya fame, Peh-ya and his sympathetic listener, his sympathetic listener, you know." Then he went off into a deeper reverie than ever. His head was bowed down, and he looked an age-worn man. Then he began to cough, and said, "I must have my medicine. No, not yet. Yes, I must. Bring out my harpsichord. No, what am I talking about? Yes, bring out my pipe. I must have my medicine."

They reached Hankow, now rebuilt, and looking old already in some places,—wooden houses age soon, and depend largely upon one another for support,—but with solid-looking white-washed walls every now and then, and a city wall on the land side, two years old, and thirteen years out of date, but curving round at the thin end of the wedge-like mass of houses, to display an ornate city gate, above which red flags floated bravely, and on which, so the chief boatman said, was the inscription, "Gate of the jade girdle,"—a girdle of grey brick it was, nearly five miles long. After a mile or so of houses they reached *Wu Seng Miao*, with its new gateway to the god of war on the Hankow side, and on the Hanyang bank, a somewhat similar one to the god of literary emolument,—he of the one leg.

Here it was suggested that Lung (dragon), the new under-mandarin, and his friends should take chairs, while the boats went down the Han and round to the east gate of Hanyang, a distance of more than two miles. And in chairs the party went, a little procession of somewhat imposing character. Camilla had been told to look out for the Moon Lake on the right, fully visible for half a mile, the Ancient Bell Tower,—the bell ever tolling to arouse men's consciences,—the triple-arched Moon Lake bridge,—the Chinese always mark bridges on their maps,—the pavilion on the lake erected for tea and wine drinking in memory of Peh-ya's sympathetic listener, the Tortoise Hill on the left, and after passing an umbrella maker's village at its "tail" (we say foot), a two-storied pagoda to a virtuous woman, which is called the "Virtue Completing Pavilion." All of which sights were familiar to

FATHER AND DAUGHTER. 429

the head boatman, and as familiar to Mandarin Lung, and even to Camilla herself, as the graphic picture map of the Hanyang official records could make them. Besides all these objects of interest, they were to pass a tomb to a third-century hero, hard by the city walls.

Having reached Hanyang, entering at the west gate,

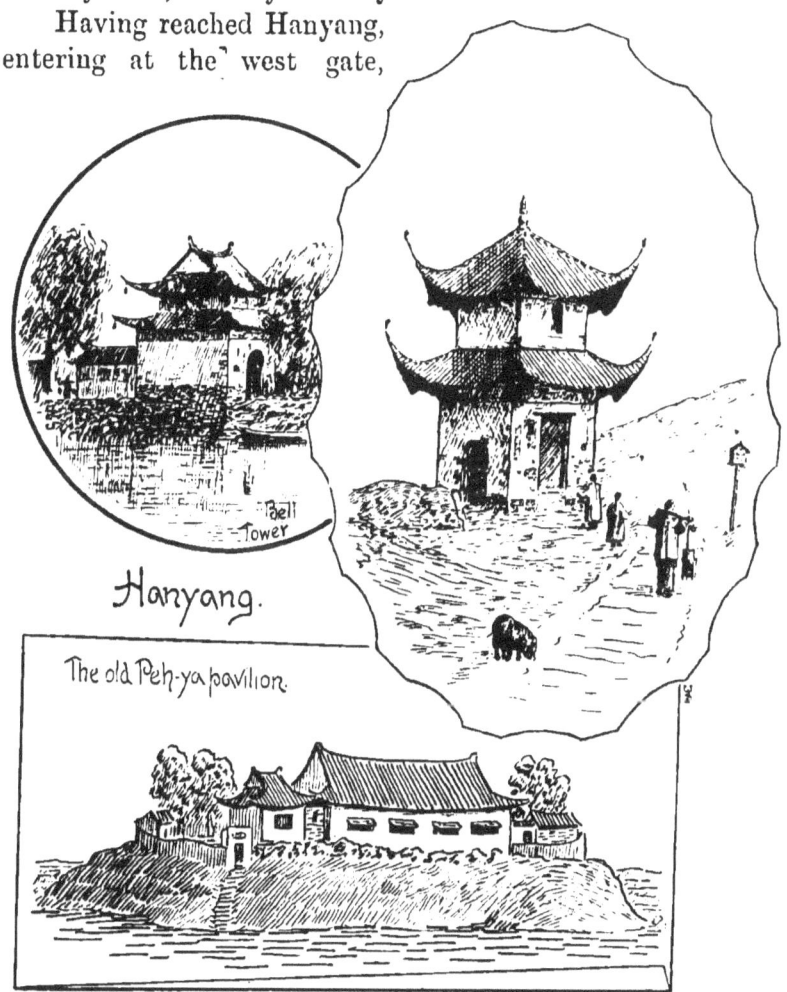

Bell Tower
Hanyang.
The old Peh-ya pavilion.

along the wall street, which had once been a moat, they found the old-new residence of the man who was going to dispense justice in a small way for a consideration. The same gentleman-constable, however, was received in a manner which seemed to Camilla well-nigh Imperial. He went up into the "great hall" (20 feet by 15), knelt gracefully, and knocked his head majestically before a box on the table, which box contained the imperially-granted seal, whose supreme value Nieh might have said was only apparent when it was lost. Then lighting three sticks of incense in a side apartment, gentleman-constable Lung worshipped the idol of the *yamun*, and sat down to the feast

provided for him by the outgoing mandarin. He invited Nieh Sheng-seng, while Camilla sat down with Mrs. Lung to a similar feast in another apartment.

This over, the newly-fledged dragon told Nieh that the luggage should be sent to his inn on the morrow, unless he had a house. From which Nieh gathered that he was not to live on the premises after all. Camilla, however, could be provided for for the night by Mrs. Dragon. As she could not well put up at an inn,—a mere shanty at best,—and he could not remain there, he consented, with much apology for troubling his benefactor hitherto. He must not offend Lung. All his prospects depended upon him. "Come not between the dragon and his wrath," says Shakespeare by the mouth of King Lear, and Nieh yet hoped against hope that this particular dragon would resemble those with the pink beards twined round the pillars of paradise, gloriously friendly and suggestive of further glories in the penetralia beyond.

It was now afternoon as Nieh Shen-seng, soliloquising upon human undependableness, passed out of the west gate, and wandered down the street, far more busy than that in the city. He would seek the lodging he had occupied at examination times years before. It was not to be found. It had been burnt. But, wandering on to the right, he found a new house which commanded a view of a lotus lake (pond) and of the Tortoise Hill. On the garden (yard) door was an inscription, "Auspicious house [desirable residence] beckons a renter" (to let). The landlord lived next door, and to him Nieh Shen-seng repaired, offering to take the house for a day or two, and, if he liked it, to come to terms as to its purchase. To this the landlord agreed, and accommodated him with some old bedding for the night. But Nieh had no opium utensils with him. His landlord did not seem to be a smoker. He was red-faced and somewhat corpulent; he loved wine instead. As the sun set, therefore, the scholar was fain to proceed forth, and try and find an opium den, guided by his nostrils. He discovered one not far off, and, with a few coolies, yes, and one beggar, assumed the horizontal position, and began to satisfy his craving upon very poor opium indeed.

He had a restless night, and at early dawn he proceeded to the *yamun* to fetch his daughter and his boxes. The latter he found stacked up in the inner "heaven-well courtyard,"—they had not even been put under the eaves. The mandarin was out—to him, but his daughter appeared before long, and soon they were both to be found in their new house. The grumbling coolies had been paid, and the landlord provided the breakfast, entertaining them with the legend of the well opposite the garden gate (yard door). This was to the effect that a celebrated Taoist had once lived on the spot, and as his hair began to turn white, felt sundry drawings to the land of perpetual youth. He, however, was not going to die. He was to become an Immortal. And being of no monopoly-loving character, he pointed out to his disciple a heap of wet coal, and said, "Eat

The Well of the White Crane.

that." The youth demurred. He might have eaten his peck of dirt already, but the coal did not look specially nutritious. His master disappeared, however, and the disciple began to look at the coal with inquiring glances. But refrained from even tasting it as yet. At length his mind was made up. He would try; his teeth were sound, and he was no dyspeptic. But some days had elapsed, and when he put forth his hand to touch it, lo, the heap of coal suddenly changed to a white crane,[1] which, having found the well, took a dive therein, and was seen no more. But the same well has been called the "Well of the White Crane" ever since.

Then followed a story of a little shrine at the "mouth" of the "Great Alley of the Wu family," an arrow's-shot from the house. There was once a fishmonger named Lieu, who became extremely poor, and so having no other shelter for the night, curled himself up to rest in the same shrine. As he slept, he dreamt that the wife of the earth god (could it be the wife of the noble Confucian Han Wen-Kung, the idol-hater of the Ta'ng dynasty 768–824?) informed her demisemi-deified husband that the eight Immortals might be expected shortly, and asked him to arouse and prepare to salute them as they passed. The fishmonger awoke, and anon saw eight beggarly forms approaching. He made a grab at the clothing of the eighth, who, finding himself identified, scratched his head (O gentle reader, I am, like Confucius, "a compiler, not an originator"), and gave him a clot of Celestial incrustation therefrom, telling him to buy stale fish and place them in the water into which this "treasure" had been dropped. He went forth in the morning, and gained some putrid fish for the asking,—that is, for old acquaintance sake,—and putting a portion of his "treasure" in a borrowed tub with a little pond water, found that the fish were all but alive. He sold them, and bought a fish tub, and having prospered in business, grew old and feeble, when he bethought himself of the

No more Stinking Fish.

---

[1] For the Taoist himself to have become a white crane would not have appeared wonderful, for, according to an old Taoist book, those who swallow the "divine elixir of nine revolutions" are thus transformed.

"treasure." If it renewed the freshness of putrid fish, it might make him at least ten years younger. He swallowed some of the stuff, and forthwith departed this region of fish nets and fish tubs to become an Immortal himself!

The landlord was evidently of Taoist leanings, but the stories were found to be corroborated by the neighbours, and they helped to make the neighbourhood interesting to the new-comers.

Nieh Shen-seng had more than enough to purchase the house, but felt the need of some remunerative employment in order to sustain him and his daughter. He therefore went into Hanyang, and presented his card at the *yamun* doors. The tall sugarloaf hats of the runners were on the pegs, a sure sign that the mandarin was not out. He was not at home, however, to him; and as Nieh waited, he heard a familiar voice saying, "The opium devil wants to borrow money, I expect. Don't ever bring in his card again." Nieh Shen-seng went off without hearing more. He came home livid with rage, and had to take a special quantity of "medicine" to console him. Nor did the "medicine" seem very consolatory now. His savings would hardly last many more months.

His daughter did her best to cheer him; and seeing him directing wistful eyes toward the Tortoise Hill, proposed that they should go thither. He could not walk so far. It would kill him, but he went nevertheless.

They had a fine view of the three cities from the top— one of the sights of the world. But both had their heart-aches. Camilla came back to turn up once more the pages of the familiar *Book of Odes*, for she was a good scholar, and loved poetry—

> "I ascended the southern hill,
> Gathering the sweet aspidium;
> My lord I have not seen,
> Grief wounded is my heart.
> If I had but seen him!
> If I had but met him,
> My heart would be at peace."

How the old-time words came home to her! Then as

434   A STRING OF CHINESE PEACH-STONES.

the evening shadows gathered, and the rush-pith lamp was lit, she came to the words—

> "The fowls roost on their perches
> In the evening of the day;
> The goats and kine come home,
> But my husband is away."

It was a moonlight night, and, escaping from the sickening fumes which filled the little room, she went out into the yard to look around. There was the moon nearly full, and in it was the old man that folks said bound together the feet of those destined to marry, with a red cord. Where was that red cord now? Had it for ever snapped?

There was another legend which seemed more appropriate to her sad destiny, which represented the man in the moon as perpetually hewing away at the branches of a cassia tree, which grew as fast as he hewed. That was it. Poor father! Poor dead "husband"! Poor, poor Camilla!

Within the yard was a *fu-yung* (tree mallow), whose buds

were beginning to open. In the language of flowers, the *fu-yung* was the princely flower who wooed and won the camellia (in the days when men wooed those they loved). The tree is there with its buds of promise, but where was Camilla's lover?

Her father had told her that the Empress Wu, Li Tan's persecutor, walked in her palace garden one day, where she found all the flowers open but the late blooming camellias, which being thus tardy were ordered to be banished—transplanted to another palace at Lo Yang. What depraved empress had banished her by banishing and killing, yes it was so, killing her Li Tan?

Then again, a famous beauty of antiquity, a favourite of Li Tan's second son, the "Lustrous Emperor," was one day walking in the palace grounds to find a camellia out in bloom. She touched the petals, and left a print of her rosy fingers thereon,[1] which appeared year after year. Camilla had been touched, not too gently, by fingers the reverse of rosy, and the print thereof seemed to appear year after year. Her poor heart ached.

Her father called her in, saying it was not etiquette for a maiden to be out in the moonlight. His tones were reproachful and harsh, as he bade her rub some ink for a pair of scrolls like those which used to hang up in the house where she was born.

> "A heart of diamond [fanned by] zephyrs from the crocus;
> Righteousness for a friend, virtue for an instructor."

While rubbing the ink, a pretty conceit came into her mind concerning the complaint of the ink-block at being ground down,[2] and the reply of the ink-slab as to that grinding being but the needed preparation for a higher destiny.

"Lend me a small pen, father," she said, when he had finished the somewhat tremulously drawn characters, "and a

---

[1] See footnote on p. 243.
[2] "Ground by adversity" is a Chinese phrase in the proverb, "Good men suffer much grinding." (This footnote and the story of the "rosy fingers" leaving a mark on the camellia are to be borne in mind when the verses are quoted at the end of the book.)

blank red visiting card." Her father seemed to shudder at the latter word, and looked well-nigh despondent. But having complied with her request, he watched her write the poem, altered one character, complimented her upon the style,

yes, and the sentiment too, and promised to write the lines on two other scrolls in the morning. After which, with mingled feelings, she retired to rest.

In the morning he had forgotten all about his promise. Father was getting very forgetful now, and, even after several reminders, the scroll would never have been written but for her soliciting the aid of a small boy next door, who for a trifle for himself bought the paper. The scholar then wrote a wrong character. He must have his opium first. She was always troubling him. Why was she not more dutiful? Undutiful enough to get another sheet of paper, then another, for the second did not match, she had at length the subdued pleasure of seeing the scrolls mounted and hung up in her room. But she would never ask her father to do her another favour.

The weather began to grow hot, and the time of the military examination approached. The burly "students" came pouring in, and the neighbourhood became quite lively with the rattling of horse bells. Camilla just remembered the sound of Seng-teh's horse bells years ago. That sound always made her sad now.

It was the eve of the competition, and her father, who felt very feeble, asked her to take his little chair outside (that one inscribed on the back, "Long life, perpetual youth"), for he felt unusually depressed. There he sat, prematurely old, and full of wearing, corroding thoughts, in which was no promise of a higher destiny. Those hateful words "opium devil" cut him to the quick, and their sting was in their partial truth. He had lost face with himself. Yes, he could not deny that. He saw his better self—not the future ideal self which you and I see when heavenly influences are most real, but his own self, the self he had actually possessed once, which had borne his name for years. He saw it, he clutched at it. But it eluded his grasp. He struggled with all the energy of Tantalus. He laid hold of its garment, but it seemed to tear; he touched the hem, but no virtue came forth therefrom to cheer the despondent man. He tried to catch its shadow, but it had passed by. The past wholly irrevocable, the future hopeless to an extent which you and I have never known even in our most melancholy moments. The opium pipe was now more and more a necessity, and less and less a satisfaction. It had been an entertaining servant once, a servant on a low wage, then a servant who took liberties and demanded more and more pay, an indispensable servant who soon had its own way, then a master who paid rapidly diminishing wages, then a tyrant who dragged a slave along in fetters, a slave with some memory at times of his former state.

Do all opium-smokers feel thus? No. Some have never had selves worth possessing. Their

> "... ancient but ignoble blood
> Has crept through scoundrels ever since the flood."

But men of the Nieh stamp, who have once been high-principled according to their light, feel eventually that all principles are mere book phrases to them. The world of men is hollow, the world of thought rotten to the core. Happy they who still possess the treasure of affection, some gentle soul whose memory of the brighter past projects itself into the gloomy present, the memory of a home perpetuating itself amidst the desolation of bare walls and empty ghost-haunted rooms.

His daughter was indispensable to him now. He loved her with a love described in Hobbes' selfish philosophy, which makes love but a form of selfishness; true, perhaps, of all the love that the cynical philosopher ever remembered; true, doubly true, of the parental "love" of Nieh.

Apart from that "love" he would try and betroth her to someone else; he would then get a few tens of thousand cash to spend on "necessities." But it would not do, though he hardly doubted her acquiescence; for a heart lost to principle regards all principle in others as a mere bogie, called in the West sentimentality. She was dutiful in her way. But then, if he died, she would have no home. Home! well, yes, she had one now, but for how long?

Then he had done his best to find Seng-teh. He had satisfied his conscience. Conscience! The word used to be real once, but, like the youth in question, it had died defeated in battle, or had sickened of ague, now a cold and shivery thing, now throbbing in burning exaggeration of life; at last, cold in death, a memory, a shade, or a haunting ghost.

His reverie was interrupted by the sight of two men approaching. One of them was a foreigner.

"Shall we go in, father?" asked Camilla.

"No; the foreigner will not hurt us."

FATHER AND DAUGHTER.

As the two approached, she retired behind her father's chair, with her eyes cast down to the ground. She felt too poorly to blush. She blushed white. The foreigner was followed by a crowd of noisy children, who cried in chorus, "Foreign devil! Foreign eye-scooper!" and the like. Camilla looked up a moment, to see the Chinaman turning round to reprove the crowd, while the foreigner walked quietly on. But the foreigner looked at her! That was enough. She seized hold of the back of her father's chair, intending to drag it and him into the house, but he fell over with a cry of pain.

The foreigner and his companion lifted him gently up, and carried the fainting man into the house. "Pardon our intrusion, but he seems ill; and I am extremely sorry that my coming along should have caused him to fall over." The words were uttered by a foreigner, a foreigner with "a whole mouth of Chinese!" There was a foreigner in their house! Had the legendary white crane emerged from the well opposite, and talked to her with the eloquence of a well-trained parrot, she would hardly have been more surprised.

"Do not fear," said the young Chinaman with a pure Hanyang accent. Then, "May I close the yard gate? the children are so noisy." She was too bewildered to say No, and the young man closed the gate. At the same time the portly form of the landlord appeared on the scene, striking terror to the hearts of the youngsters, and restoring something like quiet.

"Do not fear," the young man said once more; "the foreign Shenseng is a noted physician. He has saved many a life; he will help your father, never fear."

"But please, sir," she replied tremblingly, "his eyes!"

"What is the matter with them?" asked the foreigner gently, and proceeded to place his finger and thumb on the eyelids.

"Stop, foreign devil, eye-scooper!" she screamed. "This is my father. Go! Go at once! You shall not scoop his eyes out!"

The scream aroused the sick man, who called out faintly, "What is the matter?"

"The foreign doctor has come to heal you," interrupted the young man.

"It is well," was the languid reply. "No one else can." But Camilla placed herself before her father, and dared either of them to approach.

"My child, go behind my chair. He may have some 'thorn frost' [quinine]. That is a good medicine."

"Little sister,"[1] pleaded the young native, "the doctor has no knives with him. And if he had, he would not hurt your venerable father's eyes. That is a slander, the charge of eye-scooping. But he has some 'thorn frost' and a 'hundred sorts' of medicines at Hankow."

"Shall I retire, and let my friend give your father some medicine?"

"But I am no doctor," urged the other.

Camilla involuntarily looked at the dreaded foreign nondescript. Was he, after all, a human being? It was but a half glance, but she thought she saw some moisture in his eye. There was indeed an expression of kindly sympathy in his face. In the sudden reaction from her alarm, she felt her own tears flowing freely.

"Does your father smoke opium—much?"

"Yes," said she in a broken voice.

"For some time, I suppose? And that cough, when did it begin?"

"Years ago," coughed the invalid. "I took opium for it."

"Like many others. It helped you at first, but not afterwards. I have better medicine than that over the river in Hankow, and by and by, if you are willing, you can break off opium, but do not trouble about that now. I have a little 'thorn frost' here which will not hurt you. I will send something more suitable to-morrow morning, by my friend here, if he can spare the time."

"Certainly."

---

[1] A term for a mandarin's daughter. It is possibly the only instance in Chinese where a diminutive is used in anything approaching an endearing way. The word for sister compensates for the diminutive, for it is literally "elder sister," implying superiority.

"What is your honourable surname?" asked the sick man, looking at the last speaker."

"My humble surname is Li. Your exalted surname?"

"Nieh."

Then hurriedly, "And your honourable designation?"

"Shü-k'ing."

"The same, the same!" cried the young man, with tears in his eyes.

"Praise the Sovereign on High!" ejaculated the doctor. His tears were a reality now.

But Nieh could hardly understand what had happened. He looked bewildered.

"I am Seng-teh, your son. My father! My father!" and he knelt before him.

Camilla had retired to give vent to her tears within.

Her father called her, but she did not come. She had long since joined the "society for the preservation of modesty." She could not come.

"We will go now," said Seng-teh, who had suddenly grown bashful. "May I come to-morrow morning, father?"

"Yes, my son," and they were gone.

Chapter XXIII.

RESURRECTION.

"As the drum beats on a lofty hill, his fame is heard afar."

THE sun was setting, and as the two walked away, gong-beats were heard from the opposite side of the lotus pond. A small company carrying torches and lanterns wended their way between the grave mounds over a little rising ground to the left. Then another similar company emerged from another house, and started in the same direction. Then another along the right bank. These latter were evidently coming past the gate.

"Go and see the sights, my child; I want to think."

"But"—

"But what?"

"Do you think it is quite safe? Will they be coming here again?" She meant the two visitors. Strange indeed that feeling which is one moment aching longing, and at another nervous dread. What a queer girl this Chinese maiden must have been!

Her father, however, did not catch the point of her remark. "Well, if they do, they need not see you. Shut the gate; those military 'students' are not over polite."

"He *is* handsome. No, it is more than that, he is so kind. I can trust him. He is so good. He is noble. But that left hand of his! And his face looked worn. Has he been ill? Has the foreigner saved him too? He does not seem to be employed by him. He does not belong to the foreigner. He called father, 'Father.' He belongs to no one else. He is mine! He is mine!" All this in the very sanctum sanctorum of Camilla's heart. She hardly liked herself to hear it. It was so un-Chinese, where most folks were married first and only came to know each other after. " Yet father loved mother. And I "— But the gong-beats came nearer.

She could hear voices. What were they saying? "That old head yonder "—a pout of the prominent lips indicated the house—" has a pretty daughter. Such delightful little dots of feet. Teeny weeny feet they are. When I get my degree, I mean to employ a middleman to get her. Her father is an 'opium devil,' and will soon be glad of a cash or so."

This was enough. She darted inside. " They are talking insultingly."

" About whom ? "

" About me."

" Yes, you are better inside. Put three wicks in the rush-pith lamp, my child There are three of us now." The words were uttered in a kindlier tone than she had heard for many a weary day. But they were followed by, " Fetch me my medicine."

Seng-teh had taken his foreign friend on to a low hill beyond the execution ground, the nearer side of which was the little stone monument to the " Pomegranate blossom woman." The open space was also the parade ground for the soldiers of the camp, that camp from which Seng-teh had once released a lame hunchback. From the foot of the rising ground upon which the camp stood, there ran a straight shallow trench. This was the racecourse for the morrow. When it was dark, about five hundred little companies had gathered there. There were a thousand lights, lanterns or torches. Before the proceedings began, Seng-teh told his friend how that even in the athletic competitions the young men were to undergo, there was opportunity for cheating. The proportion of rich folk who got their degree was always somewhat high. The target at which they shot, from foot or from horseback, had a teller near with a drum; the examiner might turn his

Eve of Military Examination.

blind eye thither, and the well-paid drummer strike up even without the arrow hitting the mark. Moreover, in lifting the heavy weights, some "candidates" were known to have a silk rope concealed within their garments, which somewhat distributed the burden. Such things were notorious.

But while he was speaking, the companies were gathered into one compact mass, and the two drew nearer to see one of the sights of China. The future competitors unsheathed their swords, and followed by lanterns and torches, rushed with a war-whoop along the shallow ditch, hacking right and

left at unseen enemies. This was to dispose of any haunting ghosts, who otherwise might trip up their horses on the morrow. Arrived at the end of the course, each man turned aside, planted three sticks of smoking incense in the ground, and fired off a string of crackers ("Get along with you—please"). It was a wonderful sight, flames and racings, sword brandishings, wild yells of a most heathenish nature, and the perpetual volley of crackers. After half an hour of such sightseeing they turned homewards. Seng-teh pointed out on the right a great curio, a granite table with seats on either side. This, he said, was for the accommodation of the ghosts of folks killed in the Rebellion, and buried there *en masse*. But his

Table for Ghostly Feasts.

eyes seemed to turn frequently to a spot behind where he said the table was to be seen in daylight. "Let us kneel down here," said the doctor. "This has been a wonderful day in your history. The Sovereign on High is good. Let us thank Him." And there in the darkness among the graves, almost unheard by his companion amid the firing of the crackers, the doctor poured out his heart in a few simple words.

Next morning Seng-teh was up before daylight, though daylight came early. By the light of a red candle—he must have a candle, nothing less, and a red one—he read once more the 26th chapter of Leviticus, then took down from the shelf the last volume of all, and read a few words marked in the margin with red circles. Later on, by force of habit, he took his signboard and hung it outside, but, on second thoughts, brought it in again. Then he roused up his little assistant,— a schoolboy whom his friend the doctor had recommended to him,—told him to look after the shop, and with a final look in the rather wavy glass he went off towards *Wu Seng Miao*. His shop was not as yet in the main street, but business was good. He had had to renew a large part of his stock, and had procured some blanks of various sorts from the potteries to engrave in his unoccupied hours.

Receiving two bottles of medicine and a small basin of a half-solid, half-liquid something, he proceeded toward the landing-place. But here a bright thought struck him, and he went back home, to find an intending customer examining his wares. The man, who seemed well-to-do, bought a few cups and gave an order for the engraving of some blanks, telling him that if they suited in quality and price he would recommend him to the *Tao Tai*, the chief mandarin of Hankow. He had never seen that kind of work before. "Nor had Peng the admiral," said Seng-teh modestly. "You have done work for him? I am his [distant] cousin," said the stranger. This seemed a good omen. And selecting a pair of vases, his own work, which he had procured through a friend, and two engraved cups, he put the jelly in one of the latter, and started off through the archway of the god of war, "the one man of Shansi," to the one house in Hanyang. But as he went along, he almost trembled. He would rather have met the inexorable P'eng, or even the god of war in his most awful moments, than face someone in that one house. He could not proceed, but yet he did. Strange fellow, this young Chinaman!

But he really could not go straight to the house, he must wander round the lotus pond. He must cheer his jaded spirits with a cup of tea, and one of the "scald-back" cakes. Having paid for which, he was accosted by a burly man. "You are the man who went into old Nich's house yesterday with the foreign doctor, are you not? I live next door. Tell him I will be back soon with the meat; here are the vegetables."

Seng-teh's spirits revived at the sight of this powerful contingent. He insisted the man should retain the meat for himself, while he purchased a larger quantity for Nich. Keeping close by his side, he at length managed to come up to the citadel. He would rather have had the Feuliang episode over again, however. As he entered, the last corner of a blue mantle was seen disappearing into a side apartment. The enemy had retreated! "Who's there?" asked a now familiar voice.

Seng-teh replied in person. He would have raised the siege but for that voice. And now hearty, but somewhat laconic, greetings were heard on both sides—by someone yonder. She had half a mind to stop her ears, but did not. The young man commenced operations by taking a little jelly and putting it into his "father's" mouth, who swallowed it before he knew what he was doing. He could not but ask for more, even when he had heard that a foreign lady had made it.

"A veritable goddess of mercy," he exclaimed, "if she were not a foreigner."

Seng-teh suggested that the "goddess of mercy" being from the West, might herself be considered as a foreigner. Whereat someone in the opposite room began to feel certain emotions, not very favourable to even the most superlative goddess of mercy. She would not have worshipped that deity on that day, under any compulsion whatever. She would rather have committed suicide by swallowing opium.

"Is this spoon hers?"

There was a breathless pause, during which someone thought she would swallow opium after all. But such a catastrophe was averted by the words "No indeed. I have a porcelain shop, you know, and this is out of my stock." Then, happily for Seng-teh's future prospects, "I have never seen her. It was her husband the doctor who gave this stuff to me. I drew the picture on the cup myself." The maiden now felt injured by the fact that, owing to the unalterable laws of optics, no human eyes, however bright, can possibly see through the cracks of two walls fifteen feet distant from one another!

"Why, it is Peh-ya and his sympathetic friend. Well drawn. Excellently written. And the other?"

"That is the 'empty city stratagem.' I had the honour of presenting one like it to the Admiral of the Yangtse."

"Not his Excellency Peng, surely?"

"The same."

And Camilla—here the writer begs to remind his readers, that he never promised to describe that which passes description, but merely to string together a few dry-as-dust peach-stones he has picked up along the highways and byways of China.

"And those vases?"

"I painted them myself. They are painted, the others engraved."

Seng-teh was buried alive in superlatives.

"Camilla!"

But Camilla answered not, still less put in an appearance.

"Camilla! Where can the girl have gone? Come at once, foolish child."

The child did certainly look as foolish as any maiden of her calibre could possibly do, when she appeared at length.

Seng-teh "did not notice" her; he suddenly became absorbed in thoughts of breakfast. He bolted out, and was nearly mistaking the outer door for that which led to the kitchen.

"Two fools!" was the scholar's comment thereon. Then to his daughter, "Is the rice nearly done?"

"I will go and see, father." But she too forgot the geography of her own domicile, and found herself in her own room. She could not face that terrible young man in the kitchen! The impossible had to happen, however, after her father had called no less than three times.

"Yes, father," she said, almost crying.

"Well, what about the rice?"

"Oh! the rice?" Had Camilla become a victim to the opium-smoker's forgetfulness? "I do believe he is cooking it."

"Well, I expect he has learnt to do that."

"But his wounded hand, father?"

"It is not wounded now, and it is his left."

"Oh, his left, is it?"

"Yes, go and help him! Are you mad?"

The awkward pause—a mere instant—which followed was broken by the appearance of the victorious and virtuous hero, who asked if there was anyone next door who could buy a few things more.

"I have already sent him for a pound of meat. Why has he not come back?"

"I have a pound or two, Nieh Shen-seng. I intercepted him, but I want one or two trifles to flavour it." Camilla went out and returned with the juvenile from next door. The directions given him related to the purchase of a little powdered ginger, some thickening, a water chestnut or two, also a few other things, and some pepper, unless there was some of the latter in the kitchen.

The youngster having been despatched on his errand, Camilla had to go by parental orders and show Seng-teh where the little jar of pepper was. She did so very inarticulately, and quickly returned to look at the pottery, for want of something better to do. She looked askance at the contents of one of the cups, then almost complacently at the spoon, and finally—it cost her an effort—she took up the cups one after the other in her hand, then the vases. There was a distinct trace of pride in her blushing face now, and almost tears in her eyes. The soliloquy of the previous evening was repeated for the hundredth time, but now with distinct additions. It was too good to be true. She had breakfasted, she had feasted already.

The lad came back with the articles enumerated, as well as some dried mushrooms, dried daffodil flowers, "ears of wood," otherwise edible fungus, and a few ounces of liver. Then followed a great deal of chopping and those varied hissing sounds so familiar to the Chinese, all of which promised a delightful meal. Anon a grateful fragrance filled the house, and eventually the whole result of the new culinary artist's efforts appeared in detachments.

"Shall I go, father?" asked Camilla, but not with impetuous earnestness.

"No, foolish child; stay, of course."

"What, and eat with him!" thought she. But like many other undertakings beneath the skies, to refer to the rebels' proclamation, it had to be done.

The meat balls were delicious. They might have pleased the palate of the immortal Elia himself had he lived in China—in a house with a dried earth floor, until he had become as practised with the chopsticks as he was with his pen. Yes, in order to the full enjoyment of these delicacies, the floor must be of earth, and the clothless table slightly rickety. Given these conditions, the verdict must inevitably be a foregone conclusion, so spicy, so "short," and so tender are the meat balls prepared by Seng-teh's recipe.

"Where did you learn this?" exclaimed the delighted parent. "At the Kiangsi potteries," was the reply.

"You know how to fill bowls as well as how to paint them. But how did you get there? And why did you not write?"

Seng-teh hid his left hand under the table, and related the chapter in his history already known to the reader. But, like the Chinese stories, it came out in small chapters, for there was a danger of the breakfast getting cold.

A Chinese meal is eminently a social affair. The chopsticks go into the common property bowls, and it is highly correct to put delicate morsels therefrom on to the rice in your neighbour's private property bowl. Unless, perhaps, the "neighbour" be the long-lost lady of your dreams. Seng-teh had helped Nieh Shen-seng thus; he could not quite bring himself to help "father,"—that word died out almost from his thoughts, it was too familiar now. But yet, with a supreme effort of mechanical force, he managed to put one of his meat balls on to the rice of Miss Nieh,—no, it was into the bowl of little Camilla. She gave a just audible scream, and seemed to scream louder inside. It was not correct. She would frown the offender down; and in doing so, their eyes met for the first time since he had nursed her as a child. Then she suddenly found that one of the rice bowls needed replenishing, and glided off with it into the kitchen.

The history proceeded. "And you were really the first to scale that wall, my son?" said Nieh, wiping away a tear with his coverlet. "And you say the Admiral Peng accepted one of our bowls. When was that?" Seng-teh had to relate that episode too, and the end of Lieu Fah.

"He was always hateful; but go on about the potteries." It all came out; even the story of the proffered hand of the maiden. The reader must be prepared for more tears, nay, they were almost sobs, from Camilla. The reverie of the past evening was repeated for the hundred and first time, only on this occasion all the words seemed to be underlined, that is, marked with double red circles down the columns. At the opium chapter, Seng-teh stopped short. It would be heartless to go on.

"Proceed, my son. Tell it all. I could add more." And so, in a subdued voice, Seng-teh related the collapse of young Tai, and his own tastings and testings.

"Bring my pipe, Camilla," interrupted her father. She looked horrified. The contrast was too great. Her filial obedience forsook her. "Bring it at once, I say, and all the apparatus, and the kitchen chopper too. Shall I be outdone by my own pupil?"

"But I had not felt the craving, father."

"Take this pot at once, I say, and throw it on the kitchen fire, pot and all." A sickening odour filled the house.

"Now, hew away at these things as though you had a rebel before you. There! there! there! I will be free, if it costs me my life. Now, the lamp and the tray. Down, you rebels! There! there!" And he sank back exhausted.

Seng-teh administered a dose of the medicine, and said he

would relate no more just now. But that look which rewarded him! The unutterable gratitude of a girlish heart, of a long-despondent daughter, triumphant too, and full of that mysterious something which went to his once desolate heart. It was not a Chinese look, it was wider; it was from the depths of human nature stirred almost to an agony of rapture.

"And did the foreigner make you swallow his doctrines?" the sick man inquired at length. It was Camilla now who put a spoonful of jelly into her father's mouth.

"No; for days he said nothing. But there was a scroll on the wall with an inscription, 'Our Father which art in heaven.'"

"Then the foreigners worship their ancestors after all?"

"That Father is the Sovereign on High, the Ancestor of us all." Nieh Shen-seng seemed about to speak, but again Camilla anticipated any further words with a spoonful of jelly. Seng-teh must be right.

"One day, however, the foreigner came in, and pointing to the two last petitions, said, 'Do you know, my brother,'— yes, he said brother,—'who has preserved you from many a temptation, and who will deliver you from evil?' I suggested my former teacher, Nieh Shen-seng. Then said at length, 'Heaven.'"

"That was better, my son. 'The Emperor Shuin had the Empire. Who gave it to him? Heaven gave it to him, was the answer.'"

"'Yes,' he said, 'Heaven, your Heavenly Father, and mine, the Heavenly Spirit who, as the *Imperial Dictionary* says, "leadeth forth all things," the Heavenly Spirit whom we trust for daily rice; who created us and gave us a conscience; who loves us; your Father and mine. We are brothers in His family. "All within the four seas are brethren."'

"'But you are from outside the "four seas,"' I said. 'You are outside the five relations—sovereign and prince, father and son, elder and younger brother, husband and wife, friend and companion. Why do you come and help me? I called you "foreign devil" once. Such kindness is unprecedented.'

"'Not unprecedented,' he replied, 'for One in old time, God's only Son, came to us men from outside the five relations, for we had broken them and disowned our Father, came to be cursed and wronged and killed. And He came to embody all the five relations; to make God our Sovereign, and we His statesmen; to make us sons of the Heavenly Father; to be Himself our elder brother; to make all who trust Him His friends; to be our faithful Friend for ever and ever.'

"'How is that?' I exclaimed. 'I never heard it before, nor did my ancestors.'

"'Nor did mine many hundreds of years ago; but, knowing it, they have taught it me, my father and mother did. And I cannot help telling others about it. But you are weak yet. I will tell you more when you ask me.'

"'Now!' I exclaimed. But he had gone."

"My son," said Nieh, "'The hungry think any food sweet, and the thirsty the same of any drink,[1] and thus they do not get the right taste of what they eat and drink. The hunger and thirst, in fact, vitiate [the palate]. And is it only the mouth and the stomach which are vitiated by hunger and thirst? Men's minds are also injured by them.' You remember those words of Mencius?"

"Yes; and I have heard that those who seek after righteousness, like hungry and thirsty ones, shall be filled."

"That is not how the sentence in the classics runs. It is, 'The superior man seeks doctrine, the mean man eatables.' But the meaning is right. Except that it does not say they shall be filled. That is, not in any commentary I have read. But I am weary now, and must rest. Will you come to-morrow?"

"Yes, I am busy to-day. I have a great deal of work before me for someone who calls himself a cousin of Admiral Peng. But I rest to-morrow." And so the conversation ended, except for another eloquent look, half-wondering, but fully trustful, from Camilla.

When Seng-tch came again next morning, he found that Nieh Shen-seng had not had the most pacific time possible during the long hours which had elapsed. Long they had seemed to all three. As for Nieh, that terrible craving had come upon him in the midst of the reaction after the morning's

[1] Cf. Prov. xxvii. 7.

excitement, that awful *must*, which seemed wrought in fire upon every bone and muscle, that hunger, that starvation which seemed surely to be the very agonies of death. Then, in his unhinged state, the wretched man had been taking overdoses of the medicine supplied him, and that had complicated matters. Dose is an element almost unknown in the popular mind. If ten pills be a help, twenty will be a double help. But the bottle was distinctly labelled, " Three times a day; only one small wine-cup." And Seng-teh had repeated the cautions again and again. Camilla was very distressed about it; she had to take the bottle away, and received some bitter reproaches. " She did not care for her father now. It was all that child Seng-teh. He himself might die; he was dying. The agony was intolerable. Medicine was to heal a man. Why did not the doctor heal him? Why did he put him off with that useless stuff?" It was a dreadful day; it was a terrible night.

She did not run away this time when Seng-teh came. He would save her father, she knew he would. She was watching at the door for him, and Nieh Shen-seng was anxious for him to come.

When he arrived, he gave his " father" a dose of another sort of medicine he had brought. He explained that the doctor had not anticipated that his patient would give up his opium at once, and so had sent nothing to compensate for its sudden removal. He had only met him the previous night—too late to come over. The doctor lived a very busy life, and on the " sixth day after worship" (Saturday) he—had to use special means on some patients. It was too early yet to say that it had been operation day.

The sufferer took the medicine eagerly, and pleaded for more—pleaded almost as a spoilt child might for another lump of rice sugar (glucose) when mother had only bought him a cash worth. The relative position of the two men seemed reversed. Nieh moaned like a fretful baby, but after taking the draught he grew quieter, if not more amiable. Camilla would cook the breakfast; she did not care for him now. Seng-teh could go and swallow "foreign tea," eat foreign doctrines, and "worship" on their wine and meat. He would not forbid his staying, however. So Seng-teh stayed—the bright schoolboy, now a man of twenty-eight, whose varied experiences have developed his character far more than twice the number of years would have done in the case of a sedentary student or stay-at-home farmer. It was not fossilisation in a rocky mould; it was not deossification of the mental bones—a reversion to the invertebrate type of existence. It was growth. Each year had added something, and the troublous years had added most. Each year had meant a ring of tough fibre, not perhaps in an oak,—the *robust* characters are found chiefly in Hunan, the home of the Chinese oak and Chinese timber trees generally,—but perhaps the willow. And in the midst was the little tree protected by those of later years. He was still the little scholar in heart.

And here was that little scholar's once idealised, almost deified teacher, not as he once was, but still assumed to be so. The promise of that life had been broken, but he would cling to the promise nevertheless. And in no wise interfering with his old-time reverence, nor quite absorbing all his present-time thought, was a sweet little promise almost unbelievably fulfilled. We have seen that Seng-teh readily took the colour of surroundings when he felt at home in them, sometimes weakly so, but not now. He fell into his present circumstances as naturally as though he had been in them for years instead of twenty-four hours. It is this adaptability to circumstances in the non-*literati* Chinese which has in it at once the possibility of life and living, of mental and spiritual education, and also, if the circumstances be ignoble, of hypocrisy, of deceit, and final ruin. Opium full often softens the fossilised student, to leave the man in the same mould, with only the solidity of a mass of gelatine, as yielding as opium paste itself.

Nieh Shen-seng had lost all grit, but he had the form. He was the scholar still in the form of a staunch Confucianist. He had all the phrases still, and it was the very influences which had come upon him of late which gave his soul body enough to protest against some of those influences.

When breakfast came, he was " superior man " enough not to " seek eatables "; his appetite had gone. He was virtuously superior by necessity, and proudly superior as far as pride was possible to him now. Moreover, his superiority had a positive side; he " sought doctrine," that is doctrinal dogmatism, and found it within.

" You mentioned the word 'worship' just now [he omitted " my son "]. You rest to-day; it is a special day, the foreigners' worship day, and that of the rebels too, who massacred your father, and you follow them. I have no patience with you."

Seng-teh replied by saying that he was a Chinaman and an Imperialist, but that he thought the worship day was a good old custom—" old custom " was Chinese enough. Custom is a demigod, old custom is one of the supreme deities.

" Did Confucius observe it? Was the seventh day special to him ? "

" I do not know; but you yourself once said that seven was a special number in the very ancient *Book of Changes*, to the study of which Confucius said he would give fifty years if he had them, that he might be without great faults."

" And do you suppose that you, child, have found out what the sacred Sage failed to learn ? Can you elucidate the *Book of Changes* ? He could not."

" I am far from saying I can. But I have a book which is said to be the oldest in the world; the opening chapter throws light upon some sentences of the Taoist philosopher Chwang-tsz, which you quoted the day I became your son. It is from that book that the number seven in the *Book of Changes* comes, and the custom of ' worship day.' "

" If there be such a book, of course it is binding. But Confucius had never heard of it, and shall the Western barbarians be wiser than he ? do they know anything he did not know ? " Here the medicine bottle was awkwardly in the way. Seng-teh removed it, to make its existence still more obvious. " I do not want to learn doctrine from the barbarians. It was they who stirred up the Longhaired with their heresies."

" Stirred the leaders up against idols, not against their emperor. And it was the foreigners who put the Rebellion down at last."

"The foreigners? You deluded child, it was the god of war who came to the help of Cheng Kwoh-fan, came down in a visible form. Why are you not orthodox, read the classics, and worship him if you are a Chinaman?"

In reply, Seng-teh pulled forth from his neck the old string of peach-stone charms, untied the string, and held it forth in his left hand. The unexpected appearance of that old necklace, held out as it was in the maimed hand, had a visible effect. From the brave deed of the wall-scaling, and the glitter of the Admiral Peng's twenty taels, Nieh's mind's eye wandered back to an old conversation on the subject of worship; when, having demolished all the gods which the murdered Li had honoured, that usually happy-go-lucky farmer had posed him with a pleading face, posed him with a question he could neither answer nor disallow. There was that face before him. There were those searching eyes behind the whole-hearted look on Seng-teh's face. Why did that uncomfortable episode come back to him now, to him who had lost all Confucianism even, except the phrases? It was too much. He sank back exhausted.

And Seng-teh had not left him to go to worship. Of course it was Camilla. It must be. It could not be any care for him. Yet again, as he opened his eyes, he saw in that face the face of the bright little boy who had reverenced him once. What was there in him to reverence now? Seng-teh must have noticed the change. He must loathe him, as he loathed himself. There could not be anything besides selfishness in the world. He himself was all selfishness, and he was a staunch Confucianist. But was he?

Chapter XXIV.

For Better, for Worse.

"If one has not the bones of an Immortal, it is hard to meet with the Immortals, and even if one rubbed shoulders with them, one would not know it."—*Chinese Saying*.

It was now the eighth month (September 1867), the "chrysanthemum month," and a row of painted porcelain pots in Nieh Shen-seng's little garden saw their art glories fade beneath the loveliness of flowers which no Chinese artist could paint, blossoms painted by the Great Artist.

Seng-teh had now solved a little problem with the aid of his Camilla. Chiefly sympathy that help was, but in return for it he had called her the "Fire Maiden." He had erected a temple to her—in his heart. The worship therein was not idolatrous; it was but the old English word worship, still surviving in the marriage service. He had made a small kiln in his backyard. He could now paint and fire his own wares. These would be more attractive to the general public than the rather too æsthetic thin black lines of the laborious engraving process; half the price too, cheaper to him than the painted cups and vases of other men, and perhaps more conscientiously painted. He would have to move into a better-known street, and his juvenile must be his apprentice, while another juvenile might become shop-boy.

It was the day before the autumn solstice, and Nieh Shen-seng was arrayed in his long plum-black silk robe, the robe he had been married in, which had accompanied him in one of his boxes in his travels. He cherished it as a woman may cherish her wedding-dress. It was more than a wedding-gown; its value did not lie there. It was the sign of his life-long adherence to the doctrines of Confucius. Everybody wears those gowns now on state occasions, because everybody knows that all ultimate respectability is Confucian. The gown belonged to him. It was the princely robe of the princely man, whose princeliness was evidenced by the graduate's button, "on fortune's cap . . . the very button," but with a meaning unknown to any Western dramatist. Shakespeare had only the phrase, Nieh had the reality transcending all phrases, the jewelled crown of the princely Confucianist, who could weave Confucian phraseology into a mosaic of princely style;

The East Gate Hanyang

and who now was free from opium, except as far as a couple of "opium-curing pills," not supplied by the foreign doctor, were concerned. "A couple" in Chinese, as in Hebrew, stands for a few. But what with tonics and expectorants, he was on his feet again. He was going to worship Confucius. Not at the Hanyang temple of the sages, for that hateful Lung of unspeakable memory would be there, but at Wuchang, where the ceremony was as imposing as at any place in the Empire. If Seng-teh was too far gone to become a Confucianist, he would still see what Confucianism was like. No foreign "worship" ceremonies could be named in the same day.

The two therefore went off in the afternoon in at the west gate, and through the city of Hanyang, past the abode of the Dragon, where we wince and inwardly maledict; past the red-coloured walls of the temple of the Sages, where we grow large as we point out the stone which commands all mandarins on horseback to dismount here; past the memorial arches to noble widows who refused to marry men who were doubtless noble; past the county *yamun*, then the large præfectural *yamun*, with its wall opposite to guard against evil influences, and to display in wonderfully glaring colours a beast called a *ta'n* (a pun upon the word covetousness), who is trying in vain to swallow the moon, which, as all Chinese scholars know, is an especial pill, and anon an emetic for the heavenly dog whose voracity causes the eclipses. A mighty brute that, but of extreme sensitiveness as regards the sound of gongs and drums upon earth, or a fraction of earth, just a few—well, thousand *li* away. Mighty brute, but mightier gong!

The Cause of the Eclipses.

Then at last they came to the east gate, whereon are the characters, *Ts'ao Chung*, which embody one of the oldest metaphors on record in the mundane universe. "Lo, this mighty current hastens to its audience with the Ocean," as the *Book of Odes* (following the *Book of History*) has it.

"*Ts'ao Chung*," repeated Nieh, as they crossed over the

flowing waters in a little sail boat. "How ancient, how grand, how appropriate the metaphor! It must have warmed the heart of the sacred Sage himself."

And there before them was the Yellow Crane Tower, beyond the mile-wide Yangtse, that tower beneath which the famous drunken poet of China (who came to the front in the reign of Li Tan's "illustriously Imperial" son) had drunk wine and written marvellously lawless and marvellously musical verses. Beneath which tower, also, as Seng-teh remembered, the indomitable Hu Lin-yi, he of the strange  smile and the birthmark on his left cheek, had watched the defeat of P'ao Ts'ao, and had ordered the lictor to be in readiness to administer forty blows. It stood upon ancient walls, dating back in some parts to the Sung dynasty (tenth century A.D.). Where are your Western barbarians now? Nieh felt himself again, and himself meant his Confucian self.

They ascended the steps, and entered in at the gate of the Placid Lake, not far from which lived a scholar who had taken his degree with Nieh, and was therefore a brother in Confucius. They were to spend half the night here, for the ceremony is just before dawn. The "brother" received him with that artistic politeness in which the *literati* seek to outvie one another. He prophesied for him official posts, glorious fame, and the like. It seemed all present tense to him, and he honoured his guest accordingly; then managed to squeeze into the much-belarded conversation the fact that he

had heard that Nieh's "virtuous son-in-law" had eaten the foreign religion, adding, as sugar to the pill, that Confucianism and it were exactly alike. The pill proved to be as indigestible to Nieh, however, as the moon to the heavenly dog. He was disgraced by a disgraceful hypocrite, not Seng-teh, who could hardly have helped himself, but by a Confucian and a graduate who had wilfully forgotten the "three character classic" (we say A B C) of all politeness, acknowledged by the barbarians even, in their barbarian way, which is to make your guest as comfortable as you can. All this passed through his Confucian mind in a flash, a rather scathing flash; but from the depths of the Chinese nature, practised from generation to generation in the adaptation of self (and the truth too) to circumstances, he replied, with a polite smile, that his "unworthy son-in-law" ("unworthy" matched "virtuous") had had some intercourse with the Western barbarians for the sole purpose of teaching them the rudiments of Chinese politeness (that was cutting!) and the doctrines of the sacred Sage, to whose temple he was about to take him,— it was already late,—to impress upon him that he in his turn might impress upon the said barbarians the supreme majesty, the "heaven and earth equalling" virtue of Confucius. At which, having had the last word, he bowed himself out. No, he would not be back for the night, as he had hoped, but had to make another call, a peremptory necessity, for the friend in question had known his father at Fancheng. All of which his host rightly understood to mean that he was too ashamed ever to darken his portals again.

"Thus," said he to Seng-tch, "you would separate chief friends." To which the young man replied not. His very silence cut Nieh. Seng-tch had no expostulation, no reproach to make outwardly. Nieh coughed, and the cough reminded him of the foreign medicine he had forgotten to take before he came; and the foreign medicine of the foreigner, to whom he probably owed his present ability to walk. He had felt grateful to him, for the man was kind. He seemed kinder at every visit. And all that Confucian politeness had done for the graduate was — But even his reverie was interrupted by violent coughing.

His attention was now taken up by the sight of a cross marked with ink upon the pavement. He saw in it the character "ten." All characters were sacred as having been used with reverence by Confucius. The reason of its having been written there was soon apparent, for, as the two stepped aside to avoid treading upon it, two or three men standing up against a wall near cried, "Foreign religion eaters! Foreign devils' sons!"

The Cross Character Sacred.

Nieh Shen-seng had self-command enough not to reply, otherwise than by ordering them to bring a basin of water. " I'm a graduate," he said, "and will appeal to my friend the mandarin, if you do not bring it at once." It was quickly brought, and, robed as he was, the scholar stooped down and washed out the sign, saying, "'Reverence written paper'; have you mean fellows never heard the words? Do you not know that characters written anywhere are sacred?" Then he walked on. He felt he had partly atoned to Seng-teh for his words about the foreigners; there was a bond of union over that sign, though perhaps for different reasons, and, moreover, Seng-teh seemed condemned that he had not said anything about it. So they were quits.

Arrived at the gate of the temple, they passed through one or two courtyards, then turned to the left, and came to an open space in front of the large enclosure which holds the temple proper, and after noticing the marble bridge which spans an ornamental piece of water, found themselves within the great quadrangle. At the north side stood the actual temple with a terrace of stone before it, the ascent to which is gained by broad steps divided in the centre by a sloping block of granite, with the Imperial dragon sculptured thereon in bold relief. At the foot of the steps, on either side, stood a pair of stone tablets, each supported on the back of a massive tortoise. Behind these, on the terrace itself, were ornamental wooden frames, two of which supported very ancient and sweet-toned bells, the others having musical stones and other relics of bygone ages suspended therefrom.

They then entered the temple building, facing the entrance of which was the great central tablet to Confucius, curtained with yellow silk. The effect of the whole was certainly sublime, as far as Seng-teh's artistically susceptible mind was concerned. It did really seem to body forth the greatness of Confucius. Of course Seng-teh owned him to be great. So did his friend the foreigner. He would have liked to have come with them, had it been possible. Nieh turned away from the curtained tablet, sublimely large in the gathering gloom, and said slowly, " I am a disciple of Confucius, Now let us look at the offerings."

The chief of these was an ox, with a sheep and a pig on either side, shaven after slaughtering, each lying in a separate trough.

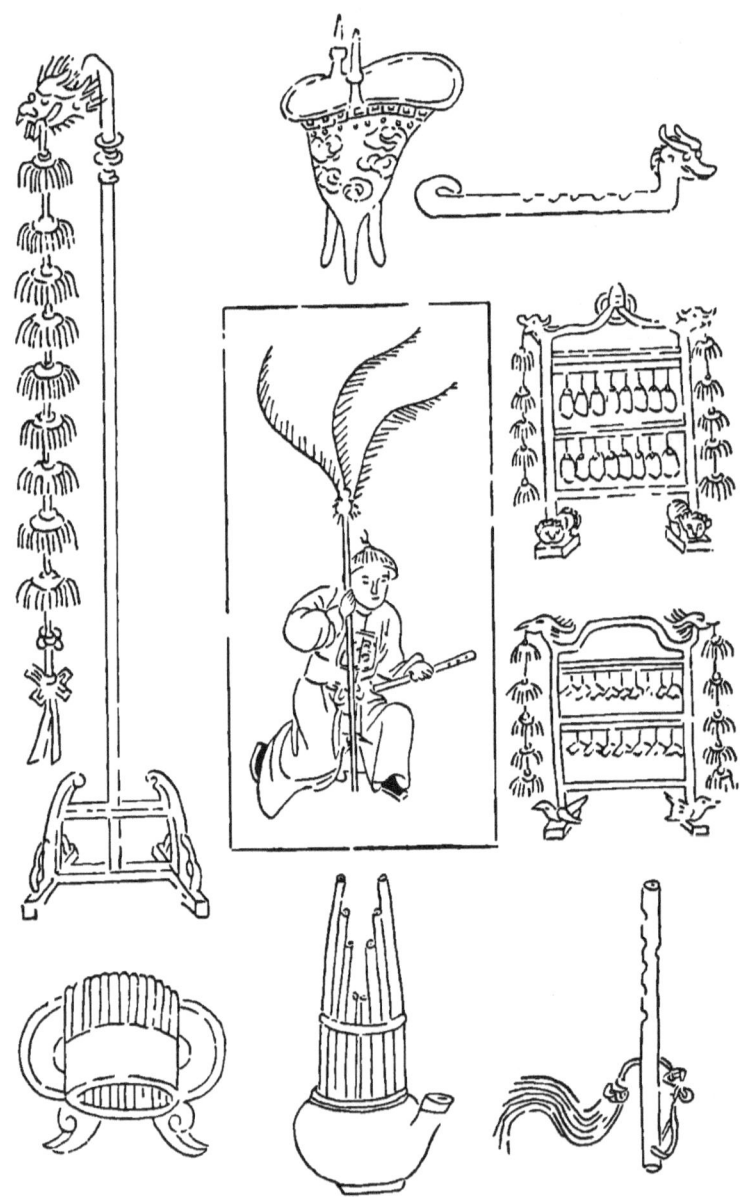

Here the sublimity began to give a little. No rebel bands would have run away with that ox. And on Nieh Shen-seng's vouchsafing the information that the Viceroy has to fast for three days before offering his tribute to the memory of Confucius, Seng-teh made a mental note that the poor brute before him seemed to have fasted for a much longer period still, and that the fast seemed to have ended fatally. The avarice of the underlings who had bought it would have some sort of an evil retribution, as far as their masticatory apparatus and their digestive organs were concerned, for they were to try and pick these fleshless bones afterwards. None but a painter of Pharaoh's lean kine could make anything sublime out of that mass of skin and bones. It reminded Seng-teh of the ancient dream.

On high tables to the right and left were spread out, in ancient shaped bowls, a number of foodstuffs. On the central and smaller table was the altar of incense. Against the walls on either side were tablets to Mencius and to Confucius' more immediate disciples, before which were more lean sheep and pigs, and other collections of eatables. Three ancient bronze wine-cups rested upon a stand near the doors, while another table hard by had a newly composed ode to Confucius, attached to a board lying thereon.

They then entered an apartment on the east side of the quadrangle, where they examined the ancient pattern musical instruments which were to be used that night, the most notable of which consisted of thirteen reeds of unequal length inserted in a gourd, also several varieties of flutes and flageolettes.

Having seen all that was to be seen, Nieh Shen-seng told Seng-teh that they must seek some inn and rest there, instead of spending a literary evening at his friend's house where he had been disgraced. And to a dismal lodging-house they accordingly went, leaving it in the fourth watch of the night, after vain attempts to rest upon the somewhat densely populated beds, from which the exceedingly interesting, zoologically interesting, wadded quilts had been removed.[1]

---

[1] A certain emperor was once the subject of treasonous plots. One night a statesman approached his couch to assassinate him, but certain loyal attendants of his slumberous hours bit so vigorously that he awoke in time to save himself. Upon which he conferred a patent of nobility upon the loyal multitude, saying, "Be prolific, and increase from generation to generation."

By this time a number of folks had gathered around the entrance to the temple. The least excitement seems to be such a welcome relief, that Chinese loungers are instinctively attracted thereby. Not all who stood or squatted there would go inside, fewer still would get a chance job, but in the blackness of the small hours, while the watchmen were noisily announcing their fidelity to their all-important duty of gong-beating, the little crowd lingered around those red portals.

The quadrangle was now dimly lit with lanterns. A band of soldiers had already taken their places, to add the dignity of a patch of military red to the proceedings. They had not yet fallen in, but were squatting, laughing and smoking to their hearts' content.

After long waiting, the message came that the *Tsz Tai* (Viceroy) was approaching. The red lanterns were quickly lit, and the unofficial ones extinguished. At the four corners of the quadrangle large bundles of tall reeds were set on fire. The redcoats fell into line, and bands of young men emerged from the eastern chamber, clothed in robes of light blue silk, and wearing the graduate's gilt button upon their hats. Very few of them had taken their degree, Nieh Shen-seng said. These pseudo-graduates were preceded by a leader, who bore a long red rod, crooked at the top in the form of a dragon's head and neck. From the dragon's mouth depended a chain of red tassels. The blue robes arranged themselves to the left and right upon the terrace, each holding an instrument of music and a wand tipped with a long pheasant plume. By this time the corridors were crowded with sightseers, and anon the Viceroy stood without.

A herald standing at the top of the dragon steps cried aloud, inviting the Viceroy to come and worship. He advanced as directed, accompanied by a few high mandarins, civil and military, all of them clad in robes of state, above which hung the Buddhist rosary.[1] Leaving the rest in the

---

[1] The apparent inconsistency of such an adornment is more than paralleled by the remarkable fact that Buddha is a canonised saint of the Catholic Church. "St. John of Damascus in the eighth century wrote a religious romance, of which the narrative is taken from the *Lalita Vistara*, the story of Buddha's life. It became very popular in the Middle Ages, and the hero was canonised.

centre of the court, the Viceroy approached the temple proper, accompanied only by the master of ceremonies. At the same time the *Fu Tai* (second provincial mandarin), accompanied by an attendant, made his way to a building on the east side, and the *Fan Tai* (third provincial mandarin) in like manner to the west side, where were the tablets to the disciples not honoured with a place in the large temple.

Meanwhile the ancient pattern drums were beaten, and the music began. It was strange and weird, and really sublime in effect. From the highest tone in the Chinese scale, the musicians descended with long-drawn notes, tone by tone, repeating each note twice,[1] while the bearers of plume-tipped wands assumed one or other of the ninety-six postures prescribed by ancient usage, returning to their original position to change it for a fresh posture as each note sounded.

The Viceroy had now reached the temple, and first of all lit the incense. As the blue smoke curled upwards, the music was hushed, and he knelt before the great tablet, bowing his head to the ground three times. He rose, and again knelt, bowing thrice as before. The whole being repeated the third time, he rose with a majesty all the more marked because associated with seeming humility, and returned to take his place in the centre of the quadrangle once more, the music starting afresh.

The herald again cried aloud, and the high officials went their ways as before, to offer the first cup of wine. This they did by lifting one of the three antique goblets above the head, and then going through the thrice-three prostrations once again.

Then more music and posturing, a return to the centre of the court, and the herald's invitation to offer the second cup. On their return this time, the ode to Confucius was read on bended knee by a scholar with a clear musical voice. Again the herald's voice was heard proclaiming that it was

He has his festal days in the Roman Communion on the 27th November, and in the Eastern on the 26th August, under the name of Josaphat, a corruption of Bodisattva" (See Max Müller, *Chips*, iv. 174-179; Beal's *Fahian*, p. 26, n.).

[1] After the style of the third line in the tune "Claremont."

time for the third offering of wine. This over, the high officials again returned to their places. A fire of paper was lit in an old-time brazier on the south side of the quadrangle, the ode torn off its tablet and committed to the flames. Meanwhile the morning had begun to break, and the grey light of dawn lent a climax to the imposing ritual, which terminated with that act.

ANCIENT BRONZE WINE CUP USED IN THE WORSHIP OF CONFUCIUS.

It was an ideal scene to Nieh Shen-seng, and he felt so thoroughly absorbed therein as to be within a measurable distance of the ideal man of China,—a fairly ideal man himself after all, a man of diplomacy, perhaps, for it was an ingenious explanation that of Confucianising the foreigners; not that any foreigner had great capacities that way. He would himself study the doctor a little, not as the vulgar, to find out the side most susceptible to imposition,—an easy task that (for where *our* city walls have their weak places, they seem to have no walls at all),—but to find out his susceptibilities for taking the Confucian mould and the Confucian polish. It was a pleasant fancy that. The barbarians! should he after all deign to teach them? A brilliant career could hardly be expected in that direction. No, he would go his own way, enlightening Seng-teh, whose foreign religion tendencies must have had a severe blow to-night. He would get his next degree in the spring. It was the year of the great triennial examinations, and he deserved an official post. Look at that mean fellow Lung! Was he not a princely man compared with him? He would get the honours prophesied by the man who had tried to disgrace him the evening before. He would fill out those phrases until the name Nieh should be a name indeed, and that far and wide. During which soliloquy he had half unconsciously been feeling for the "anti-opium pills" wrapped up in a cloth in the recesses of his left sleeve, and transferring a couple or so to his mouth.

"Why is Confucius never spoken of as a deity?" asked Seng-teh as the proceedings ended.

"A deity indeed; why should he be? The 'Imperial Kwan,' with his title of 'Sacred Spirit' [a term now familiar to Seng-teh in connection with the Holy Spirit of Scripture], cannot compare with Confucius. He was but military, though he did put down the Rebellion, that is, assisted a literary official to do so. Literature comes before matters military. An essay is a grander thing than a victory. Confucius' simple 'Sacred Man' means more than the Imperial Kwan's 'Sacred Spirit.' Even the emperor who deified Kwan took the title of Elder Brother. The Emperor is above all your deities, but Confucius is high above all emperors except one or two—Yao and Shuin, for instance, who lived ages before he was born [which in English might be very freely rendered, Why make Shakespeare an LL.D. of a university no one knows anything about?]. Han Wen-kung, the illustrious statesman and scholar of the Ta'ng dynasty, was deified into a miserable 'earth god,' to govern a few paddy fields here and there. No, the 'Sacred Man' is far above all your 'Sacred Spirits.'"

The breeze which had brought them over the flowing Yangtse had now increased into a high wind, and the wind had brought on a fine rain. The temperature had fallen very considerably. It was almost chilly to the two men who had come over the river on a scorching afternoon as thinly clad as possible. There was not much beneath Nieh Shen-seng's robe.

"Had we not better go to your friend's house?" suggested Seng-teh. "You were going to make another call, you know."

"Simple child, I have no friends in Wuchang now. I had one, but you disposed of him. We must return. The company has nearly all gone, and he among them. I hope he has not seen us."

They went out from the temple, Nieh Shen-seng turning to quote the inscription over the red gate, "'Virtue comparable to that of heaven and earth,' and yet you would have Confucius made into a god!"

As he uttered the words he commenced to cough violently. It was only raindrops on the stones. No, there were red spots among them! He was alarmed. "Call a chair and three bearers; the roads are slippery," he gasped.

At the moment a chair passed. It was reversed (as in old London in the sedan chair days), to show that it was empty. It was stopped. A dozen coolies struggled for the third place, and struggled very volubly. More coughing and more red spots. The rain was increasing. "Get another for yourself." "No, I will walk." "But you will get wet, and the bearers hurry along so." "Never mind, I shall be nearer you walking."

They reached the Yangtse, and paid the bearers, who wrangled furiously for more cash: "Wet weather, slippery paths," then curses on some folks' ancestors. A large "mandarin ferryboat" was just crossing. They gave the bearers a few cash more, who clamoured for more still, but they had only the normal two cash each, which should carry them across, according to the regulations of the same "mandarin ferryboats." Tearing themselves away from the excited coolies, who clutched at their sleeves, and would like to have had their fingers in their queues, they walked up the swaying plank, with boat-hook for banisters, Nieh Shen-seng coughing more violently than ever, and with more alarming result than before.

The boat was dancing about upon the heaving waters. The "Son of Ocean" (as the word Yangtse means according to some) seemed to emulate his hoary sire [1] in large white-tipped waves. "Only half sail! Only half, I entreat," cried the nerve-shaken man. And not without some reason, for every high wind means some overturned boats. Those who go up and down the Yangtse dread the wind, but the ferrymen are well-nigh foolhardy. More than foolhardy they seemed to the terrified man, who clung to the upper side of the boat—clung for dear life. They took no notice of his cries, regarded him not, he who was a graduate and a future mandarin. He felt curses rise to his tongue, but they were checked by the violent coughing. He moaned at every lurch. He screamed more than once, while the boatmen merely let out the sail for a moment and muttered "Coward." It would go over, it was going over! There! But no, they reached the other side at last, and he proffered his two cash, which were small ones. "Two!" they cried; "did you not hear us say four when we started?" While another man quoted the proverb, "Talk big words, use small cash." Seng-teh at length discovered a few others in the recesses of his purse at the girdle. He gave them to the men, who followed them up the steps, cursing all the ancestors of the men who owed them one twenty-fifth of a penny.

"Another chair, quick!" moaned the scholar. That cough and its attending symptom were terrible. Reaching home, the bearers were dismissed, the juvenile next door was sent out for wine and ginger, which was administered—to make matters worse.

"Let me call the doctor, father."

"Yes, call in Fung Shenseng," a native practitioner who lived near.

[1] ". . . while mighty rivers, the sons of ocean, deep resounding, lash the hollow shores, . . . agitated by a tempest" (Klopstock's *Messiah*).

Seng-teh whispered something to Camilla, and ran over to Hankow, bringing the foreign doctor back in a chair.

"He will have to come over into the hospital if I am to do anything."

The invalid protested, and in waving his arms there dropped out the paper of black pills, which smelt strongly of opium.

"Yes, he must come over," said the doctor, looking at the scattered pills, adding, "I thought as much."

"Call in Fung Shenseng," moaned the scholar. Then after a worse fit of coughing than ever, "Anything to save life."

Four men were fetched, and the invalid was taken over on the bed as he was. Camilla had the chair, the two walked behind, after locking up the house and giving the key to the landlord.

Nieh Shen-seng opened his eyes eventually, to find himself lying upon a bed in a room hung with tablets from grateful patients, "The wizard hand brings back the spring," "Grace equal to that of a new creation," "Kindness pervading three generations"; they were all read at a glance. But what were those words yonder, so deficient in literary intricacy, beginning "Our Father"? He could read no more, easy as the inscription was; he closed his eyes. And kindly hands ministered to him until he went off into a needed sleep, dreaming about the majesty of the Confucian worship.

Camilla was allowed to stay for a while. The doctor had brought in a large folding screen and placed it on one side of the bed, then another for the other side. They sat down, the "son" and daughter on either side of the sick man's bed. Camilla felt confidence in the doctor now, for Seng-teh did, and the foreigner seemed a very brother to her father.

Nieh woke at length with a start and a cough, then heard another patient who was now cured say, "A thousand thanks, doctor; my relatives will not know me now. I am twenty years younger."

"Let me see that man," the scholar gasped faintly.

It was Chii, his wife's brother! The shock of recognition proved too much for Nieh, and the doctor had to interfere.

He and Chii went out to find a lodging near in an old woman's house where uncle and niece might be accommodated, and Camilla was taken thither.

They came in every day, and after some time Nieh was well enough to converse about the old days. That frivolous Chii was serious now. Had he "eaten the foreigner's doctrine"?

"No, not that," he said; he but knew the Heavenly Father.

"I thought you were going home."

"Not till you are well."

"That will be a long time."

"Never mind."

Did the Heavenly Father make men unselfish? Nieh wondered. Everyone was kind. And that thoughtless brother-in-law as kind as any! Strange!

. . . .

It was now the tenth month, the eighteenth day of the foreigners' eleventh month. "Strange folk those barbar— those foreigners, but somewhat indispensable now." The three were beside him. He was better now, able to sit up in bed. He would be able to go home after a few days. Chii was going to wait on, until, on Nieh Shen-seng's return, Seng-teh should be married. A blush reddened the cheeks of Camilla. Her heart was at peace with regard to her father, and Seng-teh was—

When a terrific bang shook the place, shattering one of the windows and loosening a large piece of plaster, which fell with a crash, happily into the centre of the room, where there were no beds. Never thunder-peal came so suddenly. Camilla fainted. Seng-teh tremblingly raised her from the ground, while Chii rushed out to see what had happened. No one knew, but over in the direction of Wuchang there arose a huge cloud of white smoke. "The Wuchang powder magazine!"[1] arose the cry, as the crowds rushed hither and thither about the street laden with their portable belongings.

[1] "A voluntary statement made by one of the powder-sifters, since dead from frightful burns, runs to the effect that one of the *Wei Yuens* (small mandarins) was an opium-smoker, and that on rising from his lamp his cotton

474   A STRING OF CHINESE PEACH-STONES.

The doctor came in to see after his patients. They had all fled except Nieh Shen-seng, on whose person the shock undid all the work of the kindly physician.

He lingered some days, until one afternoon his friends might have been seen watching around the dying man. Seng-teh bent over him to hear him utter the sounds *Ts'ao Chung*, then " East Gate."

" Flowing toward the ocean," suggested Seng-teh. Yes, that was it.

Then faintly, " Read that to me." The screen had been removed to give the dying man more air, and he was looking at the red scroll on the wall.

They knelt around him, and repeated softly, " Our Father which art in heaven."

Before they had finished it, they seemed to feel that a

sleeve was seen to be smouldering, and dropped some tinder into the heap of powder by the side of this man. . . . The man was perfectly calm and conscious when he made this unsolicited statement" (newspaper cutting pasted into the MSS. diary of the late Dr. W. F. Porter Smith, W.M.S., Hankow).

certain silence had come. A life river had reached the ocean—that Imperial Ocean which we call "Our Father."

. . . .

A few weeks had passed, and three chairs proceeded through the *Wu Seng Miao* archway one morning. They were plain chairs, but there had been a marriage that morning. The ceremony had been a happy combination of that familiar to us and the non-heathen essentials of the Chinese bridal-day. The chairs were put down and reversed, so as to go into the boats back foremost. But there was another reason,—a large crowd had assembled on the steps. The reason thereof was a ghastly head in a wooden cage hung up against the wall. Seng-teh looked from that cage to the inscription, and saw the name of Lieu Fuh-t'ang thereon, and the charge of having attempted to stir up the country people in privy conspiracy and rebellion, also of having been a villainous thief for many years. Seng-teh hurried his bride away. Such a sight was not fit for her. But from that ghastly background his own lot seemed to shine forth with added lustre.

Chü had many a comment to pass as the three crossed the river. One of the bearers in the other boat was voluble also.

"Up the Tortoise Hill, did you say, sir?" asked the bearer just noted. His name need not be given; it was that of the former apprentice of the priest-monk on the Nine Recluses Hill.

"It is a shame to make you carry me."

"I am delighted to do so, Li Shen-seng."

The little procession passed along the "Moon Lake path," through the "Ancient Bell Tower," over the bridge, through the umbrella maker's village, then into the valley of graves, where Seng-teh had last seen the retreating form of the rascally Lieu years before, then up the hill.

"Yonder is the camp. Over there used to stand the temple which had a tablet to Li Tan. You know his history?"

"I know *him*, my princely husband!"

Chü followed at a little distance, and said, "Yonder is the place where the boats start for the Nine Recluses Hill. I will go there now, with all respectful congratulations."

476 A STRING OF CHINESE PEACH-STONES.

"Without partaking of our pot-luck? We have no other guest. It is so soon after the"—
"I have feasted already," was the laughing reply, and he was gone.

That afternoon Camilla showed her husband, her "princely husband," the two scrolls on which her father had written her own verses.

The lines thereon may be rendered—

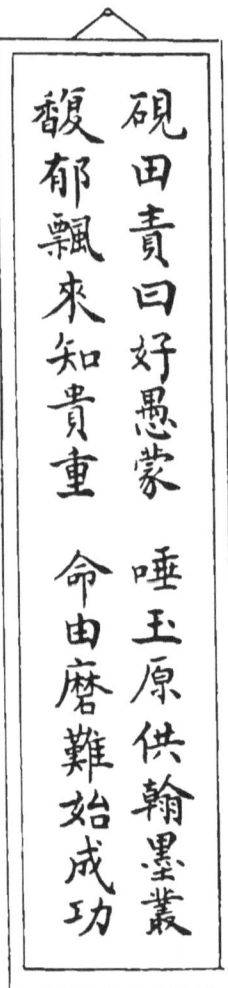

"Alas," moaned the ink-block, "ground down day by day,
My cloud-circled landscape full soon will be gone,
My former companions, how brilliant and gay,
By sorrow's white fingers, my comeliness worn."

"O fool," cried the ink-slab, "the more thou art ground,
The more are the gem-words by masterhand writ,
The sweeter the perfume that floats all around:
By grinding thou'rt made for thy destiny fit."

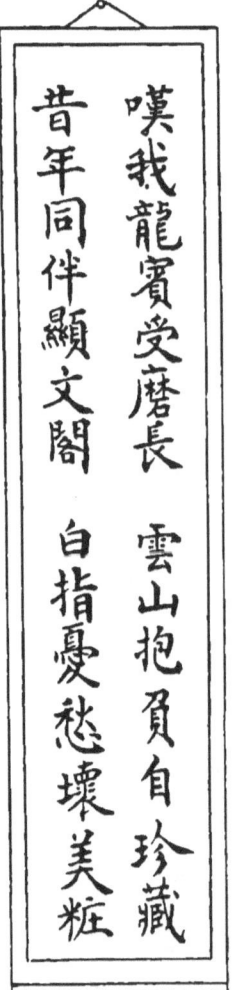

"And now, my Li Tan, will you write me another scroll

FOR BETTER, FOR WORSE. 477

to hang up in the middle? Those prayer-words you know, that father"—

"Yes, my Fung-kiao, but first I must take off this robe. It is tight at the neck. Why, it is the old necklace I have worn so long which presses. Rub the ink for me while I go out and buy the red paper," he added, as he divested his person of the marriage-robe and the

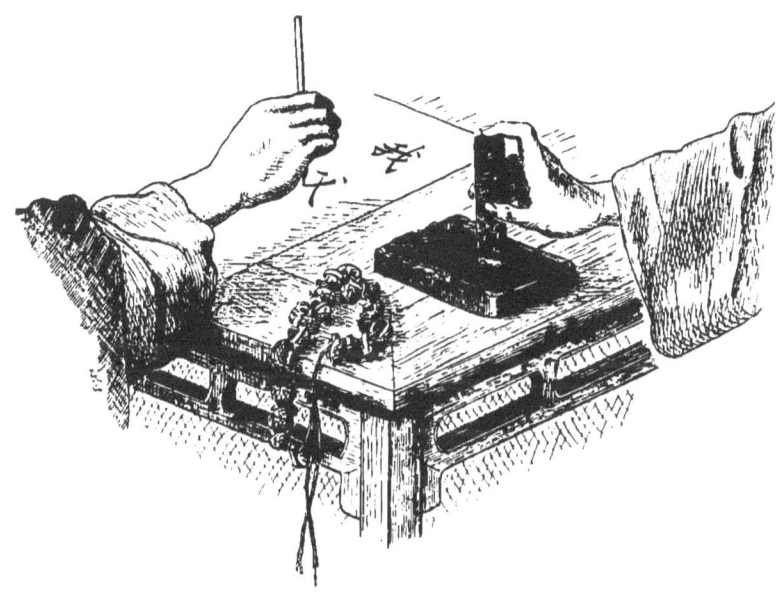

STRING OF PEACH-STONES.

Appendix.

THE EARLY WORSHIP OF THE TAIPINGS.—The hymn sung in the Taiping Camp (p. 248) embodies all the lines which are now remembered in Hanyang county by ex-rebels and country folk generally. But by the omission of any reference to the Holy Spirit it is evident that one line has dropped out. The whole as first sung reads thus:—

"We praise Thee, O God, our Heavenly Father;
We praise Jesus, the Saviour of the World;
We praise the Holy Spirit, the sacred intelligence;
We praise the Three Persons, united as the True Spirit."

After this doxology came the following hymn:—

"The true doctrine is different from the doctrine of the world.
It saves men's souls, and affords the enjoyment of endless bliss.
The wise receive it at once with joyful exultation.
The foolish, when awakened, understand thereby the way to heaven.
Our Heavenly Father, of His infinite and incomparable mercy,
Did not spare His own Son, but sent Him down into the world,
To give His life for the redemption of all our transgressions.
When men know this, and repent of their sins, they may go to heaven."

Then followed the Ten Commandments.

In the book of religious precepts from which the above is translated,[1] there is also "a form to be observed when men wish to forsake their sins."

"They must kneel down in God's presence, and ask Him to forgive their sins; they may then either take a basin of water and wash themselves, or go to the river and bathe themselves [self-administered

[1] *Impressions of China*, by Captain Fishbourne, 1885, p. 261.

baptism]; after which they must continue daily to supplicate Divine favour, and the Holy Spirit's assistance to renew their hearts, saying grace at each meal, keeping holy the Sabbath Day, and obeying all God's commandments, especially avoiding idolatry. They may then be accounted the children of God, and their souls will go to heaven when they die; all people throughout the world, whether Chinese or foreigners, male or female, must observe this in order to salvation."

The prayer to be used by those who wish to forsake their sins:—

"I, so-and-so, kneeling down with a true heart, repent of my sins, and pray the Heavenly Father, the Great God, of His abundant mercy, to forgive my former sins of ignorant folly, in repeatedly breaking the Divine commands, earnestly beseeching Him also to grant me repentance and newness of life, that my soul may go to heaven; while I, from henceforth, truly forsake my former ways, abandoning idolatry and all corrupt practices, in obedience to God's commands. I also pray that God would give me His Holy Spirit to change my wicked heart, deliver me from all temptation, and grant me His favour and protection; bestowing on me food and raiment, and exemption from calamity; peace in this world and glory in the next, through the mercies of our Saviour and Elder Brother Jesus, who redeemed us from sin. I also pray that God's will may be done on earth as it is done in heaven. Amen."

In which Amen surely every reader of this early Taiping prayer will join, adding a further prayer that the great overturning in favour of Perfect Peace and the Kingdom of Heaven may speedily be accomplished in China.

www.ingramcontent.com/pod-product-compliance
Lightning Source LLC
Chambersburg PA
CBHW021417300426
44114CB00010B/525